PRAISE

"I have lived through my fifteen seconds of fame, albeit not without scars. But what about the 16th second? What happens then?"

Trauma and homophobia in Richard's hometown of Lafayette, Louisiana, led him to Houston, Texas, where he found a vibrant, welcoming gay community—and where he discovered exotic dancing. Performing under the name Colt Michael, Richard became a highly-recognized, award-winning stripper. He spent years living a double life, using drugs and alcohol to bridge the gap between the fabulous, debonair performer and the lonely, insecure young man he truly was. Unfortunately, his wild lifestyle caught up with him, and HIV/AIDS, as well as his rampant substance abuse, took their toll on his body and mind.

Returning home to die with his family in Louisiana, Richard spent years waiting for the disease to take him the way it had killed so many of his friends and lovers. However, Richard began to find reasons to live. He would soon become a pillar of his community, helping HIV+ people live with their disease, organizing Pride festivals and fundraisers, and running for public office. His memoir shows just how much a life can change and how fame—and recovering from fame—can help a person grow and persevere.

The gay community has few elders because of the AIDS epidemic, and with this memoir, Richard steps into that role. He provides an insider's social history of gay men in the American South during the 1980s and 1990s. Though there are many solemn and heartbreaking moments, Richard also writes with great humor and cheer. The most delightful part of this book is the author's conversational tone. It reads like oral history, with chatty (and sometimes catty) asides throughout the narrative that bring the reader into his world. Photographs and newspaper clippings provide context and further insight into Richard's tales. With important lessons that can appeal to all, this memoir is a celebration of a life fully lived. –**Sarah Poulette,** *US Review of Books*

Ted A Richard's *The 16th Second* recounts the fascinating social and cultural life of gay men in Louisiana and Texas from the late 20th century to the present, through the autobiographical lens of a performer, organizer, and activist.

Ted A Richard has worn an astounding number of hats. He came of age as a gay man in the 80s and 90s, pursuing a successful career in retail management while moonlighting as an exotic dancer in a dazzling world muralled with sex, drugs, and alcohol. *The 16th Second* follows the author through and beyond his "fifteen seconds" of fame – first the travails of a young man whose social and romantic relationships are ended all too soon by AIDS, and second the hard work of an HIV-positive gay man choosing service to his family and community over his former self-aggrandizing pursuits.

Richard's project is explicitly personal. He lived through the trauma of the onset of AIDS in America, and after receiving his own HIV diagnosis he had good reason to expect the same untimely end as too many of his lovers and friends. In this regard, the tone of *The 16th Second* makes sense: this reflection on a fortunate life is told in a personal and personable way, with an almost conversational style – complete with winks and nods to the reader, historical side notes, and a few prickly airings of grievances.

The text's underlying struggle is with the sheer volume of material it covers. *The 16th Second* takes a maximalist approach to its subject matter (boasting no fewer than three subtitles), covering everything from Richard's high school years to the present, enlivened with numerous reproductions of personal photos or published paper ephemera of gay culture. On the one hand, this leads *The 16th Second* toward a narrative style leaning heavily on summary to move through time. This autobiography does not use a novelistic style to . . . render scenes.

IR Verdict: *The 16th Second* is well worth reading for its portrayal of forty tumultuous years in LGBTQ history, as told by a funny, flawed, and human man. *–IndieReader*

The 16th Second **is the inspiring memoir of a stripper who became an activist.**

Ted A Richard's encouraging memoir *The 16th Second* concerns his work as a stripper during the 1980s and 1990s, as well as his experiences with alcoholism.

In his youth, Richard was a popular student. He was also closeted. By his twenties, he had found work as a dancer in Texas gay bars. Though his book covers his chases for pleasure and fame, and mourns losses that came because of alcohol and cocaine use, it also celebrates his achievements: Richard won numerous awards as his alter ego, Colt Michael. And even after being diagnosed with HIV in 1987, he continued to gain acclaim and notoriety as a dancer across Louisiana and Texas.

But Richard's rambunctious, fun outward appearance belied his melancholy mindset. He recounts how many of his friends died of AIDS, suicide, and overdoses. Eventually, he surrendered to the idea that he would die in a similar manner. He was often lonely: "everyone wanted to be with Colt Michael, but nobody wanted to be with Ted A Richard." When his HIV became AIDS in 1994, he realized that "those 'seconds of fame' were actually 'seconds of shame.'" A return to his parents' home in Louisiana enabled him to begin treatment for the illness, though he was still entrenched in alcoholism. Many years and DUIs later, he achieved sobriety, beginning a second life in charity work.

Each of the book's first fifteen chapters details a "second of fame," or a memorable and formative moment that moved Richard in a dangerous direction. The "sixteenth second" comes after he writes about retiring as Colt Michael and beginning HIV treatment. A suggestion that life is at its fullest after a person's "fifteen seconds of fame" are over dominates, complemented by the clear record of how Richard's fame led him down a path of destruction. This work is amplified by the book's friendly and familiar tone: the book flaunts Richard's endless charm to its benefit.

Distinctive sensory details make the scenes all the more intimate, amplifying their ranging feelings of joy and sorrow. Richard's sense of despair after receiving a diagnosis that he'd come to regard as inevitable is tangible. So, too, is his ecstatic disbelief at winning second place in the Texas Male Stripper of the Year contest. **–Aimee Jodoin, Clarion Review for** *Foreword Reviews*

The 16th Second is a vulnerable, autobiographical account of Ted Richard's life—by turns raucous, debauched, joyous, isolated, and ultimately redeemed. Each reader will find something with which to identify in their own lives. **–Jules Jernigan**

THE 16TH SECOND

THE 16TH SECOND

The Wild Life and Crazy Times of Colt Michael
Navigating the End of Fame
and the Beginning of Life

Alcoholism, Drug Addiction, Sexual Abuse, HIV/AIDS
Defying Death, and Delusions of Grandeur

What Really Happened

TED A RICHARD

W. Brand Publishing
NASHVILLE, TENNESSEE

Note: This work is a compilation of the author's recollection of these events. Some names, people, places, and incidents have been changed for privacy. Locales and public names are sometimes used for atmospheric purposes.

Copyright ©2022 by Ted A Richard

All rights reserved. No part of this publication may be reproduced, distributed or transmitted in any form or by any means, including photocopying, recording, or other electronic or mechanical methods, without the prior written permission of the publisher, except in the case of brief quotations embodied in critical reviews and certain other noncommercial uses permitted by copyright law. For permission requests, write to the publisher, addressed "Attention: Permissions Coordinator," at the email below.

j.brand@wbrandpub.com
W. Brand Publishing
www.wbrandpub.com

Cover design by designchik.net

the 16th Second / Ted A Richard —1st ed.

Available in Hardcover, Paperback, Kindle, Audiobook, and eBook formats.
Hardcover ISBN: 978-1-956906-12-7
Paperback ISBN: 978-1-956906-13-4
eBook ISBN: 978-1-956906-14-1

Library of Congress Control Number: 2021923030

This book is dedicated the memory of those who never got to enjoy their 16th Second.

CONTENTS

FOREWORD..XIII

PREFACE XVII

CHAPTER 1: FIRST BASE (THAT TIME I DID A CARTWHEEL)....................... 1

CHAPTER 2: GREEN ROPES (THAT TIME I DRANK SCOTCH)..................... 11

CHAPTER 3: WELCOME TO FANTASY ISLAND (THAT TIME I GOT HIGH) 25

CHAPTER 4: A DOZEN ROSES (THAT TIME I WAS FORCED OUT)............... 31

CHAPTER 5: SHIRTLESS JOE (THAT TIME I TIPPED A STRIPPER)................ 39

CHAPTER 6: HAPPY BIRTHDAY (THAT TIME I MET MY SOULMATE) 53

CHAPTER 7: SPECIFICALLY UNINVITED (THAT TIME HE DIED) 65

CHAPTER 8: SEX ON THE BEACH (THAT TIME I CAME OUT OF HIDING)............. 73

CHAPTER 9: LEATHERMAN (THAT TIME I MADE A VIDEO) 81

CHAPTER 10: I'LL BE BACK–I PROMISE (THAT TIME I WAS RAPED)........... 89

CHAPTER 11: COVER BOY (THAT TIME I WENT TO THE CLINIC)............... 103

CHAPTER 12: TALLULAH TWILIGHT
   (THAT TIME I WAS A PEARL OF A SEA-MAN)......................................117

CHAPTER 13: MR. MAGOO (THAT TIME I WAS A PROSTITUTE).............. 129

CHAPTER 14: FAME ADJACENT (THAT TIME I WAS IN A PARADE) 143

CHAPTER 15: WATER TIGER (THAT TIME I GOT A SUNBURN).................. 159

CHAPTER 16: THE 16TH SECOND–WHAT HAPPENS NEXT
   (THAT TIME DOLLY SANG FOR ME)...171

CHAPTER 17: AWAKENING (THAT TIME I WAS A POSTER BOY) 181

CHAPTER 18: JUSTICE (THAT TIME I DONATED BLOOD) 191

CHAPTER 19: HONOR (THAT TIME I SAW A RAINBOW)..........................197

CHAPTER 20: SERVICE (THAT TIME I WATCHED A CARTOON)............... 207

CHAPTER 21: LEGACY (THAT TIME I WAS A DADDY)............................. 219

CHAPTER 22: TRUST (THAT TIME I ALMOST KILLED HER).....................227

CHAPTER 23: REDEMPTION (THAT TIME SHE DIED) 237

CHAPTER 24: FELON (THAT TIME I WAS SANTA...AGAIN) 249

CHAPTER 25: RESPONSIBILITY (THAT TIME I RESCUED MYSELF)..........261

CHAPTER 26: MISSION (THAT TIME I WORE ORANGE) 273

CHAPTER 27: FAMILY (THAT TIME I GOT A TATTOO...OR TWO) 285

CHAPTER 28: PRIDE (THAT TIME I LOVED A BISCUIT) 297

CHAPTER 29: INSPIRATION (THAT TIME I MET THE GOAT) 311

CHAPTER 30: ADVOCACY (THAT TIME I WAS AN IDOL) 325

CHAPTER 31: INTEGRITY (THAT TIME I ATTENDED A FUNERAL) 337

CHAPTER 32: BE YOU–BE FABULOUS (THAT TIME I RAN FOR OFFICE) 347

AFTERWORD 363

POETRY 369

    HAIKU COLLECTIVE

ABOUT THE AUTHOR 373

REFERENCES 375

RESOURCES 379

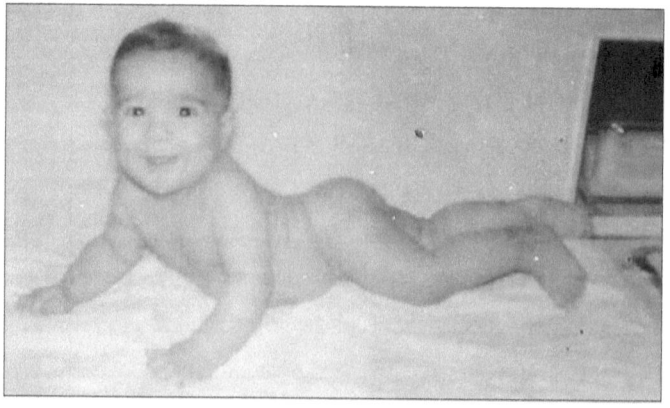

Ted at six months old

FOREWORD

It has been quoted (and misquoted) that the eccentric artist and gay icon Andy Warhol once declared that everyone would be "world-famous for fifteen minutes."

I believe that we often take credit for thoughts or actions not originally our own, allowing others to think that they are. We are raised to have good manners and to be courteous to others. One of these common courtesies is to not correct others in public while they are speaking.

So, we let them continue their conversations, though their stories are not entirely correct. We intend to pull them aside later in a private moment more conducive to assisting them in correcting their stories for future accuracy. That's what we intend to do. But we never do. It's just a silly story, after all, and it really doesn't matter if whoever is regaling it is embellishing a bit. The "tiny fibs" make the anecdote funnier anyway, and no one is the wiser.

Hence begins the life of a lie which, though began as unintentional, remains a lie.

And while Andy Warhol's words from 1968 indeed were prophetic, I take exception to the "fifteen minutes" rule. In these days of intense social media and fast-trending topics, our attention span has rapidly been diminished to the six-second (up to 180 seconds) view of a TikTok video.

To live in a world where self-worth is determined by the amount of "likes" received on an assortment of social media platforms is not reality and can actually do irreparable harm to anyone who subscribes to that mentality. Being "famous" in the twenty-first century does not mean the same thing as when I was growing up as a Baby Boomer (1962) in the deep South.

With that in mind, I decided to "update" the famous quote to properly reflect on life in the twenty-first century.

"In life, ANYONE can be famous for 15 seconds."

What is "fame" anyway? Is it wealth and status? Is it power and prestige? Is it perceived notoriety and a recognizable name? Or is it something else?

And what does "fame" really mean? How and why is your definition of famous different than mine? And why does it matter? Or should it matter at all?

As a society, we allow situations, culture and over-exposed media attention to determine for us who is famous and who is not. Why do we do that? I've never really understood that concept. The fact that we unwittingly allow outside circumstances and events to bend the definition of fame, creates an environment in which we find it difficult to see the fame within ourselves. And when did we decide that we attribute our value only to the fame to which we aspire?

As my definition of fame has evolved over the years, I have come to learn that fame can only be defined by what YOU describe as "someone or something that rises above the set standard of accomplishment in the field for which they are being recognized."

I believe that the basic premise of the original quote is correct. "In the future, everyone will be world-famous for fifteen minutes."

ALL of us should see FAME when we look in the mirror.

I certainly have had my fifteen seconds of fame many, many times. But sometimes the fame that you want is not the fame that you get. Not all fame is good fame. Sometimes, *infamous* is a more accurate term, and sometimes embarrassingly forgettable is what you hope for. I have experienced both "fame" and "infamy" several times during my life. I have been fortunate enough to achieve success as a retail hotshot, as an entertainer, as a singer, as an actor, and as a politician. Miraculously, I have lived through my fifteen seconds of fame, albeit not without scars.

But what about the *16th Second*?

What happens then?

What happens when the "fame" is gone?

Is there life *after* fame?

After years of struggle, self-loathing, and self-sabotage, I learned that what happens in the *16th Second* is the most important time of our life, because the *16th Second* IS the rest of our life!

The *16th Second* is our new beginning, and only we can define its outcome.

Once I came to realize that I had completely fucked up my first fifteen seconds, I knew that I had to do better. I had to make my *16th*

Second worth something. This time not for everyone else but only for me!

This cathartic process of finding and defining my own faults, and the lies I told about them, have opened windows to my sordid past which had intentionally remained closed for years. The lies I told in the name of covering my shame were so convincing that they became widely accepted as truth. And the actual truth was blurred between my own reality and the reality I wanted others to think I was living. Because of this, I felt the need to share some of my stories from the perspective of those whom I have lied to or mistreated; and show insight into how their truth helped me to find mine. It is time for me to acknowledge that my fifteen seconds are over. (Or was I truly ever famous at all?)

I deliberated about the inclusion of several stories in this book, but I know their exclusion would not eliminate the fact that those things happened. I would never want anyone to repeat many of the things that I've done. So perhaps these stories can be a lesson in what NOT to do! Of course, I have changed some of the names and/or locations to respect the privacy of those involved. Those individuals can choose to claim their identity in this book if, and when they so desire.

I have taken an inventory of the people, places and events that have had a significant impact on the trajectory of the life I had not yet lived. I have described each *"second of fame"* as a specific chapter in this book. As my personal life, private life, family life, and business life have become intertwined throughout the years, many of the same people appear throughout the book. Understanding that some of the people you meet today could play a part in your life story ten, twenty, or even thirty years later should remind us always to be kind and courteous to each other. I wish I would have learned that lesson sooner.

Now begins my life in the *"16th Second!"*

My sincerest hope is that you will be inspired to create your own fifteen seconds of fame, seizing the courage to create fame in your own world, and believing in yourself so very much that you see fame in the person staring back at you in the mirror!

Life's most rewarding achievement is to be proud of the person whose evolution has inspired self-growth and self-worth. I encourage you to do something every day that inches you toward your goal of what

YOU define as fame and success, so that the fulfillment of your life in the *16th Second* validates the fame you always knew you had.

Be proud of your *16th Second*!

This is my discovery and the evolution to mine.

Ted A Richard

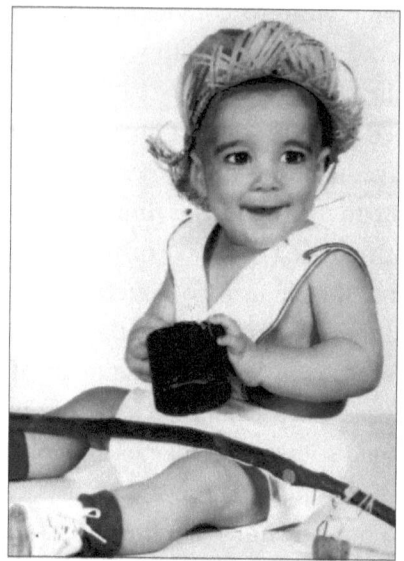

Fishing Ted at three years old

Cowboy Ted at four years old

PREFACE

About halfway between New Orleans and Houston, somewhere between the Atchafalaya River and the Bayou Contraband, is a quiet little country town; that neither is quiet, nor is its country lifestyle well-defined. Lafayette, Louisiana is known as the heart of Cajun Country and often is called the Pride of Acadiana. [Acadiana is the large region of south and southwest Louisiana which was home to the "rebellious" people of Acadia, Nova Scotia (Canada) who refused to sign an oath of allegiance confirming their loyalty to the British Crown, and, by extension, Protestantism. Many of these Acadians exiled during what became known as the Great Expulsion (1755-1763) found refuge and comfort in the enriched farmland and familiar cultures with the Creoles who had also inhabited there.]

I am an eighth-generation Cajun. My charm and personality almost certainly come from the French and Irish heritage of my mother. My wit and passion almost definitely come from the French and Native American (Seminole) heritage of my father.

I grew up in a small dairy farm community about ten miles from Lafayette in a tiny village with no discernible city limits called Ossun. At the time I was growing up, there were at least seven dairies within one mile of my house, and we were friends with all of the dairymen.

But on our farm, we raised more than just dairy cows. We also raised Shetland ponies, a few chickens (at times), and sheep. Yep ... *SHEEP!*

Farm life was a complete joy for me. We had fresh milk every day, fresh eggs when we had chickens, and home-grown beef whenever one of the cows was butchered. Watching newborn calves frolicking in the fresh spring grass and seeing the baby lambs hopping around the pasture wild with excitement and curiosity made for many memorable childhood moments.

Each year, I got to hand-raise a calf and a lamb. I got to bottle-feed, nurture, and cherish them as if they were my own children. I even gave them names so that they knew they were loved. The most difficult part of this process was the knowledge that, at some point, this calf and lamb would grow into a cow and sheep, and become meat in the freezer. But I guess that's farm life. It's just not something that I ever got used to. I only wanted to remember their infancy in which I had always played a major role. Maybe that made the butchering more tolerable. *Maybe.*

But my favorite time on the farm was hay baling season. Every year, each of the nearby farmers baled hay for storage to feed to the cattle, horses, and sheep through the winter. In those times (mid-late 1970s) most farmers were still making square hay bales.

My job was to pick the bales up from the ground and throw them up onto a rolling wagon. I was paid a quarter per bale, and we usually picked up between 200-300 bales per day. I always have enjoyed the outdoors, and hay baling season gave me a great reason to get outside and bask in the sun.

The work was very hard, but Joe, my older distantly related cousin who lived just up the street from us, always made it worthwhile. And Joe would always take his shirt off while loading the hay, and he usually was the guy on the rolling wagon to whom I would throw my bales. Shirtless Joe was always proud to flex his sinewy muscled arms and ripped chest and abs as he picked up the bales I was throwing to him. (On some days, I swear that the smell of his manly sweat still lingers in the Louisiana summer heat; though I know it is only in my wishful mind.) There was something distinctive about Joe. He wasn't like the other guys I knew, and he seemed to think I was a bit different too. I liked him, and he liked me; and he would always give me a little sideways wink when nobody was looking. Maybe he was just wiping the sweat from his eyes or was he really winking at me? I would never know. In the meantime, I just enjoyed the view of Shirtless Joe's tanned and hirsute body and threw him another bale of hay.

Summer came and went, and I couldn't wait until the next summer to be close to Shirtless Joe again. Shirtless Joe would have a major impact on my life as a young adult, and he would play an instrumental role in navigating me through my *"next second of fame."*

CHAPTER 1

FIRST BASE

(That Time I Did A Cartwheel)

Standing in the middle of the Parc International stage, I just stood there for a moment to relish in the spectacle we had created. It was the Acadiana area's inaugural PRIDE (People Representing Individual Differences and Experiences) festival, and I was the emcee. We had worked diligently for the past year to see our dreams of this event to fruition, and the day was finally here.

Postured next to me was the pastor of the local Universalist Unitarian Church. As he was addressing the crowd which had now gathered closer toward the stage, I summoned all "married" couples to a pre-selected spot directly in front of the stage. Once the pastor welcomed those in attendance, he blessed all of their civil unions. (Marriage equality would not be legal until over a year later, June 26, 2015.) It was heartening to see the joy and passion of those gays and lesbians who had chosen to spend the rest of their lives together.

I looked out into the crowd and felt their love for each other and the love of the community that I thought I had been missing for so long. Homophobia was not welcomed in this sacred space we had created just for US and our allies. I looked down from the stage and saw my parents and other family members seated near the front row of chairs. They always supported me and never failed to let me know just how proud they were of all that I accomplished. Seeing the smiles on their faces, though exciting, was somewhat bittersweet. It reminded me that this type of event would have been impossible over thirty years before, when I was coming out of the closet, and needed a community to welcome me. Homophobia in the deep South is rampant; some say it is taught, some believe it is inherited. Sadly, not much has changed.

I hoped that this little festival could help to change people's minds in the tiny hamlet of Ossun, Louisiana and Lafayette Parish where I grew up. This little town had come a long way from my years as a closet queer, but there was still much more progress to be made.

I think I can barely remember when Scott, a small village just west of Lafayette, got its first traffic light in the middle of town. This most highly trafficked area of the quaint community was flanked by the local Roman Catholic church, a regional bank, an elementary school, and a village gas station that also sold hunting supplies, fishing tackle, and bait; and had a section for ladies' toiletries and essentials. The school, L. Leo Judice Elementary, was named after one of the visionaries of small-town education. He dedicated his life to the growth and progress of Scott, which was, at the time, a major railway depot. Louis Leo's father, Alcide Judice, renowned as the "Father of Public Education in Lafayette Parish" was the person who originally conceived the idea of transportation of children to schools via horse-drawn carriages and wagons. The present-day school bus transportation system is an enhancement of Mr. Judice's original idea.

L. Leo Judice is where I spent first and second grade. I always was a fairly intelligent student, even at a young age. But my boredom frequently got the attention of my first grade teacher, and not the kind that I wanted; so, I always was given extra work to keep me busy. My teacher often said to me, "Ted, always be your best you!" I only remembered that because she had to tell me that so many times. I wouldn't say that I was mischievous; it's just that I usually finished my work before the other students, and I became a bit rambunctious from boredom.

My life today would not have been the same without the structure and discipline of my elementary teachers, who had such an impact on my childhood. I do not think that teachers get enough credit for the valuable jobs they do in creating an environment where each student can excel and can explore the world at his, her, or their own pace. I want to thank all of those educators who recognized my potential and allowed me to expand my horizons (without being a disruption to the rest of the class). I wish to credit them for enabling me to be challenged and teaching me ways to overcome obstacles that, at the time, I thought were impossible. Their influences in my younger years allowed me to experience life and not just live it. And their insistence that I remain productive while not being a disruption was a lesson often repeated throughout my lifetime, though that wasn't always a good thing.

My life on a stage began as early as first grade. I always was one of the featured performers in school plays. My first grade teacher recognized my talent as a singer/dancer/performer long before I did, and I apparently had a very large repertoire. In reviewing pictures from first and second grades, I portrayed George Washington, a Native American warrior, a Japanese geisha, and an Native American woman.

My earliest recollection of first grade, other than constantly being told to shush, was the annual spelling bee. There was a category for each grade, and the winner would win ice cream and candy for the class. (Imagine me, as spastic as I was already, hyped up on a million calories of sugar.) I really wanted to win, but not for the treats. I wanted to be the best. I wanted to prove to the entire class that my best version of me was better than anybody else's. I don't know why I felt that was so important to me, but I remember, at the time, that this was the most important thing in the world. I just HAD to win!

The first round had sixteen contestants, so we were separated into two groups: the boys and the girls. I made it through the first three rounds rather easily. Then we were down to the final two boys; me and my best friend at the time, Troy Box. Troy was given the word "clue" and spelled it C-L-E-W. While I felt bad for Troy because he got it wrong, I knew exactly how to spell that word ... "clue, C-L-U-E, clue;" like the color blue. That's how I remembered.

I had beaten out the rest of the boys in the spelling bee. Now I was up against the winner from the girls' team, Terri Fabacher. We went back and forth spelling word after word and neither of us ever missed, until I was given a word that I had never heard, much less spelled. The word was "butch." I did the best I could ..."butch, B-U ... uh, C-H, butch." Through my peripheral vision, I could see that Terri's eyes had immediately lit up. She knew the word, and spelled it with ease ... "butch, B-U-T-C-H, butch." Then, looking directly at me, as if to spite me, in a taunting voice, she said, "T. Ted, you forgot the 'T' in it, there's a 'T' in 'butch.' " So, adding insult to my already injured pride, this first grade girl knew how to spell "butch." Whether or not she knew what it meant, she knew how to spell it, and that was all that mattered in a spelling bee. My deflated ego headed back to my desk. I wanted to find the word "butch" somewhere.

The dictionary read, "BUTCH (adjective) having the appearance or other qualities of a type traditionally seen as masculine (i.e. a butch woman in a baseball cap)." Crap, now I had to look up the word "masculine." There, I found it, "MASCULINE (adjective) having qualities or appearance traditionally associated with men."

Now I felt even worse. I couldn't even spell a word that meant that I was a man. But the girl knew how to spell it. Now I wondered if she knew what it meant. She didn't either. I said, "Terri, it means man-like, not like a girl; but like a boy, that's what 'butch' means. Oh, and Terri is a man's name!" I felt better for a little while, but the sting of being the second-place loser still hurt.

I never told my parents that I had participated in the spelling bee, because I would then have had to tell them that I placed second. That just was not going to happen; not that they would have been surprised. After all, I was born second, too; for the rest of my life, I knew that I could never be first.

Second grade was my saving grace, or so I thought it would be. Continuously trying to "be my best me," I found other outlets to release my boisterousness. I found myself singing under my breath during class; yet another disruption. So, my second grade teacher said I belonged in the choir. To this day, I don't know if she really meant it, or if it was just a way for her to get me out of her class for the next forty-five minutes.

That year, during the elementary talent show—which was actually a competition, though I didn't know it—I was already singing on stage. I had been rehearsing a duet version of this song called "Sixteen Candles" with, you guessed it, my first-grade nemesis, Terri Fabacher. "Sixteen Candles" was a song written and recorded by The Crests, who, in 1958, was the first interracial mixed doo-wop singing group.

Terri and I had mended fences since my spelling bee flub. It seemed that winning the spelling bee didn't mean as much to her as it would have meant for me. And by second grade, we had both "matured."

That Saturday evening, we both sang our hearts out to be certain that our parents in the audience could hear us singing, as we attempted some kind of stupid little choreography that, apparently, the choir instructor thought was cute. Terri had a rather soulful voice for a white girl. She sounded kinda like Aretha Franklin, whose song "Respect" I had heard on the local radio station. And I was thinking that after our first grade rivalry, I did owe her some R-E-S-P-E-C-T. As for me, I sounded more like a cross between the countrified version of Elvis Presley and, with my soprano-ish voice, a little bit like Patsy Cline. After all of the performances were completed, the administration began handing out awards. Our rendition of "Sixteen Candles" won second place. Again, second grade, second place. I still think that we would have won *if not for those meddling kids*. [Oh, no, that's from that new *Scooby Doo* cartoon I had seen on television this morning during breakfast. Now back to the story.] I still believe that if our choir director had not forced us to learn those silly little dance steps and non-sensical facial expressions that we could actually (and should) have won.

Never in my wildest dreams could I have believed that my short-lived life of "stardom" in elementary school could prepare me for the life of excitement for which I was destined. I knew that I belonged on a stage. But stage life was not for me. At least not in second grade. Soon my day would come. I hoped!

I also began writing at a very early age. It was one of my elementary school teachers who taught me that "words mean something." From then on, I began writing down the things that were important to me and things that bothered me. I figured that if I wrote about it, then I could remember the good things and forget about the bad things. I often wrote notes to myself, and then threw them away as discarding them meant that they no longer had any effect on me. This seemed to work for a while, but somewhere along the way I was sidetracked, and the writing stopped, and my troubles started.

Academically, I excelled in the classroom. I was a stellar student of reading, writing, and arithmetic. The only class I ever failed was P.E. (physical education). I could do jumping jacks, and squats, and push-ups, but the one obstacle that I could not conquer (at the time) was balls. If there was a ball involved, I failed miserably. (Except for dodge ball because I was so tiny the opponents couldn't find me.)

As a youngster, I tried to play little league baseball for a very short time. Problem is, I sucked at it! I couldn't throw the ball, I couldn't catch the ball, and with a bat that felt as though it weighed more than I did, I most definitely couldn't hit the ball.

But my little league coach allowed me to still play a minor role in the team's lineup, just so that I could have a chance to play. And since I could barely hold the bat, the coach would always tell me to bunt. He never explained to me why I had to bunt, nor did he ever show me the proper way to bunt. He'd say, "Just hit the ball into the ground with the front of the bat." Which I always did, and I always was called "out." That made me so mad! (Of course, "out" would come to mean something totally different in my later years.)

When it was my turn to bat, I got the same call from my coach: two touches on his chin, then a tug on his ear, then a shift of his cap, and often wondered how the other teams never figured out those hand signals. Later, I realized that the other team always knew that I was going to bunt. They'd seen my lack of athletic abilities at many other games. *Ted's gonna bunt, and he's gonna be out.* The play and the outcome were a foregone conclusion.

But I finally got tired of always being out. So, during this time at bat, even though I knew I was supposed to bunt, I HIT that damned ball, and got all the way to first base. I was so excited that I did a cartwheel onto first base. I distinctly remember that I had to gauge my run and begin my cartwheel so that I would land firmly on first base. And I did! It was perfect! I was so proud of myself for not only hitting the ball and being safe on first base, but my magnificently planned acrobatics on the baseball diamond deserved a standing ovation. And I got it; yes, a standing ovation. But not for the reasons I would have wanted.

The umpires tried to call me "out," as they had done several times in the past. But this time, they were calling me out for sliding into first base. While the crowd was on its feet wondering what the hell had just happened, I was arguing my case with the umpires. I recall explaining to them the difference between a "slide" and a "cartwheel." All three of them looked down on me with both astonishment and anger; while trying to not laugh at my incredible, yet seemingly unconvincing, argument. *Who the hell was this little kid pretending that he knew more about baseball than the umpires?* Admittedly, I didn't know much about the rules and etiquette of baseball, but I did know about cartwheels. Finally, after chatting with the coaches of both teams, the umpires relented; probably out of pity, for both me and my parents. I was safe. I had finally made it to first base! (Sadly, the word "safe" would come to have a very different meaning later in my life also.)

The entire crowd looked at my parents in disbelief, but more so in disgust from the parents of the other team. My parents remained absolutely silent. That was my *"first second of fame,"* and my last game of little league baseball. The entire city of Scott, and possibly all of Lafayette Parish, was relieved.

And I was okay with that. I had spent almost two years in little league baseball, and I cannot name one other person on my team. If little league is supposed to be an exercise in team building, then this team particularly failed miserably. I did not make any friends on the team, and many times I felt as though the rest of them avoided me. I often felt ostracized because I wasn't as good at baseball as they were. And I could see the look on theirs and their parents' faces every time I got up to bat. If we lost the game, it was always my fault. And though that wasn't the case, that is how I felt.

So, in making it to first base, I felt some sort of redemption. A validation that I didn't always suck at baseball. And the "cartwheel of excitement" was my way of congratulating myself for a job well done. I deserved that standing ovation, regardless of its intention. It was mine, and I earned it!

Football, anyone? Absolutely NOT for me! I wasn't good at that either, even with the coaching I got from my Dad. But some of my fondest memories of my childhood were when my brothers and I would play football in the front yard. I had one older brother and one younger brother, so they figured that since I was the middle brother, it was only fair that they play two-on-one against me. It sounded legit at the time, so I agreed to the rules. For each play on offense, I could hike the ball to myself and run for a touchdown. For each play when I was on defense, they had to hike the ball to each other, and they always had to throw a pass, so at least I knew what their strategy was. It may seem as though our rules were a little off-kilter, and they probably were, but they worked for us.

Later in life I realized that I actually learned a lot about myself during those days. I learned about teamwork (watching my brothers plot against me), about independence, the strength of my own resolve to win, and the importance of patience and good strategy when the deck is stacked against you. And because I lost almost every game, I became very comfortable with the term "losing gracefully."

I have been very competitive since an early age; and while I love the competition, I never seemed to be able to win; and I certainly did not want the word "losing" to become a part of my ever-expanding vocabulary. My place in life already had been determined; I was the second born of four siblings. I was destined to always be second. It was my birthright!

I won second place in the first grade spelling bee.
I won second place in the second grade talent contest.
I won second place in the third grade jump rope race.
I won second place in the fourth grade obstacle course.
I won second place in the fifth grade reading aptitude challenge.
I won second place in the sixth grade Science project rally.
I won second place in the seventh grade track and field competition.
I won second place in the eighth grade Social Studies rally.

I was extremely talented in all of these areas, but I wasn't the best at anything. And I wanted to be the best! One of the lessons that I learned from all of these second-place finishes is that when you're constantly coming in second, you try even harder. So that's exactly what I did. Maybe high school would be different. *Maybe.*

High school was also a time when I started exploring, or at least trying to understand, my sexuality; I always thought that girls were pretty, but I really had no desire to date them, let alone have sex with them. My sexual appreciation always gravitated to fit, buff, muscular young men. My high school crushes were the usual suspects: the blond-haired, blue-eyed quarterback; the black-haired, brown-eyed baseball pitcher; and the red-haired, green-eyed track star. I guess I thought it was normal, and that everybody goes through this "phase," but my "phase" never went away.

I vividly remember my teenage years, looking through the JC Penney catalog at the men's underwear section for "inspiration" during my early masturbatory experiences. When my mother caught me perusing the catalog, she must have figured that I was "in need," because the following week I received brand new underwear from the latest JC Penney catalog. I often wondered if she noticed that the catalog pages were stuck together, and why those pictures aroused me in ways that would send me straight to hell.

I knew that there were other guys in my class that had the same kinds of feelings that I did, but I was never bullied like they were. Maybe it's because I wasn't more effeminate, or maybe it's because I wasn't so unintentionally obvious. It took me a long time to understand that I was guilty of the same type of homophobia that they were experiencing. I looked for tell-tale signs of gayness that seemed shameful to me. I certainly did not want to be one of "them," so I continually distanced myself from anyone who might be one of "them." Guilt by association is the thing that I dreaded most. I feared the hatred of the muscle-bound athletes that I lusted after. I feared the betrayal of the student government jocks who had garnered my unrelenting admiration. I feared the anger of the high school girls who thought that I was the "it" guy. If they knew that I was like "them," would I no longer be "it?" For someone who always prided himself on being strong and confident, I was precisely the opposite, and I allowed myself to remain that way for most of my high school years.

A turning point for me occurred on September 21, 1979, when Mark Simon, a great friend of mine, was killed in a motorcycle accident on his sixteenth birthday. The driver of the motorcycle lay comatose in the hospital.

Mark and I double-dated for homecoming in the fall of 1978. He was a sophomore, and I was a junior. Once homecoming was over, we dropped off our respective dates at their homes. We were in my car, so I took the long way home, talking about all sorts of things—school, teachers, boring classes, and catching up on the latest teen gossip. Throughout the conversation he kept saying that there was something that he wanted to talk to me about. The conversation was interesting and engaging, but I wondered if I was intrigued by what he was saying, or just in awe of his chiseled handsome beauty, blond hair, and green eyes. Again, he reminded me, and himself, that there was something that he wanted to share with me. And then, almost a year later, he was dead; and I never knew whatever it was that he wanted to tell me.

At Mark's wake, I found a napkin on a side table and just started writing. I was compelled to purge myself of this grief, and writing was the only thing that could console me. I had meant for them to be words that I had written "just for me" to help me get over this devastating loss of a great friend, but when some of my classmates came over to comfort me, they noticed that I was writing something and asked to read it. It was because of their insistence that I had the distinct honor of delivering those words of healing and hope as the eulogy at Mark Simon's funeral; my writing was also featured in Mark's *In Memoriam* in our high school yearbook.

Grieving over the death of someone very special to you, especially at such a young age, was devastating. I, too, was only sixteen years old, and never had really learned how to process death. I never could have imagined what it must have been like to not live past your sixteenth birthday. I needed a shoulder to cry on, an understanding person to comfort me in my dreadful time of sorrow.

Little League baseball practice at home

CHAPTER 2

GREEN ROPES
(That Time I Drank Scotch)

I found the consolation I was searching for in the arms of one of my high school teachers, Mr. MacIntosh. He was extremely understanding and gave me the support that I needed during this difficult period of my life.

Those days of heartbreak and healing led to more of an emotional connection than I ever could have imagined. Mr. MacIntosh seemed to know more about me than I knew about myself. We had deep conversations about the meaning of life, the absoluteness of death, and reaching for the stars in the meantime. We had *kismet* that I couldn't fully grasp, but I think that he did. Did he know that I had a huge crush on him, too? *Maybe.* Maybe not.

Earlier that past year I was selected by our high school's administration and staff to be a member of the Carencro Commodore Club which, at the time, was a nationwide organization focused on volunteerism, community service, and leadership development. As fate would have it, Mr. MacIntosh—my everyday man-crush—was the sponsor for our local Commodore Club. At that point, I didn't know if I was in love with him or if I misconstrued his compassion during my time of need as affection, or if it was just pure, unadulterated infatuation. Regardless of what those feelings meant, I was very happy to now have a reason to spend more time with Mr. MacIntosh. And since I was also the editor for our high school newspaper, I was elected to be the reporter for the Carencro Commodore Club.

The annual Commodore Club convention the following year (March 1980) was held in Jackson, Mississippi; as the reporter, I felt an obligation to attend. Once again, fate would play a role in this, as I was the only Commodore Club officer able to attend. It would be just me and Mr. MacIntosh for an entire weekend out of town.

The drive from Lafayette to Jackson took more than five hours. We talked constantly throughout the drive, but I can't recall anything that we talked about. The radio constantly blared out songs of the disco era, from artists such as The Bee Gees, Donna Summer, Michael Jackson, and Rod Stewart. We pumped up the volume on songs we liked, and I am fairly sure that I sang along, but he didn't. When the hype of the previous song ended, we'd lower the volume for more conversation.

Before arriving at the hotel, Mr. MacIntosh stopped at a local convenience store to grab some soft drinks and snacks. We shared a hotel room that night. As he jiggled the key into the failing lock on the door, we entered a shadowy room that, even with the lights on, still felt dark and dirty.

As I pulled back the moth-eaten bedspread, I suddenly detected the rank smell of old musk and pine freshener. The combination of smells made me nauseous, but I gathered myself and tried to mask the smell with douses of the Paco Rabanne cologne I had tucked away in my overnight bag. *How in the hell was I supposed to sleep in this filth? Was Mr. MacIntosh actually expecting me to get a good night's rest here?*

But Mr. MacIntosh had other things in mind when he stopped at that convenience store, he also had purchased alcoholic beverages. His selection for the night was Old Milwaukee beer, mine was Southern Comfort with strawberry soda. I was no stranger to alcohol by this time in my life, but hard liquor had not been my *forté*. However, I figured that I was out of town, with my teacher/sponsor, no one would find out anyway, so I decided to try something new. And at least if I was drunk, I wouldn't notice the stains on the pillowcases nor the holes in the sheets.

Needless to say, I got a bit drunk. I blurrily remembered waking during the night to go to the restroom, and when I returned to bed, I couldn't help but notice Mr. MacIntosh's chest heaving up and down, and his wife-beater T-shirt clinging tightly to his well-sculpted abs. I could see his muscles stretching the wales of the white cotton fabric between breaths. I stood there for a minute and stared at the beauty of this ginger Irishman. When he jostled in his sleep, I hurriedly hid at the foot of his bed.

As I arose slowly, I began to notice the excitement forming in his JC Penney white underwear. *Dare I breathe? Dare I look? Dare I touch?*

Somehow the liquor had given me the courage to act upon a latent instinct that I had intentionally concealed for at least two years. I carefully nestled my way into Mr. MacIntosh's bed and began rubbing my fingers over his hairy chest. I had never been with a man, naked, in the same bed. *Would this be my first?*

Then I felt Mr. MacIntosh wrap his strong shoulders around me. The same shoulders that once comforted me after the death of a friend were now pulling me toward him ... my lips to his. And as our lips met, our eyes stared straight into each other's souls. *Should we really be doing this?*

We kissed for what seemed like hours as we explored each other's bodies. We both knew that our "love" was taboo, but it didn't matter. We enjoyed each other over and over again that night and attended the Commodore Club convention the following day as if nothing had happened, but for the hangovers.

My first sexual experience with another man was more satisfying than anything I could ever have imagined, and I definitely was not disappointed. I never told Mr. MacIntosh that I was a virgin, but I think he figured it out at some point during that first kiss. His actions became gentler and gentler so as to be sure that I was comfortable. I appreciated that he accommodated me that night in every way, both physically and emotionally.

The ride back to Lafayette was extremely awkward. We both knew that we could never tell anyone about our weekend of sexual exploration. He would certainly have lost his job, and possibly risked jail time. Thankfully, the school year was almost over. Although I had not planned anything beforehand, what happened over the course of that weekend was exactly what I had hoped would happen. We continued seeing each other in secret for the rest of my senior year, and we both agreed that we would never mention this to anyone, but this venture of exploring my sexuality had such a profound effect on me that my coming out story would not be complete without it.

The fact that I was involved sexually with one of the high school teachers during my senior year has been a deeply held secret up until now. Mr. MacIntosh was the sponsor of the Commodore Club, I was a Commodore Club officer, and I was as in-love with my teacher as any hormone-racing teenager could be ... only I couldn't tell a soul. It was a struggle every day to be in love with someone, yet unable to share that love with anyone outside of the relationship. I soon learned that Mr. MacIntosh—*Charlie, to me*—was very popular with a few of the other students. I was heartbroken to learn that I wasn't his only lover. However, the excitement of my upcoming senior prom helped me to forget the pain of a relationship that I never really had with a teacher who never was really in love with me. (For you locals running to check the high school yearbooks, don't waste your time; he's not in them.)

Across the street from my elementary school was the Sts. Peter and Paul Catholic church. I was raised a devout Catholic, and my parents drilled this religion into me. (They didn't know that I was gay, and that I was having a near-traumatic experience each time I set foot into the church.) My brothers and I were also altar boys from the time we were in second grade until we were seniors in high school. Father Michael Guidry, the parish priest, knew all about my impure thoughts, the JC Penney masturbatory experiments, my salacious dalliances with Mr. MacIntosh, my lustfulness toward my best friend, Hank Steuben, and many of my other tawdry thoughts and actions; he heard all about them during confessionals.

Yes, I was committing sins all week long, then repenting for them on Sunday morning. He would usually assign me a penance of one *Our Father* and three *Hail Marys*, and then the *Glory Be*. Penance was supposed to be a sorrowful time of reflection when you prayed for absolution that God would protect you from the evilness of your sins and give you the strength to refrain from committing those same sins again. For me though, it was just a way to make me feel better about myself. If I told someone, even a priest behind a curtain, then everything that I was feeling was real; and I truthfully wasn't sorry about anything. I was just going through the motions (like many other Catholics I know).

During my senior year of high school, I was asked to become an acolyte, an honorary term for "advanced" altar boys. At the time, it seemed like a distinct honor to bestow upon anyone in the Catholic faith. I desperately wanted out from under the thumbs of the Catholic church, but I didn't want to disappoint my parents by turning down this prestigious offer. What bothered me about the Catholic church was the actual mass.

Every Sunday morning, I would hear so many congregants mispronouncing words clearly spelled out for them in a missalette; and I always thought, *if they can't even pronounce the words, then they most certainly can't know their meanings, nor their context.* To me, the entire mass was exaggerated pomp and circumstance combined with robotic traditions which meant something to those devout Catholics, which I was not. It all was irrelevant to me, and I was just going through the motions. Pray, kneel, pray, stand, pray, sit, pray, repeat. If this is what the Catholic church meant to define as prayers, I never grasped the concept; they were only words repeated *ad nauseum* for reasons I failed to even want to understand. It was simply a waste of my time.

With equal amounts of politeness and frustration, I accepted the acolyte designation; and from this day forward, I would get to wear a green rope around my waist and not a white one like the "regular" altar boys. It wasn't until later that I realized that the only difference between an altar server and an acolyte was a green rope. And, at least in this church at this time, the only people that wore the green rope were the ones whom the priest liked and wanted to keep in his flock. *Yep, you know exactly where this story is headed.*

I had been a member of the youth ministry at Sts. Peter and Paul Catholic church in Scott since I was a freshman in high school. We often did extracurricular activities together outside of both school and church; each summer we would take a trip to AstroWorld in Houston, Texas. During the summer between my junior and senior year of high school we took a road trip to Arizona and hiked the Grand Canyon.

Fr. Mike was quite active for a thirty-six-year-old, and, at sixteen years old, I realized that I had athletic abilities I had not known existed. I was a damned good hiker. Fr. Mike and I were much quicker than the other non-hikers in the group. We would walk several paces ahead of them down and then back up the winding paths in the Grand Canyon. At times we would get so far ahead of them that we stopped for a break and waited for them to catch up to us. We talked about stuff in the meantime.

I liked Fr. Guidry, and during these trips we always found time for quiet moments together where we could just sit and talk. I always knew that he was the man behind the curtain during my confessionals, so I knew that he knew the turmoil of emotions I was experiencing. I never told him that I was gay, and he never asked; but when I confessed about those impure actions with my high school teacher, he didn't seem shocked. Once again, one *Our Father*, three *Hail Marys* and a *Glory Be*. I still wasn't sorry.

Each year during the Lenten season, the priest(s) at the church assembled members of the youth ministry, which included the altar boys, the choir, and some of the catechism teachers. We met at the rectory's dining hall each Friday during Lent to discuss the Passion of the Christ, the significance of the Resurrection, and say grace over our Lenten meal of rice soup. On this particular Friday, the one before Good Friday, Fr. Guidry had invited me to spend the night at the rectory (the priest's home while serving in that parish) as I had done on a few occasions as an altar boy. My parents dropped me off at the church, suitcase in tow, and waved good-bye to me and Fr. Mike. They were so excited that I was getting to know the priest better. Maybe I was going to join the priesthood, they thought? My willingness to please my parents forbade me ever to correct them when they talked of ordination and such. I felt it was better to say nothing than to see their burgeoning dreams deflated.

With the money I made from my part-time job at the local grocery store, I enjoyed going to Keller's Bakery once a month to buy a chocolate cake and a lemon meringue pie, still two of my favorite sweets. But this school year I had been saving up for a Sony Walkman, a portable cassette player with headphones. This accessory for others was an absolute necessity for me. I just HAD to have one! By mid-spring I'd saved up enough money to buy the Walkman and five cassette tapes: Air Supply's *Life Support*, Boston's 1976 self-titled debut album, Dolly Parton's *Best of Dolly Parton*, Louisiana's LeRoux's self-titled debut album, Three Dog Night's *Joy to the World–Their Greatest Hits,* and the soundtrack of *A Star is Born* starring Barbra Streisand and Kris Kristofferson. In case you haven't yet figured it out, my musical selections must have set off more than a few "gay-dars" at Raccoon Records, the local music store. But I didn't care, I had bought my Walkman and my music with my own money. I was happy!

I brought my new Walkman to show off at the Lenten dinner; it wasn't so much the Walkman itself that excited me, nor the music. This was the very first major purchase that I made using only my own money. It was more a sense of pride than a feeling of boastfulness. (Pride would come to have a much deeper personal meaning later in my life.) The others could see the joy in my face, and they were happy for me too. I also talked about how excited I was to be going to my senior prom with Hank Steuben and his date, conveniently omitting the part about my huge crush on him. Fr. Mike Guidry commented about how proud he was of my accomplishment, and how happy he was for me regarding my senior prom; for a country bumpkin like me to get accolades from the parish priest was quite unexpected. I was excited.

The regular Friday Lenten meal was meant to be a time of reflection and repentance. I often reflected on my happier times with Mr. MacIntosh, and I had absolutely nothing to repent. I went only because I got to sit in between Bart Mosely and David Zeringue, and we'd play footsie under the table. They were both straight, but they had been at least pseudo-bisexual with me on more than one occasion, though we never went all the way. Neither of them knew that I had been sexual with each of them, so the flirting was especially exhilarating for me. I tried to think about what it would be like if all three of us were together in bed. A clink of a glass before grace brought me back to reality. I would never know.

The dinner ended, and in short succession, all of the members of the youth ministry left the rectory. Then it was just me and Fr. Mike. I helped to clean up the kitchen, and then retired to his bedroom as I had done before.

But something about this night *felt* different, *smelled* different, *was* different. Not that different was a bad thing, it just was *different*. I smelled wine. (Until now, the only wine with which I was familiar was Boone's Farm Strawberry Hill that I drank at a swim party.) But this wine smelled rich and sweet, kinda like the church wine we drank on Sundays, but it wasn't. As it turns out, what I was smelling wasn't wine at all. Fr. Guidry had opened a bottle of Glenlivet Scotch Whisky. Not knowing what Scotch whisky smelled like, I could understand how my senses were confused.

I wondered if this was some sort of belated indoctrination into the brotherhood of acolytes and wearers of the green rope. Had all of the previous brethren acolytes been treated this welcomingly into the advanced ministry? I figured they had and accepted it for the honor that I supposed it was. Since I was the youngest of the acolytes, I assumed that my "initiation" had arrived closer to the end of my service to the ministry. I was wrong on both counts.

    I had slept at the rectory on more than one occasion; Fr. Mike usually tried to introduce me to classical music. (*Is that how he mentored the others, too?*) I didn't know much about—nor care for—classical music, but I did know about Beethoven, Brahms, and Bach, oh, and the "William Tell Overture," which I always thought a funny piece of music. He usually educated me by pulling various albums out of his collection and my ears appreciated the sound of putting the needle on the record before I heard the upbeat tunes of Beethoven, Tchaikovsky, and Mozart. (I had a better understanding of Fr. Guidry's love for classical music when the movie *Amadeus* premiered in 1984.) Seated together on the floor, Fr. Mike let me read the album covers and inserts, which I knew to handle with care as they were some of his most cherished treasures.

    The mood of the music that night was different too, and when he put the needle on the record, the songs sounded a bit more somber, and sometimes even romantic. Maybe I was imagining things or the Glenlivet was having an adverse reaction with the merlot I'd had earlier with the rice soup. I viewed the album covers of Chopin, Liszt, Verdi, and Wagner, not knowing that these artists were renowned for their romantic, classical repertoires. I didn't know much about classical music, but even my young ears could recognize the difference in the tone and cadence of this music compared to the times before.

    And, probably unrelated, but for the first time I noticed an enormously thick book with lots of red and black colorings, and a swastika symbol on the front cover, *The Rise and Fall of The Third Reich*. I remember thinking that it was rather odd for a Catholic priest to be interested in Nazi Germany; but I digress.

    We listened to music for a while longer and soon the wine and the Glenlivet had finally made me dizzy enough to stumble a bit while walking about in the small room with two twin-size beds on either side of one wall and a bathroom on the opposite wall with the living area in between. Fr. Mike asked me how I was doing since the death of my friend,

Mark Simon. With my words slurring a bit, not knowing if it was the liquor or something else, I told him that I was still a bit heartbroken, but that I was getting better. My senior prom was only a few weeks away, and I was double-dating with my new best friend.

I sat in the small wingback chair enjoying the music and ate the melted ice left over from the last serving of Scotch. I noticed the bottle was almost empty and the wooziness in my head had the room spinning. Too many emotions and too much alcohol (one glass of wine and one drink of Scotch), told me that it was time for bed; I didn't usually get this drunk this quickly. *Was the liquor really that strong, or was it something else?* I would never know.

I fumbled around to find my pajamas in my suitcase. While Fr. Mike was in the bathroom getting ready for bed, I undressed down to my skivvies and by the time he walked out, I was already wearing my brand-new JC Penney blue-and-white seersucker pajamas, which I had also bought with my own money. It was rather difficult getting into my PJs with all the lights out; shirt buttoned, and drawstring pants tied into a pretty little bow, I was ready for bed.

I was quite stunned when the bathroom door opened, and bright fluorescent lights suddenly flooded the room. From the backlighting, my eyes quickly adjusted; I was aghast to see Fr. Mike in his tighty-whitey underwear, rubbing himself. *Was he putting things in place; did he have an itch to scratch, or was it something more? Was Fr. Mike trying to seduce me?* I didn't know, and I didn't want to know.

The sight of my priest without the pajamas he normally wore when I was there disgusted me. *Where were his PJs? And why wasn't he wearing them? Why was what is usually hidden under his robe now on full display, only covered by a thin layer of white ribbed cotton?* That I DID want to know but figured that avoiding confrontation was the best option on this night. Turns out, I may have been wrong.

I immediately turned my body away from the view that I didn't want to see and threw on the headset from my new Walkman. I had already put the soundtrack of *A Star is Born* into the cassette player. As Fr. Mike approached, the song "With One More Look at You" was playing. I pretended that I never noticed him approaching from behind, and I fast-forwarded the cassette tape to the final song, "Evergreen."

He tapped me on the shoulder to get my attention and gave me a "priestly" hug good night. I ignored what I knew was the beginning of his erection pressed against my thigh, and abruptly ended the hug.

I fell asleep quickly, mostly on purpose, probably aided by the alcohol (and maybe something else). Sometime during the night, I noticed a shadow that seemed familiar though the profile was vague. It was then that I saw that Fr. Mike was saying his prayers; but he was knelt directly over my bed. I wondered why he would be praying on his knees at my bedside, especially while I was asleep. I let the thought escape me and fell back to sleep; I must have been having some sort of disturbed dream; or maybe not. I didn't know, nor would I ever.

As the nightmare continued, I could feel his hands fumbling with the drawstring on my pajama pants. Slowly, he began fondling my crotch, hoping for some type of physical "rise" from me. In my deep sleep, I fought off the urge to get an erection, and rolled over. Soon, I again felt his hands trying to engage me, which I again refused. I could feel the bed trembling; I knew that he was masturbating. I chose to ignore him. I curled up into a fetal position; the nightmare was over, for now!

When I awoke early the next morning, my pajama shirt was buttoned wrong (I don't recall him unbuttoning my shirt), and the string belt on my seersucker trousers was untied. Maybe the wine and the Scotch had more of an effect on me than I had originally thought; I don't remember alcohol having had this much of an adverse effect before.

This morning *felt* different, *smelled* different, *was* different. But this time, I had the distinct feeling that *this* different was bad. My head was still spinning a bit; and even at seventeen I already knew what a hangover felt like. This was NOT a hangover! Had Fr. Mike slipped something into my drink? I would never know; this oblivion would be the downfall of most of the rest of my life.

I suddenly remembered the vivid nightmare from last night; that's when I realized that the nightmare was REAL! I said nothing and did nothing, I just couldn't believe what had happened to me and was extremely disturbed. I didn't take the time to shower and just put on my next day's work clothes. I shoved everything else back into my suitcase; and I don't remember if I said good-bye to Fr. Mike. (He may have had a 6:00 a.m. mass on that Saturday, but I don't remember that either.) My brother picked me up in time for us to both be at work at the grocery store on Saturday morning–7:00 a.m. sharp.

When I returned home after work, I dug in my suitcase, and pulled out my only-worn-once JC Penney seersucker pajamas and cut them up, then threw them into the garbage. I knew that's where they belonged, though I had no clear explanation of why. I knew that they were dirty, and my whole body felt dirty too. I was so angry to throw away my hard-earned money, but the throwing away wasn't about the money. I hopped into the shower to wash off the filth from the night before.

As the only altar boy with the green rope, my *"second second of fame"* was being the recognized acolyte at holy mass on Easter Sunday, which I found quite ironic considering the not yet alleged event(s) of the prior weekend. I conducted my regular churchly duties during the mass, then went home and did some studying before bedtime. Tomorrow was another school day; only a few more weeks and I'd be free. I'd finally get out of high school, escape the obligations of being an altar boy, and finally end the façade of pretending that I enjoyed church at all. I did not attend a regular church service for the next few years, especially not Catholic (unless it was a funeral).

On Thursday, June 14, 2018, Reverend Michael Guidry, then seventy-five years old, turned himself in to the St. Landry Parish Sheriff's Office and confessed to providing alcoholic beverages to and sexual molesting a sixteen-year-old boy in his church parish rectory.

EPIPHANY! Suddenly the word *epiphany* meant something totally contrary to the Catholic version; because at that moment, as I began to put the blurred pieces together, I realized that I had not absolutely lost my mind; something bad *had* happened and I knew it. It is amazing the amount of clarity you get when all of those repressed memories start coming back; especially when you never wanted them to. Although I still couldn't recall the totality of what had happened, my entire life I had wondered what happened on that night, and now I KNEW that I had been sexually assaulted. Epiphany in the Catholic church is a celebratory feast of the revelation as God incarnate as Jesus Christ. My personal epiphany was that I realized that former priest Michael Guidry was a pedophile, and that I had been one of his many victims. And this motherfucker was smart enough to wait until he knew I was seventeen years old. Is that how he got away with his sexual abuse for so long? Regardless, he knew, and I know, that I did not agree to anything sexual with him at any time ever!

My only thought now was I wish I could have hanged him with that fucking green rope. But it was too late ... the damage was done.

The reigning leader of the Roman Catholic Diocese of Lafayette, Bishop Joseph Douglas Deshotel stated, in reference to the arrest, "I pray the victim finds healing." *REALLY!* VICTIM! JUST ONE! HELL NO! FUCK THIS!

What Fr. Michael Guidry did to me happened in 1980; it was now nearly forty *fucking* years later. Do you really believe there is only ONE VICTIM? FUCK YOU, Catholic church!

This was further proof that even after the Lafayette Parish calamity that became the trial of Gilbert Gauthe, the first priest in the United States to face a widely publicized criminal trial for child abuse, the Catholic church was still operating under the same *modus operandi*: relocate the priest before the congregation found out; forgive the cause and silence the symptom.

This time Michael Guidry got caught, but how many others like me had he molested over the past several decades? I know of at least three others: one committed suicide (Bart Mosely), and one died of HIV/AIDS-related complications (Harold Decourt). The other (David Zeringue) is currently divorced with grown children, and just like me, has had several run-ins with the legal establishment since those days after we were molested by the person our parents thought they could trust.

At his sentencing in April 2019, the former priest Michael Guidry stated, "I would like to say I'm very sorry for the things that happened. I know what I did was wrong." *Too little, too late, motherfucker! Fuck you too!*

He was sentenced to seven years hard labor followed by three years supervised probation.

I would still have preferred using the green rope! But that's just me.

[Update: In August 2021, the former Reverend Michael Guidry was unanimously denied bail by the Louisiana State Parole Board.]

Disgraced Catholic priest Michael Guidry Mugshot (courtesy Daily Advertiser)

CHAPTER 3

WELCOME TO FANTASY ISLAND

(That Time I Got High)

I returned to school after the Easter break as if nothing had happened; the only person I could have told about my experiences that night at the rectory was Mark Simon, and he was now dead; and no one would ever have understood. (I don't even know if I did.) I was still in a fog but didn't understand why. I just knew that something bad had happened that night, but how could I tell anybody anything if I just didn't want to remember? There was absolutely no story to tell, so I remained silent.

I was excited about my high school senior prom, but not for the reasons you may think. The chosen theme for the evening was *Welcome to Fantasy Island*; and I was certainly living some sort of dystopian fantasy that night. [*Fantasy Island* was a television series that ran from 1977-1984, with each episode centered around a wide variety of characters who had paid for the "fantasy" experience of their dreams on a tropical island.] My biggest fantasy would have been to have Mr. MacIntosh escort me to my senior prom, but we both knew that would never happen. In my worst nightmare, my fantasy never looked like the night I was about to experience. I needed an evening to remove those vile thoughts of what had happened to me at the church rectory just two weeks before. This night would not disappoint.

My best friend, Hank Steuben, and I decided to double-date for the evening; we began the evening at some fancy-schmancy restaurant, and I thought it would be a great idea to drink a Tom Collins, or two or three; a cocktail made with London Dry gin, club soda, and lemon juice. I probably thought those cocktails made me seem high class, but I soon learned a very important lesson.

Once dinner was over, it was time to head to our senior prom, but there was a slight change in plans. Since we had taken separate vehicles,

Hank asked if my date could drive my car so that he and I could ride together. My heart instantly melted. I had been in love with Hank since the day I met him. Coincidentally, he and his family lived in the same subdivision as Mark Simon's parents, so I had the opportunity to visit him often. I cherished the moments that we shared together, and we formed a bond that I thought could last forever. As I handed my car keys to my prom date, I remember thinking to myself, *is this the day that he is going to tell me that he loves me too? Is Hank finally gonna kiss me?* That couldn't have been further from the truth. My heart shattered again.

I had never in my life seen marijuana before, so I had no idea what it looked like or smelled like. But by the time we arrived at the prom, I most certainly knew what it tasted like. During the forty-five minute drive from the restaurant to the prom, Hank and I had smoked more than enough pot to dispel all of the hurt feelings I thought I had, and I almost forgot that I was still in love with my best friend, although he didn't feel the same. I was HIGH, HIGH, HIGH!

I was so high and more than just a little drunk, that my date abandoned me for most of the night, and rightfully so. But most of my memories, though foggy at best, were from the time I spent in the bathroom with all of my friends trying to sober me up so that I could get into the prom. I was mumbling and stumbling over myself, and the best my friends could do was to keep me out of sight in the bathroom. I recall being steadied up against a bathroom wall, and as I slid down the wall, someone would try and prop me up again. There was absolutely no hiding the fact that this stellar academic and *Who's Who Among American High School Students* was undeniably wasted, drunk, and high.

There are vague memories of our high school principal trying to talk to me, and I vomited on his shoes before being sent outside (with chaperones) to get some fresh air. Mr. MacIntosh watched from inside the building, and I tried to avoid his stare, but it was inescapable. He feigned concern for my predicament, but I knew that his only concern was for fear that I say anything about our relationship that never was.

After about twenty minutes in the warm spring South Louisiana air, I was back at the prom as if nothing had ever happened, but everyone knew exactly what had happened. I pretended as though no one knew I was drunk and high, but no amount of Paco Rabanne cologne could have covered that smell. For the last two weeks of school, several teachers pulled me aside to counsel me about the dangers of drinking. I really should have listened.

I guess one could say that prom was my *"third second of fame,"* but that certainly is not something of which I am proud, nor anything for which I would like to be remembered. And how ironic was it that Mr. MacIntosh, the teacher I had been sneaking sex with for the past few months, was suddenly concerned about my well-being.

In retrospect, I understood how my lack of sexual identity, my fear of being labeled queer, and the juxtaposition of being "in" and "out" took its toll on my mental capacities. I had been in a relationship that had existed only in my head, and I missed that feeling of being in love.

I missed Mark Simon, and I wish that I could have been there for him in the way that he wanted me to. *But Mark was dead, so why was I still living?* I never realized how much Mark's death had impacted those formative years of my life, and how learning to live without him, without learning his secret, would haunt me for the rest of my life.

I still wished that Hank would have been in love with me. But that was wishful dreaming, just like Mr. MacIntosh, and just like my senior prom. I was now alone on Fantasy Island!

I graduated from high school in the spring of 1980 with a $1,000 "Distinguished Freshman" Scholarship to the University of Southwestern Louisiana (now, University of Louisiana–Lafayette). I was truly looking forward to college life, with aspirations of a double-major of English (Journalism) and Pre-Law. While that may have seemed like lofty goals for a seventeen-year-old, I had the intelligence and fortitude to succeed. Memories of my first grade teacher's advice resonated with me and I strived to "always be my best me." I started college in August 1980 with renewed spirit and the vigor to become someone better than I thought I could be; definitely something better than the person that currently existed.

[Sidebar: My paternal grandfather was a United States Army medic who was killed on the beaches of Normandy, France, during World War II; though his body would not be recovered until a year or so later. To honor his service, I wanted to join the military and see the world; the military would also have been my escape from the hatred of my own sexuality. *Maybe.*

My interview with the Army recruiting office lasted fewer than five minutes. He asked, "Are you a homosexual?" I sheepishly affirmed, "Yes, I am." (Long before Melissa Etheridge penned that album.) Immediately, I was escorted out the front door. I was not "eligible" to serve our country; and the roller coaster of discrimination began.]

Though I thought that I was ready for college, my personal life was chaotic. I had the smarts to excel at college, as most of my course load was advanced placement classes. (With an Academic College Testing score of thirty-one, I "tested out" of most of the basic courses.) I was a smart, driven, and confident person, but my daily stressors—that included coming to terms with my homosexuality—had overcome my need for academic success. I was academically gifted, but not at all focused. I needed balance.

A great diversion from the doldrums of college life was the excitement of fraternity life. I decided that joining a fraternity would help me to make new friends, study more effectively, and receive assistance from my fraternity brothers to make college life not only tolerable, but interesting. I was completely wrong; there were no new friends, no improved study habits, and no fraternity brother assistance. Three strikes *... was I back in little league?* I slowly gravitated away from college studies and toward fraternity parties and alcohol.

I opted to join Sigma Nu, mostly because I knew absolutely no one in the fraternity, so I figured they wouldn't know my secret. The Sigma Nu house was located near the USL campus and was convenient for study time throughout the day. The fraternity was also well-known on campus for having some of the greatest parties. The fact that I was still only seventeen years old didn't really seem to matter. A party was a party, and I was happy to be there.

Exactly one year after Mark Simon's death, on September 21, 1980, I met the person who was driving the motorcycle on that dreadful night. Thomas Steinle, a motorcycle enthusiast, was, as it turns out, Mark's boyfriend. Thomas was a year younger than Mark, but he portrayed himself as being much older. He was strikingly handsome and gave off a vibe of James Dean meets Elvis Presley crossed with Tarzan. He had been comatose for about nine months after the accident and didn't know that Mark died until he recovered.

Mark's family welcomed him as one of their own. On that day, I also learned that Mark's family knew he was gay, and that Thomas was his boyfriend; something I wished I would have allowed Mark to confide in me. Thomas and I sat on the patio of Mark's parents' home and shared some quality time. We talked about the shared friendship we had with Mark, and how his tragic death deeply affected us. Thomas regaled me with stories of the many special times that he and Mark shared. I told him about Mark's and my long trip home after homecoming night, and that Mark never got to tell me what he wanted me to know. Thomas told me that Mark spoke about me often, and that Mark had always wanted me to meet him; but the opportunity never presented itself. We hugged and cried and cried and hugged, then we talked some more and hugged and cried again. Wiping the tears from each other's eyes, we consoled each other with one final hug.

I saw Thomas once more at a Halloween house party in 1985. Both alcohol and drugs were readily available; I decided that Crown Royal and cocaine would be my poison for the night. He and I cruised each other most of the night in this dingy studio apartment that could barely fit the queen-size bed, but we each pretended that we didn't notice. It would have been taboo for me to sleep with him; he was my best friend's widower. Mark would surely have struck me with lightning for even considering the thought!

That would be the last time I saw Thomas Steinle. I do wish I could have visited with him more. Sadly, he fell down the rabbit hole of despair and destruction with alcohol and drugs after Mark's death, and no amount of recovery could save him. I had been told that upon his HIV diagnosis, he moved to New Orleans, then on December 13, 2002, I received a phone call from Mark's parents telling me that Thomas had died. He was only thirty-eight years old. I hope that perhaps he and Mark have found each other in the next life, and that their love will finally be everlasting.

Knowing now that THAT is what Mark wanted to tell me gave me peace in acknowledging that he would have entrusted me with such insight into his personal life. I only wish that we would have had more time to share so that he would have been able to confide in me his true feelings. But I know that Mark, through his own transition to the afterlife, helped me out immensely as I navigated my own path of discovering my own sexuality.

His death troubled me so much that I found it within myself to tell the girl I was dating that I thought that I was gay. We were coming home from a date, and I pulled over on the side of the road. I was still reeling from Mark's death, and I just broke down and cried in front of her and said, "I think I might be gay." She said, "Oh honey, I already knew that. I was just waiting for you to figure it out."

That very special person was Jocelyn Rae Jensen. She was the very first person to whom I was able to admit that I was gay. I was so relieved that she understood me and never judged me; and we have remained best friends to this very day. I often tell others that "we never really broke up, we just both started seeing other guys!" (And as long as it wasn't the SAME guy, we were gonna be okay!)

It truly hurts my heart to believe that being gay is something that you have to admit to. When, exactly, did straight people begin having to admit that they were straight? I now recognize that I was born gay and that nothing that anyone could do or say was going to change who I loved. I was a man who loved other men. No one should ever have to admit to that. It's just another fact of life. But life just isn't that simple. Maybe one day it will be. Until then, I decided to live in my own Fantasy Island where I could openly live as my true self regardless of others' opinions; at least that's what I told myself.

Senior Prom – Welcome to Fantasy Island – 1980

CHAPTER 4

A DOZEN ROSES

(That Time I Was Forced Out)

My coming out was not so much a traumatic experience (for me) as it had been for so many of my gay and lesbian friends. I had known that I was gay since high school; Mr. MacIntosh definitely helped to solidify my absoluteness about my own sexuality. But because I was so involved in school activities and school government, there was never a target on my back. I was not bullied in high school; but I saw it happening to others who were perceived to be gay. And (sadly) I consciously distanced myself from those people because I did not want to be guilty by association. I never had to address my sexuality in high school, because I hid behind my popularity.

During the summer of 1980, shortly after I had graduated high school, two very dear friends of mine, Brian Richardson and Greg Salvatore, took me out for the evening. I really didn't know where we were going, but I was happy to be with other guys who I thought were just like me. Soon afterward, we arrived at a small bar on University Avenue in Lafayette, Louisiana. I remember driving in front of this bar many times and I would often see strange-looking women hanging out on the front steps, but I didn't understand why. It was clear to me that these were men dressed as women, and I didn't understand that either.

The bar, I later learned, was named John's *C'est la Guerre* (That's War). But the meaning behind the name was exactly the opposite. *C'est la guerre* became a rallying cry during the years of World War II (1939-1945) to express frustration that while doing everything "right," the outcomes were always "wrong." This French phrase of resignation provided a universal excuse for anything that was broken, no longer functioned, was unavailable, or could not be accomplished. It also explained away any and all unusual behavior. Regardless of where the name for the bar was originally derived, it was extremely appropriate for a gay bar. And while the bar has now been closed for many years, our struggle for survival continues.

As we entered this bar, I noticed that all of the walls were painted black, which made the already-small bar seem even tinier. There was a pool table in the far corner, and a small bathroom tucked away just beyond the pool table. I immediately noticed that the men's urinal was in full view to the other patrons shooting pool. That was quite odd, but weirdly intriguing. It also seemed that this bar was not very popular, since very few people were there, which made no sense, since the parking lot was full. I remember feeling uncomfortable and a bit ashamed to be in this dingy little bar. But I was happy to have my friends with me.

Someone soon bellowed over the loudspeakers: "Showtime in ten minutes ... ten minutes 'til showtime!"

We were then escorted into a huge back room that was packed. I was about to see my very first drag show. Within seconds, I was immediately singled out of the audience at the hands of that night's emcee, Miss Charlene Barberra. And I distinctly recall Miss Barberra saying something like, "I can tell you've never seen a man in a dress before. But, give it time, one day you'll be up here in a dress too." And she was right! (More about my "drag" experience later.) I remember feeling out of place but welcome at the same time. I wore a very brightly colored Hawaiian shirt, and thought I was looking pretty good; however, when I saw how everyone else was dressed, I realized that I tried a little too hard to fit in. Despite this, I met other people who were just like me, and it felt wonderful!

I spotted one of my fraternity brothers at *C'est la Guerre* that night, and could tell that he was trying to mingle in the crowd to avoid eye contact. (So was I!) But the second Miss Barberra put the spotlight on me and my fabulously flamboyant shirt, my cover was blown. If he hadn't yet seen me, there was no mistaking it now.

It was also on this night that I got to first enjoy the talents of Miss Naomi Sims, a female impersonator who would play a major role later in my life. To this day, I still thank Brian and Greg for introducing me to a new world of self-awareness, familiarity, and acceptance. This one night changed my life forever. For the first time, I learned that there were places for "people like me" to go and feel welcomed and safe, without fear of homophobia and retaliation.

The following morning, my parents were curious about how my night was; I told them that I had a great time, and told them where we went, but never mentioned that it was a gay bar.

My parents suddenly had a look of fear and concern on their faces; I didn't understand why. They proceeded to tell me the story of a cross-dressing man who had recently been murdered nearby that same bar. They implored me to be safe, and made me promise to never go there again. They informed me that the victim liked to dress up in ladies' clothes; they called her Tammy Lynn; when police found him, he was already dead, with his penis slashed off and put into his mouth.

They also informed me that Tammy Lynn was my cousin on my stepgrandfather's side of the family. Someone was arrested and convicted of the crime, though he always claimed his innocence. It would be a myriad of occurrences later in my life that led me to believe in his innocence. I would unearth the fact that my uncle knew a lot more about this incident than he had let on at the time; he'd feign drunkenness each time I brought it up; I knew he was lying.

Unfortunately, my first venture to a gay bar, or whatever they were called, affected my sister in a very sad and perverse way. At the time this occurred, I had already graduated, but she was still attending Carencro High School. One of her classmates told her a completely fabricated story and outed me to her. She was so traumatized by this revelation that my parents had to pull her out of school for the rest of the day because she was inconsolable. The reason that I am including this story is because I feel it is very important to recognize that others in my family were bullied because of me, and for that I am truly sorry. And honestly, I did not know this story until thirty-something years after high school. This is how my parents relayed the (mis)information to me.

One of my sister's classmates told her that he worked for a local florist, and on this exact night, they were hired to deliver flowers to someone at John's *C'est La Guerre* bar. They stated that someone had purchased a dozen roses to be delivered to me personally at the bar.

(For the record, to this date, I have NEVER received a DOZEN ROSES from ANYONE EVER in my LIFE!)

[Even from the outset, the story doesn't make sense. Why would a florist allow a minor to deliver flowers to a bar where liquor was sold? And how would this person even know who I was, or if I was even at that particular bar on that exact night? I had never been to this bar before, and the only two people who even knew me there were my two friends, Brian and Greg.]

I remember being furious when my parents told me this story because I knew that it wasn't true. So, my next question was, "Who told my sister this story?" And I was told that my sister didn't want to say, because this person was her friend. [I never understood that either. I would not want to be friends with someone who caused me to be bullied because of their actions.] To this day, my sister has never revealed which "friend" told her the story that caused her so much pain.

My *"fourth second of fame"* is compliments of false teenage spite on a school campus which I no longer attended, about an event that never happened, in a place the gossip monger should not have been, which lead to my sister being bullied. This person took away *my* privacy to protect *theirs* and damaged my sister in the crossfire.

Actually, I have always known exactly who this person was, but I will not mention their name here, and will instead opt to extend to this person the courtesy that they never gave me. I will not out that person now, even though they have since acknowledged that they are homosexual. But there is another reason that I will not reveal this person's name.

You see, I completely understand *why* they did what they did. Because they did what I did when I was in high school by hiding in the shadows; though I NEVER acted maliciously toward anyone because of their perceived sexuality (or lack thereof).

In their effort to hide their own shame about their own homosexuality, it was much easier to cast doubt and shame on others. And while I never outed anyone, I was painfully aware that I was able to keep my homosexuality hidden because those other perceived homosexuals were taking the brunt of the bullying. And by this person talking about me and my homosexuality, it deflected the bullying away from them.

And that's the defense mechanism that they thought was appropriate. Not only was it NOT appropriate, it hurt my sister tremendously.

I forgave this person many years ago. I have learned that forgiveness is for yourself, and not for the person being forgiven. In most cases, the person to whom you bestow forgiveness usually doesn't need nor want your forgiveness, and in most cases, they don't even care. For years, I held a grudge toward this person; a person who wasn't even in my social sphere. I was only hurting myself by holding on to the anger and guilt I felt for what they had done to me and, by extension, my sister. I no longer have any animosity toward this person.

But I DO believe that this person owes my sister an apology. Because of their actions in an attempt to defame me, they created an environment where my sister was bullied simply because her brother was gay. And my sister deserves a heartfelt apology for what they put her through.

It is NEVER okay to hurt others just to make yourself feel better!

As my sister is reading this, she is just learning that I did not know this story at the time it occurred. So, if I seemed uncaring or uninterested in what was going on with her at school, I sincerely apologize. I just didn't know! This situation could have and should have been handled much differently!

So, call me homo! Call me gay!

I AM those things! I OWN those words! And I am PROUD of who I am!

But I wasn't then.

That summer night in 1980 was the first of many nights at John's *C'est la Guerre* bar, where I continued to meet others who were just like me; I opted to ignore my parents' request. I was young and my sexual experiences were nuanced and exhilarating. (Until that point, Mr. MacIntosh was the only person with whom I'd been "all-the-way" sexually.)

I would often tell my parents that I was staying at a friend's house on the weekends, so that they didn't worry when I didn't return home that night ... even though, many times, I didn't know which friend I'd be spending the night with. Chances were, I had not even met him yet. On those few nights when I actually had a date, we would have dinner and drinks, and/or head to the movies with drinks, then bar hop for even more drinking, and then enjoy each other for the remainder of the evening until we fell asleep.

My Dad used to always ask, "Where did you go?" and "Who were you with?" and "What did y'all do?" And I remember telling my Dad, "One day you'll ask me, and I'm gonna tell you. So, don't ask me anything that you don't really want to know the answer to."

He finally asked me those questions one too many times, and I answered each of them in detail. And I recall him telling me, "Well, at least you were *the man*." While I'd like to pretend that I did not know what that meant, I absolutely understood. He could handle the fact that his son was gay, as long as he was still "the man."

And then he said, "So now you're queer?" My immediate response was, "No, I'm not queer, I'm GAY; there is a difference." And over the next few days I had long explanations with my parents about my homosexuality. (This was at a time when "queer" was a derogatory term used to minimize and slur homosexuals.)

I learned that my parents equated gayness with girlishness (more specifically, wanting to be a girl like Tammy Lynn), which is exactly what I was afraid of. I assured them that I loved all of my "parts," and that I was not a girl. (I later explained transgenderism to them, but that would have been information overload for them initially.) My parents always accepted me and loved me unconditionally, and my coming out did not diminish their love for me.

"Hell Week," a common hazing initiation for the freshmen pledges, forced pledges to play various drinking games, with each of them rigged so pledges would lose and have to drink whatever alcohol was put on the table. I didn't mind losing the drinking games because they blurred my memory of that unfortunate night with Fr. Mike at the rectory and that painful afternoon shared with Thomas Steinle lamenting Mark Simon's death. But the partying life seemed to disagree with me.

After losing one of the drinking games, I fell asleep in my car with the ignition turned on. My intention was to sleep it off in my Little Green Frog, a nickname we had given to the car my brother and I had inherited from my grandmother after her death. With alcohol-thinned blood,

I was cold that night, so I left the car and the heater on while I napped, unaware that the headlights were also on.

I was startled awake by campus police, and I remember the police officer's flashlight blinding me through the driver's side window. What I did not know, was that the campus police had already called my parents, and they were there to "greet" me, as well. My parents scolded me, then drove me home. The following morning, we discussed the dangers of drinking and driving; and how I could have killed myself being in that car with the ignition turned on. There would be many more bad decisions to follow.

By the end of my first semester of USL, I was already disenfranchised with college life, and was no longer excited with continued education. Even Sigma Nu couldn't keep my attention. I told my parents that my grades had dropped to below a "C" average, so I was dropped from the pledge class. But that's really not what happened.

My fraternity brother who had seen me that night at *C'est la Guerre* outed me to the other Sigma Nu brothers, and I was denied entry into the fraternity by a majority vote of the current members. Once again, I had been scapegoated for being gay by another gay person attempting to conceal his own homosexuality.

I enrolled for a second semester at USL, and was determined to remain focused on my studies, especially since I was no longer in a fraternity. But that forced determination was short-lived, and I never completed my second semester of college, even though I was excelling with a 3.8 grade point average. That didn't matter. I was miserable, and I needed to figure out why!

I wanted to explore life and it was obvious to me that my head was just not in the right place. After a semester and a half of college, I realized that I had had enough. I was moving on. But where, and how?

a dozen roses I have never received

CHAPTER 5

SHIRTLESS JOE
(That Time That I Tipped A Stripper)

As for nightlife, I had become rather bored with the gay scene at John's *C'est la Guerre* and needed another outlet in my search for my next gay friend/conquest for the evening. During my semester-and-a-half of college I had found a hometown, old-timer's hillbilly bar call Frank's, a mixture of misfits and ne'er-do-wells where there was always a card game to join. Price of admission to join was free, but that was just to sit at the table. The real gambling started after that. I spent many nights playing Bourré, Cadillac, or Spades. I almost always lost, but I was getting drunk, so the money didn't matter.

Most days, I would hang out by the pay phone. I always enjoyed a friendly game of pool, and the pay phone was conveniently located by the pool tables. Often, random men would call the pay phone to find out who was there, or if there were any cuties around. The person on the other end of the phone was usually a closeted gay guy, or a downtown businessman wanting some discreet fun after work before going home to his wife. I was always happy to oblige.

At the time, I had no idea that Frank's Bar had been a constant in the gay community. While other gay bars were constantly opening and closing, Frank's remained the only bar that was ALWAYS there for ALL of us. A straight female patron once told me, "It don't matter if you're white, black, homo, straight, pink, yellow or purple, at some point you're gonna end up at Frank's." She was right. (Unfortunately, Frank's was a victim of arson in the late 1990s and was destroyed. No suspect was ever arrested. It was, of course, a gay bar.)

Most weekends I started out with a couple of drinks (Crown Royal and Coca-Cola) at John's, then headed downtown to Frank's for a few more drinks and some fun with some straight guys before I headed back to John's to watch the midnight drag show before finally ending up at Leaping Lena's.

Leaping Lena's was a split-level bar on the outskirts of town within Lafayette Parish, but outside of any city limit restrictions and the 2:00 a.m. closing law. The first time I walked in, I noticed that all of the walls were painted black, reminiscent of John's *C'est la Guerre*. The footpath around the bar area was lined with black linoleum tile. The rest of the bar, except for the dance floor, was covered with carpeting that looked as if it had been discarded remnants of an old hotel. The patchwork patterns of purple, pink, orange, black, and white were splattered with many spilled drink stains from years of neglect and several cigarette burns which the club didn't even try to hide. A fog of smoke (cigarette, cigar, and marijuana) greeted guests, and the only escape from the dank smell was a visit to the upstairs outdoor patio. While "upstairs outdoor patio" may describe the portico of some upscale establishment, this was far from being that. Leaping Lena's upstairs outdoor patio was the four-foot-square fire escape landing that hid patrons' lewd and sometimes illegal acts. Enclosed within ornate wrought iron left over from the previous tenants, the fire escape was connected to a small balcony that went halfway around the building, with no lighting, which helped us hide from the police when they sometimes arrived unexpectedly.

We almost always spent the night at Leaping Lena's, and with the help of the alcohol and a few black mollies (a concentrated form of the amphetamine MDMA, or Ecstasy), a baggie of cocaine, and maybe a hit of acid, we were still wide awake and partying by morning when the roosters crowed and signaled that it was time to go home. I usually had random hookups at Leaping Lena's, so my man-craving was satisfied ... for the moment.

[Sidebar: I'm realizing that I must sound like I was the "cock of the walk" or something like that; far from it. At university, I took Psych 101, so often times when I was headed out for my (almost) nightly "rooster" hunt, I'd bring a legal pad and a pencil. That way, if I ran into anyone I knew whom I didn't want to know that I was gay, I'd tell them that I was doing research for a project in my Psych class. It was simply insane for me to believe that I was fooling anyone, and many of my friends today still remember that "cute little boy in the tank top and the short shorts."

They still remind me, "Girl, you know you coulda left your notes in the car!"]

By then I had become a barfly ... studying during the day, then partying all night long. I still lived with my parents during college, so all of the money I made from my part-time job at the movie theatre was mine to spend. Though I was making really good money for a college kid, my need for drugs weighed heavier than my other responsibilities. I had champagne taste on a beer budget, but could usually tag along with generous benefactors. The atmosphere in Leaping Lena's was so dark that we didn't even bother sneaking off to the bathroom; we'd just use a car key to grab a bump of cocaine and snort it in the middle of the dance floor. It was always great to have a drag queen for company because then we could all use her extra-long fingernails as coke spoons. High on cocaine and whatever other substances we had taken that night, and after I had used up my tag-along friends' drugs, I was on a manhunt. I didn't like the thrill of the chase; I knew what I wanted, and I wouldn't stop until it (he) had been conquered. I'd hook up with a random stranger or strangers from the bar and enjoy myself for the rest of the night.

Since I had selfishly shared other people's drugs for the evening, I usually had some leftover cocaine that I kept for myself so I could stay awake for classes and work. I had become what I thought was a sexual delicacy. Realistically, I was a sexual deviant. In less than a year, I'd made myself well-known in the gay community as the "go-to" guy for sex; but I was hard to get. Although some of it was salacious gossip, most of it was true. I was a voracious sex addict. I enjoyed the rush of anonymous sex, and yearned for the attention, not realizing the negativity that came with it. I wanted men and they wanted me, and all those I refused would call me names like "skank" and "filthy tramp;" only they dared not say these things to my face. But I couldn't really be angry with them either; it was the truth.

I always wanted to be popular and finally I was; just not the kind of popular that was being talked about me behind my back. I had somehow turned myself into the hometown harlot. Lafayette's own Lush Lucy (me) became easier after each drink. Very seldom did I have to buy a drink, but little did I know, my sexual prowess and escapades would prove costly.

Though the sex was exhilarating and dangerous, and the anonymity of it all is what began the demise of my reputation; for me, it wasn't about the sex at all. It was about the power; when I was having sex, I felt powerful. I chose the people I wanted to have sex with, and I knew they wanted to have sex with me. It was MY choice and not theirs. I always wanted the power that seemingly came with striking good looks and yearned for the validation of popularity. The popularity I received was *not* the popularity I wanted nor needed, but at the time, I was oblivious to the damage I was doing to myself and my own self-esteem. I was finally popular (in my own distorted world), and THAT'S what mattered most!

Leaping Lena's closed its doors soon thereafter due to curfew laws changing, and a new gay bar named Club Fantasy opened up near the university. The small club was tucked behind the back entrance of an all-night diner, and the parking lot was shared with the strip mall that housed my favorite music store, Raccoon Records. One of the conveniences of the location is that many straight men could use the parking lot of the strip center, then scurry over to Fantasy without being noticed; so, if anyone saw their vehicle there, they would assume they were shopping. Indeed, they were, and I was happy to fill their "carts."

The bar's entrance was barely visible from the parking lot, as the lights were normally kept fairly dim, and more so on the inside. The club maximized its use of space by setting up the main bar area in such a way as to separate the billiards and rear seating areas, from the dance floor/stage and front seating area; still allowing space to create a backstage area for performers to prepare.

One summer night in 1981, Club Fantasy had a special show night featuring male strippers from Houston, Texas. I had never seen male strippers before; although I had seen some female strippers at a club called The Villa. If these male strippers were anywhere near the caliber of entertainment that night at The Villa, I'd be better off staying home and saving my money. The talent was simply dreadful ... and, NO, I DO NOT want a private dance! My brother and I left immediately when the dancer, a very pasty-skinned white girl—who we couldn't tell if she pregnant or just overweight—asked us for a tip. Maybe we should have given her a couple of dollars, because she sure could have used a shower.

The thought of male exotic (and erotic) entertainment piqued my curiosity. I wanted to see what all the chatter was about. And DAMN ... I'm so glad I went! Club Fantasy definitely fulfilled all of mine that night!

I can vaguely remember seeing the first dancer, but I was not really paying much attention. Then the second dancer came out from behind the stage. He wore a costume that resembled a unicorn, and then slowly, with the rhythm of the music, he began to shed his costume. I was entranced ... but not by him, nor his perfectly sculpted body, nor the fact that he was almost naked. This guy could dance! This stunning Cuban/Puerto Rican Adonis moved with the music so expertly that the two became one. It was beautiful. His name was Peter Casares; and this was not the last time that his journey and mine would intersect.

Then the third dancer began performing. He was a sun-kissed blonde god, and blondes normally weren't really my type, but something about him kept me from peeling my eyes away. He was muscular, slightly bronzed, with short feathered hair ... and he could dance as well as Peter! I was besieged by his beauty and impressed with his talent. Though I had never in my life tipped a dancer, I quickly dug into my pocket to grab some cash. I saw others in the crowd putting money into his G-string, but I just didn't feel comfortable. As outgoing a person as I was, and as slutty as I acted, I was entranced by this male stripper. I wanted to leave a good impression without embarrassing myself in the process.

With dollar bills in my outstretched arms, the blonde bombshell slowly gyrated toward me. I don't know if I was shocked at his approach or if I was just blinded by his handsomeness, but when he pulled his G-string from his hip to allow me to put the money in, I froze. I don't know why, but I just grabbed his hand, and gave him the money.

After the show, I knew this for certain ... I wanted to become a male stripper! I sought this dancer out of the crowd to let him know how much I truly enjoyed his performances, hoping he could give me trade tips about how to get into the stripping business; but mostly just because I wanted to be near him. I never expected what happened next.

He told me his name was Dan Miller, and that he was the reigning Mr. Gay Houston. He was a recent cover model for *This Week In Texas*–

Texas' Leading Gay Publication, aka *TWT*. It was obvious that we found each other very attractive, and we laughed about how I placed the money in his hand, rather than in his G-string. That really got his attention, as he told me that no one had ever done that; he was both surprised and intrigued. I think we both were.

We spent the rest of the night together, but it wasn't enough. I wanted, no, I *needed* more. Clearly, so did he! And I was in between jobs, so I had lots of time on my hands; very little money, but lots of time.

The next day, we set off to spend the week in Houston. He took me around the city, and introduced me to his friends. It was a fantastic week and he was the perfect host and tour guide. He took me to a bar called Montrose Mining Company with very low ceilings, exposed wooden rafters, and a concrete floor littered with peanut shells. Yep, there were barrels of roasted peanuts for its patrons to peel-and-eat while they cruised the bar. As we approached the bar, the bartender turned around and recognized Dan right away, but paled when he saw me. The Shirtless Joe from my hay-baling days immediately jumped over the bar to give me a huge hug. Dan was speechless. How the heck did I know David? (His real name was Joseph David, or J.D., but Texas knew him as David Prejean, the reigning Mr. Gay Texas 1982. I preferred to call him Shirtless Joe.)

David, Dan, and I chatted for quite some time. I'd regale stories of farm life with Shirtless Joe, and David would say that he always wondered when I'd find my way to Houston. Dan listened in astonishment and smiled with happiness knowing that he had inadvertently reunited me with my long-lost cousin. Though Dan and I never became a couple (I didn't have a job nor money, and I lived over 200 miles away ... he made the right decision), I will always thank him for showing me a whole new world that, until then, I did not know existed. I returned to Louisiana with a new attitude and vowed to revisit Houston soon.

Upon my return from Houston, I finally landed a job working at an upscale fashion boutique named Brother's. I had applied to work at this store several times before being hired and shopped there often just to show the management my excitement about their store. I was ecstatic when I got the phone call and made sure to wear all Brother's merchandise to the interview, including the brown leather zip-up ankle boots I'd purchased the prior week, only to find out later that they were labeled as women's boots. I was hired immediately, and on my first day, was introduced to my new boss, Greg Salvatore. *Yep, the very same guy that brought me to my first gay bar with his then-boyfriend, Brian Richardson.*

I loved working at my favorite men's store, but even that soon wore off, and I started drinking and smoking before work. I thought I held myself together quite well, but my ruse fooled no one. Management fired me on the spot when I showed up to work both drunk and high. As tough as it was to lose a beloved job because of drugs and alcohol, I was even more ashamed of myself for embarrassing my friend and boss, Greg. He was the real reason I was hired in the first place; he found my job application and vouched for me. Not only did I let myself down, my selfish actions soured his reputation with the owners. I am forever regretful that I let down one of the people I admired most.

Without a college career and without a job, two weeks later I had packed a few suitcases to spend the rest of the summer with Shirtless Joe and his partner Rick Griffin. They had a wonderful condo on Holly Hall directly across from the Astrodome, and I woke up to a view of my childhood dream vacation every day for a sweet deal of only $100 per month in rent.

But there was another reason that I *needed* to leave my hometown to search for opportunities elsewhere. Almost my entire life up until that time had been a lie ... by living my life in a heterosexual world where a young gay boy felt unwanted and disrespected by this society with a perpetual small-town attitude toward anything they did not understand. And even though I had been out for a couple of years and was established within the gay community, I still felt as though I was hiding myself in my own little closet.

It was David (Shirtless Joe) who introduced me to Naomi Sims, the same female impersonator originally from near my hometown whom I had seen performing at John's *C'est la Guerre*. Newman (Naomi) had seen me out with Dan and David a few weeks prior on one of my whirlwind visits to Houston, and told David, "I need to meet that guy!" David said, "No problem, he's my cousin. He's living with us," and made the introduction. He came over to the condo and spent the afternoon with us, and brought cocaine and a few hypodermic needles. I had never done intravenous drugs before, but I had heard that it gets you twice as high twice as fast as ingesting or smoking. And that was right. The only problem is that the high didn't last, and every forty-five minutes or so I needed another fix. I did not know how these people were affording all of these drugs, but I was happy to be the recipient of their generosity.

With Naomi's insistence, I secured a job my first week in Houston at one of Texas' largest gay discos. The Copa offered more than 10,000 square feet of over-the-top flamboyant entertainment. The front portion of the bar—secluded from the rest of the disco—was a very upscale piano bar where the owner would often tickle the keys for sing-alongs and other gay shenanigans. The back portion of the club had four separate bar stations on three different levels, and a huge dance floor with a large raised stage for drag shows and other entertainment. I was hired as a barback, as I had no bartending experience, and I fit in with the Houston crowd instantly. (In 1981 the legal drinking age was still eighteen, and by the time Texas raised the legal drinking age to nineteen, I had just turned nineteen. The universe was obviously sending me a sign that it wanted me to drink. So, I did.)

During that summer I had many, many wild nights at The Copa as well as many other bars including The Mining Company, to see Shirtless Joe of course, The Galleon (happy hour entertainment), The Ripcord (leather bar), Brazos River Bottom (country and Western), and Mary's Naturally, one of Texas' oldest and most renowned bars of its time.

Not only was the Copa my home bar, but it was my favorite bar because it felt as though the entire staff took this newbie under its collective wing, and for that I was truly appreciative. That, and all of the after-hours debauchery we enjoyed are some of the most amazing memories that I'll never forget.

And the Copa offered something else that interested me. The bar hosted a weekly male stripper contest where the weekly winners could compete to become a monthly winner, and at the end of the year, for the "Male Stripper of the Year" contest. Sure, winning would take lots of hard work, but I really, really wanted that trophy. I usually worked on the nights of the male stripper preliminaries and would watch and learn as I worked ... and drank.

That summer, Naomi took me under her wing and showed me the ropes in Houston gay entertainment. She introduced me to important people and mentored me in ways that even she didn't know. I am forever grateful for the privilege of calling Naomi a friend. When Naomi Sims was Queen Apollo de Lafayette (a gay men's Mardi Gras Krewe) in 1988, of course, I was part of her entourage. She continually showed grace under pressure and showed me the world as she saw it, and she also showed me the struggles and pressure as an entertainer to always be a performer, and how to walk that tightrope. One of most important things that Naomi taught me was that there was a definite difference between friends and acquaintances; the difficult part was figuring out which was which.

One afternoon I was all alone in this fabulous two-story condo; using rubber tubing as a makeshift tourniquet, I injected myself with who knows how much cocaine. I laid on the floor and enjoyed the feeling of the plush carpeting on my bare skin; it felt as though my nerve endings were *outside* of my skin. I looked at my hands and swore I was touching the carpet, but the actual floor was at least two feet away. It felt as though I was having an out-of-body experience, but I was still in my body. I was hot on the inside and suddenly became super-cognizant of my surroundings. I was sensually aroused but not in a sexual way; it was more of a spiritual awareness. I danced up and down the stairs all afternoon and pretended that I was a famous stripper; not only famous, but the MOST famous. I wanted to feel what it was like to be gawked at by hundreds of adoring fans who threw their money at you. There was this mix of songs which I found in David's record collection called *Stars on 45* with snippets of songs recorded by various artists including The Beatles, with songs such as "Intro Venus," "Sugar Sugar," "No Reply," "I'll Be Back," "Drive My Car," "Do You Want to Know a Secret?" "We Can Work It Out," "I Should Have Known Better," "Nowhere Man," and "You're Gonna Lose That Girl." With this one extended-length record I tried out different dance moves, and vowed that I would one day be a star. It was on that day, in that fucked-up state of mind, that I decided for sure that I was going to be a male stripper. And not just *any* male stripper, but the Texas Stripper of the Year. On that day, in June 1982, I became Colt Michael.

My *"fifth second of fame"* was that afternoon all alone at David and Rick's condo sashaying up and down those stairs, mostly naked, enjoying my body and the movements of the dance, envisioning throngs of adoring men transfixed on me in amazement. Of course, the fame was only a fantasy, but so was Colt Michael!

While still living with David and Rick, I entered the Male Stripper of the Month contest at the Copa-Houston, and won for the month of July, which meant I could compete for Texas' Male Stripper of the Year in August. It was truly an unforgettable experience.

There were sixteen contestants; one for each month of the year, plus the next four highest preliminary scorers. At that time, I was still very uncomfortable with myself as a young gay person, and with my own self-image; but I always knew that Colt Michael could "put on a show." And that HE DID!

That night, I wore a space odyssey-type outfit; a triangular silver Mylar top that ripped apart at the sleeves, black skin-tight satin pants with tear-aways on the side seams adorned with silver fringe, and short black cowboy boots embellished with silver sequins and black fringe. The opening song was the beginning of "Reflections" by Diana Ross and the Supremes. It was a slow, melancholy song that allowed the audience to get wrapped into the performance as I removed the top part of my costume. That song slowly morphed into "The Visitors" by ABBA. I danced up a storm as I seductively brought the crowd into my performance. I tore away the black satin pants to reveal a black leather jock as the music was now mixing into "We Can Work It Out" by Chaka Khan. (Remember *Stars on 45* from earlier that summer?) The final look was revealed as I slowly unsnapped the leather jock strap, wearing only a very thin G-sting embellished with red fringe, and nothing else (except those black fringed boots). I couldn't remember exactly what I was doing during each song segment, nor could I recall anything about the crowd or their reactions. I was so focused on the performance that some might say that I forgot to have fun; but for me, the enjoyment came from dancing for hundreds of people and have their (mostly) undivided attention as they watched me do what I did best ... DANCE!

As winners were named, I remember being extremely nervous. I desperately wanted to be in the Top 6, but everybody else was so good too. I felt defeated even before the announcements began. And when the emcee started calling names, mine was not one of the names called; but my name HAD been called, and in my nervousness, I never heard. I had actually made the Top 3. Then they announced the third-place winner, and it wasn't me. So, there I was on stage with only one other contestant, who happened to be someone with whom I had become dear friends, Peter Casares; who was a professional dancer and choreographer by trade. (Yes, the same "unicorn dancer" Peter Casares I met at Club Fantasy in 1981.) There was no way that I had a chance to win. And then the drum roll, and the emcee announced that the first runner-up was Colt Michael, and the Winner of the Male Stripper of the Year for 1982 was Peter Casares. To be honest, I was just shocked to win second place, but then I found out that I had only lost by one point (or so I was told). It had been the closest contest ever; I considered myself a WINNER anyway. It's the first time in my life that I was second place and I was okay with that. Peter and I remained friends for years, until his death on April 20, 1990 at age twenty-seven; another victim of the AIDS epidemic.

(Oh, and I almost forgot to mention ... the head judge was ... Dan Miller! YES! *That* Dan Miller!)

The very next day, I learned that David and Rick had been evicted from their condo for having not paid the mortgage for months. Rick was a banker and had not been to work since I arrived in Houston in late June. It was then that I understood where all the drug money had been coming from. Indeed, I had not paid my $100 in rent since the first month, spending it instead on alcohol and drugs.

With no money and no place to go, I returned to Louisiana to live with my parents and Rick went back to wherever he had come from. I lost touch with Shirtless Joe when he moved to the West Coast in the 1990s.

Neither David nor I knew of the depths of his boyfriend's addiction until we saw that notice on the front door while Rick was supposedly at work. Coincidentally, the bank called that day to find out if Rick was feeling better and when he thought he might be coming back to work. Having now learned about the treacherousness of addiction, it is difficult for me to fathom what Rick must have been going through to lose absolutely everything to alcohol and drugs. Rick died penniless shortly after he moved home ... of an accidental overdose. Perhaps there was a lesson to be learned that I should have heeded as a warning, but I missed all of the caution signs and flashing red lights. Maybe I just didn't want to see them.

But as tragically as the summer of 1982 ended, I KNEW that I was going to find my way back to Houston. SOON! Very soon!

[Update: Joseph David Prejean died May 29, 2006. At forty-nine years old with graying hair and a distinguished appearance, David died under mysterious circumstances. He was found face-down in a swimming pool in Palm Springs, California. I chose to remember him as Shirtless Joe, my cousin who helped me out of the doldrums of my closet to find a new life in a new city to call home.]

Now back in Louisiana, I got a job at JC Penney in the Northgate Mall in Lafayette and worked in the display department and sign shop, charged with dressing the mannequins, decorating for holidays, and creating signage for the entire store. The job was amazing, but my boss was not. He was married with kids, but I always had the unnerving feeling that he undressed me every time he looked at me. I don't know if that was really the case, or if it was only in my mind, but after more than a year of working in the display department, I requested a transfer to the sales floor and was immediately named the merchandising assistant for the Young Men's department.

I'm certainly not lost on the fact that I'm now working for the same company that provided my first masturbatory experiences via its annual catalog. But life became even more ironic.

During the late 1970s and early 1980s, the JC Penney men's restroom on the first floor was so well-known for homosexual "cruising" that it was listed in *Bob Damron's Gay Men's Guide–Cruising Areas*. While I was in college, I had visited that JC Penney bathroom on several occasions on the suggestion of Mr. Damron. And he was right; as soon as I walked into the restroom, the other patrons were eager to show me their packages. I gladly showed off mine too, since mine was usually bigger. I had my pick of willing participants. I didn't mind if the others watched, they were just not getting any; at least not today, at least not from me.

It was all so exciting because it was all *so* forbidden. Not only the homosexual aspect of it, but the publicness of it too. One person watched the door for any intruders who needed to use the restroom. By the time the door creaked open, we all were back to our respective stalls or urinals as if nothing lascivious was transpiring. As soon the "intruder" left, the fun resumed with vigor.

Never could I have planned that my new office as the JC Penney Merchandising Assistant would be behind the catalog department with a direct view of the men's restroom from behind my desk. Oh, the cruelty of it all!

As a JC Penney employee, I no longer participated in the festivities going on in the men's room, but it was still fun to see the cruising techniques of those still-in-the-closet gays swapping "activities" with complete strangers directly across from my office. The risk and taboo of it all made for some very interesting workdays. I loved my job!

And after only a few weeks at this new position, I knew that retail was my destiny, my calling. I truly loved this job, and did *not* repeat the mistakes I made at Brother's. I was very dedicated to my job at JC Penney and saw a future career with the company. I monitored my drinking and quit smoking marijuana. The cocaine remained a constant, and now that I had a regular job again, I could better afford it.

During my time at JC Penney, I also made a name for myself as a male stripper in Houston named Colt Michael; working in Lafayette during the week, and dancing in Houston on my weekends off. (Yes, I was already *Magic Mike* when Channing Tatum was still a toddler in diapers!)

I had danced around the Lafayette area as a newcomer male stripper a few times but was often told that I "wasn't good enough," and I believed them. My lack of self-esteem was probably the root cause of my sexual proclivities; if men desired me and wanted to have sex with me, then I could trick myself into thinking that I had the power of validation that I so desperately desired. But I was always being made to feel like somebody or something was better than me, especially in the gay community, and even more so when it involved stripping. In hindsight, my mind was so warped by drugs and alcohol that I never realized that those who shunned me then actually sent me a message: *Get your shit together, dude.* But my blindness to the obvious constantly had me believing that I wasn't the best, and if I wasn't the best, then I wasn't worth anything. I learned (much too late) that I wasn't angry with others for challenging my talent, but rather with myself for believing them and not believing in myself and in my own abilities. I needed to find confidence ... and some cocaine.

Houston's Stripper of the Year contest with winner Peter Casares (courtesy of This Week in Texas magazine)–1982

CHAPTER 6

HAPPY BIRTHDAY

(That Time I Met My Soulmate)

Having placed second in the contest in Houston, I was now a bonafide male stripper, and that's where my delusions of grandeur began to take root. On that night I proved to myself that I could be a performer and demanded respect. I started my own dance troupe, The Hunted, and parlayed my Houston experience as collateral to book dancing gigs throughout Louisiana; the tour was very successful. The Hunted was so popular because it featured gay and straight, male and female dancers. We were an equal-opportunity dance group, and always insured that every dancer was comfortable in their surroundings; a tenet of which I have always been proud. With such a variety of dancers, we catered to almost any audience.

One of our first gigs, in the fall of 1982, was a performance at Ladies' Night at a straight club in Lafayette named The Sting ... a tribute to the 1973 motion picture, *The Sting* starring Paul Newman and Robert Redford. The Sting was a college crowd favorite and frequented by a mostly straight crowd ... although behind the scenes, it was a regular hangout for "closet gays" who wanted to be perceived to be straight. But we all knew better.

[Disclaimer: Very often, I am asked why I am so proud of my life as a male stripper; especially since many people consider the "profession" to be somewhat demeaning. It is important to note that being a male dancer in the 1980s was significantly different than the strippers of today. I was always professional and courteous to everyone, and when anyone tried to touch me, they were immediately escorted away. My job was about dancing and entertaining and had absolutely nothing to do with sex; although I'm not so naïve as to not recognize the sexualization of male dancing.]

When I walked into The Sting that night, I realized that the "stage" side of the club was completely blocked off by long black curtains. The pool tables were covered with plywood to serve as a makeshift stage. I was less than impressed; but I was paid to be there, and I gave the best show possible, given the circumstances.

After a while, I kinda got accustomed to the plywood bowing and popping beneath my cowboy boots as I danced and grooved for an excited all-female crowd. It allowed me to move with the rhythm of the music, while simultaneously avoiding the "soft spot" in the middle of the plywood board, so as to break neither the board nor the pool table.

Throughout the night, ladies shoved dollar bills into my boots while I gyrated my hips to the music that was preselected by the club's resident deejay. It was definitely not the same type of music to which I was accustomed to at the gay clubs; but music is music, and as long as it's got a beat, I can figure out how to dance to it. Being sequestered to the four corners of this raised pedestal that was sure to collapse at any moment made performing difficult and inhibited my ability to perform some of my signature moves such as the "straddle" and the "strut." I cleverly maneuvered myself within the confines of a pool table, and the audience of hyped-up women didn't seem to care.

But my night was saved when I saw a familiar face in the audience. As she approached to tip me, I realized that it was my own cousin, who had no idea that I was one of the dancers, or that I was a male dancer. As she handed me the dollar bills, she laughingly questioned, "Do your Mom and Dad know you're here?" With a Cheshire cat-like grin, I quickly replied, "Do YOUR Mom and Dad know that YOU'RE here?" We both laughed out loud at the hilarity of the moment, especially since we were both aware that we each "batted for the other team," and we have never spoken about it since.

As soon as the event was over and I got paid, I made a beeline for the exit. I needed to find some men to be around; gay men specifically. At the time, there was a very large gay bar in downtown Lafayette called Pharaoh's, with ancient Egyptian-themed décor. It was quite decadent and much more upscale than any of the other gay bars then or since. Truthfully, it wasn't the ambience of the bar in which I was most interested; it was the men! MEN! MEN! MEN! I was in desperate need of a man for the evening. I enjoyed the admiration and adulation of all of those women earlier in the evening, and I especially appreciated the almost $500 in my pockets; but right now, I needed the pleasure of a man!

As I jumped into the Green Frog to leave the venue, headlights blazed in my rearview mirror. I thought it was some girls from The Sting who had followed me, so I swerved in and out of the lanes trying to lose them in the traffic, but somehow those headlights kept following me. I most surely did not want them to see me headed straight to the gay bar.

As I pulled up to a parking spot directly in front of Pharaoh's nightclub, I saw the blue lights of the city police flashing in my rearview mirror. *DAMN, I was getting a ticket!*

The police officer, via the speaker of his squad car said, "Sir, please step out of the vehicle and keep your hands where I can see them." Of course, I obliged. He stepped out of the cruiser and approached me. "We've been following you since you left The Sting and you seem to be driving a bit erratically; have you been drinking, sir?" My response, "Yes officer, about two beers." Which was true, but I don't even know how many shots of tequila and peppermint schnapps were handed to me throughout the night. I drank every single one of them along with a few bumps of coke.

The policeman then said, "Well sir, it seems as though maybe you've had too much to drink, we're going to do a field sobriety test. First, I want you to put one foot directly in front of the other and take ten steps, turn around and walk back." I completed the task and even attempted a pirouette on the turn. I noticed the cop trying his best to not laugh and to keep his composure; it was obviously not my best performance. Then he said, "Okay, I want you to raise your right leg and hold it up and count to thirty out loud BACKWARDS ... one Mississippi, two Mississippi, three Mississippi, and so on." I am now certain that he actually never said backwards, but somehow that's what I heard; so, instead of holding my right leg in front of me, I put my right leg behind me and started counting "thirty Mississippi, twenty-nine Mississippi ..." the policeman, now trying to contain himself from exploding with laughter stopped me in mid-"Mississippi." "No, No, No," he snorted, "Mr. Richard, why are you doing it backwards?" It was then that I realized I had completely misunderstood the instructions. So, thinking maybe humor would make things better, in response to his question, I replied, "Because I can!" Immediately, the officer said, "No, you can't!"

Evidently he didn't appreciate my attempt at comedy as he spun me around and handcuffed me. "Mr. Richard, you are being arrested for driving under the influence of alcohol," followed by the reading of my Miranda rights and placing me into the back seat of the police cruiser. This was definitely *not* the type of cruising to which I had become accustomed; and while I've always loved a man in uniform, considering the aforementioned circumstances, I knew better than to try my luck.

So, I just sat there quietly with my hands handcuffed behind my back. I had never been arrested before and had no idea what would happen next. At the age of nineteen, I was arrested for the first time. I could have and should have been arrested several times before ... for drinking while driving, illegal drugs, lewd and lascivious acts in public spaces ... I do not know how I was able to avoid the long arm of the law for so long.

He drove me to the downtown police station for booking including mugshots and fingerprinting, though I was never put in jail. Instead, I was given a ticket for "Driving While Intoxicated." My parents were waiting for me in the police office parking lot, as the car was still registered in their names. I got into their vehicle, and we once again had a very deep conversation about the dangers of drinking and driving. My parents thought that I had been smoking pot (remember my senior prom?), but I wasn't. They had no clue that I was high on cocaine too.

The police station was only about a mile from where my car was parked, so my parents drove me back to Pharaoh's, where my car had remained during my arrest; they did not know that I had parked in front of a gay bar. I got out of their car, they handed me the keys to Little Green Frog, and I drove home ... still drunk and high on coke. I somehow fooled my parents into believing that I had not been driving drunk at all, and they believed my story about being followed by those girls from The Sting.

Fortunately, my mug shot was never published in the local news; a benefit of "friends in low places," so my very temporary police detention remained unknown to the general public.

It was shortly thereafter that I met my first boyfriend. I was still working at JC Penney and moonlighting as Colt Michael as often as I could. Most of my dates were one-night stands with whomever I felt like being with that night after I had probably already had sex at the club, and probably with somebody else. While my sexual escapades made me desirable as a conquest, it made me unwanted as a boyfriend.

But that all changed on the night that I met Dennis Thetford. It was Friday, September 17, 1982, and we had each been invited to a dinner party with mutual friends in Baton Rouge. However, neither one of us knew that everyone else at the party knew that this entire event was planned just so Dennis and I could meet each other.

Dennis was an auburn-haired, hazel-eyed, muscular bodybuilder; the kind of guy whom I never thought would give me a second look. But from the moment we locked eyes that night, we both knew that our friends were absolutely right for setting us up on this blind date. At the time, he had just turned thirty-nine years old and I was still a teenager. I had just experienced a love-at-first-sight moment; and this would be a relationship I would never forget. Dennis already had a lover, and prior to meeting me, had already booked a cruise with someone else, who also was *not* his lover. Oh, and Dennis' lover was at the same dinner party. But I was nineteen years old, and quickly falling in love; the rest just didn't matter.

At the time, there were a group of men and women in Lafayette who were creating a brand-new gay Mardi Gras krewe in Lafayette. The only gay Mardi Gras krewe at the time, the Mystic Krewe of Apollo de Lafayette was, and still is, specifically for gay men only. This new group wanted Louisiana's Acadiana area to be seen as a bastion of inclusivity, so this mostly-gay krewe would include both men and women, and welcome members of the bisexual, transgender, and ally communities also. This new all-inclusive LGBTQIA+ alliance would become the Mystic Krewe of the Royal Order of Unicorn. A description from its website states, "ROU was founded on the ideal that everyone is welcome to join—we hold no labels here. We want to encourage people within the community, no matter their identity, gender, race, or philosophies to come together and be a part of something wonderful." After that incredible Houston summer with Shirtless Joe and

Naomi Sims that ended rather tragically, I was excited to become a part of the ROU family.

In October 1982, the newly formed ROU held its first pageant. With my new boyfriend, Dennis, on a cruise with someone who wasn't his lover and definitely wasn't *me*, I decided to enter, either out of spite or jealousy, I don't know ... and vied to become Mr. ROU by competing in the categories of interview, sportswear, formalwear, and talent. I knew that I would do well in the interview portion, and probably in formalwear also. I had no idea what sportswear was, so I just made up some type of construction worker's outfit.

I had been performing as a male exotic dancer all over Louisiana but had not yet performed at a gay bar in Lafayette; it seemed that being local is not what the gay bars were looking for. But I decided that my talent for this contest would be the debut of Colt Michael in gay Lafayette.

Created specifically for this competition, Colt Michael invented a new routine, performing to the song "Red Light" by Linda Clifford (from the soundtrack of the movie *Fame*). I danced while wearing a cowboy outfit, complete with hat, snapped shirt, tight jeans and boots. I seductively removed my clothing until only a few strategically-placed bandanas covered my mid-section. I then pulled out a pair of scissors that I'd tucked inside my jeans and begin cutting off the bandanas one-by-one. It was very erotic, very nuanced, and very dangerous. Yes, I was comfortable with my body, but still second-guessed my abilities. I began to feel comfortable and relaxed, yet invigorated, as the performance progressed, and more and more bandanas were stripped away. Finally, I was down to the second-to-last bandana. Just one more snip, and the crowd went WILD!

I continued dancing and the crowd noise grew louder and louder. *Damn, I must be doing really well.* Then I saw one of the female judges looking straight at my crotch. I inadvertently had cut off the wrong bandana, and was fully on display to the entire crowd. For some reason, I was not embarrassed at all. I quickly corrected the issue, and the audience actually booed at me. While I may have been horrified in the immediate moment, I thought the slip-up was actually quite hysterical. I guess I needed more practice on my routine.

Who knows if my unintentional wardrobe malfunction and "display of affection" had any bearing on the outcome of the contest. But I am still honored, to this day, to have been the very first Mr. ROU in 1982-83 and bragged about my big win to Dennis when he returned home from his cruise.

On the following weekend, Dennis decided we would stay at his New Orleans apartment to give me a break from my parents. My Dad had come over for lunch and noticed a very large purplish mark on my neck. "Ted, what is that?" he asked. And Dennis, without skipping a beat, said, "Oh, I'm sorry Mr. Richard, I must have put that there last night." If my Dad had any questions about my sexuality before, definitely he knew the answer now!

Upon arriving in New Orleans, we drove to a parking lot on Toulouse Street. It was then that I realized that Dennis' apartment was next door to Club New Orleans, a gay men's bath house that I had frequented on several occasions; and from his terrace there was a great view of its clothing-optional patio.

Of all my relationships, this was by far the weirdest. I hadn't really had a true boyfriend before, and Dennis currently had a long-time boyfriend whom everyone knew, and he was rich … very rich! Dennis owned a very upscale antique shop in Baton Rouge, and his partner, Rex, owned a high-end hair salon. Though we lived in different cities, we saw each other as often as possible; the distance and the age difference were never a problem. But the money was!

I was a nineteen-year-old just getting started in life, and he was already a powerful and successful businessman; who, for lack of a better term, was already married to another man. And his husband knew exactly who I was, and actually really liked me. Coincidentally, his husband had a much younger boyfriend, too. We would often double-date, and those were always the weirdest nights for me. *How could anyone be in a long-term committed relationship and agree that each other could have a boyfriend on the side?* This open relationship concept was something new to me. I didn't understand, but at the time, it didn't matter. I was as in love with Dennis as any other nineteen-year-old who falls in love with an older man could be. Of course, I never saw it that way.

We often got those awkward glances when we were out in public. I knew that our age difference bothered some people, but we were comfortable with each other, so no one else's opinion really mattered to Dennis, nor me. But there definitely were other things with which I was much less comfortable, and I knew it wasn't Dennis' fault; it was probably just my own insecurity. I never knew if people stared because of our age difference, or if they thought he was cheating on his boyfriend. I often wondered if they thought that I was some kind of "paid-for" boy toy or if I was just his "hustler" for the night. Or did they think that he was my daddy, and I was his son? [Dennis was only about three years younger than my Dad!]

The only real argument that Dennis and I ever had was about ... you guessed it ... MONEY! And the fact that he had lots of it, and I had almost none. I always felt uncomfortable going out to dinner at these fancy-schmancy restaurants which we both knew I could never afford. So, even though that wasn't Dennis' intention, sometimes I DID feel like the "little pageant boyfriend"... with the Mr. ROU trophy and sash to prove it.

Dennis explained that the reason he always treated me so extravagantly is because he knew that I couldn't afford it, but that he still believed I deserved the finer things in life. When I explained to Dennis how it bothered me that the restaurant server would ALWAYS put the bill toward his side of the table, and how I felt under-recognized in the relationship, he understood exactly what I meant. So, we came to an agreement.

Once a month, we would go out to a restaurant that I could afford, and I would pay the bill. It was never anything fancy on a JC Penney paycheck, but it made me feel as if I was also contributing financially to our relationship. And it let him know that I loved HIM and not his money; though I must admit, the gifts were very nice.

One of the other things that I really appreciated about our relationship was that he never questioned my faithfulness, even knowing that I was often dancing half-naked all night for strangers. Indeed, it would have been a bit hypocritical for him to expect fidelity while he was being unfaithful in his own relationship. But I was always faithful to Dennis and accepted our relationship as it was defined by us; as long as he was honest with his long-time boyfriend, Rex, I was okay with the situation.

November 20, 1982 was my "big" birthday ... turning twenty on the twentieth. I was so excited to be spending this very special day with the man that I loved. Dennis knew that this was a very special day for me, but he had already planned a buying trip to Paris for his antique store. My little nineteen-year-old heart was shattered!

I immediately called Jocelyn Rae and told her how crushed I was that Dennis couldn't be with me for my special day. She said, "Don't worry, honey. I got this!" She always knew the right things to say and the right things to do at just the right times, and she knew me better than I knew myself. I thought that I shielded her from my alcoholism, drug addiction, and voracious sexual appetite; but she always *knew*. I am forever indebted to her for her kindness and sincerity. She spoke to me as a human being, while most others at the gay bars spoke to me as if I was a plaything. Yes, I realized that I did that to myself, but Jocelyn saw past that attention-craving exterior, and found the innocent, hurt, and betrayed little boy inside. I am so fortunate to have her always in my corner.

Jocelyn took me out to Bennigan's, an Irish pub/restaurant where she worked. I had been there many times to visit her while she was working, so I knew most of the staff, and of course they knew it was my birthday. About midway through our meal, I heard all kinds of raucous and hullabaloo coming from the kitchen area singing "Happy Birthday."

I immediately just gave Jocelyn that "eyes rolling to the back of my head look" that said, "no you didn't." And she *swore* she didn't do anything. But all those people kept walking toward our table with that damned little cupcake with the candle on it made "especially for you." My face kept turning redder and redder as the "Happy Birthday" cackles got louder and louder. When the Bennigan's party makers finally got to our table, they turned around and handed the cupcake to the guy sitting at the next table. As it turns out, he was celebrating his "big birthday" too.

Up until this time, I had never met anyone who had the exact same birthday as me ... November 20, 1962 ... but there he was, at the very next table. His name was Kevin Nunez. And we even shared the same middle name of Anthony. As we left the restaurant, we all exchanged pleasantries and talked about our plans for later in the evening. They were just going to take it easy for the night. Jocelyn and I were going out to the new gay club on the Breaux Bridge Highway called The Old School. We all hugged each other and laughed about the coincidences of having the same birthday and being seated at tables directly across from each other at the same restaurant, then parted ways.

Jocelyn and I had been at The Old School for about an hour or so, and we were twirling on the dance floor, when simultaneously we looked across the bar. Right there, standing at the front door, shaking like a frightened sheep, was Kevin Nunez, my birthday twin; he looked at me as if to say, "*How do you know what you know? You can see right through me,*" and like the Paul Parker disco hit revealed, we were "Right On Target." Jocelyn and I immediately bolted from the dance floor to welcome him "out." The three of us danced away the rest of the night and Kevin and I remained friends for the next several years. I was so happy to have been there to greet Kevin and make him feel comfortable in his new surroundings and I wouldn't have had it any other way.

Just as Brian and Greg welcomed me into the gay community, my "*sixth second of fame*" was the honor of welcoming Kevin Nunez into the Lafayette gay scene. It was an evening and event that I will always hold close to my heart, recognizing the significance that comes with helping someone finally come out and become the person they always knew they were!

Our paths crossed many times over the next several years, and we always reminisced about the night that we first met. We never dated because we both knew that we were much better off as friends. Cherished friendships are often very difficult to gain, grow, and flourish, sometimes especially in the gay community; and we each valued our eternal friendship and that special bond for a lifetime. Of course, we always called each other on our birthdays.

Colt Michael performing the "bandana act" at the MR. ROU contest–1982

CHAPTER 7

SPECIFICALLY UNINVITED

(That Time He Died)

Celebrating my "big birthday" with Jocelyn and Kevin was one of the most memorable nights of my life. I thought that my night would be ruined without my new boyfriend by my side, but the universe soon showed me that I was wrong.

The next day, Dennis called me from his European antique buying trip to wish me a happy birthday, not realizing he was a day late. I told him about my night and that Jocelyn took me out to eat and how we met Kevin Nunez. He was excited for me, although we both wished we could have celebrated together.

Then, there was an odd pause, and he asked, "Do you know a Charles MacIntosh?" I know my jaw must have hit the floor. *How the hell did Dennis know Mr. MacIntosh? There was no way they could know each other, and why would he ask me that now?* It must have been very important to him, since he was asking me this question on a long-distance phone call which, at the time, was about $3.60 per minute.

I chose my next words very carefully, and replied, "Yes, Mr. MacIntosh was one of my high school teachers. Is that who you're talking about?" Then Dennis said, "Well, you won't believe this, I ran into him yesterday at one of the antique shops. He recognized my American accent and asked where I was from. I told him that I was originally from north Texas, but now lived in Baton Rouge." They must have had a much longer conversation, because somehow Lafayette and Carencro came up in the conversation, which prompted Dennis to ask Charlie if he knew me. Mr. MacIntosh said, "Ted Richard? Of course I know him; he was in the Commodore Club at Carencro High School when I was the sponsor. How do you know him?" Dennis replied, "Ted is my boyfriend."

Dennis learned that Mr. MacIntosh was teaching English as a Second Language (ESL) at the local university and had lived in Paris for the past year. Sometimes the world was just a little too small for me. What were the chances that my current boyfriend would meet my high school crush almost 5,000 miles away? I didn't ask Dennis any more questions about Charlie, and he didn't offer additional comments about their meeting. I didn't want to know if they compared notes, and allowed myself to believe that Mr. MacIntosh would never have divulged our secret trysts in high school to a total stranger.

Dennis returned from Europe the following week and invited me to spend the weekend with him at his New Orleans apartment. As a belated birthday present, he had purchased a leather-covered backgammon set with genuine marble dice; I know this gift must have been extremely expensive, but I never asked. I kissed him and hugged him to let him know how much appreciated the gift, but more importantly, how much I truly loved him. Dennis and I made love and I fell asleep in his arms in the middle of the afternoon. Later that evening, he took me out to eat at Brennan's Restaurant. We never spoke about Mr. MacIntosh again.

I was still working full-time at JC Penney in the Northgate Mall and trying to further establish the Colt Michael brand and The Hunted dance revue. Then, in the early 1980s, a new gay bar, Strokes, opened in Lafayette, and the bar owner, Ken Richard (no relation) wanted an all-male, all-gay dance group to entertain the ever-expanding gay population in Acadiana.

Keller Berchman and I had known of each other since high school, but we really didn't know each other since we didn't congregate with the same group of friends. "K," as we nicknamed him, was active in drama club and speech club and was very popular in theater circles. For reasons unbeknownst to me at the time, I resented him. It wasn't until I bumped into him one night at Leaping Lena's that we reconnected and became friends. We had several heartfelt talks about our high school days and our fears of being exposed as gay. These conversations made me realize that my resentment wasn't about my dislike for him; it was my jealousy that he was much more comfortable with his sexuality in high school than I ever was, and I resented the fact that he could be himself while I chose to stay in the closet.

Keller and I got together a group of about six or seven gay (or bisexual) male dancers, and we became The Strokers. This new form of all-male, all-gay entertainment became very popular very quickly and soon we were doing shows across the state, including our weekly gig at our hometown bar.

In an effort to promote The Strokers, we had an open-to-the-public photo shoot. The event was held on a Saturday afternoon sometime in the spring of 1983. Strokes charged a $5 admission fee to attend the photo shoot, and the bar was standing-room-only. Each dancer provided his own costumes, or lack thereof, the bar's dance floor had been converted into a studio, and we hired a professional photographer. My photo session was, by far, the most salacious, as I was the only dancer willing to pose nude. Let's be real, by now most of Lafayette had already seen me naked, so this was nothing new. Though I was always careful to not show any of my privates in the photos, I had forgotten that the far side of the dance floor behind the studio area was a wall of mirrors, so the entire audience got views of my entire body that the cameras never saw. Personally, I didn't see what the big deal was all about; but apparently there were some nude pictures of me that other people have in their possession. To those people, please enjoy the photos; I already know what I look like naked.

As outgoing and adventurous as I was as a dancer, I absolutely abhorred having my picture taken, especially as a model. I disliked the way I looked in the pictures, but don't know why. There weren't any glaring flaws or obvious disfigurations, I just didn't like them; but this photographer, Jimi Haines, was superb. When I received my copies of the prints, I was extremely satisfied; he made me look so good in the photos that I almost didn't recognize myself. It was the first time in my life that I remember liking the way I looked in a photograph. He made me look like the model that I never saw myself to be. These pictures liberated me and made me come to life, and I felt as if nothing could stop me.

Our photos were used statewide to promote The Strokers, and wherever we performed, we usually packed the bar. We performed at dive bars and hole-in-the-wall bars as well as mega-gay bars such as New

Orleans' Bourbon Pub, but we consistently gave the best performances regardless of the size of the crowd or the bar. We were there to entertain, and that's what we did.

Although most of the other dancers focused on the tips they were getting, I did not. We all got paid when we arrived, so anything we made in tips was just a bonus; and while I always appreciated the extra money, that wasn't my main goal.

First and foremost, my objective was to be the most creative and vivacious entertainer that the crowd had ever seen. I'd harken back to the night that I met Dan Miller, and I remember how he made me feel while he was out there on the dance floor. I wanted to make each and every crowd feel the same way that Dan made me feel on that night. And while I loved traversing the state of Louisiana entertaining hundreds of fans each night, I still knew that my future was in Houston; but my heart was with Dennis in Baton Rouge and my career was still with JC Penney in Lafayette.

[Sidebar: I was so happy to have reconnected with Keller Berchman, especially since we never really got to know each other in high school. As founding members of The Strokers, we forged a friendship through our mutual love of dance. Sadly, on September 7, 1991, Keller became the second classmate of mine from Carencro High School who died of HIV-related issues (though it wasn't mentioned at the time). Keller died much too soon, and the world missed out on the talent he would have brought to our generation. I still admire him for his passion and courage, but most importantly for teaching me that I had something to offer and helping me to believe in myself.]

Dennis and I had a wonderful and loving relationship for a little over a year; we saw each other as often as possible in between my dancing and work schedules and his business trips. I always tried to schedule at least one show in Baton Rouge and one show in New Orleans every month just so that we could spend those nights together. It was always a treat to put on a performance just for my boyfriend whenever I was out of town, but I always had a strict rule of never leaving the bar with anyone; that is how I chose to separate my public life from my private, personal life. It also furthered the fantasy that perhaps I was available and there was a chance for them to get to know me better. There wasn't, but they never knew that.

It was during one of my weekend trips to Baton Rouge on September 17, 1983, when I was staying at Dennis' house, that the awkwardness began. Both Dennis and Rex were at their respective jobs, and the house was empty, except for the housekeeper and me, or so I thought. I was taking a shower so that I could be ready for dinner when Dennis got home. Suddenly, I noticed the lights in the bathroom flickering on and off and thought it was the housekeeper, so I said, "Dorthea, it's Ted, I'm in the shower." No response. Then the lights were dimmed very low; I knew someone had to be in the bathroom with me because that was the only way to dim the lights, and I knew that it wasn't Dorthea. I hurriedly turned the water off and reached for a towel but it wasn't where I left it. Instead, there stood Juan, Rex's eighteen-year-old Spanish-Italian boyfriend. He was naked and actively caressing himself for what he *thought* was *my* pleasure. He tried to jump into the shower with me, and I shoved him away while asserting that I was in love with Dennis. He said, "It's okay, they know." I knew he was lying.

That night, Dennis took me to dinner at Ruth's Chris Steakhouse for our one-year anniversary. I *had* to tell Dennis about the incident with Juan, and there was no way that I could do that without ruining the evening. I waited until after dinner to alert him that I had something very important to discuss. By this time, I figured that he thought I had a big surprise for him. The surprise part was true, but it was nothing like what he expected; I couldn't believe that this is how our first (and only) anniversary date would end.

While Dennis and I never spoke about that afternoon ever again, I could tell on our future get-togethers that something was amiss. He began treating me differently, especially whenever Rex was around. (Rex and Juan broke up after he learned about Juan's indecent proposal.) It seemed as though Rex blamed the entire incident on me because I was "being too sexy" around the house. Maybe I should never have said anything, but I felt Dennis needed to know what had (not) happened. I was in love with Dennis, and not with Rex's boyfriend; how did all of this suddenly become my fault? Thankfully, Dennis' love for me never waned, and he apologized profusely to me for being blamed for something just because I was up front and honest.

It was early November 1983, and Dennis was on a two-week business trip in Germany; I was so excited that he would be back in time to celebrate my twenty-first birthday. In the middle of his buying trip though, he called to let me know that he was very sick and was coming home early to go to the hospital. He told me that he had a severe sore throat that just would not go away; but he said that he would call me as soon as he was back in Baton Rouge to let me know how he was feeling. I worriedly kept waiting for a phone call that never came. Dennis died almost two weeks later, November 18, 1983, just two days before my twenty-first birthday. He was only forty years old.

To make matters worse, Rex called my parents' house to give me the bad news, but refused to speak to me; instead, he instructed my parents to inform me that I was not to attend any of the funeral or memorial services. He forbade me from sending flowers and totally erased me from Dennis' life and his death. Even though my family and Rex's family knew that Dennis and I were in a relationship, I was specifically *uninvited*. The looks on my parents' faces showed me that they were just as confused as I was, and they consoled me with hugs of support and compassion.

While I blamed Rex for my dismissal at the time, I later realized that my exclusion was specifically from Dennis' family. To add insult to injury, in Dennis Thetford's full obituary, the names of his long-time partner and his parents weren't even mentioned; it was as though Rex never existed, and his parents did not want any association with this abomination of a son. His long-time partner was omitted due to homophobia and hate; the parents' names were omitted due to embarrassment and shame. Dennis had died from GRIDS (Gay-Related Immunodeficiency Syndrome, the precursor to AIDS), and his family apparently did not want their name associated with their own gay son. And the obituary disrespected Dennis even more so by not providing a proper photo. Shameful!

Years later, I wrote prose about my *"seventh second of fame"* and being specifically uninvited to the funeral of someone I was absolutely in love with, and being denied the courtesy of sharing my love for Dennis with his other family and friends. I called it *My Sympathy: Because You Need It*. That was one of the first times in my life that I remembered being truly personally hurt by the hatred of others. I was never given the opportunity to properly grieve, but had to navigate that path to acceptance and forgiveness on my own.

My wild and crazy life continued, having learned a few more important lessons. Life isn't fair, so buckle up and get back in the saddle. There are more roads less traveled to explore; and opportunities easier said than done, since some of those roads were never meant to be explored.

Strokes' photo shoot–1983

CHAPTER 8

SEX ON THE BEACH

(That Time I Came Out of Hiding)

In April 1982, a new gay bar, JR's, opened in Houston and quickly became one the hottest bars in town for the best in male dancing entertainment. JR's was named for the famously infamous and villainous character, JR Ewing, on the hit primetime soap opera television series, *Dallas* (1978-1991); as of June 2022, JR's is currently the oldest gay bar in Houston. JR's was well-known for its Tuesday night "jock strap" competitions; though I have no idea why they called it a jock strap contest because absolutely no one ever wore an actual jock strap. But I digress. This weekly Tuesday night contest would bring in competitors from across the state.

On one of my many prior trips to Houston I met Randy Marslon, a jet-black-haired, hazel-eyed muscle-bodied god of a man who entered a male stripper contest that I judged; of course, he won. After the competition, all of the dancers were performing around the bar on oddly placed podiums. I quietly walked up to his podium and placed a $100 bill in his hand and congratulated him on his much-deserved win. I knew that there was instant chemistry between us, but I was still with Dennis in Baton Rouge, so, without an explanation, I hurriedly left the bar after I had tipped him. I figured I'd probably never see him again, anyway.

In the spring of 1984, I went to Houston for Memorial Day weekend to visit friends and attend the annual gay event, Splash Day, in Galveston, and decided to enter one of the preliminary contests for the jock strap contest. Out of the six dancers competing, I was fortunate to win first place and automatically qualified for the finals to be held during the summer.

Imagine my surprise when I saw Randy Marslon at JR's that night of the finals contest as a contestant! The moment we saw each other, we instantly confirmed that the connection we made on that first night was mutual. He wondered where I'd disappeared to and why I left so abruptly. I explained that I had a boyfriend at the time, and although we shared mutual chemistry, I didn't want to get either of our hopes up. While it was a very pleasant surprise to see Randy again, I quickly realized that he was also my competition, so we talked a bit more before we headed off to our respective dressing areas to prep for our performances.

Tuesday, June 5, 1984, Houston was now my second home, even though I had no permanent place to live. The city was always so welcoming to me. I loved the people and felt as if they loved me back; it was *kismet*, I belonged in Houston!

The finals contestants were extremely competitive. There were fifteen professional male dancers from across Texas, and Colt Michael visiting from Louisiana. As was customary for each competition, contestants drew numbers for their order of performance, and I picked number sixteen, the last dancer. Drawing last gave me the benefit of watching all the other performers, while I tried to figure out what I was going to do. To be completely honest, I do not remember most of that night; between the mixture of Jack Daniels, Jell-O shots with vodka, and cocaine, most of the evening was a blur. However, I was cognizant enough to realize that on that night, Colt Michael became a real person; and my delusions of grandeur were allowed to manifest within the confines of only my own mind.

I chose the song "Coming Out of Hiding" by Pamela Stanley to dance to, and my outfit was a grunge cowboy look with a G-string made of tan chamois cloth (what you wash your car with), so that when it got wet it became nearly see-through. Some audience members had seen my chamois dance before at The Galleon, another well-respected gay bar in Houston, and brought spray bottles to squirt water onto my G-string each time they tipped me, which ensured that the chamois clung to every ridge pattern on my package as only a wet G-string could. All of the other competitors watched my performance, and my chamois G-string was soaking wet by the end of the song.

Then the deejay replayed my song, so I continued dancing, and all the other contestants came out to tip me and congratulate me. The crowd chanted, "Colt Michael, Colt Michael, Colt Michael!" I didn't know what was happening; I just knew it was obviously something to which I was completely oblivious. *Did I win?* The emcee, Brandi West, wasn't even back on stage; it felt like pandemonium. Then finally the crowd subsided, and the emcee reappeared. All of the contestants were now back on the stage with me again as she started naming the winners. Fourth runner-up (not me), Third runner-up (not me), Second runner-up (not me), First runner-up (not me). And again, I started doubting myself. I guess it just wasn't my night. And then the emcee says, "and your *WINNER* is" ... long pause ... "*COLT MICHAEL!*"

I was in complete shock, and there was total chaos in the crowd; at least that's the way it felt to me. I thought it was because they disagreed with the results, but next thing I knew, my music was cued up and I was asked to perform again. It was truly a feeling that I could never put into words. Winning this contest was the most important thing to me at that time; I competed against some of the best of the best, and I WON! Who knows why I needed a trophy to prove to myself that I deserved accolades? It's as if I finally KNEW that I was good enough; I was relieved but stressed at the same time.

Then, immediately I remembered what Naomi Sims always said: "Always be grateful for what you have achieved. From this point forward, you are a recognizable name, and there are responsibilities that come with any title." I completely understood exactly what she meant.

I also remembered her advice about winning: "Success is not always forever, so be sure to always thank the people who got you to where you are." And I did just that, lingering after my shows to chat with patrons and thank them for their support.

The following week, the bar used my picture for its weekly advertisement. This was long before social media, and I really did not do any self-promoting because it made me uncomfortable. So when any establishment used your photo for its advertising, it was truly a big deal.

While I was now finally "somebody," once I stepped off the stage and the applause stopped, I still felt the same emptiness and anonymity inside. The contradictions in my head had me feeling excited yet depressed at the same time without a good explanation as to why. Alcohol and drugs still quelled those directly opposing feelings, at least for the time being.

My prize for winning the competition was an all-expenses-paid trip for two to Puerto Vallarta. Throughout my entire performance at JR's that finals night, I felt Randy's eyes on me from behind the backstage curtain. Apparently, our mutual affection was obvious to the bar patrons, so much so that it was assumed we'd go to Puerto Vallarta together. But I had other plans.

My Puerto Vallarta vacation couldn't come soon enough; I needed some alone time on a sunny beach to clear my head and figure out where my life took such a wrong turn. How was it that my professional life was on an upswing while my personal life was in a tailspin? I was sure that alcohol and drugs were not the culprits; it most certainly was something else. As soon as I returned to Louisiana, I called Jocelyn Rae to invite her on the trip, but she was in the middle of rehearsals for an operatic performance in Washington, D.C.

My decision to go alone was a great one, which is not to say that I didn't wish Jocelyn could join me, but I *needed* to get accustomed to going places all alone, and learn how to enjoy myself, on my own time, and on my own terms. Ever since then, almost all my vacations have been solo; and were very freeing and exhilarating. I met people that I normally would not have met if I had been with a boyfriend or group of friends, and the locals always loved to show off their city and take me to hidden gems that tourists don't usually know about. That's exactly what happened in Puerto Vallarta.

This was my first trip to Mexico, and the Aeroméxico plane trip there was more of a roller coaster ride. While the views from the plane were stunning, flying so high over the mountainous terrain made for a bumpy ride. Several of us made plans to meet for dinner on the first night after we all got settled in, and our vacation began.

I met a very handsome young man on the plane who piqued my interest, but he was with friends and I didn't know if he was gay or not. Still, I exchanged introductions with him as I had done with all the others, and was ecstatic when he showed up to dinner alone and sat right beside me. As he sat down, his legs brushed up against mine, and with his left hand on my thigh, he outstretched his right hand to reintroduce himself. "Hi Ted, I'm Ross, Ross Wyrick; nice to meet you." I sensed that Ross had not forgotten my name, as I had most certainly remembered his. How could I forget that sexy Kentucky bluegrass twang? Ross and I had an immediate connection and we enjoyed sharing many wonderful times together over the weekend.

We took a boat ride to a remote island off the coast. I had taken a hit of acid before I left my hotel room; the clear, blue-green waters and the golden rays from the cloudless skies made for some kaleidoscopic trances on our way to this "secret" island. Ross and I were nearly inseparable, and explored the island waterfalls, and hidden lakes, and each other.

As I reeled from the effects of the acid, the boat ride back to the beaches was a totally different experience. There were free margaritas for everyone, and suddenly the faint smell of pot engulfed the boat. Suddenly, our three-hour tour had turned into an oblivious afternoon and my acid trip became a journey of twisted emotion as Ross got high on pot and I slurped down several margaritas to keep from getting cottonmouth.

That night we visited several clubs, including a bar called The Lion's Den. It was the only gay-friendly bar I could find (but the others didn't know that). It was famous for ... actual LIVE lions IN the bar; they were in a huge cage behind double- or triple-paned glass; and the tourist attraction was feeding time. Feeding times were posted so tourists could watch the lions devour their meals; it was quite the spectacle.

We took taxis to get to all of our destinations up until that point. But, if you've ever been to Mexico, when you do that, you never know what happens next. Cabbies drive on the sidewalks, honk bicycles out of the way, and I'm positive that we almost hit a cow.

It was nearing the end of the night (perhaps 4:00 a.m.) and Ross followed me out of the bar. I thought he wanted to share a cab, but I was totally wrong; he wanted to walk along the beach back to our hotel rooms. I said, "That's over a mile away," and after the day I'd already had, I was exhausted.

He said, "Trust me, it'll be worth it!" Ross' plan for us was ultimately more than anything I could have ever expected. As much as I love romance and passion as a feeling, I'm usually not the type of guy that plans the most romantic dates. I was always afraid to plan something romantic, for fear it would not turn out the way I planned, so I just chose to never plan at all. I have always enjoyed spontaneity and this sudden date was both perfectly planned (by him) and totally spontaneous (for me). Ross must have been trying to plan this evening since shortly after we had met on the airplane. Although we had planned many excursions together, I found it curiously odd that he would often appear at random events which I had not planned, but there he was, and I was always happy to see him.

I had never strolled along the beach holding hands with another man in my life. So this romantic gesture from Ross was new territory for me, and both welcomed and thrilling. For a while, we laid on the sand and stared at the stars; and then this kiss came out of nowhere. I felt a surge of emotion when I realized that our bodies were now entangled in spontaneous passion. We made love for what seemed like hours; we were lost in time as we noticed the brightening of the horizon to the east. We witnessed the most beautiful sunrise ever shimmering over the azure blue Puerto Vallarta waters. Our hands remained intertwined as he walked me all the way back to my hotel room, and then another kiss, and another tryst, then he left to pack for our return trip. How I wished this "dream come true" would never end, but we both knew that sunrise would be the sunset of whatever relationship we both wanted. Once we landed in Houston, he was going back to his Kentucky straight life and I was going back to Cajun Country, Louisiana; we both recognized it for exactly what it was, a weekend fling!

That night, my *"eighth second of fame,"* Ross made me feel as though I was the only man in the world. I had never enjoyed that feeling of being someone's "everything," even just for a weekend. (My first boyfriend, Dennis, always made me feel extremely special, but I had come to the realization that I never was, and was never going to be, his "everything.")

We had a very late breakfast together that morning, then took the shuttle back to the airport separately, as he rejoined his traveling companions. Ross and I stayed in touch for the next few months, but we never saw each other again. And yes, that one night in paradise was absolutely worth it!

The Aeroméxico flight back to Houston seemed much less choppy than the flight to Puerto Vallarta, but I was still high on leftover acid and a love hangover to notice the difference.

JR's advertisement (courtesy of This Week in Texas magazine)–1984

CHAPTER 9

LEATHERMAN

(That Time I Made a Video)

Since Dennis' death, I fell back into the same patterns of excess as before ... alcohol, sex, Ecstasy, sex, cocaine, sex, acid, sex, pot, sex, cocaine, sex, sex, sex.

Then, a few months after I returned home from Puerto Vallarta, I met my second boyfriend. I was celebrating my twenty-second birthday at Club Cadillac, a recently opened gay bar; maybe this could be my "lucky" birthday. Dennis had been dead for over a year, and I wanted someone special in my life again.

I wanted another relationship, but almost no one who knew me thought that I was relationship material, and they had every reason for believing so. My over-the-top sexual escapades offered no reason for them to think otherwise. Mitchell Mahfouz was thirteen years my senior, recently single, and had not yet been privy to the mostly true small-town gossip. He was that right guy at the right time, and I fell head-over-heels in love with him, but he just had left a long-term relationship and didn't want anything permanent. I figured that I was ready for another relationship, but he was not.

It was Valentine's Day 1985, and Mitchell said that he had something very special planned for our romantic evening. He took me out to eat at The Landing, a waterfront restaurant and my favorite eatery at the time, on the banks of the Vermilion River. As we lingered over post-dinner cocktails and watched the river flow by on the candlelit pier, I saw him reach for something in his front pocket. He pulled out a small box, and said, "Here, open it!" My hands shook as I unwrapped the decorative foil paper to reveal a velvet-covered ring box. Inside was a beautiful gold ring encrusted with diamonds. My jaw dropped; was I now engaged? Mitchell was quick to define the ring as a gesture of his affection for me, but that he was not ready for anything serious. Wow!

A gorgeous ring, and then a stab to the heart; how was I supposed to understand these mixed signals?

Mitchell was most certainly as emotionally calloused as he was passionate, and mine was not the only heart he broke. He meant it when he told me that he really liked me but didn't want a relationship; obviously the ring meant much more to me than it did for him. After about six months of monogamous dating, at least on my part, Mitchell crushed my heart. It would be several years until I spoke to him again, but once my hurt feelings healed, we remained friends until his death in 2007. And, yes, I kept the ring. As a matter of fact, I still wear it today.

Back in 1982 during my whirlwind of a summer in Houston with Shirtless Joe, I met another Joe that definitely made my eyes water and my Levi 501s tighten so much I nearly popped a button. His name was Joe Varvaro, and he "welcomed" me to Houston several times that summer. Joe was the epitome of Italian handsomeness with a rugged jawline, stealthy brownish-green eyes, and a body that could charm the pants off many men, as he did mine.

Joe and I lost touch for a while when I was dating Dennis, but we reconnected on the night of JR's male stripper finals in 1983; he won, and I was first-runner up (second-place loser again). He would go on to become the current third runner-up to Mr. Gay Texas, and, coincidentally, had been sponsored by JR's.

Joe and I continued to see each other on each of my subsequent visits to Houston; though we never officially dated, he held a very special place in my heart and I was excited when he was chosen as the next *TWT* cover model. *Damn, what was it with me and these Mr. Texas guys and TWT cover boys?* It was also Joe who was right there in the front row to cheer me on during the male stripper finals at JR's in the summer of 1984. Following that exhilarating victory, I was booked almost every other weekend to perform in Texas, so between work at JC Penney and my Colt Michael career, I was extremely busy. But my life was falling apart despite my success in both arenas.

Spending time with Joe came as a welcome distraction from the stressors of retail management and the grand delusion that I was now somehow famous. Joe always kept me grounded and sane. And part of that equation was a whole new world to me. Joe introduced me to the world of leather, bondage, fetishes, and fantasy; in our land of leather make-believe, Joe and I enjoyed each other in ways I never knew were possible.

In May 1985, I was formally welcomed into Houston's gay leather community via Texas' Southwest Drummer competition. One of the categories for this competition was "fantasy," and Joe had this insane idea to recreate (simulate) some of our sex acts on stage. As intimate as we were, I wasn't ready to share that life in public; but I consented, and we practiced our routine several times. Joe worked diligently to ensure that his fantasy was a complete secret to the rest of the competition as well as the judges.

At the reception held on the evening prior to the Mr. Southwest Drummer contest, I was introduced to everyone as "Joe's hot friend from Louisiana;" and while I was very well-known on the male stripper circuit, I was completely unknown in the leather community. I was Joe's best-kept secret. That night at the after-reception at the Ripcord, Houston's famous/infamous leather bar, I was unexpectedly called to the stage while Joe was being interviewed. The emcee asked me to turn around and show off my best "asset." I obliged, and grabbed Joe's hand to let the audience know that I was *all* his, and tomorrow night's show at Rich's (a downtown gay mega-bar) would prove it.

Joe's fantasy concept was to search for and find the man of his dreams, capture him, whip him into submission, and possess him forever. I was not accustomed to being the less dominant partner, but this was Joe's fantasy, and I wanted him to feel the power that he had over me. He dressed in black leather from head to toe: barely-there chaps, jeans, a vest, boots, a policeman-style captain's hat, spiked arm bands and wrist bands, a spiked dog collar, and a grey bandana showing above his back left pocket. I wore a tattered white tank top, ripped Levi's 501 jeans, black cowboy boots, with a grey handkerchief flung from my back right pocket.

The music started and I wandered onto the massive stage alone as I pretended to be lost and afraid. The music faded, and within a split second, a bullwhip snapped right next to my ear. I spun around and stared at Joe longingly as he snapped the bullwhip again before circling the leather strap around my waist. I grabbed the tip of the bullwhip just before it snapped and revealed an angry red welt on my forearm ... just as we had practiced. As Joe tried to wrangle me into his arms, I pretended to resist and crawled away, but he grabbed my ankle and used the bullwhip to tie my hands behind my back. He ripped my clothes off and left me onstage completely naked, then walked off. The audience was aghast and silent. Joe then reappeared with electric hair clippers and straddled me over his knees. He massaged my back and glutes; then he flicked on the power button and the buzz of the clippers ignited the audience once more.

He twisted me around and we kissed passionately, then he knelt on one knee and straddled me over the other and flogged me mercilessly as I writhed in pain. Joe was relentless in his determined infliction of combined pain and pleasure; the audience stood silent yet again. Once he whipped me into submission, he lowered me onto the floor, naked and now bruised, then sealed our relationship with a sweet, soft kiss. At that moment, it felt like an earthquake inside of that bar; it was so loud it felt as though the walls could have crumbled. Joe then lifted me up off the floor, kissed me, and carried my bruised naked body offstage.

To quote the *Houston Forum* newspaper dated May 31, 1985, *"Joe Varvaro, sponsored by Hooters, left little to the imagination as he whipped and shaved his fantasy subject to a frenzy as the crowd screamed, yelled and otherwise raised the decibel level at Rich's to a hitherto unknown peak."* The article goes on to discuss the other contestants and winners; first runner up was Peter Casares (yes, my "unicorn dancer"). The article continues, *"...and then an expected hush fell over the crowd as they announced Mr. Southwest Drummer 1985–Joe Varvaro. The crowd went wild as they really made the acoustics quiver."*

I was so very proud of Joe and was excited for him; he had worked so hard for this, and I knew that he deserved it. Part of me was secretly happy that we beat Peter Casares at his best game; I don't know why I still had such jealousy for Peter; we were friends, I know I shouldn't have felt that way, but I kinda' did.

However, there is a part to this story which has never been told ... until now. Joe and I practiced this routine for weeks. The part of the fantasy that scared me the most was the bullwhip; I had to catch the tip of the whip just before it would have snapped across my back. As it turned out, that should have been the least of my concerns. I was then twenty-two years old and had never been shaved before in my life; I had no idea what that would feel like, but I wanted to help Joe fulfill his fantasy and also win this competition. Being completely exposed, literally and figuratively, I did not know what a flogger would feel like. And while the entire crowd that night thought that I was writhing in pain as Joe manhandled me with the flogger, I was actually laughing hysterically, as the leather straps actually tickled me. Fortunately, the entranced audience was none the wiser since, apparently, the body's reaction to "writhing in pain" and "laughing hysterically" are very similar ... just like the metaphor of the agony and the ecstasy. I never even told this story to Joe; I would never have wanted to diminish his "fantasy."

Joe Varvaro died on June 19, 1988, at age twenty-seven; yet another casualty of the AIDS epidemic; I feel honored to have been able to help him see some of his dreams come true and let him get the recognition and accolades of fame that he so richly deserved. This was one of his "*seconds of fame*" and I wanted this evening to be specifically for *him*. Joe gave me a night that I can never forget; nor would I ever want to; he unwittingly helped me to fulfill some fantasies I never knew I had.

Simultaneously, my hard work and dedication at JC Penney were paying off, as in the year following my reassignment to the Young Men's department I was recognized as one of the Top 5 JC Penney Merchandising Assistants in the country. At the time, I was also the only merchandising assistant from the Lafayette, LA area to have ever received this award, and, at only twenty-two years old, I was also the youngest.

For winning this prestigious award, I was given an extra week of paid vacation and a silver humidor. I never smoked cigars, so opted to use the small container in my bathroom as a cotton swab dispenser. Although I never used it for intended purpose, and the sheen has tarnished into a patina, this little silver bucket remains one of my most prized possessions. But my life was still not complete. As successful as Ted A Richard was at JC Penney and as popular as Colt Michael was as a dancer, there was something missing; and I still relied on alcohol and drugs to fill the void between the two.

But winning the Merchandising Assistant of the Year the previous year gave me the confidence boost that I needed to ask for a promotion to upper management. While my boss supported my efforts to move up within the JC Penney company, there were no management positions available in Lafayette. The only management opportunity at the time was in ... Houston, Texas ... but the company would not pay for moving expenses. Finally, I was being offered the chance to move to Houston, and I already had a guaranteed job. The universe was smiling down on me.

I knew of someone who had recently moved to Houston who was now looking for a roommate. Neal Landry and I hadn't really been friends, but our common circles of friends comingled often. On one of my dancing trips to Houston, I stopped by his apartment to have a look around; it was located in Rosewood Estates which, at the time, advertised itself as "Houston's Largest Gay Apartment Complex," and coincidentally was only a few exits off the freeway to my new job at JC Penney in Meyerland Plaza. Truthfully, it really didn't matter, and I could have lived in a shack fifty miles away; I was moving to Houston!

It was during this trip in October 1985 that Neal and I went to the clubs on Houston's Pacific Street. We started the night at JR's for a few cocktails, then moved on to the Montrose Mining Company where I was greeted with a huge hug and a kiss from the doorman whom I didn't even know! Apparently, he was a fan, and let us in for free.

I soon found myself immersed in some of the hardcore porn that played continuously on the many video screens around the bar. I jokingly called it "fruit on a loop," and Neal doubled over with laughter.

I leaned over the bar to refill my drink when a stranger tapped me on the shoulder and asked, "Hey, is that *you*?" as he pointed to one of the screens. Neal and I looked up simultaneously to view the monitor with this stranger. "Holy shit," I said, "Yep, that's me!" I had no idea that Joe's and my entire performance for Mr. Southwest Drummer had been recorded and was now a part of the "fruit on a loop" reel at Montrose Mining Company.

Suddenly, it all made sense; the entire staff knew *exactly* who I was. Although I always yearned for fame, I certainly did not expect my "intimate" performance with Joe to be replayed over and over at the local sleaze bar. My *"ninth second of fame"* was truly a case of, be careful what you wish for! Of course, notoriety has its privileges; Neal and I enjoyed free admission and drinks all night long, and maybe that made his decision to accept my roommate application a no-brainer. It is my sincerest hope that the "fruit on the loop" reel was discarded and/or lost when the Montrose Mining Company closed in 2016.

I returned to Ossun from that trip with renewed vigor, and my parents noticed the excitement in my voice when I told them that I was finally getting a chance to live out my dream by moving to Houston. But as excited as I was for this new experience, I was a bit apprehensive; I would quickly learn that "living" in Houston was definitely NOT the same thing as "visiting" it.

with Joe Varvaro, Mr. Southwest Drummer
(courtesy of this Week in Texas magazine) –1985

CHAPTER 10

I'LL BE BACK – I PROMISE

(That Time I was Raped)

I moved to Houston, Texas during Thanksgiving week of 1985; although Neal had been there for about a year before me, he was still new to the area, and had only recently been open about his own homosexuality. We both were able to enjoy new life experiences without the dreaded fear of cultural bigotry and persecution. We were able to live OUT LOUD for the first time in our lives. Living as our true selves was a new feeling for each of us, and our shared moments of "learning the ropes" together was a time I would always cherish.

    I met my next boyfriend that very first night out on the town alone after officially moving to Houston. It was Thanksgiving Eve 1985, and I had just walked into a new gay club called Heaven; at the time, it was THE place to be for anything and everything in gay music and entertainment. Unusually crowded for a Wednesday night, I was waiting at the bar for my good friend and bartender, Chuck Roberson—yet another *TWT* cover boy—to order a drink, when this random guy approached and said, "Hi, my name is Patrick McCarter and you are the hottest thing in here. I need to bring my drunk friend home now, but I promise I'm coming back just for you. Please don't move." I was in complete shock; I'd just arrived, and it was my first night out as a resident of Houston; besides, there was no way that I was the "hottest guy" in there. After all, I was waiting on Chuck Roberson (a future Mr. Gay USA), and life didn't get much hotter than that! His candor and confidence bore no conceit, and I was intrigued. Patrick wore a gaudy, oversized denim jacket with extra-long dark brown suede fringe that swayed with the music as he walked and moved. I stared at his hips purposefully shaking back at me in his new Z. Cavaricci jeans. So, of course I stayed and waited, and waited, and waited.

I was already on my third Jack and Coke, countless tequila shots, and more than just a few keys of "happy dust" while chatting with Chuck as he slung cocktails for the crowd. Finally, I saw this curly-haired, muscle guy wearing a slinky tank top and almost painted-on jeans sauntering closer and closer. *Holy shit!* It was Patrick; this Greco-Irish, black-haired bodybuilder with the mesmerizing sapphire-blue eyes did a complete wardrobe change; I was in awe of the stoic yet gracious beauty that had been hidden underneath "the hot guy with the denim fringed jacket." Damn, he looked great; and while the fantasy of what I hoped our night would be swirled in my head, I had to keep it together so that he wouldn't know just how high I was. I'm so glad I waited.

Our mutual interests included dinner and a movie, the theater, the opera, and he also enjoyed partying just as much as I did. We became Houston's hot new couple, and I certainly enjoyed the attention. I became so enthralled in what was the "Patrick and Ted Show" that I knew I would be devastated if it ever came to an end, and I thought it never would; Patrick was my forever love, my soulmate.

My life with Patrick flourished, but furthering my career goals in Houston with JC Penney were short-lived, as the position which had been promised to me never materialized; there was no offer nor explanation. I continued working there for a while, but the deceitfulness of being assured a management position that never existed sent me into a deeper tailspin of substance abuse and self-doubt.

After about six months at Meyerland JCP, I was promoted to supervisor—a lower position than the one promised me—and the $520-per-year raise didn't even amount to a cost of living adjustment. I was furious, but I needed the job, so I said nothing. Additional gigs as Colt Michael helped supplement my income, but even that barely covered rent and my penchant for alcohol and drugs.

As a supervisor, I had access to the money tills and had to balance them after my shifts; it wasn't very long until I had figured out a way to steal money from the registers and still have the tills balance before the beginning of the following business day. At first, I was taking $5 or $10 per day, then, since I had not yet been caught, I upped the ante to stealing $20 a day. By the time I finally was called in to the security office to be fired, nearly six months later; I had been working at JCP Meyerland for almost a year and stealing close to $200 per shift to the tune of about $1,000 a week. Thankfully, the company did not press charges and did not make me pay restitution, since they had no idea how much money I stole.

Two security guards and the store manager escorted me to my vehicle, and I was banned from the premises; I had successfully destroyed a nearly five-year career in favor of my addictions. At the time, I completely blamed JCP for my actions, because it was the company's fault that I didn't get the job or salary that I was promised. In my own warped mind, I'd done absolutely nothing wrong, and I wasn't sorry, either. But, here's the silver lining, I have to thank the company for the opportunity to move to a city where I finally felt as if I belonged. I am still angry that the management position never really existed, but I am thankful that this offer was extended because the rest of my life would never have been the same; so, I guess I do owe JC Penney a bit of gratitude. Kinda.

With no full-time work, Colt Michael performed more often and at higher payouts, which didn't go over very well with some of the bar owners; especially since some of them were also my drug dealers who paid me in cocaine instead of cash. I applied at several of the local bars to become a barback or a bartender, or really anything. I did not get a single response; it seemed as though I was great for entertainment, but that was the extent of my qualifications. They couldn't recognize my brains and talent beyond my show-biz skills; I guess I should have seen that one coming.

In mid-December, I finally got a call from a manager at Heaven; Chuck Roberson, fresh off his much-deserved win as Mr. Gay USA 1986, saw my application and gave me a great reference. New Year's Eve was fast approaching, and they needed someone to work in coat check. I really wanted a bartending or barback job, but I figured at least I'd have my foot in the door.

I visited my family for the Christmas holidays and never once brought up the fact that, not only was I now unemployed, I had been fired for stealing ... for alcohol and drugs. It was during this trip to Louisiana that I booked a gig with a dance troupe called Erotic Dance Company (EDC) that included both male and female strippers. That week, EDC was booked at The Broken Wheel in Bayou Vista, Louisiana, over sixty miles from Lafayette. Luckily, Miss Melissa, the group's manager, lived about halfway between the two towns, so we were able to crash at her house for the night.

   The Broken Wheel is exactly the type of bar you would visualize in a town named after a swamp, and a name that warns you that you're entering a bar with parts that are already broken; with aged wood on nearly every visible surface, dimmed fluorescent lighting, and bourbon barrels substituted for tables surrounded by short wooden stools made to look like old wagon wheels, obviously made by a less-than-skilled carpenter; and the bar had installed temporary curtains to separate the men's side from the ladies' side for the night. The clientele was mostly country and farm-hand folks with a few yippity-dos pretending to be living high on the hog; it was clear that they were there for the alcohol and not necessarily the entertainment, since most of the patrons were already drunk when we arrived at around 9:00 p.m. for a 10:00 p.m. showtime.

   I don't know how much the other dancers nor Melissa were being paid, but I know that my fee was $150; maybe that's why there were only two male dancers and two female dancers. It wasn't a very profitable night, as most of the people had probably spent most of their money on Christmas gifts; they just needed a reason to get out of the house. As always, I performed with the same energy whether there were twenty people in the bar or 200 people. But this crowd was different, and barely paid attention to me as I was gyrating and romancing my way across the dance floor; it was often that I could see women sneaking off to go outside (during my performance) to refill their drinks, being too cheap to belly up to the bar. (Why anyone would be allowed to wear a tube top in late December when their titties hang lower than their belly buttons is a concept I will never grasp.)

   The other male dancer, Adam, was a straight (pronounced "bi-sexual"), 6'4" tall, bald, tattooed muscle-bound hunk; his experience that night was completely different than mine. Realistically, by comparison, I would have wanted him rather than me, too; even though Adam couldn't find the beat to the music if it hit him on the head; he needed only to stand there and twist back and forth displaying the massive package barely concealed by his G-string. I subtly (pronounced "overtly") flirted with Adam while we were backstage; not that I thought he ever noticed, since he mostly ignored me. But onstage, he stole my thunder and my applause; and it's not as if I could just magically "grow" to better fill my G-string. I had become so accustomed to the cheers and adulation of the gay guys at the clubs in Houston, that I was disappointed when I didn't even get one autograph request. I was glad when the show was over, everyone got paid, and we packed up to head back to Melissa's for the night.

Aside from Adam's lackluster performance, I still thought he was hot, although "pretty but dumb" usually wasn't my taste. Luckily, there actually was a bright side to the evening; I met a young lady who was a great conversationalist, and she took an interest in me.

Her name was Theresa DeLuca, a melding of Italian brawn and Southern charm, masculine musculature and feminine curves; she was opulently beautiful. She and I struck up a very pleasant conversation during the ride together down to Bayou Vista from Melissa's house. She was intrigued about how a gay guy made money in straight bars, how I performed for straight girls when I didn't find them sexually appealing, and, most specifically, what made a gay guy gay; all questions to which I had no real answer.

Her stage name, Honeycomb, lent itself to her schtick, which involved dressing up as a honeybee; as she undressed for the attentive, horny, men, she'd "sting" them whenever they tipped her pretending to be searching for their "honey." It really was a cute and very effective gimmick, which she told me she had thought of after hearing the song of the same name on one of her Mom's cassette tapes. Theresa's "Honeycomb" performance as the honey-seeking queen bee garnered her hundreds of dollars in tips that night.

The half-hour trip back to Melissa's house took forever; Theresa fell asleep in my lap as Melissa drove; Honeycomb had her fill of "honey" for the evening. As we arrived at Melissa's house, I came down from the Ecstasy I took several hours earlier and went to bed.

I don't know how long I had been asleep, and at the time, I thought it was part of a drug-induced hallucination, but I could hear the twisting of the rusty doorknob to the bedroom. I concocted a scenario in my head where Adam sneaked into my room to let me play with the "rooster" he'd been hiding from me all night. I heard his raspy voice whisper, "Ted, are you awake?" I didn't answer. *Could it be that he was actually paying attention to my earlier flirting attempts?*

I temporarily forgot about my boyfriend, Patrick McCarter. (Our relationship had been unsteady for quite some time now, and our sex life was non-existent; with such strong feelings for each other, neither one of us wanted to declare "the break-up," but it was bound to happen, and soon.)

I soon felt Adam's warm hands caressing my legs, slowly making his way upward until I could feel his lips envelop me. I kept my eyes closed and enjoyed the experience; I still couldn't believe it was happening; this would have to be mine and Adam's secret; his girlfriend could *never* find out about us.

He leaned in to kiss me; I felt the softness of his sweet lips and the moistness of his tongue touching mine, but suddenly felt two bulbous orbs hitting me on my chin which I knew didn't belong there; Adam's chest was not THAT big!

WAIT! What the FUCK! Fuck ... it WASN'T Adam ... it was Theresa! *Was I being RAPED by a WOMAN? How the hell could I allow this to be happening to me?* YES, and I don't know. The entire incident was over before I could wrap my mind around what just happened.

At the time, there was a popular porn movie called, *Debbie Does Dallas;* well that night, "Theresa Did Ted!" She apologized, saying that she thought she could change me. I shouted, "Theresa, you're barking up a tree that's already been pissed on!"

Melissa, hearing the commotion, burst in through my bedroom door as Theresa covered herself with the bedsheet. She quickly ran out of the room, and left Melissa and me speechless. I immediately got dressed, picked up my stuff, got in my car, and drove back to my parents' house. Theresa would need to find another way home.

I knew that Theresa had no idea that I had been flirting with Adam, since I always made certain that she was out on the dance floor whenever I was making moves; but I always wondered if Adam had put her up to this, or if this was just something she devised on her own. I never saw either of them again, but I chose to believe that Adam was completely innocent of any wrongdoing. On that night, Theresa Deluca indulged herself in her own claim to fame; she *had* Colt Michael; a feat no other woman had ever accomplished, before or since.

My family was happy, and so was I, that I could spend a little more time with them before returning to Houston. I know that they saw my despondency, and I allowed them, and myself, to *believe* that I was sad to be leaving, but that couldn't have been further from the truth. I wanted to get as far away as possible from that slutty, straight girl who thought that she could turn me straight by raping me. I drove back to Houston as quickly as I could; surely the new year would be better than the last one, and the Heaven to which I was headed was a welcome reprive to the Hell I just experienced. I never again spoke of the incident ... until now.

Wednesday, December 31, 1986, I arrived at Heaven (the gay bar) at around 5:00 p.m., an hour earlier than my first shift began. Chuck, Mr. USA, fixed me a Jack and Coke and, of course we did a shot of tequila and I dropped some acid and did a line of coke. Having not made much money at The Broken Wheel, I was thankful for receiving gifts of money for Christmas; being otherwise broke after fueling up my car for my return trip, I still found money for my addictions.

The bar opened at 6:00 p.m., and the beginning of the evening was very slow; it was New Year's Eve after all, and the crowd wouldn't get going until at least 10:00 p.m., giving me time for at least a couple more keys of coke. Either it was an unusually cold night, or the gays decided to all wear their brand new Christmas present coats. Coat check was overwhelming; so much so that by 11:00 p.m., management sent someone to help me.

The chaos started at about 12:30 a.m. when many of the patrons who'd already celebrated the new year arrived to collect their coats. After realizing I had made mistakes on the first few customers, my coworker realized that I had completely messed up the entire coat check system. I truthfully don't remember exactly what happened next, I just remember no longer being at the bar.

My next recollection was being questioned by the doorman at Patrick McCarter's high-rise apartment complex in downtown Houston. I was buzzed in and staggered to the elevator trying to appear as un-drunk and un-high as possible. I knocked on Patrick's door and heard sporadic mumbling, but figured it was the television. Patrick opened the door in only his underwear and a bottle of champagne. Standing right behind him—also in his underwear—was Patrick's ex. Their expressions told me that my visit was VERY unexpected, and that their plans for the evening did *not* include me. That's when I knew that our relationship was definitely over.

But a few weeks later I called Patrick to come over and visit; he made sure that I knew this was not a conjugal visit. There was no one else to talk to since Neal and I barely spoke to each other. In retrospect, Neal had many other reasons to disregard me and my actions; I had become toxic to him. For years, I waited for an apology but was too caught up in myself and my addiction to realize that it was *me* who owed Neal the apology.

Angry with me for lying and hurt that he could no longer trust me, Neal moved out and left me alone in the apartment we once had so happily shared. Although I know we left on what was not the best of terms, I do have some of the fondest memories of our fun times together in my first Houston apartment. This big step would never have happened without his help ... and my parents, of course. [Neal and I lost contact over the course of the next several years; he never got to know the person I ultimately became. Sadly, he passed away on July 24, 2020, at the age of fifty-six, regretfully never getting the apology from me that he so greatly deserved.]

At my wit's end, broke, depressed, and nearly homeless if I didn't come up with ALL of the rent, I told Patrick what was really going on with my job; but I lied to him, too. I never explained to him the real reason why I was no longer employed; I merely told him that my job hadn't been working out and that I had just quit because they weren't treating me fairly. I know that he'd heard about my outrageous behavior at Heaven on New Year's Eve, but he never questioned me about that night, so I never gave answers. I never questioned *his* New Year's Eve antics either; it was for the best.

Patrick was a very well-known hairdresser in the Houston Montrose area (gay mecca), and as fate would have it, one of his clients was the general manager at Foley's Department Store in Sharpstown Mall. He said that he would put in a good word for me but couldn't make any promises. The following day, I drove to meet with Kathy Knott, Patrick's client and Foley's store manager; and after three consecutive interviews on the same day, I was hired immediately, and started training the following day. I was ecstatic that no one did a background check on my previous JC Penney employment. Fortunately, Kathy Knott trusted Patrick to not steer her in the wrong direction, so now I had to prove to her, Patrick, and the rest of the Foley's executive team that they made the right decision.

With this new job also came a rejuvenated spirit that had been missing for some time; I enjoyed my life again, and no longer worried if I was going to have a place to lay my head at night; and I do owe Patrick a debt of gratitude for introducing me to the store manager of Foley's-Sharpstown. That introduction opened doors for me in the retail world that would not otherwise have been available to me. *Thank you, Patrick.*

Soon I would have a new roommate, Dennis Derwin. Dennis was small in stature but large on personality. He always had a smile and a welcoming heart. Dennis had lived in Houston for a while but needed a change of scenery. We had chemistry right away. No, not the sexual kind, but the friendship kind.

Dennis was from Hudsonville, Michigan, a small town of fewer than 8,000 people. It didn't take long to realize that Dennis and I were going to be not only great friends, but exceptional roommates. We shared lots of common interests, but also were intrigued by the differences in growing up in a small town in southwest Michigan compared to a homophobic town in south Louisiana. All in all, we realized that there wasn't much difference at all. Homophobia is embedded everywhere ... it is not particular to weather nor circumstance ... and we had both learned that moving away was the best thing for each of us to do at that time.

We both enjoyed the nightlife, but we were also mostly broke, so every year we purchased season tickets to AstroWorld and the Greater Houston Zoo. There was a group of about ten of us who did this, so that whenever we felt like going out but didn't have any money, we could always go enjoy thrill rides at the park or a summer day at the zoo. Either way, we only had to pay the $5 for parking.

[Flashback: As a young kid, our family vacation was almost always a trip to Houston to go to AstroWorld. Advertised as the Eighth Wonder of the World at the time, it was our family's summer escape. I'd have never thought, as a kid, that I would actually live in the same city as AstroWorld. Look at me now! I'm movin' on up!]

Dennis and I had loads of fun together and shared a million laughs; I was introduced to many of Dennis' friends, including Rusty Clark. Rusty was from Alpine, a very small southwest Texas town with a population of fewer than 6,000, flanked in the foothills of the Davis Mountains to the north and the Glass Mountains to the east; nestled near Big Bend National Forest. Rusty and I also shared a lot in common with each other, aside from our friendship with Dennis. Somehow these three small town transplants to Houston found each other amongst four million others; we have remained friends throughout the years and have always kept in close touch.

It was Valentine's Day, Saturday, February 14, 1987; Patrick and I were both single, and since we had remained such close friends, we decided to have a V-Day pity party at his high-rise condo; it was the first time we had been out together since the breakup. The evening was very simple; we just went out to dinner, had a few drinks; I had taken a hit of Ecstasy but didn't tell Patrick; and picked up some ice cream to bring back to his place. (Okay, that's a lie. We actually had brought back some popcorn. Patrick and I enjoyed watching porn while eating popcorn and constantly critiquing the acting. We jokingly called it "attention whoring." It was our guilty pleasure.)

As Patrick was about to put the video into the VCR, there was a breaking news story on the national news; a female stripper in Utah had performed for a judge in that state's Third Judicial (Salt Lake County) District Court to prove that her performance was not "lewd and lascivious" in an attempt to prevent the shuttering, or fining, of the strip club in which she worked. But it's not the story itself that caught my attention; it was the girl; I KNEW her … it was Theresa DeLuca, my rapist from last December.

I almost immediately called 411 (directory assistance) to request the phone number of Diamond Dolls Cabaret, the club which, according to the television information, Theresa had been "representing" in court. I got Patrick's permission to make a long-distance phone call from his apartment and called the club and left a message for "Honeycomb" to return a phone call to "Colt Michael." The Dancing Dolls Cabaret "office manager" informed me that "Honeycomb" would receive the message at 2:00 a.m. the following morning at the end of her shift. (I was happy that her "bee sting" gimmick hadn't changed; it made it easier for me to find her.)

Patrick never questioned the urgency of these phone calls, and I never offered a full explanation, ever; I only told him that she was one of the dancers from my visit back to Louisiana last Christmas. We laughed about the spectacle of being a stripper in a courtroom. At the time, I was able to laugh about it; it was the only way to hide the contempt I truly felt for her.

That was the last Valentine's Day Patrick and I shared; we had an incredible evening, laughing at the gossip we created by going out as an un-couple. I even spent the night with Patrick, at his insistence, because he didn't want me to be alone for Valentine's Day. It was nothing sexual; just a shared compassion for each of us that we were able to remain cherished friends even though our "boyfriend" relationship had come to an end.

I left his apartment very early on Sunday morning to be certain I'd be home in case Theresa called; and sure enough; my house phone rang before noon ... it was her. I tried to exchange pleasantries with her, which was nearly impossible, considering the awkwardness of the situation; but I wanted her to know that what she did to me had traumatized me.

She seemed uncaring about the entire situation, and then startled me with the following statement, "Oh, and I got pregnant that night, but I had an abortion, so you don't have to worry." I'm fairly sure that I dropped the phone, although the rest of that conversation was a complete blur. Not only had she raped me, she also took away from me the chance to be a father; something I had always dreamed of.

My *"tenth second of fame"* was a chance meeting of a slutty woman who wanted so badly for me to be straight that she raped me, and then destroyed the evidence by getting rid of the one thing that I have missed having all of my life: a child and the opportunity to be a father.

In my own life, I have always been pro-choice when it comes to a woman's body and her right to choose, but in this case, Theresa took EVERY decision away from me. SHE made the decision to rape me, and

SHE made the determination to end the pregnancy resulting from that rape. I feel as though, in this particular instance, MY rights had been infringed upon. Yet, I still must protect her right to privacy. Kinda doesn't make sense to me, at least not in this case.

In retrospect, I could easily have reworded the prior statements to profess the love for a child that I now will never have; because I was specifically uninvited (yet again) to serve any role in the decision-making process; but the outcome would still the be the same ... I am now childless.

The following week, my parents visited for a VERY belated birthday celebration (three months late). Mom baked a fig cake for every one of my birthdays and placed numbered candles on the cake for me to blow out to make a wish. Her cake that year tasted especially sweet; I knew I was never going to get my wish; Theresa had already assured me of that. But I knew I was going to be okay because Mom and Dad said so, though I never told them what had happened to me. I decided to never let this incident consume the rest of my life; there is no doubt that the loss I felt further contributed to my already rampant alcohol and drug abuse and made me less caring about my reputation as the sexual deviant I had become.

To this day, I have never told anyone this story. It is much too painful to know that I could have had a child, and that choice was stolen from me. I have always wondered what kind of a father I would have been and how having the responsibility of a child could have changed the course of my life for the better. I would never know!

(HIS name would have been Coulter Anthony-Thomas in honor of my friend Colt Thomas, 1983 Mr. Gay Texas and 1983 International Mr. Leather, who would become the very first model for the cover of *Advocate MEN* (Premier Issue–1984). I first met Colt shortly after his *TWT* cover story and had the opportunity to visit with Colt several times during my many travels to Houston; at the time, he was doing his doctoral residency at the University of Texas at Galveston. Colt and I became fast friends, but never dated. A doctor, cowboy, and leather man, Colt later revealed to me that he was humbled when I told him that he was the inspiration for my own alter-ego. Coulter "Colt" Thomas died of complications from HIV/AIDS on September 6, 1992. Yet another friend gone way too soon. We will never know of the many lives this doctor could have saved, yet the research was not yet available to save his own.

HER name would have been Michaela Antonia.)

Colt Michael performing at The Broken Wheel–1986

This Week in Texas cover – (courtesy This Week in Texas magazine)–1987

CHAPTER 11

COVER BOY
(That Time I Went to the Clinic)

I started my new job at Foley's-Sharpstown in early 1987; and decided that this was going to be the year that my life would get a much-needed boost in confidence and financial reward. For the past several years, I lived a devil-may-care life of wild abandon where I used alcohol as a remedy, drugs as a cure, and sex as a weapon. I knew that my life HAD to change, and the burden was all mine. Of course, this was before the life-changing Valentine's Day debacle, and I am beyond thankful that Patrick remained one of my dearest friends throughout the chaos that was my life. I regret that I never told Patrick what had truly happened with Theresa DeLuca/Honeycomb, as perhaps he would have known how to be a bit more of an empathic friend; but that was my fault too.

On a much more positive note, my moonlighting job as Colt Michael was now on the upswing; and here's the backstory. During the early months of our relationship, Patrick regaled to me about the night that he and some friends went to this dive bar near downtown Houston and saw this really hot stripper from Louisiana named Mike. He wasn't far into the conversation before he realized that "Mike" was Colt Michael, and that Colt Michael was *ME*. I asked, "Why didn't you tip me? I certainly would have remembered you if you had." He gave me some lame excuse about how his friends were ready to go and some kind of "Money for Nothing" bullshit, but I digress. [Ooh, wait, it's kinda like that Dire Straits song. Only in the 1980s could a song with lyrics mentioning a *"faggot"* wearing makeup and an earring become a No. 1 song on the *Billboard Top 100*, be one of the Top 10 songs of that year, AND get nominated for two Grammy Awards. Using "faggot" as a derogatory term for gay men was commonplace, and the fact that this song garnered the accolades it received further explains why so many young men chose to remain "in the closet."]

That dive bar that Patrick McCarter and his friends visited that night was The Lazy J. I had danced there on a few occasions, though to this day, I have no clue what the heck "The Lazy J" means. Having lost all respect from any of the bars on Houston's Pacific Street (the gay strip) due to my outrageous drunken and disorderly behavior on the past New Year's Eve, I was willing to take a gig almost anywhere that would have me. Due to my keen adeptness at self-sabotage, The Lazy J was the only bar that offered me a job as a male stripper on a regular basis. (Although I now also had a retail job, I still needed the extra money for other expenses; living in the big city ain't cheap, and neither were the drugs!)

The fact that Colt Michael was no longer a "star" (just me assuming that he ever was) was a humbling experience for me. *What the hell had happened?* Just three years before, I boasted about being Texas' Male Stripper of the Year (more delusions of grandeur), then two years ago I was Joe Varvaro's hot Cajun guy, and now some little dive joint was the only bar in town offering me a regular gig.

I knew *exactly* what happened, and I knew that it was all my fault; I allowed myself to believe that I was famous and that "normal people" rules didn't apply to me. I now believed that my persona of Colt Michael was real and the "fame" that "he" had acquired was worth something; but I was just a well-endowed guy in a G-string. I quickly realized that my status as an "out-of-town" performer came with its own perks; but now, I was a local, and the rules completely changed. They *did* apply to me. Being an "out-of-towner" held some type of allure that got the attention that "locals" did not. And although Houston was a much bigger city, the "out-of-town" allure faded; I had to prove my abilities, to both myself and to the Houston crowds, all over again. The pedestal I had placed myself upon was crumbling quickly, and I had to start over from the bottom (no pun intended).

As part of The Lazy J promotion for that week, the owner asked if I had any recent pictures so that they could feature me in that week's advertisement in *TWT*. I told him that I did a photo shoot when I was a part of The Strokers back in Lafayette a few years before, but that I didn't think the photos were very good.

The following day, I met with the manager of The Lazy J at the *TWT* offices and brought my photo albums to see if any of my old head shots were good enough for the advertisement. I will never forget the bar manager's expression when he saw my portfolio. He said, "Are you nuts? These are fantastic! Those eyes get me every time!" Over the years, people often complimented my eyes; I even recall the photographer saying, "Do that thing with your eyes," but I had no idea what he was talking about. It's not until The Lazy J bar manager pointed it out, that I noticed how big and beautiful my dark brown eyes were. I am forever grateful to staff and management of The Lazy J for giving me the opportunity that, at the time, no one else would.

On Saturday, January 24, 1987, The Lazy J was standing-room-only; on this night I noticed the similarities between this bar and Frank's Bar in Lafayette. It was a true "locals" bar that hosted patrons of every color, creed, culture, and sexuality; a real cornucopia of Houston's gay culture in a very nondescript, discreet location on the outskirts of the downtown area, just like Frank's. It was one of the first times that I felt truly welcomed by the club and the community as a whole; not because I felt un-welcomed anywhere else, but because this bar made me feel like I was "home" again.

On that night, when the emcee introduced Colt Michael, the uproarious applause was almost deafening; but it wasn't a fandom type of applause, it was more of a "welcome back." And I was even more excited when I peered down, and there, in the front row, was Patrick McCarter and the friends whom he had come with the last time they were at The Lazy J; but this time, they ALL tipped me. My Houston homecoming came a couple of years later than I had expected, but the feeling I had that night was worth the wait!

After the show, I stayed in the bar for a while, and signed autographs; I made it a policy to always do a meet-and-greet after each performance, as (in my mind) it made Colt Michael a "real" person, and not just a slab of meat on a stage. Conversely, having so many genuine, adoring fans made me feel special; I wanted to somehow live vicariously through Colt Michael, and enjoy his fame and the benefits that came with it. I became addicted to the high every night while I was onstage and as I signed autographs after each show, and lost myself in the fantasy that *was* Colt Michael and found myself getting depressed that Ted A Richard wasn't HIM!

The last person in line that night to get an autograph was a strapping, older man, wearing ripped Levi's 501 jeans and a leather vest revealing the brawny, sculptured body and hairy chest of someone who had spent more than just a few years at the gym. His *TWT* magazine opened up to the page on which my ad appeared, he introduced himself; Steven Meert, the manager of Outlaws, another gay bar in the Houston Montrose area. He asked if I would be willing to dance at his club sometime, and I explained that I would need to discuss it with the management at The Lazy J, but that I was sure we could figure something out.

Saturday, March 14, 1987, I was cleared by the Lazy J for a one-night gig at Outlaws. I remember opening the front door (there was no back entrance), and the entire crowd just turned and stared. Steven came out from around the bar to greet me and escort me to the dressing room; the consummate professional, I arrived at 9:00 p.m. for a 10:00 p.m. show. There were three other entertainers that night, all drag queens (using the term loosely), and I was the featured performer and only stripper.

I heard the emcee, Christi Storm, announce, "Welcome to the stage, our very special guest for the evening, on loan from The Lazy J, Mister Colt Michael." As soon as I appeared from behind the stage curtains, I could see that the crowd was already on their feet, and, once again, I was happy to see Patrick McCarter and his friends there to support me. Wearing a black kimono jacket with silver sequins and fringe, I danced to "Open Your Heart" by Madonna, and performed my signature move of completing ten high kick straddles consecutively, and having the audience count out the straddles; it was always such a crowd pleaser and garnered lots of tips. I was not naïve enough to not know exactly what thoughts were going through some of the patron's minds; I KNEW they'd wish that I would straddle them; I was the only one that knew it was never gonna happen.

The crowd was completely engrossed in my performance as I completed my signature straddles. However, as I stomped around the stage to transition into my next dance move, one of the speakers fell from the ceiling exactly where I stood only seconds before. Steven Meert, who was also tending bar that night, jumped over the railing of the bar and rushed to stage to make sure that I was okay. I assured him that I was fine and told him that I hoped the speaker wasn't damaged; he politely said that he was more concerned with me. He gave me a gentle hug as I felt his hairy chest meet mine. The caress went no further; it was paramount that I allow the audience to lust in the fantasy that was Colt Michael. I performed my second and third acts with no technical difficulties and did my standard meet-and-greet after the show and signed autographs, having made over $300 in tips.

I stayed longer than planned because I really wanted to know more about this Steven Meert fella. He was HOT for sure, and tonight was one of those nights when adhering to my policy of not leaving the bar with anyone would prove to be extremely difficult; but it just had to be that way. I chatted with Steven over a few more Jack and Cokes. I learned that his ex-partner was a guy named Paul Comeaux, who, in the "it's-a-small-world department" was a brother to the same guy who was Mitchell Mahfouz's ex-partner before me. Yep, my second boyfriend's ex was my soon-to-be next boyfriend's ex's brother; even I still sometimes have a hard time wrapping my head around that one. I'll give you a minute to grab a pencil and draw it out on paper. Got it? Good.

The very next day, Steven called me, and I was so excited that he was asking me out on a date; but I was wrong. A freelance photographer wanted to know if he could have my number. He was interested in updating my portfolio; of course, I said YES! I was so excited that I hung up the phone before Steven got a chance to ask me out. I was going to get new photographs for the "new and improved" Colt Michael, plus, *This Week in Texas* wanted me on its cover!

[Sidebar: *This Week in Texas* (*TWT*) was a free weekly gay magazine serving the entire state of Texas. This gay rag featured news, current events, local gossip, homo-scopes, and sadly, obituaries. But the main feature of *TWT* magazine was the weekly cover story. Each week the magazine selected a Texas starling to grace its cover and centerfold spread. While the magazine did make for interesting and informative reading, it was the cover story that most people wanted.]

The weird thing about the magazine cover and the stripping and all of that other stuff is that I never really considered myself to be very attractive. Yes, I thought I looked okay, but that was just me; my looks weren't anything very special. I never really liked to be photographed, so, those photo shoots were treacherous to me; I never thought I looked good enough. As a matter of fact, I was well aware of all of the photographers in the crowd whenever I was dancing, and the strobe of flashbulbs (you youngsters will need to GTS ..."Google That Shit," compliments of my nephew, Dominic) from their cameras was sometimes blinding, but there was probably not a single photograph from any audience member who got a shot with me facing the camera. As soon as I noticed that the camera was about to flash, I would turn my head away. I certainly wasn't going to let some amateur catch me at a bad angle. Was that vanity, or just nonsense? Either way, it was the truth!

My last photo shoot was nearly five years before with The Strokers; it was time for some new pictures, but I still hated having my picture taken, especially when I had to pose for them. Carl Davis, the *TWT* photographer, was extremely professional and took his time with me to get the best shots possible. I had made one thing clear; since most of gay Texas had already seen me nude, I thought it would be a great idea to be photographed fully clothed. Mr. Davis agreed, saying that he wanted my eyes to tell the story. I told him that I had absolutely no idea what he meant.

The photo shoot began and then almost ended as abruptly as it started. Mr. Davis asked, "Ted, what's wrong? You look so scared." I sheepishly replied, "I'm petrified!" as I told him about my aversion to cameras. He reminded me that I had already done a photo shoot since I was able to provide a head shot for the magazine advertisement. I said, "Yeah, but that was different. We were in a bar, and we were all drinking, and it was just for fun; actually, that head shot was one of the few good pictures from that shoot." He got back behind the camera and said, "Look, just follow my directions and be yourself." Laughing now, I replied, "At the same time?" Now, we were both laughing, and Mr. Davis allowed me to believe that I was in control of the photo shoot, giving me very little direction. After about two hours or so, the shoot ended, and Mr. Davis seemed pleased; I was still petrified.

I had a meeting with the *TWT* magazine editors and my photographer on Thursday, April 2, 1987; they were both excited about how the cover had turned out. So was I, but I honestly didn't think that the picture actually looked like me at all. I remember asking the *TWT* editor, Chuck Patrick, who had air-brushed my pictures. He said, "Ted, we didn't do ANYTHING! That's ALL YOU! Do you not realize how attractive you are?" I admitted to him that I seldom took photographs because I hated the way I looked in "posed" pictures; then I thanked him and photographer Carl Davis for making me look so good. Mr. Davis said, "Ted, I just took the pictures, I hope that one day you can see how beautiful you are, and just appreciate it for what it is." I blushed and thanked them again as, together, they handed me the first copy of my new *TWT* magazine cover, just prior to the next day's distribution.

On Friday, April 3, 1987, the worlds of Ted A Richard and Colt Michael would soon collide; and my "double-life" escapade would be blown when the *TWT* magazines with me on the cover circulated across the state of Texas. The centerfold text stated, "Ted A Richard is a warm, spicy Cajun dish just right for chilly evenings. The twenty-four-year-old Houstonian, a native of Lafayette, Louisiana, is a merchandising assistant in the young men's department of a major department store, and sometimes works as a male dancer under the name Colt Michael. He enjoys dancing (especially to Country and Western), reading (currently *Ancient Evenings* by Norman Mailer); and, true to his sassafras roots, he likes Cajun cuisine (crayfish *étouffée, filé* gumbo, etc.)" Obviously, that was a very busy week for me, and I was booked solid (at my "dancing" job) all week, in addition to working my full-time job as a salesperson at Foley's-Sharpstown.

[Sidebar: There were some fantastic outtakes of when Mr. Davis asked me to "do that thing" with my eyes; I saw exactly what he meant when I previewed the photos for the magazine.]

On the Thursday following the release of my *TWT* cover, I was booked at a fairly new gay bar on the outskirts of the Montrose area, Rooster's, to be a guest dancer with the Fantasy in Motion dancers. I had never danced there before, but I was paid "extra" (pronounced "cocaine") for that night to promote the new club with the celebrity of my new magazine centerfold. As usual, I arrived at least an hour before showtime; I was scheduled for two sets, but I always brought an extra costume for encores, which there usually were, and tonight's encore was almost assured. Having arrived earlier than expected and being already prepared, I decided to do a short meet-and-greet before the show and sign a few autographs promoting my new *TWT* cover.

This night's performance was no different, except when I looked out into the audience, my boyfriend of the past few weeks, Steven Meert, had taken the night off from his job at Outlaws just to show up and support me. He tried to be discreet by hanging out in the darkness, away from the lights of the dance floor, but I spotted him within the first few seconds of being on stage. He was the only person I allowed to kiss me on the lips that night, but I don't think anyone noticed. They only cared about the fact that I was mostly naked; Steven saw me as more than that, and always reminded me that he wanted the brains behind the physique, and I loved him for that.

But Steven wasn't my only surprise that night; when I looked down into the audience, I saw many of the sales staff from Foley's-Sharpstown, including my boss. Little did I know that the magazine had somehow made the rounds of the store, and now all of the employees knew exactly who I was. I had only worked there a few months, and should not have been so shocked that the staff figured out who I was; I mean, after all, I have a very distinctive look; even though I barely recognized myself in any of those photos, and the magazine almost exactly revealed where I worked.

The previous night's show at Rooster's was a rousing success, and I was proud to be a part of it. I showed up promptly for work at 7:00 a.m. the following morning at Foley's-Sharpstown and almost immediately was summoned to my boss' office. She and I had a very long talk about professionalism as she explained to me the importance and "definition" of "being an executive in an executive world." I affirmed to her that I understood completely, then I showed her the money I had made the night before; it was more than her salary. So, we made an agreement that I would be promoted to General Area Sales Manager at Foley's-Sharpstown and get a twenty-five percent raise in salary within the next two weeks if I promised to not dance in the Houston area anymore. Promise made, promise kept; and everyone was happy. Although I did sneak in a few Houston gigs (courtesy of The Lazy J), I was performing so well at my new job as GSM of the entire Men's Department, that the Foley's management turned a blind eye; I was grateful.

My love life had also taken a turn for the better; Steven and I were officially a couple. In our few short months of dating I learned that Steven was no stranger to the "centerfold industry" either; in addition to being named Houston's Mr. Leather in 1982, he was also featured in *Drummer* magazine (a monthly print magazine for the gay leather community) in November 1982 and was *Numbers*' (a gay porn magazine) cover boy and centerfold in August 1984. As it turns out, my ex, Patrick McCarter, was also featured as *Honcho*'s (a gay porn publication) Man of the Year in 1986 and was also on the cover of *Drummer* magazine in May 1987; coincidentally the same week of his *TWT* cover. Somehow, my paths kept crossing with some of the elite members of the Houston leather/porn community, although I still never thought that I fit in.

[Sidebar: Little did I know that one chance meeting with Joe Varvaro in the fall of 1983 would introduce me to a world where I belonged but never felt a part of. I never revealed this to Joe, but on the night before the Mr. Southwest Drummer contest, I had sex with one of the guys I met at the reception; we were very discreet, as I usually was. His name was Richie Mullan, an icon of the Houston leather community in his own right, and also the head judge for the next night's contest.

Richie and I were instantly attracted to each other. In the "it's-a-small-world" department, I discovered later that Joe had dated him once also, as well as Peter Casares. The attraction between Richie and I was strictly sexual, and we both knew it. But how could we sneak off into the night without anyone knowing? Turns out, it was easier than we thought. While both Joe and Peter were being introduced to the crowd, Richie and I snuck off into the bar manager's office. In less than a second, we were both stark naked and exploring each other. It was during this tryst that Richie began testing my limits of leather kink. With his lips filled with mine, he commented, "I'd really love to shave you!" I questioned, "Now?" He replied, "No, next time."

Whew! I dodged a bullet. There's no way that I was going to tell him that shaving was tomorrow night's "talent" in fantasy. It was then that I realized that Joe knew exactly what the head judge's fantasies were, and he intended to reveal them to him on the main stage on the following night.

I choose to believe that Joe Varvaro won Mr. Southwest Drummer 1985 on his own merits, as he deserved it; but if my little tryst with the head judge tilted the judging in his favor, then I was happy to "help." Richie and I did stay in touch over the years, and he was one of the first people to call me when he saw my *TWT* cover. He told me that wanted an autographed copy and I was excited to oblige. Only three months later, on July 11, 1987, Richie Mullan would be dead at the age of twenty-nine; yet another cherished friend taken too soon by complications from AIDS. A bittersweet loss since I had not made the time to bring him the autographed *TWT* cover he had requested.]

In retrospect, I can now look back at those pictures and recognize that "damn, I was kinda hot." But back then, I never saw it. I think a lot of people had the perception that I was a bit arrogant. But honestly, I was never very convinced that anyone really wanted to talk to me, so, on most nights when I went out, I just sat in the corner and drank or did coke. Onstage, I was someone else for a little while and lived this exciting life, but offstage, when I was just Ted A Richard, I was just as insecure as everyone else.

Steven and I had been dating for about four months, and I was aware of a secret that no one else knew about. Steven had tested positive for the HIV virus about six months before we met. He informed me of his status on our first date, and told me, "if you can't handle it, I'll understand." But I knew that I had already fallen in love with Steven even before our first official date; we had spent enough time getting to know each other at the bars that I knew he was "the one." Unfortunately, for me, that wasn't the case.

Sometime in mid-July Patrick McCarter visited me at my new Montrose digs in Westmoreland Square; an oasis of an apartment complex complete with a kidney-shaped swimming pool just outside my front door, palm trees galore for shade (and ambiance), and of course, pink flamingos. He always loved visiting my apartment for the "scenery" (pronounced "hot available men"). The complex was very well-known as a mecca of the "see-and-need-to-be-seen" crowd of the younger gay community. Many years later, I realized how incredibly racist and sexist the management was. The entire apartment tenant population were handsome, WHITE men; there were no Blacks, no Hispanics, and no Asians; there was the one token Jewish guy, though. And, of course, there were no lesbians; there were no women at all.

[Sidebar: I never did understand why so many gay men seemed to hate the lesbian community. After all, we're all on the same sinking ship of inequality. We should be building each other up, and not purposefully tearing each other down. Why can't we all just get along?]

I lived in a corner apartment on the ground level; I lovingly called my apartment "the fishbowl" because the pool's waves refracted in my extra-large paned glass windows. It was Apartment #123, which garnered me the nickname of "123 TED," because of the supposed revolving door of dates I had. And although I never thought my dating habits were anything out of the ordinary—especially since I currently had a boyfriend—apparently my "lewd and lascivious" life was great fodder for poolside gossip, even though the gossip wasn't always about me. Imagine my surprise when a neighbor asked for Patrick's autograph on his centerfold in *Drummer* Magazine while handing me the magazine with Patrick's pages already stuck together ... just like the men's underwear section of those JC Penney catalogs when I was a teenager. There was no hesitation in my response, "NO, absolutely NOT!"

On this particular day, Patrick and I skimmed through the most recent *TWT* magazine when I noticed there was a recent uptick in the obituaries. We lamented about how sad it was that so many people were dying, and that it seemed as if no one outside of the gay community cared.

There was a specialty facility called the Montrose Clinic that provided free, anonymous HIV testing, and it was so anonymous that you were assigned a random number when you arrived. We walked into the clinic together, knowing that we needed to be ready for any outcome, but, in those days, it took up to two weeks to get test results, and all that time waiting and worrying certainly didn't help my mental health. In addition, the ONLY service the clinic provided at this time was HIV testing. There was no counseling.

Two weeks later, Patrick called and said the clinic needed to take another blood sample because they needed "to make sure" the test was correct. Not only had I *not* told Patrick about Steven's diagnosis, but I also never told him that I received the same phone call from the clinic. (We also saw our preliminary results published in the Montrose Voice, a local gay newspaper; I never told Patrick my "anonymous" number, either, since our assigned numbers were not sequential.)

I wanted to be a great friend to Patrick, and I didn't think that telling him about my phone call would have helped to comfort him. Of course, Patrick's final result was that he had tested positive for the HIV virus, and so had I, but I never told him. I didn't tell anyone (not even my best friend, Jocelyn Rae); I still don't know if that was the right decision.

My *"eleventh second of fame"* came in late July 1987, sitting alone in Westmoreland Square in Apartment 123 staring at the ripples of the water waving across the pool with the palm tree fronds fluttering in the wind; I was on the phone with a nurse's aide from the Montrose Clinic. She verified my anonymous number, 026415 (that series of numbers etched into my brain); the tears were already streaming down my cheeks when she told me the news that I already knew, "You are HIV-positive, so please schedule an appointment with a physician at your earliest convenience." And that was it, no counseling, no "How could I help," just NOTHING. I was on my own. I called Montrose Clinic for a referral, and the soonest appointment available was more than two months later. (In retrospect, I now realize that the reason there were no appointments available is because so many people were testing positive. That sad confirmation would play out like a movie over the following few years, as so many of my friends and acquaintances died.)

At the time, I knew very little about this virus; but I knew that this was the same illness that killed my first boyfriend, Dennis. I want to make it perfectly clear that in no way am I blaming Dennis, nor anyone else, for contracting this virus; this was new to ALL of us; we now call it HIV/AIDS.

The irony is that, although all of our positive test results were being sent to the CDC (Centers for Disease Control), the United States government was doing absolutely nothing to combat this virus. To quote a homophobe from the 1980s, "It's killing all the right people." Yes, someone actually said this, but I refuse to state this person's name; it doesn't deserve recognition. This person only said the silent parts out loud!

As a matter of fact, then-president Ronald Reagan, did not even mention the word *AIDS* until September 1985. By that time, the AIDS crisis was already more than four years old, and the federal government still (seemed to) refuse to acknowledge its existence. From the mouth of the American president whose own son was gay, you would have thought the response would have been quicker ... but NO!

To further clarify, Patrick and I got tested in July of 1987. By that time the "crisis" was more than six years old. And still, Houston, the fourth largest city in the country, did not have adequate health care for HIV/AIDS patients. SIX YEARS!

[Sidebar: In 2020, a pandemic called COVID-19 decimated the United States, killing more than 400,000 people in less than one year. Our federal government—albeit too late—created a task force called "Warp Speed" to develop a vaccine for this virus. Coincidentally, on that task force was Dr. Anthony Fauci; the same doctor who led the fight to find a cure for HIV/AIDS. Within nine months, a vaccine was created by two different American companies and began to be administered in late December 2020. This just further demonstrates that had those same efforts and monies been spent toward the 1980s AIDS crisis, perhaps the outcome would have been different.]

Once I got off the phone with the Montrose Clinic, I grabbed some Jack Daniels from the kitchen cabinet and drank a few shots straight from the bottle; luckily, I still had a few keys of coke left from the night before. Within a few hours, I was just drunk and high enough that the shock of what had just happened was now a B-movie reel appearing in an alternate universe; I called Steven and told him the news. I made certain he knew that I didn't know how I had acquired the virus; so, I had to tell my new boyfriend intimate details about my past, including my past IV drug use. He hugged me so tightly that I almost couldn't catch my breath, but he instinctively knew that's exactly what I needed. He was right!

I never went to my scheduled appointment at Montrose Clinic, nor did I ever see a doctor for my newly diagnosed death-sentence; going to a doctor's appointment most certainly wasn't going to keep me from dying. Many of my friends and neighbors who saw these doctors were dying anyway, so, to me, there was really no point; the outcome would be the same. I would soon die just like Dennis Thetford, and the rest of them ... painfully, horribly, and alone.

Steven and I forged ahead with our relationship; our secret deeply held between only the two of us. As the months flew by in our relationship, we fell more deeply in love, and our mutual HIV status seemed to bring us even closer together; it kinda became something we bonded over; it was the one thing we shared that we felt we could speak about only with each other.

Sometime the following year, a receptionist at *This Week in Texas*, Dan Wibel, called me and asked if I had any additional copies of my *TWT* magazine cover; unfortunately, I did not. He said that my cover must have been *TWT*'s "Cover of the Year" for 1987 (Volume 13). Indeed, there was no such thing as "cover of the year," but he informed me that my edition of the magazine was the only one which the company had absolutely no record of, since all of the copies, both in all the bars across Texas, and in their archives were gone. Thanks to JD Doyle and his website, *houstonlgbthistory.org*, for downloading my personal copy so that at least there would be a digital version available.

Though *TWT*'s "Cover of the Year" never existed, I convinced myself that it did, because I HAD to; it made me feel important and wanted, furthering my delusions of grandeur. I never told my "cover of the year" story to Patrick either; our friendship was much more important than my own vanity.

Lazy J advertisement – (courtesy This Week in Texas magazine)–1987

CHAPTER 12

TALLULAH TWILIGHT

(That Time I Was a Pearl of the Sea-man)

Along with the fame that came with the *TWT* magazine cover was the unsavory aspect of stripping and being asked repeatedly to enter the porn industry. The money was tempting, but I was in love with Steven, and I would never have done anything to damage or destroy our relationship. I was pursued by a variety of male erotic pornographers, and offered thousands of dollars, but nothing—especially money—was ever worth losing the love of my life. Not delving into the porn industry also assured that I would never have a neighbor ask me to autograph sticky-paged magazines ever again. In addition, entering the porn industry meant my HIV-positive status would be publicized; even with all the safeguards of anonymity, many of the 1980s porn actors were outed as HIV-positive; and I was unwilling to be exposed to criticism and risk the almost certain fate of losing my executive retail career.

[Sidebar: On a much sadder note, every single one of my friends who opted to get into pornography (both print and film) are now dead. In my head I thought, *Yeah! I dodged a bullet*! But my heart was filled with sorrow that so many of my friends were lured into this world of "instant success" without proper health standards to ensure their protection from contracting the HIV virus. To the contrary, many pornographic studios secretly paid their male models premiums if they agreed to do bareback scenes (without a condom); that is, until the federal government stepped in and established safety guidelines and began making the studios responsible for the well-being of their models.]

Since my stage name was Colt Michael and one of my dearest friends was Coulter Thomas, many people assumed that I had derived my name from COLT Studios, a nationwide porn distributor. For the past several years, hundreds of acquaintances scoured the internet searching for my sexual escapades on a myriad of websites. I'd never confirmed that I did porn, but I never denied it either; they just believed their fantasies, further precipitating my delusions of grandeur. But the joke was always on them; I always knew that those porn movies never existed, but I needed for people to believe that they did.

Simultaneously, the gay community was in a state of chaos; so many people were dying, and it seemed as though no one was doing anything to make the situation better. It felt as though the whole world was against us. Very quickly, it became apparent that we, the gay community, were going to have to help ourselves.

In 1976, Mr. Tag Kowis (aka "Flash Storm") and a few of his friends began hosting The Garden Party in his back yard, an event principled on the reasoning that it would be a day when it didn't matter what your outfit consisted of, whether you were "real" or just "convinced," as long as it pertained to DRAG (dressed to resemble a girl), and you had a great time in doing so. The Garden Party established itself as an extremely "campy" affair, billing the event as a "whore-to-culture extravaganza." The small *soirée* soon became an annual event that grew so quickly that larger venues were needed to accommodate the crowds. While the first few years were just about having tons of fun in dresses, by 1984 it had become clear to the hosts of The Garden Party that they wanted to do more for the Houston gay community which was being decimated by this horrendous disease and began donating proceeds from the event to local HIV/AIDS organizations; in excess of $125,000 over the next several years. Meanwhile, over fifty or so friends and acquaintances had withered away and died from complications of this dreadful disease.

Unless you lived through it, there was absolutely no way to describe those feelings of desperation, loneliness, and helplessness as I watched my friends die. In the course of one year, the population at Westmoreland Square had become nearly half vacant, with the leasing manager struggling to fill the empty apartments. The once happy and gay complex and the 123 TED apartment had become a place where no one wanted to visit, much less, live.

Being on the cover of *TWT* magazine did, however, come with its own perks; by the following week, I was suddenly welcomed with open arms at all of those Pacific Street clubs who shunned me after my recent New Year's Eve debacle. More importantly though, it garnered me an invitation to The Garden Party events, which at the time was by invitation only.

[Flashback: Miss Charlene Barberra was absolutely right when she said on that infamous night that I didn't come out, that, one day, I would find myself on the *C'est La Guerre* stage wearing a dress. It was autumn of 1980, and the movie *Fame* was a huge box-office hit. But it wasn't the storyline of the movie that got my attention; it was the music and dancing. That morning I had gone to a discount store and purchased a very short black satin dress and matching low-heeled pumps; the entire outfit cost less than $20, so you can almost imagine the horrendousness of my drag look. I had a dear friend of mine decorate my face with make-up and he let me borrow a Lucille Ball-red curlicue wig.

And Tallulah Twilight was born. Yes, that was my drag name, and Tallulah was fabulous; just ask me (her)! That night Miss Charlene Barberra introduced me to the stage, "And coming out of chute number two, our newest virgin child, Miss Tallulah Twilight." The song "Red Light" by Linda Clifford from the movie soundtrack of *Fame* started playing and I danced my way onto the stage; turns out that dancing to this song made for great practice, since it's the same song to which I would dance the night that I became the first Mr. ROU just two years later. It took a while for the audience to realize that Tallulah Twilight actually was ME, and many were shocked, though not surprised. I sashayed my way across the stage and collected dollar tips along the way; until that night, I didn't realize exactly how long six minutes and eight seconds was, especially in heels. The song ended with both my ankles still intact, though a bit worse for wear; I received a standing ovation, and I made more money in tips than all of the other "girls" combined. At the end of the evening, I distinctly remember one of the performers, Tamyra Colbert, telling me that I was much too attractive as a man to be hiding my beauty with a dress. But for me, it was not at all about wearing a dress; it was all about being on a stage, any stage. And I never wore another dress again ... until The Garden Party years.]

This fundraiser was much too important an event to be concerned about being perceived as a "drag queen," and I definitely did not do the drag community any favors by showing up in a dress. I was not gorgeous as a woman, but it didn't matter; we were raising money to help save our own lives! I am forever thankful to the drag community for always stepping up and stepping out anytime they were asked for assistance in the continuing fundraising efforts to support our brothers and sisters still afflicted with HIV/AIDS. I've always admired the talents of female illusionists, but I certainly never considered myself to be a drag entertainer. My hideous ensembles during The Garden Party years proved that; though I am so happy that I was able to contribute to the needs of our community in such a special way!

My roommate Dennis and I (and Rusty, too) always made it a point to attend this annual grand gala. Rusty hated drag, but he acquiesced, realizing the importance of the event. Sure, everything about the experience was over the top, and over the top was where I always felt most comfortable.

Shortly after one of these Garden Party extravaganzas, Dennis became very ill; neither of us knew exactly what was wrong with him (at least that's what we pretended), but by the look in his eyes, I could tell that this was something serious. After very little discussion and absolutely no debate, Dennis decided to move back to his hometown in Michigan. As much as I didn't want to admit it, I knew that this would be the last time we would see each other. And so did he. A huge hug, some lingering "love you, friends," and that infectious smile is what I choose to remember (... only the good times ...).

[Update: Dennis died in his hometown on July 30, 1991. Rusty made "the big move" to New York City and lived with me for a few months beforehand; we most certainly kept in touch. Great friendships are hard to come by, and we should never let distance diminish that connection. Rusty has been happily (legally) married to Glenn for several years now, and I have always wished them all the happiness in the world.]

In addition to the fundraising efforts of The Garden Party, many local bars organized other events to raise monies to support the fight against HIV/AIDS. Back when I was dating Patrick McCarter, he introduced me to a few members of a group, "The Happy Hour Daddies," sponsored by a gay bar, The Galleon. Patrick was already a member, and I was happy to join in the camaraderie and assist in their fundraising efforts. Each Sunday, The Happy Hour Daddies hosted different events to raise money to help those who were suffering in our community; on many occasions, Colt Michael was invited to appear and help the cause. Of course, I happily obliged; and on those nights, ALL of the tips made by ALL of the entertainers were donated to HIV/AIDS organizations. Over the course of the next few years, my tips alone totaled several thousand dollars. I was so happy to have been able to contribute to help my friends; little did I know, that soon, I would be the one needing their assistance.

As part of The Happy Hour Daddies entourage, I was extremely honored when The Galleon asked me to be a part of their "Under the Seamen" float in Houston's June 1988 Gay Pride celebration and parade. The float was set as an underwater adventure complete with bedazzled shells, glittery pink and turquoise foil fringe, subterranean palm trees and mermaids ... err, I meant Mer-MEN. As the float rolled through the streets of Houston's Montrose area, the crowds cheered and applauded as The Galleon's presentation won Best of Show for its creative concept and colorful display. I sat at the rear of the parade float completely naked, wearing only the neon rainbow-colored flippers that designer Paul Peacock specifically made for me. Not visible to the crowd until the float had already passed, I was the *piece de resistance* that garnered the most attention for my extremely provocative costume. I was partially hidden from the rest of the float with a huge, sparkled seashell that opened just wide enough to see me straddling a starfish waving my "flipper" to the throngs of parade-goers. I had forgotten just how hot Houston summers could be, and with my legs compressed together in sequined Spandex, my glistening skin from the sweat made it look as though I was ready for the beach; and I was. I also didn't factor that I would be doing abdominal crunches for two solid hours; and I had just worked out my abs that morning at the gym. By the end of the parade, I was spent and ready to not be a mer-man anymore, ever; the accolades and applause I received was worth the temporary pain of exhaustion.

It was during one of The Happy Hour Daddies' fundraising events that I met a guy who told me he had seen me on The Galleon's float and that he was a photographer, handing me a business card that read *Rob Weatherly–Let My Pictures Tell Your Story*. He was a skinny little guy, probably in his late forties, with a balding head revealing only a few wisps of ginger hair, wearing wire-rimmed glasses with attached flip-down sunglasses, and his spindly alabaster legs showing from beneath his seersucker shorts revealed that he spent very little time outside. He seemed nice enough, for sure, but after he handed me his card, he disappeared into the crowd.

It was as few months later, and I had completely forgotten about this chance meeting; I always had guys putting their business cards and phone numbers into my G-string, which I never called. As I rifled through my closet to prepare for my family's Thanksgiving visit, Mr. Weatherly's card fell onto the floor; it had been over a year since my *TWT* cover, and I figured it was time for some new head shots, so I called him. Soon after, I drove to his home, and he ushered me upstairs to this large white room with staged lighting and large professional-looking camera on a tripod.

He produced a bottle of Jack Daniels and handed me a baggie of cocaine; it was obvious that he'd done his research. I did a few lines of coke as he fixed my cocktail; I drank a few sips as we discussed the upcoming photo shoot: what I wanted to wear (or not wear), proper lighting, and other mundane photography jargon that I didn't understand, so I just agreed. The photo shoot lasted about two hours, which gave me plenty of time for another few cocktails and more cocaine; he had that perverted look in eyes which I often saw in some of the patrons when I was stripping.

I know that he thought he could get me just drunk enough and just high enough to get me naked. I knew that getting naked for him was not going to happen. It's not that I was averse to taking nude photos; I had modeled nude before, and I was actually proud of my body and confident in the fact that I looked good enough (or at least decent) naked. It was Mr. Weatherly with whom I was quickly becoming uncomfortable; I just didn't trust him. The longer I allowed the photo shoot to continue, the more I felt that he was undressing me with his eyes to the point that I could almost swear he was salivating.

Once the photo shoot was over, I thanked him, got dressed quickly, and left; I was drunk and high, but I had to get out of there. He said he would call me back in a few of weeks when the proofs were ready, I paid him $100, and he told me that I could pay him the remaining $100 when he brought me the finished pictures.

Sometime around mid-December, Mr. Weatherly telephoned me to let me know that my photos were ready. We scheduled to meet on the following weekend at the food court in Sharpstown Mall; I really didn't want him to know where I worked, but I certainly didn't want to go back to his place and most definitely didn't want him knowing where I lived. All I wanted were the photos and to give him the $100 that I owed to him.

The photos were absolutely amazing; I guess my drunken and high "seductiveness" had found its way through the lens of his camera. As someone who rarely likes taking pictures and especially hates posing for them, I must admit that these photos were incredible, and I looked HOT! I reached into my pocket to pay Mr. Weatherly, who was now sipping a lemonade from the corn dog stand; he said that the photos were free of charge. I tried to refuse his "donation," but he insisted, then asked for a favor; he told me that he had a contact in Odessa, Texas who needed help in opening a new gay bar. I reminded him that I had a full-time job, but he assured me that we could plan my trip, being paid for by the new bar owner, so as not to interfere with my work schedule. Being it was the height of the Christmas shopping season, I asked Mr. Weatherly if there was any way that we could postpone the trip until February of the following year, so that I wouldn't have to ask for time off work during the holidays nor during preparation for our annual inventory.

He called me a few days later and told me that the new bar in Odessa wasn't going to be open until mid-February, so the timing was perfect. I would earn $800 to assist the new bar owner with the lighting and sound system installation, which I knew nothing about; but he wanted my opinion on how the bar should be set up, since I was going to be the premier dancer once the bar opened. He wanted to be certain that everything measured up to the standards I expected. I was looking forward to this new experience, but was even more excited that I would soon have a regular dancing gig which was not in Houston, and the new bar would fund my travel expenses in addition to my performance fee; I had finally become the celebrity I always knew I was. I found it difficult to escape my own delusions of grandeur.

By the end of 1988, my boyfriend of almost two years, Steven Meert, was now working at a different bar, Cousin's, in Montrose's Pacific Street area. I really liked this new bar, because it reminded me so much of The Lazy J; it was always a warm and welcoming environment, just like Frank's in Lafayette. One of my favorite things about Cousin's was the weekly Friday and Saturday night drag shows. Any time out-of-town friends visited, I always brought them to Cousin's for the "good/bad" drag show. They would always ask me what that meant; I assured them they would know once I introduced them to the "premium" performers. The entertainers for the weekly drag shows were normally D-list "celebrities" or newcomers to the drag scene; so the drag shows were usually either really, really good or really, really bad. If it was a good show, you would be impressed with the talent; if it was a bad show, you'd spend most the night laughing at the lack of talent; either way, you'd be entertained. Occasionally, Steven hired me to dance there so I could make some extra money; it was a welcomed (and necessary) diversion from the monotony of the drag show, and I was happy that none of my co-workers ever went there. I was always excited to dance at Cousin's, since it allowed me to spend a little more time with Steven, and the money I made on those nights had often already been spent on cocaine to keep me up through the night and full of energy for work the following day. To my knowledge, Steven still didn't know about the depths of my alcoholism and drug addiction. He soon found out. Remaining in an alcohol and drug-induced fog allowed me to negate that my "celebrity" now was also on the D-list.

New Year's Eve 1988 was on a Saturday, and Steven would be busy working at Cousin's; I booked a show at The Lazy J for that night with the understanding that it would not be advertised, at the risk of my boss at Foley's discovering that I had reneged on our agreement. Steven and I had discussed spending the night with each other (we didn't live together), and we decided that I would stay with him at his apartment to celebrate the new year, even though it would be after 2:00 a.m. on New Year's Day before each of us got off work.

As expected, The Lazy J was packed to celebrate the new year; the drag show started an hour later than usual; we call it "drag time." I arrived at about 9:00 p.m., as usual, an hour before the scheduled show time. While the bartender fixed my first Jack and Coke of the evening, I snuck off to the bathroom for a key of cocaine. I meandered randomly throughout the bar chatting with friends, acquaintances, and a few fans; Naomi Sims had taught me to always sort out people into those categories, and to remember the difference between them.

It was about 11:45 p.m., and I had only a few minutes until midnight; I was on my fifth drink, and had snorted most all of the cocaine I had with me. The drag show was now in full swing; I went backstage, and with all of the commotion, no one noticed me doing another key of cocaine. Then, I heard the emcee begin the countdown to the new year, "... three, two, one ... Happy New Year 1989, and welcome to the stage Mr. Colt Michael." Yes, I was the surprise entertainment for the evening. The song "Wishing Well" by Terence Trent D'Arby (a Michael Jackson wannabe) began, then morphed into the real Michael Jackson singing "The Way You Make Me Feel." And that's all that I can remember from the rest of that night.

The stories of what people told me I had done were tragically disgusting. According to scuttlebutt around the bar, I stripped completely naked and allowed patrons to grope me, and even more, for higher tips. Ringing in 1989 was a complete blur; that night I was a drunk, an addict, and a complete whore. But my night would get whole lot worse.

The next thing that I remember is that I was seated all alone in a darkened booth in the "party and play" area of a local adult bookstore. I didn't know how I got there, nor how long I had been there, nor what I had done. I slowly opened the door of my tiny 3'x4' room; thankfully, I knew one of the employees and asked for help. He told me that it was now almost 7:00 a.m. on New Year's Day and that I had been there for several hours. He knew I was drunk and high after seeing my car parked sideways in the parking lot. He saw me stumbling through the dim hallways of the bookstore, nearly naked and carrying my clothes in my hands; and escorted me to a private booth for my own safety. For my own sanity, I had to believe that he was telling me the truth, and that I had not had any dalliances with any of the other New Year's Eve castaways. If I had done anything sexual with anyone at that bookstore, my relationship with Steven would most definitely be over. Maybe it already was.

I drove home and immediately took a shower to wash away the skank, and the guilt, of whatever did or did not happen the previous night. Steven had left several messages on my answering machine; the first few were out of concern for my safety, but I could hear the anger in his voice in the rest of them. I'd just screwed up the relationship that meant the most to me in my life. I was still in love with him, and I couldn't bear losing him after the conversation we were about to have. I knew that I couldn't blame him if he didn't believe me; our entire relationship that was built on honesty was about to crumble, but I knew that lying about it would make it worse.

I downed a few shots of Jack Daniels and licked some cocaine dust from an empty baggie before I called Steven. I apologized profusely for my behavior on New Year's Eve and told him EVERYTHING ... as least the parts I remembered, the way I remembered them. I confessed to him that I had blacked out after partying too hard, conveniently omitting the cocaine. Steven said he'd waited all night for me because he was so excited about ringing in the new year, albeit a few hours late. He was furious that I completely ruined his evening because of my selfishness. I cried into the phone and begged for his forgiveness as I swore that nothing happened at the bookstore. My *"twelfth second of fame"* came when Steven abruptly stopped me and said, "You know, there's a saying that whatever you do on New Year's Day is how you will spend the rest of the year. I refuse to live the rest of this year with a slut. Good-bye!" and he hung up.

I had spent the past eighteen months building and cherishing a healthy relationship with the man that I truly loved unconditionally, and I thought he felt the same way. But I stretched the meaning of "unconditionally" a bit too far this time, and what I expected from him in this moment is more than he could give.

I had no one to blame but myself. I had just lost the love of my life for good; there was no reconciling this time. I was devastated. I reached for more Jack Daniels which was now sitting on the kitchen counter. DAMN, I was out of cocaine; I was ready to die.

Houston Pride – The Galleon float, winner Best Commercial Float (courtesy www.houstonlgbthistory.com)–1988

Tallulah Twilight at The Garden Party–1989

CHAPTER 13

MR. MAGOO

(That Time I Was a Prostitute)

Steven and I didn't speak for at least two weeks, so I was shocked when he called me on some random Sunday morning to invite me to dinner. We chatted for a little while, then I asked him why he changed his mind. I was terrified of the answer. The phone went quiet, and the seconds of silence felt like a year. He finally explained, "Well, that guy that you knew from the bookstore was at Cousin's the other night, and he told me about running into you on New Year's Eve. He told me how messed up you were and that you could barely walk, so he put you in a room so you could sleep it off. He said you could barely function, so there was no way that you could have had sex with anyone, and that he was monitoring you on the cameras to be sure that you were okay." I immediately started crying and thanked him for being so understanding.

He was adamant that this was just a dinner date, and that we would see where the relationship was headed from there; we would take it slow and get to know each other all over again. After the disaster I made of our relationship, I was willing to follow ANY rules that he deemed necessary. I had to prove to him that I was not the person who had destroyed his New Year's Day (even though I was), and that I deserved a second chance.

Steven and I went out to my favorite restaurant, Baba Yega, for our "get-reacquainted" meal; we arrived separately, since neither of us knew the outcome of the evening. He greeted me at the entrance, and, as if no time had passed since we had last seen each other, he hugged me tightly and surprised me with a warm, gentle kiss. I was immediately comforted by Steven's compassion, considering that the last time we spoke, he called me a slut. I guess it's true that even beauty can be marred by ugliness, but his true kindness in this situation proved to me that every sinner could be redeemed. I hoped that tonight would be the beginning, the reawakening, of the relationship I thought for certain was lost. I had tried not to hurt him, but I knew that I had; his forgiveness in this moment meant more to me than words could express. As difficult as it must have been for him, Steven demonstrated to me the true meaning of unconditional love; I didn't know that I deserved such benevolence.

Once we were seated, our waiter, Jack, stopped by our table to get our drink orders; Steven was already rubbing my inner thighs under the table; I pretended to be oblivious, but reacted by coyly shifting my head downward, then lifting my eyebrows just high enough so that he could see me winking at him. When the waiter recognized me, he immediately asked, "Mr. Ted, your usual Jack and Coke?" He always remembered my drink, and while I'd like to believe it's because it was the same as his first name, I knew that it was more so because I drank so much of it. He then looked over at Steven, and realizing that they had never met, I said, "Jack, this is my boyfriend, Steven." They exchanged congenial pleasantries, and as soon as Jack turned away from the table, Steven looked at me with a rather heavenly/devilish grin. Had I overstepped my boundaries by introducing him as my boyfriend? Had I misread the signals he had been giving me under the table? He removed his hand from between my legs, then leaned across the table to give me another kiss. I was stunned; who was this new Steven Meert sitting across from me? The old Steven Meert would seldom hold hands with me in public and now he was kissing me in the middle of a crowded restaurant. I didn't know who this new Steven Meert was, but I REALLY liked him.

Steven then grabbed both of my hands into his, and said, "You know, Ted, we went out for over a year before this whole situation happened, and you never told anyone that I was your boyfriend!" He could tell by my facial expression that I was shocked, but he was right. Though we had been in a monogamous relationship for nearly two years, we never put a label on it. I knew he was with me, and he knew I was with him, and the gay community knew that we were a couple; I thought the label was unnecessary.

He then continued, "It's nice to hear you actually say it." Until that moment, I had no idea how much my boyfriend truly needed to hear that he was my boyfriend, and that I was proud to call him my boyfriend.

Then it dawned on me that while I had been seeking validation from my family, my friends, the gay community, and basically anybody else, I was completely blind to the fact that my own boyfriend needed validation from me. I sheepishly lowered my head, realizing that what had hurt him the most was that he never felt validated by the one person he loved the most. I wanted to cry, but couldn't; I had victimized him enough, and I didn't dare make this about me.

As we were finishing our meal, Jack and several of the other service staff promenaded to our table with a miniature cake, singing "Happy Birthday." Steven was flushed red with embarrassment; his birthday wasn't for another four months. He looked at me with that same look of confusion as the night that I had met my birthday twin, Kevin Nunez. Steven's look was priceless when I sang, *Happy Birthday,* **My Boyfriend,** *Happy Birthday to you!* It was then that I was moved to tears, seeing the sheer joy on his face and the happiness in his smile; it was the first time he told me "I love you." On that night, in the middle of my favorite restaurant, surrounded by complete strangers, Steven and I held each other in an embrace that neither one of us wanted to end; we had each gotten the validation that we needed.

We shared the cake and went directly to his house for the dessert we had both been missing since my tragic New Year's escapade. I didn't need another Jack and Coke or cocaine; I only needed Steven to give me that high. I was ready for the rebirth of the love I thought was lost; Steven went searching for my heart and found it where I dared not look. *Why was I so afraid to believe that he was truly in love with me? Why did I, so consistently, sabotage healthy relationships with alcohol and drugs? How could I learn to make love overcome addiction?* I vowed to change; Steven deserved to be in love with the person he knew as Ted A Richard, and not the disastrous mess that had become Colt Michael.

Steven and I awoke the following morning to a rainbow of emotions, excited that we had each received the validation that we didn't know had been missing from our relationship. We vowed that we would never again take each other for granted and relished our recommitted "boyfriend" status. He told me that he wanted to plan our Valentine's Day together; I happily agreed. I would finally get to redeem myself from the disastrous New Year's Day only six weeks ago. *Maybe!*

The photographer, Rob Weatherly, called me during the first week of February 1989 to say he spoke with the owner of the soon-to-be-open gay bar, Kaleidoscope/S.R.O., in Odessa, Texas. We coordinated my itinerary so that my flight departed on Friday afternoon, returning on Sunday morning; this timing was perfect, since it was my weekend off from Foley's and I would be back in time to spend Valentine's Day with Steven.

I was excited to be traveling to a brand-new city and looked forward to creating new memories and expanding my Colt Michael fan base (assuming there already was one). I also felt honored to be singled out to be the featured dancer for its grand opening night; I soon learned that I would be the ONLY dancer that night.

The tiny, twin-engine prop plane landed at an airport surrounded by prairieland as far as the eye could see, and I swear there was an oil rig visible in the distance. I disembarked and made my way to the baggage claim where I saw a uniformed man with a sign that read "Colt Michael." *Holy shit, Sherlock,* I told myself, *I AM famous*! I wasn't even impressed that the owner had sent a limousine to pick me up, more so, that they used my stage name on the calling card at the airport. The limo driver gathered my bags and escorted me to the black luxuriousness that would be my ride for the next hour or so; I saw passers-by taking photos (assuming that I was famous), so I stopped for a few seconds and waved for the cameras. In Houston, I was a celebrity, but in Odessa, I was a STAR!

The driver, Devon, opened the back door for me so I could get comfortable while he loaded my bags into the trunk. I sprawled across the spacious seat, happy to be free from the constraints of seat belts and tray tables and rowdy children. Devon got into the driver's seat and pressed a button that lowered the darkened privacy window separating him from the back seat. He told me it would take about forty-five minutes or so to get to the hotel and handed me a "welcoming gift" from across the seat; the card read, *Welcome to Odessa. Mason Dixon.* I didn't know whether to be impressed or insulted when I opened the gift and saw a bottle of Jack Daniels, a six-pack of Coca-Cola, and a baggie of cocaine. Oh, who am I kidding ... I was always happy when my clients did their research, and did my best to conceal my excitement when I noticed the baggie-in-a-bag. He pressed the button again, and the tinted window rolled back up; over the car intercom he said, "There's ice and glasses in the sideboard." I thanked him and reached in my front pocket; I needed a key, and quick!

The limousine pulled into a regional five-star hotel; perhaps I shouldn't have been surprised that one of the largest oil-boom cities in the country would have at least one upscale hotel, and I was staying at the finest of them. Devon escorted me into the hotel, checked in for me, and brought my luggage up to the room for me.

As previously scheduled, at 10:00 p.m. sharp, Devon knocked on my hotel room door; he was there to chauffeur me to Kaleidoscope/S.R.O. As the limousine pulled up in front of the club, I saw a small crowd waiting in line to get into the club. Devon parked directly in front of the main entrance, then walked around the limo to open my door; I most definitely had never been treated like such a celebrity in my life.

I stepped out of the vehicle, having pocketed my "special" baggie and carrying my cocktail. A very large gentleman whom I had never seen before walked up to greet me; "Mason Dixon," he introduced himself, "Colt Michael, it's so nice to finally meet you. Everyone's waiting, let's go inside." Mr. Dixon and I were ushered into the entrance, bypassing the onlookers and my "adoring fans;" at least that's what I needed to believe for my fantasy to be real.

Mason was a Mr. Magoo-looking kind of fella, chunky, but not fat, with a fatter than normal nose. Probably in his 50s, it was easy to surmise that he was probably very attractive when he was younger, but the years had not been kind to him. His bulbous nose, a tell-tale sign of his alcoholism, was a trait I saw in many of my own relatives. I was more intimidated, though, by his height; he must have been at least six feet, six inches tall, and his fancy Stetson cowboy hat made him look even taller.

I found the atmosphere of the bar to be a bit confusing; I mean, I knew it was a gay bar even without the customary rainbow signs everywhere. It was Mason Dixon, rather, that seemed oddly out of place. The photographer, Rob Weatherly, said that I was going to be meeting with the owner of the bar, but I immediately recognized that Mason Dixon (the patrons referred to him as "Buddy") could not be the owner. During our brief conversations, I noticed that he knew very little about the bar business (not that I knew much more), and the staff often treated him as a "regular" customer who spent lots of money, rather than someone from whom they took orders. Regardless, I was treated like royalty, the "cock of the walk" some might say, as Buddy paraded me around to meet his friends and acquaintances.

The bar had even set up a VIP area where I could sign autographs; Mr. Weatherly provided the establishment with several of my recent head shots which I later learned the bar sold for $1 each. I kept none of that money, but I remember being so angry when I realized that my "celebrity" had been reduced to a one-dollar photo. I NEVER perceived myself to be that cheap, but maybe I was, and just didn't know it. Regardless, I was being paid $800 just to be there, and I got a free flight and travel accommodations, too; perhaps I shouldn't have felt slighted by an obvious "celebrity" *faux pas*. Buddy, the staff, and crowd at Kaleidoscope/S.R.O. made me feel like a star that night, and it was unforgettable.

It was a little after 1:00 a.m., and I was drunk and high but felt that I still had my wits about me. Buddy signaled that he was ready to go, so I signed a few more autographs and we headed toward the exit. I fully expected to see Devon and the limousine waiting for us outside; instead, I followed Buddy into the parking lot to a late-model Ford pickup truck that probably doubled as his work truck. I didn't question it at the time; but it didn't make sense that someone with the means to rent a limo, pay for airfare and an upscale hotel, and pay an $800 booking fee would not have used the limo service back to the hotel, especially since we were both intoxicated.

Like me, Buddy was probably a high-functioning drunkard, or maybe I didn't notice that he was struggling to drive since I was just as inebriated as he was (maybe more ... definitely more). He parked under the archway entrance of the hotel; I thanked him for an awesome evening, kissed him on the cheek, and said good night. Tomorrow was another day, and I was the headliner in the following night's show; there weren't enough twinkles in the sky to outshine the glow that I had after such an incredible night; but this night was far from over.

Back in my room, I had one last cocktail and took a quick shower before bed. Suddenly, there was a knock on the door. Thinking that it was probably room service, I quickly wrapped a towel around my waist and peered through the peep hole. It was Buddy. *But why was he here?* With the safety lock in place, I opened the door just wide enough to let him know that I needed to get dressed. I grabbed my pajamas out of my suitcase and hurriedly slipped them on before letting Buddy in.

However, *this* Buddy certainly was not the same Buddy that I just spent the past few hours with. This Buddy was stone-faced and had an agenda: ME. He initially tried to conceal his obvious contempt for me by being overly pleasant; I had no idea why he suddenly seemed to hate me so much.

He flung me down onto the bed and tried to kiss me, but I turned away. Buddy had become an unrecognizable monster; he was more than twice my size and the more I fought to get out from underneath him, the more powerful he became. He ripped my pajamas off, and I was so stunned that I didn't even notice that he now was somehow completely naked. I knew that I was about to be raped and there was no way that I could stop him. Suddenly, I screamed, "I have AIDS!"

Buddy went completely limp as he climbed off me; he slapped me across the face as if I had done something wrong. "You're a worthless whore!" he exclaimed. "At least Stallion knew what to do and I didn't even have to fight him. What the fuck did I waste this $800 for?" (Stallion, it turns out, was a different stripper whom he had previously "hired" for the same "position" I was now rejecting.)

Buddy got dressed and stormed out of the hotel; the following morning a note slipped under my door alerted me that my stay had been cut short and my gig had been cancelled; check out time was 11:00 a.m. I phoned the front desk to ask if anyone left a package for me; the answer was "no." Damn, that dumbass didn't even pay me the $800 he owed me, and I had absolutely no money; I was counting on that money for next month's rent.

I later recall thinking that this larger-than-life Texan had a name with a familiar ring to it; and why would this wealthy man feel the need to use a fake name? I was rather naïve to the Mason-Dixon terminology; growing up in the deep south, this geographical history was buried somewhere in the backs of our textbooks. Now, knowing the significance of this line of demarcation between the Northern "free" states and the Southern "slave" states, I should have recognized the absurdity of this "bar owner's" pseudonym; I had no idea the depths of the commonalities of Mr. Mason Dixon (using the term loosely) and his belief system that one person had the authority to own another person. Last night, I got just a miniscule taste of what slavery must have felt like, even if just for one night; I was literally sold into prostitution without my knowledge.

[Sidebar: I believe that sex work has its place in society, and I would never begrudge anyone who decided that sexual healing was the right career path for them; it just wasn't for me. I always considered sex to be a personal and meaningful experience with someone you loved, even if it was just for a night (or an hour). Rob Weatherly sold me to Mason Dixon (Buddy) at a price which was never disclosed to me; I'm sure that he received some sort of finder's fee. They both knew that I had a boyfriend and had concocted this plan just so that they could each get some kind of warped enjoyment from forcing me to cheat on him; something which I never would have done otherwise. And in my mind, I never did!]

I had absolutely no money with me, so I called the only person who could understand my predicament: Naomi Sims. She instantly knew exactly who Buddy was; she was empathetic that I had been through this horrendous ordeal and sent me $200 via Western Union, no questions asked. I called Naomi when I arrived back to my apartment just to let her know that I was okay and made her promise to not tell Steven about this situation. There was no way that he could know what had happened in Odessa, especially after the previous New Year's Eve incident; we were just getting our relationship back on track, and nothing could jeopardize that and potentially derail the progress we made.

Steven and I shared an incredible Valentine's Day; he treated me to a seven-course meal at an exclusive restaurant, Anthony's, and surprised me with a "birthday" cake (nine months too soon). I guess turn-about is fair play, and I loved him for it. The romantic night that Steven planned for us was exquisite and temporarily made me forget about the Odessa fiasco.

It was on the ride home that the song "Never Been to Spain" played on the radio (remember that Three Dog Night cassette tape I bought with my own money from my first job?), and I happily sang along. Steven was stunned, "Dang, Ted, I've never heard you sing before! You're kinda great!" I was shocked that he never heard me sing before, especially since I sang under my breath all the time; I realized, though, that he was right; he had never heard me actually sing an entire song.

He asked me to sing at his bar, and even though I doubted my ability, Steven didn't. "Yes, Ted, you ARE that good; I'll book you for next weekend. We'll promote it as 'Colt Michael–The Voice Behind the Clothes (You've Seen Him Naked, Now Hear Him Sing).'" I was scared shitless; but Steven was serious, and he was giving me the opportunity for Colt Michael to grow up.

The bar was packed that night and I was on edge. The emcee, Dyan Michaels, tried to calm me down with positive words of encouragement. Steven didn't come backstage, but I had other things to think about.

The show began with female impersonators. I was the star that night. Then I heard Dyan Michaels' voice over the microphone, "Introducing Colt Michael as you've never seen ... or heard before. I walked onto the stage having already begun singing from behind the curtains; I let my voice introduce me to the audience before ever being seen. And when I got my first glance into the crowd, I realized exactly why Steven never made it backstage. Congregating in the front rows of the audience, all of my friends (including Naomi Sims, out of drag) were seated at all of the front two rows of tables; Steven was seated at the head of the table center stage. I was in awe of what he was able to pull off without me ever knowing; I needed to put on the show of my life without taking my clothes off, AND I DID!

To this day, I thank Steven for encouraging me to explore some of my many other talents; he gave me yet another opportunity to showcase some of the better sides of me that no one ever saw, but he felt needed to be seen. Steven was always my savior, but he never knew just exactly what he was saving me from; my own naïveté sometimes still haunts me.

One of the differences between the life of "Naomi Sims" and the life of "Colt Michael" is that her onstage persona was that of a female illusionist, and *my* onstage persona was completely sexualized; though, while on stage, I never saw myself as a sexual being. I wanted to be Colt

Michael because I loved to dance and was a great dancer; the fact that I was mostly naked while dancing never figured into the performance for me. I was one of the only male dancers at that time who didn't use his sexuality to become a part of the performance; I could actually DANCE, and that was what was important to me. I love looking back at old pictures and seeing the smile on my face while I was on stage; I was happy, I was loved, and I was respected. *Or so I thought.*

Unfortunately, I failed to understand that many of my fans didn't differentiate between the two personas, and regardless of how I presented myself through dance, the reality is that I was always perceived as a sexual being to be gawked at ("my eyes are up here") and the fact that I also possessed a brain and a heart never factored into their perception of who I truly was; it didn't matter to them, anyway. So, as soon as my show was finished, I packed my belongings and headed for the nearest exit.

Buddy taught me the downside of being "famous," and I never wanted to revisit that scenario. My priority was Steven, and all of the money and notoriety I could have received by staying to sign autographs after a show were not as important to me as the time I spent building a relationship with the man I loved.

I firmly believe that, prior to meeting Steven, one of the reasons that I always had difficulty keeping long-term relationships is because anyone I was dating always thought that they were competing with "Colt Michael" for attention. Naomi Sims told me on many occasions about how lonely she was in her personal life. She said, "Everybody wants Naomi Sims, and nobody wants Newman Braud;" and for the very first time, I completely understood what she meant. Everybody wanted to be with the famous persona that everyone saw onstage; but no one wanted to take the time to know the real human being behind that persona. I allowed my life as a male stripper to totally diminish my belief that I deserved anything better. Whenever I was a single man, I was very popular; the randomness of the sex didn't matter; I used men for my needs, just as they used me for theirs. The difference is that they always had this preconceived notion of what it must have been like to have sex with Colt Michael; they expected a performance, and I always delivered. But having to be Colt Michael both onstage and in bed became extremely tiring; it made for a very lonely life.

THE 16TH SECOND

Which is why I was so glad that Steven Meert and I were in such a long-term committed relationship; even though he originally wanted to meet Colt Michael, he actually took the time to know Ted A Richard. This was something new for me; it was the first time in a long time when someone wanted to know more about *me*, was interested in my brain power and not just my sexuality; it showed that he was proud of me, and made me feel as though we were equals (because we were) and that I wasn't just some trophy boy to add to his trophy case.

It was mid-September, and I was at work at Foley's; I heard a voice on the intercom saying, "Mr. Richard, phone call on line one." It was Steven's roommate, Randy; he said, "Ted, I'm sorry to call you at work, but Steven is really sick. He's being admitted to the hospital, and he wanted me to call you." I hung up and immediately called my boss; she allowed me to take the rest of the day off to tend to Steven's needs, not that there was really anything I could do.

By the time I arrived at the hospital, Steven had been admitted, and was already hooked up to intravenous medication. I was horrified to see how frail he was and how scared he looked; I couldn't understand it. We'd spent the night together only two days before, but he was now immediately—almost overnight—emaciated, and I hadn't noticed how sunken his eyes had become. I saw a version of Steven in that hospital bed that I never wanted to see; a version of illness that I had already seen in far too many of my friends and neighbors who had already died from complications of AIDS. I reached down to rub his legs, and he flinched in pain; I looked down and saw those all-too-familiar black lesions associated with Kaposi Sarcoma. His skin was now so fragile that it hurt when I touched him, and he now looked more gray than white. I visited with him for over an hour until the fatigue ravaged him and he fell asleep from exhaustion (and morphine); I went home and cried myself to sleep, after a few shots of Jack Daniels. *Damn, I wish I had some cocaine!*

When I returned from work the following day, there was a message from Steven saying that he loved me. My heart was so full of joy to hear his voice, faint as it was, that I was devastated when I listened to the next message on the answering machine. It was his roommate, Randy, his voice shaking, "Ted, please call me when you get this message." I already instinctively knew why Randy was calling, and I was hesitant to call him, but I knew that I had to.

September 23, 1989 was the day that I was forced to say goodbye to my one true love of a lifetime; it felt so surreal to realize that my partner was now dead. The one man that I had been to hell and back with was no longer here to love me as only he could. This disease had killed too many people already, but no death had affected me as dramatically as Steven's did; he was the only person who knew the other side of me that no one else seemed to care about. I called Naomi Sims and she met me at my apartment; her sympathy and words of condolence meant the world to me in that moment; but nothing could repair the gash in my heart.

And then, there it was, my *"thirteenth second of fame,"* a final validation from Steven that he truly loved me by including me in his obituary. Alas, I spent my first night alone in a very long time, and he was already celebrating his dawn in the afterlife. I will always remember Steven fondly and have always felt that he was my one true love; his dying declaration of love to me by stating my name in his final written words restored my faith that true love does exist. Steven knew about the way I was treated by Dennis Thetford's family nearly six years prior, and for him to understand how much his validation meant to me, even in death, I knew that I owed it to him to be a man that he could be proud of for the rest of my life. At least, that was the plan; then my life got in the way, and self-sabotage reared its ugly head again.

Nearly a month later, I sat alone in Houston's Rothko Chapel for Steven's memorial service. Even though the service was packed, I felt the need to be solitary in my mourning. I didn't cry, I didn't speak, but I stood up to hug Steven's parents. It felt so good to have his parents hug me back; they made a potentially awkward moment into one that was so very beautiful. After everyone left the service, I stayed seated, still wanting to be alone with my memories of Steven. The room suddenly became almost painfully quiet, but a cacophony of thoughts spun around in my head. It was then that I could feel a spirit within me which calmed my thoughts, and the emptiness of the room seemed to fill with brightness, but I know it was all an illusion. I noticed a large bouquet of red roses left over from the service. I only wish that I could have been that rose he wanted; only with much fewer thorns.

Staring at the fourteen huge Rothko originals on the walls, I never fathomed how many shades of black existed in the world. I'd like to believe that Steven's aura helped me to see that, even in darkness there was always light; I know I felt his presence.

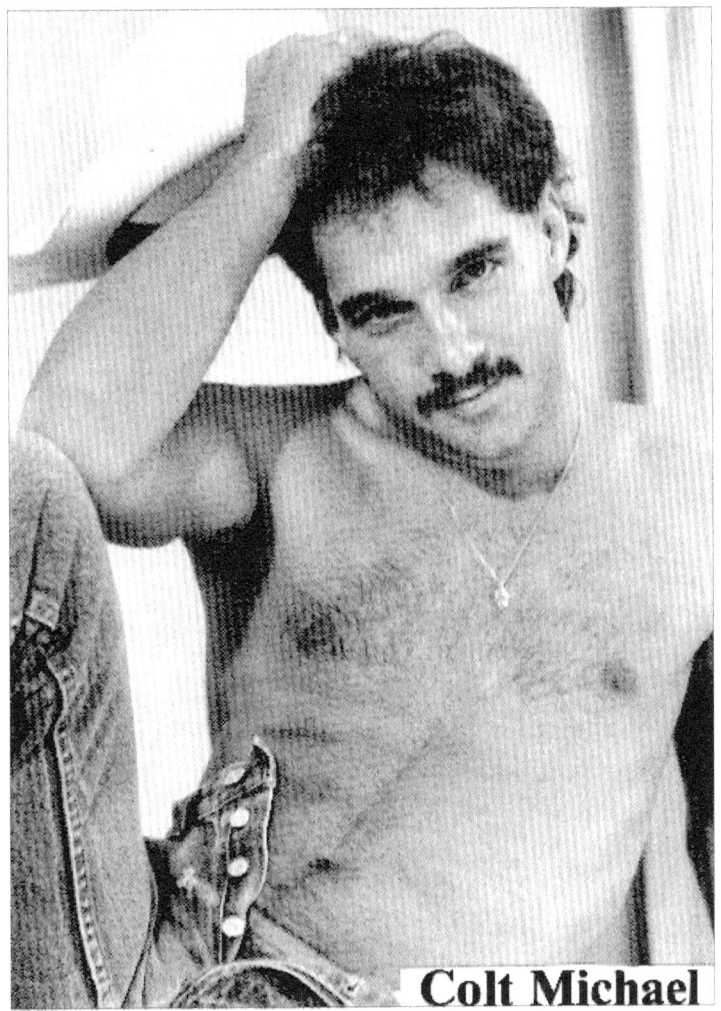

Colt Michael promo shot for Kaleidoscope/S.R.O. in Odessa, Texas–1989

CHAPTER 14

FAME ADJACENT

(That Time I Was In A Parade ... Again)

So, what do I do now? I was completely lost and clueless about how to handle this! All this death happening around me kind of made me lose my mind a little bit. I lost so many friends, my first boyfriend, Dennis, and now Steven too. I was so in love with Steven that I never noticed how pale, gaunt, and sickly he had become. I remember asking him why he didn't quit smoking. With deadpan eyes, he looked at me and declared, "Look Ted, if I quit smoking, I might have six more months to live and be miserable. I'd much rather live six months less and be happy than live six months more just to be miserable." Only two weeks after that conversation, I received that unwelcomed, but expected, message on my answering machine. I guess Steven was right; at least he died happy!

I wondered who would be next? *Would it be me?* I'd seen the way dead people look after the devastation of AIDS and I definitely didn't want people to see me looking like that! *Why was I still alive? What was the point?* To be completely honest, I did think about suicide many times. I saw so many of my friends die, and it was only a matter of time before my turn came. Suicide was something that was always far from my character as a person; and, let's face it, suicide hurts, but to say that it didn't cross my mind would be a complete lie. I could have blown my brains out, but one of my neighbors at Westmoreland Square had tried ... and missed. He spent nearly a year in rehab and was now missing the entire back side of his head; with my luck, I would have had the same fate. Then, there were always pills and other drugs; but I had seen too many people overdose, and I didn't want anyone to find me with my skin so taught it had turned purple and my body covered in my own vomit. It scares me now to think that I actually thought about all of the possible outcomes of how my suicide would affect others, but truthfully, it was only about my own vanity. To end my life would disappoint all of my adoring fans, and they deserved to see a Colt Michael who survived this disease and not someone who'd been overpowered by it. I had to make myself believe that too, especially since now my "secret" about being HIV-positive was already common knowledge in the stripper world, thanks to Rob Weatherly and Mason Dixon; who, by the way, I never saw again. I hope they both succumbed to untimely, miserable deaths, as I know that mine must not have been the only life they ruined with their ridiculous "game" of "fuck the whore."

In 1989 at the age of twenty-six, I was already a widower ... twice; and didn't know how much more pain my heart could take. So, I did what I knew I always did best; I focused all of my excess energy into my retail job, and within the following month received yet another promotion. To this day, I have no idea how executive management never suspected that I was drunk or high or both while I was at work; or maybe the cocaine and Ecstasy inadvertently helped me to do my job better. (I know that's not true, but sometimes I needed to believe things the way I wish they were so that I didn't have to face the truth.) Still, I continued to live my life the best way I knew how and learned to deal with the consequences as they came, though I often didn't recognize the consequences as such when they happened (and there were many).

The management and staff at Foley's were extremely considerate when I told them of Steven's death; they offered to give me an extra week of (unpaid) vacation, which I declined since I really needed the money. Perhaps that's why, instead of the vacation, they offered something that money couldn't buy.

From 1949 until 1994, Foley's Department Stores hosted the Annual Thanksgiving Day Parade in downtown Houston. The 40th Anniversary of the Foley's Thanksgiving Day Parade was held on November 23, 1989; the theme for that year's parade was "Celebrating Television Through the Decades." There were four major-themed floats; one from each decade: 1950s, 1960s, 1970s and 1980s. As one of the up-and-coming stars in the Foley's administration, and possibly as consolation for a broken heart, I was asked to participate in the parade.

During the time that Steven and I dated, retail became more of my passion, and Colt Michael took a back seat. Although I still enjoyed dancing and relished the celebrity that came with it, I knew that being a male stripper was not a permanent career choice. But my dedication to my retail job kept me away from my family, and I didn't get to visit them as often as I would have liked; so, each Thanksgiving, they would visit me to celebrate the holiday and my birthday.

[Sidebar: One of the oddities about being born on November 20th is that my birthday NEVER fell on Thanksgiving Day ... just some useless information which could help you to win a trivia contest someday.]

Without a doubt, my favorite treat from my family's visit was the fig cake that my mom baked for me every year since I turned eighteen years old; I still remember climbing the ladder with Shirtless Joe to pick figs from the highest branches of the tree on my parents' farm.

I was so excited to bring my family to the Thanksgiving Day parade; since I was kid, I always remember watching the Macy's parade on our black-and-white television set. I was in awe the first time I saw the parade in color, and now, I was going to be IN a parade; a surprise which I would not share with my family until the following morning.

We woke up early and headed to downtown Houston; it was unseasonably cold, and that was only the beginning as December 1989 was recorded as the coldest month on record (to date) for the city of Houston. I can certainly attest that the cold snap started in November. There were staging areas, float preparation stations, and cold beverages. But it was frickin' COLD! I needed something HOT!

Then there he was! Lawd, have mercy! JOHN STAMOS! It definitely couldn't have gotten much hotter than that! (Oh wait, I skipped a whole section there ... I was so excited!) In my head, repeating Uncle Jesse's catchphrase, "HAVE MERCY!"

So, there I was, in the staging area for the parade; everyone was freezing and hungry. I remembered seeing a little eatery close to the parade route. I was so hungry that I swear the smell of hot chili was wafting through the air; I KNEW this is where I needed to be. I ordered a large bowl of chili and a large hot chocolate. (You would think those foods didn't complement each other, but under those circumstances, they were delicious; or at least I made myself think so.) As I needed to keep an eye on what was going on in the staging area, I opted to sit on the sidewalk to enjoy my chili and chocolate.

It was then that I felt a slight tap on my shoulder; the gentleman asked where I got my food. Without really looking up, I pointed to the deli across the street. He thanked me, and then asked if he could sit with me. I said, "Of course, I ain't going anywhere;" then, as he walked away, it was difficult to not notice that hot ass in those painted-on jeans and that unmistakable mullet haircut. DEAR LAWD! HAVE MERCY! Had I just had a brief conversation with Mr. John Stamos? What the hell was this major star from the hit television show *Full House* (1987-1995) doing in freezing downtown Houston, and why would he be in the middle of a crowd asking for food? The sheer fantasticalness of it all made me certain that the chilling temperature had somehow frozen my brain into believing the fantasy that certainly didn't exist. *John Stamos? Downtown Houston? Me with chili and hot chocolate?* Even now I laugh at myself to think that I'd believe such an obscene fallacy; though, phallically speaking, I KNEW that this dream was real, it just HAD to be! I thought to myself, *there's no way that this huge star is gonna come back and eat with me sitting on a curb in the middle of downtown Houston.*

About fifteen minutes later, John Stamos returned, carrying a bowl of chili in one hand and a hot chocolate in the other; he looked just as good from the front as he did from behind. "Have mercy," I mumbled under my breath; but he must have heard me, because I noticed him trying to hide a giggle as he made his way to the sidewalk where I sat. He handed me his hot chocolate and asked me to hold it so it wouldn't spill. Of course, I did, and just as he had promised, John Stamos sat right next to me on a random side street sidewalk, and we shared a meal together. We both laughed at how disgusting those flavors of chili and chocolate were together, but we didn't care; the weather was cold, the food was hot, and we were both hungry.

[Sidebar: I'd like to believe that Steven Meert had a hand in making this impossibility possible. (With Steven, John Stamos was always my "hall pass" celebrity; you know, the person you could sleep with outside of the relationship, and not be in trouble. And Steven was okay with that because we both knew that I would NEVER meet John Stamos; and John's not gay, anyway, so it was a safe bet.) Thank you, Steven; even though my "hall pass" meeting with John was definitely platonic, you made one of my dreams come true; I was falling all over myself, still in near disbelief that I was sitting right next to John *frickin'* Stamos!]

Mr. Stamos insisted I call him "John." John and I sat on that cold Houston sidewalk as we ate chili and sipped hot chocolate and chatted. He asked me about my work at Foley's and if this was my first time being IN a parade. (I decided to not tell him about my recent mer-man experience.) I told him about growing up on a farm (omitting the part about Shirtless Joe), and that, when I was younger, we would have horse parades and go on round-ups, though I never learned how to properly ride a horse. His face lit up when he heard me talk about my childhood; he could tell that I had a happy upbringing. He then said that I reminded him of someone that he knew from his own childhood, though I don't remember him saying who that friend was.

John and I talked through the entire meal, which was probably only about fifteen or twenty minutes; we both got up from the curb, and shook hands. Then John Stamos said something to me that I will never forget; he thanked me for allowing him to eat with me. He added that it really meant a lot. I was speechless as he walked away; and we never saw each other again. To this day, I always cherish the time that, John "Have mercy!" Stamos asked to have a meal with me on a sidewalk, on Thanksgiving Day, in the freezing cold. Mr. Stamos, it meant a lot to me too! Maybe someday I will get the chance to tell you why.

At the time I had been so enamored with just meeting John that I hadn't even noticed the float he was on; he was the featured actor on the 1980s float, the same float for which I was an attendee. The float itself was an homage to everything '80s, with three gigantic golden five-point stars, at least eight feet tall, made of chicken wire, papier-mâché, and gilded fringe. Seated on each of the three stars were larger-than-life replicas of famous people from that decade; Michael Jackson, Elton John, and of course, Cher. I was all decked out in ripped jeans (thermals underneath), a black rhinestone-studded tank top, a retro jean jacket, and a platinum blonde punk-style wig. My "job" for the parade was to walk along the parade route and keep the crowds engaged and entertained as the float passed by. But once I had that brief encounter with

John Stamos, the rest of the parade, actually the rest of the day, was a complete blur. It wasn't until I saw the photos that I realized that I was also a part of what could easily have been named "The Gay Icon" float rather than just "Stars of the '80s."

The rest of 1989 was blistering cold in Houston, and once the glitterati of the parade faded, it was back to work in retail. Black Friday, the first day of the tremendously busy Christmas shopping season, was the next day, and I needed a good night's sleep. I cannot recall if I truly had a restful sleep that night, but I'm absolutely certain that I had incredible dreams, maybe even a bit moist (only because I know how much people *hate* that word!)

Meanwhile, there was a talent explosion on the Texas male stripper circuit, but I wasn't part of it. At the time, Houston had more than twenty-five gay bars, and there were strippers at nearly all of them on any given night. It didn't matter if your "scene" was disco, house music, Country and Western, trance music, or just "cruising" music; there was a stripper night just for you. "Cowboys in Action," "Fantasy in Action," "Fantasy In Motion," "Muscles in Action," "Muscles in Motion," "The Headliners," "Lone Star Male Revue," "The Men of Santa Fe," "The River Oaks Boys," "The Texas Heartbreakers," and "Urban Cowboys" were among the dance troupes entertaining gay (and questioning) men across the state of Texas. The dancers had predictable names such as "Apollo," "Hollywood," "Magnum," "Maverick," "Rip," "Rock," "Savage," "Snake" (for obvious reasons), "Stallion" (yes, that one), "Steel," "Stryker," and "Wrangler." I always thought that my stage name, Colt Michael, was original, because at least my stage name sounded like it COULD be someone's real name; it wasn't so obviously fake as all those others. I wanted my name to be memorable, and I guess it was. If someone called me "Mike," then we met "professionally," but if they called me Ted, then they knew me on more of a personal level. (When being compared to "Snake" or "Wrangler," I was often asked why I decided on "Colt." I'd tell them that I liked the name because colts were friendly, frisky young horses that could also be feisty and frivolous. Another question would usually refer to what hid under the G-string, and I'd say, "I'm not really that big, it just looks big on me because I'm little ... just like a colt.")

What a surprise when, in March 1990, my former *TWT* cover photo was featured in the *Classic TWT* section of its magazine, stating, "If you could get past this gorgeous man on the cover, Houston's Ted A Richard, you were sure to find something to satiate your appetite for entertainment and news shaping the gay community within the pages of Texas' gay gazette." Just when I thought that the hype of my "celebrity" at Foley's/Sharpstown was over, there was a whole new batch of retail staffers curious about the "legend of Colt Michael" three years later, and suddenly many of the male dance troupes who had all but discarded me just a year earlier were now begging me to tour with them. I declined, because it was insulting that, over the past few years, I was relegated to their D-List of performers; then, suddenly, *TWT* refreshed their memories. Even though I was happy with my retail job and truly wanted to be back on the circuit, I never forgot how minimized I felt when some of the dance troupes that I had helped to create no longer considered me one of their best.

[Okay, that's a total lie ... of course, I agreed to dance again when they called me. I belatedly accepted the previous offer from Foley's for an unpaid vacation. Over the course of the next week, I was booked in six cities; I kept my promise from three years before and did not book any shows in Houston. I was ecstatic to feel like an A-Lister again, all the while knowing that my sudden celebrity status was only temporary. After that week, I never got another phone call from any of the dance troupes; I wasn't shocked, but the hurt of being jilted into anonymity again stung even more this time.]

I would have loved to have been a cast member of any of those dance troupes, but truthfully, I never felt as if I fit in. Firstly, most of the other dancers were straight (pronounced "gay for pay"); I always took issue with straight guys pretending to be gay for money, especially when their girlfriends were obviously unaware that their boyfriends who danced in gay bars were also having sex with men for money. Oh, the shade of it all! But it's not the sex work that bothered me though; as someone who was living with HIV, I was more concerned about whether or not they were having safe sex. Which brings me to my second issue; the other reason that I felt as though I didn't fit in is because I was one of the few dancers NOT selling sex on the side. I took offense to being ostracized by other dancers for not indulging in the same extracurricular activities that often brought them more tips than I ever received. They made me out to be aloof and insensitive, and as if I thought I was better than they were, which couldn't have been further from the truth. I was enamored by these guys, and sometimes even a bit jealous of the attention that they received which I so craved; I wanted to BE them, I just didn't want to do what they did to get there, and that doing so would dishonor Steven's memory. Hell, I gave it away to almost anybody who wanted it; why would anybody pay for something that I was already giving away for free? For me, the difference is that I CHOSE whomever I wanted to be with, and they CHOSE me too. But whom did they CHOOSE? Ted A Richard or Colt Michael? Often, I didn't know, and at the time, it didn't matter.

After Dennis and Steven died, I once again became a sexual deviant. I didn't know how to be alone without being lonely, so *any* companion was better than none. The lines between being the cause or the symptom were blurred, and once again, I was on the never-ending hamster wheel of *use or be used*, and argued with myself over which side I was on.

It was always a liberating experience for me to have sex with someone (anyone) that had absolutely no clue who the hell Colt Michael was. And soon, Colt Michael would become a shadow hidden away in the closet for fear that if I allowed him out, he would overshadow Ted A Richard, as he always did. Why was I now so afraid of Colt Michael and who he had become? Why couldn't I be proud of him? Or had I now conflated Ted A Richard and Colt Michael into believing they were the same?

It was almost shameful how numb I became to all the death around me. I pretended as though it didn't bother me, and Jack Daniels and my other friend, cocaine, were always there to keep me company and living in the fantasy that I *wasn't* going to be next.

Death is always inevitable and emotionally draining, but when I learned that Patrick McCarter died on October 5, 1990, I couldn't find it within me to shed a tear. Yes, I was sad, but I was all cried out, always grasping for the last threads of hope that were already gone. Patrick always told me that he was not going to let people see him die ugly; he was going to die "pretty." His death, though somewhat suspect, was never investigated; he died in his sleep, alone in his apartment I was told. And yes, Patrick died before his body began to succumb to the wrath of AIDS, and he died pretty, just as he promised. At the age of twenty-seven, I was already a widower three times over; it would soon be my time to die too; and it wouldn't be pretty.

Meanwhile, I was continually recognized for my talent, attention to detail, and incredible management skills at Foley's; so much so, that I earned yet another promotion. This promotion was, by far, the most appreciated, since it was my entire staff who wrote letters to the executive office requesting to have me fill the open position in that department; they wanted their peer to become their boss; that's quite the compliment. I would be in an executive position overseeing the same managers who were once my peers; I was extremely humbled and honored that my staff thought that highly of me.

I learned early on in my retail career to never forget where I came from; very often, people moved up in a company and failed to realize that they still need their staffs to make them successful. It is this mantra, I believe, that made me a very successful executive manager; I was always empathetic to the needs of those who worked for me, and always promoted from within my own departments whenever possible. I placed high but realistic expectations on my staffs, and set my own standards exceedingly high, always leading by example. I played hard but worked even harder!

I dated sporadically, but still wasn't ready for anything serious. Often times, I would plan a date, and then just not show up because it didn't feel right. *Was I dating too soon after Steven's death?* Other times, I would be so drunk and drugged up that either I forgot that I actually had a date, or I was too ashamed to open the door when dates knocked. I stood up many dates that way, and I know the neighbors were watching, because they told me how badly they felt for those guys. Honestly, I felt badly for them too. They went out of their way to make my evenings special, but I was already too fucked up to enjoy them. So, I just stayed home alone ... and lonely ... again!

I truly do wish that I could go back in time and give all of those wonderful men a chance. That's all they wanted ... a chance to know

Ted A Richard. The one thing that I had been missing and craving most of my adult life was exactly what they wanted, but I was unprepared and unwilling to give it to them ... that's the definition of self-sabotage at its best. I didn't deserve the happiness they offered; I was so caught up in my own substance abuse that affection was not a priority. Later I learned, "Addiction is when you give up everything for one thing. Sobriety and serenity are when you give up one thing for everything." Better late than never, I guess.

New Year's Eve 1990 was supposed to be fairly uneventful. Steven was dead, and now Patrick was dead; I'd probably be dead soon too. I decided to go out to the mega-dance bar, Rich's, in downtown Houston. I figured that no one would know me there, and I could roll on Ecstasy, stay high on cocaine, and get my fill of Jack and Coke without anyone bothering me. I couldn't have been further from wrong.

From the moment I walked in the front door, I was welcomed with open arms, given free entry, and a few drink tickets; and treated with celebrity status. By midnight I was floating on rainbow clouds and chasing my watermelon-flavored bubble gum because I swore it had become an alien intent on impregnating me with its foreign seed; I remember hearing the bells and whistles and air horns in celebration, but my warped brain told me that it was ME being celebrated for "capturing the intruder." I snuck off to the bathroom for a key (or three) of cocaine, and pulled the two baggies out of my pocket, which now looked like psychedelic marshmallows. As best I could, I poured all of the contents of one baggie into the other one, then tore open the empty bag and sucked off the residue of the plastic bag.

Even after the "last call for alcohol" announcement, my night wasn't yet over. I knew exactly where Houston's club bathhouse was, but I must have circled the downtown one-way streets several times before I finally found the entrance.

I entered Club Body Center and requested a deluxe room; those were the only rooms furnished with a full-sized bed and separate shower. The attendant informed me that the only deluxe room available was the "leather room," which didn't have a shower, but had the added accoutrement of a heavy-duty leather sling that hung from the ceiling. I booked that room for the next eight hours, not for the sling, but because

I really, really needed to get some sleep. My head spun from all the acid and Ecstasy, and I keyed myself to calm the effects of withdrawal.

But sleep was far from happening. A huge, muscle-bound man loomed in front of my door, but I figured he was a hallucinogenic mirage. His name was Bob (or Robert, or Peter, or Dick ... of course, I never got his name). As I unlocked my door, I casually grazed my hand against him to welcome him inside. It would be a Happy New Year after all!

As sexually adventurous and promiscuous as I was whenever I was single, I never had the opportunity to experiment with sex on a sling; rather ironic, since I had now been a part of the leather community for the past five years or so.

The divisions of the bathhouse were tiny 5' x 8' rooms, with deluxe rooms measuring twice that size. Each room featured a small plastic mattress, sheets, a plastic pillow with pillow case, and a variety of condoms and lube on a small nightstand attached to the wall. Only the deluxe rooms had showers; all of the other rooms shared a community shower, which often ended up being just another open space for sex, as it was adjacent to the sauna and the steam room. One of the weird details about each room is that none of the walls reached the ceiling; there was an almost two-foot gap at the top, creating some pseudo-"gallery" effect so that nosey nellies could peek over the wall to satisfy their own voyeuristic tendencies.

Mr. Muscleman entered my room, and we wasted no time to make any further acquaintance; rather, we kissed as though we were on a honeymoon, slow and gentle, then rough and deliberate. Little did we know that we were inadvertently creating a real-life porno that was not of our own making; apparently the clanging of the sling chains was so loud that we attracted an audience of onlookers from the gaps below the ceiling. I could see the shadowy faces of several men and boys peering through the two-foot opening, their fingertips holding on to the top of the wall to keep their balance. Mr. Muscleman, with a stone-cold look of determination, stared into my eyes, then noticed the unwelcomed crowd; we nodded our heads in agreement to give them a show they wouldn't soon forget! When the "show" was over, he kissed me good-bye, and left.

[Sidebar: I have told this story many times over the years, and my story always stops right here; funny, right? But that is not what really happened; here's the truth about my night in the deluxe room leather sling; here's the rest of the story.]

The door to my room remained ajar, so, there I laid stuck with both the door and my legs wide open. I tried again to get off the sling, but to no avail, I was spent. It was then that I noticed several men standing in the hallway waiting for their "turn" to be "next."

Unwelcomed, the next person climbed on top of me in the sling as a crowd began to congregate in my room. They took turns holding my feet and my legs to keep me from squirming as they each "enjoyed" themselves at my expense. I have no clue how many times I was violated that night (four, maybe five or six), hating all of them but the first. I was too wasted to fend for myself, and too exhausted to make it stop.

There I was, in my *"fourteenth second of fame,"* spread-eagled with a captive audience and a standing ovation. I tried to scream, but no sound came out; I just laid there, spent, hoping they'd be too bored with my lack of interest that they would stop. But they didn't!

Thankfully, a neighbor from my apartment complex recognized me and saw that I was in trouble; I didn't know him other than as a poolside acquaintance; his name was Wayne. In short order, Wayne hurried into my room, shoved everyone out of the way, and released my legs from the leather sling. He closed the door and laid beside me on the floor. He hugged me tightly and wiped the never-ending flow of tears from my eyes.

My savior angel, Wayne Risberg, saved me from further punishment and embarrassment, which certainly would have continued had he not rescued me from the savages who were attacking me; he probably saved my life that night. Since then, I noticed Wayne even more often at the apartment complex; not really any more than before, but now we actually SAW each other. We both knew what had happened, and now, rather than just sharing a casual wave or nod, we'd greet each other with a warm embrace. I relished the comfort of those moments because they reminded me that sometimes, people just actually care about you and your well-being. Wayne knew both Ted A Richard and Colt Michael, but it was TED whom he saved that night, and he wanted me to be sure that I knew.

A few weeks later, Wayne called for me to visit him in his apartment; I had never been there, but I happily obliged. Walking in, I noticed that this formerly muscular and tanned man was now rail-thin and pale as a sheet. We never discussed the fact that he was HIV-positive, but once I saw him, we didn't have to. He told me that he was lonely and scared. His family was from Wisconsin, and most of his friends had already died; he didn't have anyone, and everyone was afraid to touch him. He asked if I would stay the night just to hold him and cuddle with him.

I was sure to hold him gingerly, since I knew that his skin was fragile and his bones were brittle. I remembered that feeling from when Steven Meert lay dying in the hospital. I had to wake up early the next morning to go to work, so I kissed him before I left, and wished him a great day, promising I'd bring him something to eat later. When I returned from work, there was already an ambulance parked in front of the apartment complex. Wayne's front door was ajar, and a medic looked at me and nodded with a graven stare. I unlocked my front door, went straight to my bedroom, and cried myself to sleep. The man who had saved my life was now dead; I'm happy that he didn't have to spend his last night alone, and I'm glad it was with me.

My alcoholism and drug abuse got worse.

It was so sweltering hot in the Houston spring of 1991 that it very well could have been the dead of summer; the entire complex at Westmoreland Square was abuzz about a new movie that was being filmed IN our apartment complex. Those were exciting times, for sure; but I was so wrapped up with work and "work" that I barely noticed the difference. Until one scorching early morning, when there was a knock on my door. It was a woman whom I did not know; she first apologized, and then asked if I could turn off my air conditioner for a few hours. She could tell that I was a bit confused as she explained that they were filming near my apartment and my A/C was making too much noise. Of course, I complied.

The woman who knocked on my door that morning was Oscar-winning producer and director, Lili Zanuck (*Driving Miss Daisy*, 1989's Academy Award for Best Picture). The movie they were making was a film called *Rush*; set in 1970s Tyler, Texas, it was based on actual events involving two undercover narcotics officers who were tasked with infiltrating a drug ring and providing false evidence while they both were getting addicted in the process.

I happened to have the day off from Foley's, but it got so hot in my apartment with the air conditioning off, that I had to get out for a while ... to a bar, of course. As I walked out of my apartment, there sat the three stars of the movie, Sam Elliot, Jennifer Jason Leigh, and Jason Patric awaiting their call for the next scene. It was then that Mr. Sam Elliot stood up from his chair, shook my hand, and apologized for the inconvenience. He was so tall, standing a robust 6'2", and his handshake was definitive and firm. In succession, both Jennifer Jason Leigh and Jason Patric did the same. I was in a complete state of awe because that encounter, which lasted less than thirty seconds, has been imbedded in my mind ever since; and I didn't even get an autograph or a picture. I don't know what it is about me that gets me so nervous around celebrities that I lose all focus and forget to do the things that "normal" people would do in these same situations.

As I left the complex, the manager handed me a typewritten note that alerted tenants to park their vehicles off premises to allow for nighttime filming. When I returned from the bar(s), the entire covered parking lot was filled with cars and trucks from the late 1960s and early 1970s. I had never seen rain machines before, but apparently, in the scene being filmed it was supposed to be a rainy night. (It was May in downtown Houston, there was no rain in sight; hence the machines.) I also noticed a very heightened sense of security around the entire area; there were additional police and squad cars, at least two fire trucks, and what seemed to be Secret Service agents. Scuttlebutt around the apartment complex was that somebody really famous was coming into town for this specific scene. So, I'm thinking to myself, *we've already got three A-List actors and an Oscar-winning producer-director ... who else could be even more famous?*

And then, Texas' newly elected governor, Ann Richards, appeared from behind the "rain." We were all awestruck; Ann Richards was an icon of the Texas landscape, especially after her 1988 Democratic Convention speech. Ms. Richards was a huge advocate for the arts and supported the entertainment industry wholeheartedly; and was also a staunch supporter of the LGBT community, though this stance was not widely recognized in her politics.

Many of the current tenants of Westmoreland Square, myself included, were asked to be extras for this scene. No, I didn't get paid, and my scene must have been left on the cutting room floor ... just a face in the crowd, anyway; but I did enjoy the excitement of it all.

The soundtrack of the movie *Rush* was composed by multi-Grammy-winning artist Eric Clapton; the movie's featured song, "Tears in Heaven," won the 1993 Grammy award for Song of the Year, Record of the Year, and Best Pop Male Performance. The lyrics, as they pertained to the movie, focused on the early and unnecessary deaths of drug addicts, and reflect on the belief that many (alcoholics and) addicts don't think they deserve anything better than the addiction with which they are struggling. The song certainly described exactly what I was going through in my life at that time, though I never considered myself an alcoholic nor a drug addict; I was nothing like THEM. I had a job, a car, and a place to live; I was better than them and I deserved better than them.

That winter, as an early birthday gift, one of my dear friends and supportive fans purchased tickets to see Joan Collins in Noel Coward's Broadway production of *Private Lives* in Houston, and also secured backstage passes. [Joan Collins had just completed a nine-year run playing the role of Alexis Carrington on the smash television prime-time soap opera, *Dynasty* (1981-1989).] The play was stupendous, and Joan Collins' portrayal of Amanda Prynne was superb; both received a well-deserved standing ovation.

After waiting backstage for twenty minutes or so, Ms. Collins opened the door to her dressing room and graciously greeted us. A phenomenal host, she offered us water and other refreshments; it was like we were visiting a dear friend, and the mood was very informal. And then Ms. Collins did something totally unexpected; she had her assistant take an instant Polaroid photo of each one of us. She then asked us to autograph her guest book, and told us that once we became famous, she would already have our autographs! I thought it was brilliant! I wonder if she still has that photo album?

Once our picture had been taken and her autograph book had been signed, I greeted Joan Collins by shaking her hand as she offered it to me, she then winced and cried out because she'd fallen behind the couch during the play and hurt her hand. I felt horrible and was stunned; so, I did the only thing I could think to do and apologized profusely and shamefully walked away with my head lowered between my shoulders.

Embarrassed, I looked behind me and saw the next person in the receiving line as he greeted Ms. Collins; he gingerly took her hand into his and kissed it ever so gently. At that time, Ms. Collins, now looking directly at ME, assertively reprimanded me that: *"That's* how one greets a lady!"

I was shaken and speechless at first, but then I realized that I had just been shadily admonished by the bitchiest of all the famous bitches, and it made my night! Now, who else can say that they were verbally bitch-slapped, in public, by the one and only Ms. Joan Collins? I CAN!

Foley's Thanksgiving Day Parade–1989

CHAPTER 15

WATER TIGER

(That Time I Got A Sunburn)

According to the Chinese Zodiac, I was born in the year of the Tiger, the Water Tiger, to be more specific. By definition, the symbol of the tiger denotes power, confidence, and strength, of which I possessed none; unless there is a sub-category within the feline description that includes scaredy-cat.

After the intense succession of tragedies that happened since the previous New Year's, I completely lost myself in the shadows of my own contempt, and allowed my anger toward the outside world to reflect internally; and lashed out at everyone who crossed my path, even in kindness. It didn't take long before alcohol became my confidence, drugs became my strength, and sex became my power again. They were the driving forces in my life, and I had lots of all three, and they were ALL *G-R-R-R-R-EAT*!! The closest that my life resembled that of a fierce feline was the cartoon character of "Tony the Tiger" (the Kellogg's Frosted Flakes cereal mascot). Tony the Tiger boasted about his strong sugary flakes of energy, however, the few flakes I had left had been frosted many times over, leaving me only wet and weak. At some point, even the "freshest" cereal gets stale and soggy, and I was about to discover what stale and soggy felt like!

In very short succession, I lost my job because of new management (I had to blame someone or something else), was evicted from my apartment (I was three months behind on rent), and at twenty-nine years old, I was now too old and unattractive to still be a male stripper. Colt Michael was dead, both my personal and professional lives were in ruins, and I was a lost soul searching for something, anything, to prove to myself that I deserved better than the life I was living but doing nothing to change it.

Then completely broke, I needed to make some extra cash before deciding which city would destroy me next. Luckily, JR's still hosted its weekly jock strap competitions. I entered as a last-ditch effort, hoping for at least a few bucks in my pocket to tide me over.

Surprisingly, there were eight contestants that night. I hadn't performed in Houston in quite some time, so I didn't know any of them. Except for one, it was Stallion; the guy who Mr. Magoo claimed was much better at being a prostitute than I was. He stared at me blankly, not knowing that I knew his secret; not realizing the abuse I endured; not seeing my hatred; it wasn't his fault, or maybe it was. I wasn't sure; and I didn't know if I wanted to be sure.

I danced through the hate as best I could, hiding my emotions in each dance move. As more and more clothing came off, I often wondered if the crowd compared me to him. I decided to not let it bother me anymore, and performed as if the rest of my life depended on it; maybe it did.

Finally, the eight contestants were whittled down to the final two ... Colt Michael and Stallion. Yes, my unwitting nemesis would be my competition for the final battle. He danced first; I watched him gyrate across the floor, sometimes hanging from the rafters, garnering the attention (and money) of his most fervent fans. I, on the other hand, had absolutely no fans in the audience; I hadn't even told my best friends that I would be there; I was too ashamed of the depths my addictions brought.

The winner would be decided by audience response; I was relegated to second-place once again, with the crowd cheering so loudly for Stallion that I could hear the echoes off the wooden rafters. I feigned happiness for his win, then heard the emcee call my name, "Y'all give it up for Mister Colt Michael!" I walked onto the makeshift stage, my face already flushed with the embarrassment of, once again, coming in second. But I was completely wrong!

The crowd erupted into a "thunderous ovation" (Oh crap, that's part of how Julia Sugarbaker from that TV show *Designing Women* regaled the "true" story of the night the lights went out in Georgia.) At least that's what it felt like. I was in total shock, and had no idea that I still had the support of the Houston community after so many years away. I learned later that my win was two-fold.

Many of those in the crowd that night were fans of Stallion, but not necessarily for his dancing abilities. It turns out that Stallion knew of my encounter with Mr. Magoo and was part of the plan all along. Throughout the night, my unfortunate incident had been the fodder of bar gossip; I had no clue. His fans were there to make me feel ridiculed, though they never showed their contempt while I was dancing; I just noticed that they didn't tip me.

I discovered later that Stallion was placed into the final two for a good reason; they wanted Colt Michael to be the one who beat him. They wanted to see the look in his face when he realized that the guy he had screwed over into a night of unwanted prostitution was the same person who had now dethroned him as "king of the stripper circuit." It was priceless, but I'm glad that I didn't know the truth beforehand. I left the bar with over $500 in tip money and winnings that night; I had $150 left by the time I got home; that would be my moving money.

I moved to New Orleans in the summer 1992 to find myself and rebuild my life but was actually only running away from my problems. Finding a job turned out to be more of an obstacle than I thought it would be. Apparently (pronounced "obviously") I'd burned several bridges at Foley's, and no amount of retail success could overcome the executive-sized hole I dug. It was a simple tale of apply, lather, rinse, repeat; and the realization that the "repeat" part kept repeating itself over and over, and I couldn't figure out how to make it stop. I wanted OFF this merry-go-round to nowhere!

Soon after, I received a call from a bar owner in Lafayette, inviting me to organize a male stripper show for an upcoming event at his club. I still had all of my Texas connections, so I was happy to assist, and contacted three of my stripper friends in West Texas who were ecstatic to be doing a show in Louisiana (Lafayette had already seen most of the Houston talent; I was both determined and excited to bring new talent to my hometown.)

The bar, Street Talk, was packed floor to ceiling; I'm sure that a few fire marshal violations were broken that night, so it didn't hurt that the Louisiana State Fire Marshal was also in attendance. The emcee, a local drag celebrity introduced each of the dancers prior to their performances; "Bull," then "Mandingo," then "Stan Studly." I was very excited that this Cajun Country crowd loved these West Texas Country men. After their second rotation, the Lafayette crowd absolutely fell in love with these dancers; I was happy for them, for the bar owners, for the customers, and especially for me! I was asked to do a job, and just proved success on every single level.

But apparently my night was not over yet. I watched from backstage, and the show concluded as the drag entertainer/emcee reintroduced the talent to re-emerge for a final bow. Suddenly, I saw Stan Studly peering through the backstage curtain, both red-faced and out of breath. He said, "Mr. Ted, you gotta come out here now, you just gotta come out here." I grabbed his arm and yanked him backstage with me. He continued, "Do you not hear that!?" I said, "What?" Stan Studly opened the curtain for me out of view of the audience; I nearly broke down in tears when I heard the entire crowd, in my little hometown of Lafayette, Louisiana, yelling, "We want Colt!" and "Colt Michael!" Most of the crowd showed up that night to see Colt Michael dance; boy, had I disastrously misread this crowd. Maybe I had been misreading signals all of my life; maybe that's why my consistent acts of self-sabotage kept destroying what I thought were my dreams and ambitions. *Maybe.*

Thinking quickly, I borrowed one of Stan Studly's extra G-strings that he packed away for "just in case." Well, this was the precise definition of a "just in case" moment, and I'm so glad that he helped me out in my time of need. I quickly sent a message to the DJ booth that I was ready, he put the needle on the record, and the bar was filled with the sounds of sirens. There was pandemonium in the building, as everyone knew exactly what was about to happen. The song the deejay was playing was a remake of a blues/rock song originally made popular by both Rare Earth and The Temptations; but now, "I'm Losing You" by Uptown Girls (from Dallas, Texas) had become somewhat of a gay anthem in the late 1980s and early 1990s. Over the next ten minutes, as I pranced and danced and gyrated my way across the stage and through the crowd, I collected more than $300 in tips for which I will always be eternally grateful; those men giving me those tips that night had no idea that they saved my life again. (I was already behind on the rent in my new apartment in New Orleans). That night was a huge success for me *and* my fragile ego, and it was the first time that I felt truly loved and honestly respected by the hometown that I thought had abandoned me when, in reality, it was I who had abandoned them. I always hoped to repay them for the well-wishes and compliments from that night; happily, I got that opportunity over ten years later. But at that time, I still didn't have a job and barely made enough money to cover the rest of that month's rent.

New Orleans quickly became a repeat of the bane of my existence in Houston! I wasn't going to make it much longer if I stayed there. As a last resort, I contacted my old boss from Foley's who was now working for a company named Jordan Marsh (ironically, now Macy's) headquartered in Boston, Massachusetts. Mike Billingsley knew my reputation as an exceptional manager with an incredible eye for detail and merchandising. I was hired, sight unseen, by the rest of the management team and was hired based solely on Mr. Billingsley's recommendation. The company even paid for my flight and moving expenses. I knew that I had something to prove, both to Mr. Billingsley and to myself, that I was absolutely worth my fantastic salary. This was my chance to earn the respect which I had at one time before I threw it all away for alcohol and drugs.

When I was still in great standing with my former employer, Foley's, I was promoted from salesperson to general sales manager over one department, then two departments then three departments. By the time I was fired for "lack of executive consistency," I managed *five* departments on two different levels of a four-story department store and was the *only* general sales manager to have ever earned that distinction. As a newly hired manager for the Jordan Marsh company, my increase in salary also came with an increase in responsibility, as I was tasked with taking over a single position that had previously been filled by two people.

I was hated before I even stepped into the store, not knowing that the previous managers were very well-loved by their staffs and were fired for "unknown" reasons. I felt the resentment and the tension in the room as my new staff and I were introduced. As it turns out, New England weather wasn't the only thing that was cold and gray; my staff gave off more cold shoulders and icy, hateful stares than I had ever seen before. I had no idea that this was a hostile work environment, but I had no other options and discovered later that I was called Mr. Billingsley's "friend from Texas," and that's all the staff knew. I still don't know what they thought that meant, but it was yet another obstacle I would attempt to overcome.

Initially, I was the general sales manager of the Ladies' Petite department and Bridge Sportswear (high end fashion lines such as Anne Klein, DKNY, Escada, Tahari, and Adrienne Vittadini) at the Jordan Marsh located in Burlington, Massachusetts. Mr. Billingsley knew my affinity for women's fashion, and was familiar with the work I had done in the Juniors and Women's departments at Foley's; but in New England, men just didn't work in ladies' departments (yet another obstacle). I only knew what I knew I had to do; I had to prove to this staff that a man could do a lady's job, and that I had to work twice as hard as they did and lead by example. It took me less that one month to bridge the gap from being "Mr. Billingsley's friend from Texas" to being general sales manager extraordinaire. Even the buyers and the executives at the home office in Boston called Mr. Billingsley to find out how the new kid increased sales by more than ten percent in just one month. The following month, some of the buyers drove in from Boston to meet me and wanted to know the secret to my immediate success. They were taken aback when they observed all of my changes, and at how I had turned the departments into true works of art; they still couldn't believe that a man could be so in tune with women. Even the women who worked in those departments told the buyers it was much easier to sell clothing and to add on sales because of the way I revamped the entire floor. On the week after that visit, I traveled to Boston to network with the buyers and other executives; and would soon teach a training class on the importance of proper fashion merchandising and creating displays specific to the customer.

But while I was growing with the Jordan Marsh company, my personal life was still in shambles. I missed Colt Michael and the person that I became as Colt Michael. To make matters worse, I lived in a little town called Woburn, Massachusetts; a quaint, lovely little place to live, but it was more than ten miles from all the gay bars in Boston, and I didn't have a vehicle. To get to Boston, I took a bus to the subway station, and usually had to switch trains at least once, depending on which bar I was going to. Then, by the time I was drunk enough to come home, I had to call a cab, since the bus lines and subways had stopped running, forcing me to pay upwards of fifty bucks for a ride home. I stiffed a cabbie more than a few times when I'd already spent all of my cash on drinks and drugs.

I was stuck in that paradigmatic belief that everyone wanted to be with Colt Michael, but nobody wanted to be with Ted A Richard. In reality, no one in Boston had ever heard of Colt Michael. *So why was I still trying to give the impression that I was once someone famous, when I wasn't at all?* In retrospect, it was pretentiousness. Colt Michael was my persona, not the reality of who I was and am. I hid behind his supposed fame, and assumed that people would recognize me from the one magazine cover that was five years old; but this pretentiousness had unintended consequences. *How dare they not extend to me the comforts afforded to me via my celebrity status?* These covert (pronounced "overt") acts to protect my anonymity made my behavior appear to be conceited or unapproachable; of which I was neither.

At work, I was a well-respected merchandiser and executive, and when I was Colt Michael, I garnered the adoration and appreciation of so many fans; but when I was just Ted A Richard, it seemed as though I was never good enough. I always ended up alone, and never met anyone of substance at the bars. *What was wrong with me? Why was I no longer attractive or attracted to anyone?* Unbeknownst to me, I was already IN a relationship; one that took me a very long time to recognize: it was with alcohol and drugs.

I needed to find other ways to get the companionship that I so desperately needed, even if it was only temporary. No longer was I searching for intimacy; I found it and lost it with Steven. His death laid bare all of my insecurities that he did his best to shield me from, fearing it would cause more harm than good. He saved me by saving me from myself.

My time in Boston was spent mostly alone, depressed, and lonely. Although I loved my job, that alone couldn't fill the hole left in me after Steven died. Steven was my safe haven, my love, and my heart. But he wasn't coming back. I had to find a way to move on because I no longer had that safe place, and didn't want another relationship. I just wanted sex ... plain vanilla, passionate but non-committal, anonymous sex. No intimacy! I just wasn't ready!

Yes, you may be surprised to learn that I paid to go out with escorts; or maybe you're not surprised at all. Either way, it's the truth. I never thought that I would ever be so down on myself to the point of hiring someone to love me for the evening. Shadow, my paid-for companion, was always there to answer my call and fulfill my needs; and as temporary as the fix was, it was all the emotion I could handle.

After a few visits with Shadow, I realized that if so many lonely people didn't exist, then neither would his livelihood. The more I got to know him, the more I realized that he was just as lonely as I was. He solved his loneliness by having anonymous sex with strangers as an escort; I solved my own loneliness by hiring him to fill an emotional void that could only be satisfied with sex from a stranger who pretended to love me for an hour or so. It was a win-win situation for each of us. But truly it wasn't!

I was still alone and kept the false belief that I wasn't lonely. *Had I really diminished myself so much as to think that the only way for me to find love was to pay for it?* Apparently, that answer was YES. I was never ashamed of it; after all, we were both meeting our needs by mutual agreement.

I justified it this way—not that I owed anyone an explanation—I could go out to the clubs all night, spend hundreds of dollars on liquor and drugs, party with everyone, and go home alone. Or, I could pay an escort $100 (plus tips) to come to my apartment; I'd cook a meal, we'd eat, and for the next hour or so, I was not lonely. The justification made sense to me. The fact that, at the time, I thought I needed justification was further proof of the insidious mind games that the Catholic church pounded into my brain during all of those misinformation-laden sermons by the priest who molested me.

Escorts often seemed surprised that someone "who looked as good as me" would need them for companionship. I later recognized that if I wasn't failing in the looks department, then there must have been something else wrong, but drugs and alcohol always made that pain go away.

I fooled myself into believing that I didn't want intimacy, but when my "date" arrived, we both understood that the intimacy was exactly what I yearned for; the sensuality was always there, but the intimacy was always missing.

I turned back to Naomi Sims for guidance, and she was there for me, as always. But by this time, we were drinking and drugging together *in absentia*, since we then lived hundreds of miles apart and called each other when we were both high and needed someone to talk to at 3:00 a.m. We had not only become friends; but we had unwittingly become each other's enablers; it was a friendship destined for disaster. But even when things were the worst for me or the worst for him (Newman), we always tried our best to be there for each other. We each had a big secret that we thought no one knew about; obviously she knew that I was HIV-positive since that unfortunate incident in Odessa, but the fact that she was also HIV-positive was something that she only confided in a few of her dearest friends, and I would never break that trust. Newman "Naomi Sims" Braud, Jr. died on November 10, 1992, and my alcoholism and drug use got worse.

Despite my addictions, I was promoted to general sales manager of the Ladies' Accessories department within six months, and shortly after that, the Ladies' Swimwear/Coats department was added to my list of departments; yes, there was a salary increase each time. (Are you now seeing the similarities between my job at Foley's and my job at Jordan Marsh?) And it was only Mr. Billingsley who knew just exactly what I was capable of; you see, he also had something to prove to those people who had hired me sight unseen, and it made him proud that I became the shining star he always knew I was. Within one year, I was promoted three times, from general sales manager over two departments, then four departments, then area sales manager over the entire ladies' fashions which encompassed most of the first floor (excluding the fragrance department). One year after that, I was promoted to divisional sales manager over the entire men's department (most of the second floor), juniors, women's, and lingerie (the rest of the second floor), ladies' furs, ladies' coats, and swimwear (on the first floor), and the children's department (on the third floor). Once again, I managed several departments on several levels of the same store, and at only twenty-nine, I was the youngest divisional sales manager. [As an example of the expanse of the departments I oversaw, on the three days after Thanksgiving (Black Friday and the beginning of the holiday shopping season) the Burlington Jordan Marsh store did over one million dollars in sales; my division alone accounted for nearly half of that. I was in charge of a $3.5

million division in a store that had more than $8 million in yearly sales. That's an accomplishment of which I was always proud.]

With all of the stress of managing such a huge swath of a successful department store, it wasn't long until I was over-exerting myself, and more symptoms of my HIV began affecting my work performance. *Was it really stress, the HIV, or my addictions?* I had no answers, but knew that I was, once again, living a circular life ... worrying about the HIV by working more than eighty hours a week to distract myself, relieving the stress of those long hours with alcohol and drugs, and recuperating from my hangovers by going back to work. Lather, rinse, repeat, repeat, repeat.

During my two-plus years in Boston, we had the worst snowstorms in fifty years. Now I'm a little Cajun boy that ain't used to snow. The first year, I kinda dealt with it, and I was ready to go home. But my staff convinced me that the severe weather was just a fluke, and that the winters were NEVER that bad. So, I stayed another year, then the following year it was even worse. I remember always telling my family how beautiful the snowfall was. And that was true, but here's the real truth. All that snow is beautiful ... until you FALL in it! So, my mom sent me a poem entitled, "A Cajun Moves North," which she had found about a Cajun dealing with New England winters. And when I read it, it was hysterical ... and absolutely the truth.

By this time, Jocelyn lived in the Washington, D.C. area, and she and I and her boyfriend, Baxter, spent time in the gay resort destination, Provincetown, Massachusetts—P'Town to those of us in the know.

Jocelyn and Baxter sometimes met me on the Boston Harbor pier, and we took the "Fairy Ferry" from Boston to P'Town; this ferry ride was an entertainment venue all on its own, offering shuffleboard, bingo, checkers tournaments, and karaoke contests. Sounds like a senior citizen ferry, right? WRONG! Imagine 500 drunk, gay men and lesbians on a rocking boat trying to play shuffleboard and sing (sometimes simultaneously)! It is an experience not soon forgotten, and, after the first time, there is a rush to do it over and over again, which we did ... OFTEN!

It was on one of these trips that I accidentally overstayed my welcome in my own hotel room. "J" and "B" went souvenir shopping for the day; but I instead opted to head down to the (mostly) nude beach. But I never made it there, although I don't remember the rest of the day. The story that Jocelyn and Baxter regaled to me was abhorrent. They found me lying face down on the bed wearing nothing but short shorts that barely covered anything. I had an empty bottle of Jack Daniels in my hand, and they were scared shitless; Baxter even thought I was dead. Then they just covered me in a blanket and let me sleep it off.

To this day, I am so ashamed of my behavior during what was supposed to be a relaxing vacation for all of us. Instead, it turned into my *"fifteenth second of fame,"* sprawled drunkenly across a hotel room bed, half naked and sunburned (though I don't remember how the sunburn happened), so oblivious to the world that I embarrassed myself in front of Jocelyn and Baxter to the point of no redemption (so I thought); and sadly, I still remember none of it.

I can vividly recall one dreary day, deep in depression and lost in my own guilt and fear, I called Jocelyn Rae. (This was after the drunken debacle in P'Town and I hoped that she would answer the phone; she had no reason to.)

Thankfully, I heard her sweet voice, "Hello?" She instinctively knew that something was wrong. I said, crying and in hysterics, "I'm calling you because I'm too drunk to go to work and I'm dying, and I don't know what else to do." It is on that phone call that I finally revealed to her my HIV diagnosis. In all honestly, she probably already knew, but to hear myself saying those words horrified me, and Jocelyn was the only person I felt I could talk to. Dennis was dead, Steven was dead, Patrick was dead, Naomi was dead. It was a comfort that Jocelyn now lived closer to me, but she was still too far away to give me healing companionship; a phone call would need to suffice for now, and it did. But I needed to get off this carousel of hell for good sometime soon; I was dying, and I knew it.

The next morning, I went in to work, and explained to the management staff (Mr. Billingsley was no longer with the company) that I had tested positive for the HIV virus; I conveniently left out the part that I had already known this for over seven years. I was told to leave for the day and to return on the next. When I returned, as scheduled, I was handed what seemed like a booklet of paperwork to sign; I knowingly signed away my rights and absolved the company of any fault regarding my abrupt termination. I knew that they were firing me for being a liability to the company, but I really didn't care, I was getting a $50,000 paycheck to get me the hell outta there, and decided to move back to Louisiana. I had no other plans, mostly because I had already wasted away any of my other options. Lather, rinse, repeat, repeat, repeat.

This was in December 1994; Boston was COLD, and it wasn't just the weather. For the past two years, I searched for "Southern hospitality" that just didn't seem to exist. The folks were all very nice and polite, but often the sincerity in their smiles was lacking, or maybe my expectations were too high. I missed the camaraderie of *home*. As usual, I excelled in my professional life—which was now over and not returning—and my personal life fared no better. Maybe it was just me needing a reason to dislike the people and places that I had grown to enjoy over the past two years; maybe I needed an escape plan, and I needed to hate the things I once loved, or maybe this was just an easy way out. Something was missing, or at least I was failing to see it, and I needed to find it! Maybe what I was missing was somewhere in Louisiana; I was dying to find out.

Then I realized that maybe I really was a Water Tiger; I had the power to sabotage even the best situation, the confidence that any good thing would go bad (through no fault of my own, of course), and the strength to continue to make matters worse by not changing my actions nor my attitude. *I was dying anyway; why did it matter?*

Colt Michael command performance at Street Talk
(courtesy Acadiana Ambush magazine) –1992

CHAPTER 16

THE 16TH SECOND— WHAT HAPPENS NOW?

(That Time Dolly Sang for Me)

Somehow, I made it through my fifteen seconds of fame, and in reflection, realized that most of those *"seconds of fame"* were actually *"seconds of shame."* For all my accomplishments—both as Colt Michael and as Ted A Richard—it seemed that the more negative, shameful events impacted my life the most. I'd love to say that I emerged from my *"fifteen seconds of fame/shame"* fairly unscathed, but in all honesty, I simply cannot. I didn't know what to expect on the other side of "fame," so I didn't know how to deal with what would happen next.

How was I supposed to deal with the aftermath of my *"fifteen seconds of fame"* when I didn't even realize that they had already passed? I was too oblivious that I was already living in my *16th Second*, and I had absolutely no game plan; after all, Colt Michael was already dead (living somewhere in eternal purgatory because I never allowed his soul to leave), and Ted A Richard would soon be dead too. I spent most of my life on a stage of one sort or another, yet almost none of the instances that I recalled as one of my *"fifteen seconds of fame"* was spent on a stage.

I could handle the truth of whom I'd become, but not the fantasy of the person I pretended to be. As confusing as my "created" life was, I didn't realize that my truth was really a lie, and gave all the credit of my perceived success to the fantasy that was Colt Michael while Ted A Richard lived in his own delusions of grandeur. *Was my squandered fame the end of the beginning or the beginning of a different end?* I knew that there was no way that life in my *16th Second* could be any worse than what I had already been through. I was so very wrong! Thankfully I would die soon, so there wasn't much time left for me to feel the pain.

I told my parents that I had been fired, was moving back to Louisiana and needed a place to stay. My parents were not wealthy by any means, but they somehow scraped up the monies to build a small sunroom addition to their house. Mom planned on using it for storage and a home office, but my parents always put their kids first and the extra room would have to suffice as a bedroom for now.

I filed for disability through the Social Security Administration. (For reference, a healthy individual without HIV would normally have a T-cell count of about 1,000-1,200 copies/ml; my T-cell count was TEN ... YES, you read that correctly, TEN.) By not taking any medications over the previous seven years, my body deteriorated to the point that I already had an AIDS diagnosis (T-cell count below 200), and was sicker than I had ever been in my life. My muscle mass withered and my skin shriveled around my bones; my face became drawn and almost gray in color. And while things looked extremely bleak, my doctor in Boston informed me that I may have probably saved my own life by never taking the toxic drug called AZT, which was one of the first drugs created to treat HIV. It killed off all of the good cells along with the bad ones.

Are you kidding me, doc? You mean I could have died a long time ago, without having to deal with this shit now? And even though I knew I'd be dying soon I still felt some type of survivor's guilt and remorse. *Why was it that all of my friends and many acquaintances had already died, and I was spared? Why were Dennis, Steven, Patrick, and Naomi all dead? Why didn't I deserve to die younger just like they did, and avoid the dreaded chaos that became the end of my life?* My ultimate destination was death and apparently, I wasn't trying hard enough. I lost the will to continue fighting what I knew was a losing battle; not that it would have mattered, since I had no map to guide me toward my destiny: Hell.

It was well past the time to have a serious conversation with my parents. They knew that something was wrong, but didn't know what. One morning, Dad asked me, "Son, do you have AIDS?" I snapped, "Yes, how did you know?" Dad and Mom noticed how extremely gaunt I was and almost couldn't recognize the person I had become. To make matters worse, I was denied disability through SSA, which, of course I appealed. The meeting with the adjudication judge did not go as planned.

THE 16TH SECOND

[Sidebar: Up until this point, I spent my entire life being defined by my excellent work ethic. I lived to work and enjoyed nearly every second of it. Being forced to beg the government for money because I physically and mentally could no longer work was the most demeaning thing I ever did. And to look as sick as I did in public ... for people to see me that sick was even more degrading. I was the person that neither Dennis, nor Steven, nor Patrick, nor Naomi ever wanted to be. I was embarrassed to be me, and hated the person who stared back at me in the mirror every day.]

I shuffled into the adjudicator's office. He sat behind a grand, Baroque-style desk, much too nice to be in a government office building (oh, so *that's* where my tax dollars went ... you needed new furniture, but I digress). I was slow and steady as I sat in the fancy leather-bound office chairs; my Dad was with me and helped me to sit, as I had become very weak during the half-hour ride to the appointment. We spoke with the judge, and my Dad helped me to explain my case for disability; the medications I was taking would often make my lips and throat parched, so I was in dire need of water, which was finally offered only after I had asked ... twice! After replying to a few questions, the adjudicating judge, the (dis)Honorable Judge Michael Caldero announced as he looked at my Dad, "If he can hold a pencil, then he can work." I immediately broke down in tears and stumbled toward the door, in desperate need of escape. I couldn't believe his words. *This couldn't be what he thinks of me.* He didn't even have the guts to look at me man-to-man while he spewed those vile words; he was just as cowardly as he was ignorant! As I left the office, I could hear my Dad's voice. I had no clue what he was saying, though I did recognize his stern tone; I had heard this same tone many times as I was growing up. Through the air vent above the closed door I'm almost certain that I heard him say, "Now listen here, Judge Caldero." That's the last I heard as I left the offices and walked back to the car. About fifteen minutes later, I saw my Dad, now red-faced, storm out of the building.

The drive home was awkwardly quiet, but once Dad parked the vehicle in the carport, I looked at him and said, "Daddy, it's okay. I know I'm dying; it'll be fine. I love you and thank you." Not another word was ever mentioned about the events of that dreadful day.

About two weeks later, I received a letter from Social Security informing me that my disability benefits had been approved. To this day, my Dad never told me what he said behind those closed doors, but I'm so happy that he did whatever he did.

For the past several months since my return from Boston, I had been on a variety of medication cocktails of Crixivan, Epivir, Zerit, Bactrim (to which we soon found out I was allergic), Reyataz, Ritonavir, and other antiretrovirals. The medication made my lab work seem as though my health was improving, but the side effects ravaged my body even worse than the disease. While my most recent blood test revealed that my T-cell count peaked to twenty-nine, I feigned excitement that it had almost tripled; but the count didn't really matter. I knew I was about to die; either with dignity or in disgust. I didn't care either way. *Why was everyone still trying to keep me alive in this abysmal life in which I became more and more miserable every day? Just let me die already!*

During this time, I finalized all of my own funeral arrangements. I saw what HIV/AIDS did to all of my friends over the past several years; I knew that my time was coming soon, and wanted to have my funeral done *my* way. I even purchased my own mausoleum plot and had the engraving done on the stone. It's up on the sixth floor in the Chapel Mausoleum at the Sts. Peter and Paul Cemetery in Scott, Louisiana. (It's not really where I wanted my final resting place to be, but it'd be only bones soon. My soul would soon be out and about, creating rainbows and butterflies, and probably wreaking havoc with more than a few people who pissed me off along the way.) I remember asking my older brother if it was weird that I was having my own headstone engraved before I died; and he replied, "No, just don't put the date you died yet!" I thought that was hysterical. It's often hard to find humor when someone is dying, and he did that for me; and I am taking this opportunity to say, "Thank you."

Being HIV-positive in Cajun Country introduced me to a whole new world of self-consciousness I never had the opportunity to explore, nor did I ever want to. The first things I encountered were the depths of fear and sheer hatred that further fueled my isolation. I understood the fear, because there was so much misinformation and disinformation about HIV/AIDS that no one knew whom or what to believe. But what I didn't expect was the harmful cruelty and divisiveness that my HIV diagnosis conjured up with people I thought *should* have known better, and in places and situations where I had assumed those present had been better educated about this deadly virus. Unfortunately, much of the isolation against people with HIV came from within my own gay community. It's the same tragic tale of guilt by association; if you were seen with me, then you must have HIV too! In retrospect, it was probably a defense mechanism for not being able to explain exactly what they were afraid of. But the shunning hurt ... it really hurt! In addition to the pain of dying, I now had to deal with the pain of rejection ... in my own gay community ... understandable, but still unforgivable.

The more I looked around, the more I saw people staring at me; it took a while before I learned to shut off my peripheral vision to save my sanity. I learned more about myself, and what it would take to stay healthy. Having the knowledge that I had gained regarding my own illness, I thought I was prepared to deal with others' deliberate ignorance and focus on my own health as a means of combatting the distance that the gay community placed between us. I always knew, though, that it would soon all be over, so I tried to not sweat the little things. As they say in the Catholic church pomp and circumstance service, "Peace be with You." And as we say in Cajun Country: "Bless Their Hearts!" (This sarcasm would be killing me if I wasn't already dying!)

It is during this turbulent time that I met a very special man who would be a positive influence for the rest of my life. I met Tommy Fontenot through mutual friends who knew that we would make the perfect couple. We dated for a while, but I wasn't in the right frame of mind to be a great boyfriend. We both realized that fairly early on; however, Tommy showed me the love and affection I needed. There are no words to express the warmth and genuine kindness that he shared with me during one of the worst periods of my entire life. Tommy loved me for who I was, not in spite of what I had, and was one of the few people with whom I could be vulnerable and brutally honest.

But even Tommy didn't know just how bad things were. We both knew I was dying, but he didn't realize how close to the grave I really was; or maybe he did and was sparing my emotions. I felt weaker and weaker, and my body was losing its vigor. My skin seemed even more discolored and gray than it had in the past; I looked more like I was sixty-two instead of only thirty-two.

Tommy never faltered. He never allowed the way I saw myself to affect the way that he saw me. Of course, he never knew what I USED to look like, so he had no frame of reference. Small victories, I guess.

On a random June weekend in 1995, Tommy and I visited some friends of his in Centerville; and since Lafayette didn't have any Gay Pride celebrations, we decided to have a barbecue and celebrate our own way. I was already getting my monthly stipend from the government, so I had some money to buy my Jack Daniels (*oh really, who do I think I'm kidding? I ALWAYS found money for alcohol and drugs*). I forgot how exhaustingly hot South Louisiana summers could get, and bourbon whiskey mixed with a hit of acid dehydrated my already withered body faster than a dewdrop in the desert. (*Do dewdrops even exist in the desert?*)

I had a fantastic afternoon with Tommy and his friends; albeit probably much more fun than they knew I was having. By evening time, we were all spent and decided to turn in early. Tomorrow was another day and we'd have leftovers from the barbecue for breakfast.

For some reason, probably because I was still wired on the remnants of the acid, I was the first one to awaken the next morning, and decided to get a head start on the others, showering so that I could assist in setting the breakfast table. I was in awe of their antique claw tub with the ovular shower curtain; I had only seen these tubs in magazines, and now I was actually showering in one. It took a while for the water to get hot; living out in the country does have a few downfalls. In an effort to shower quickly and not use up all of the hot water (*you country folks know exactly what I'm talking about*), I lathered quickly and began shaving. Suddenly, what I knew was blood splattered onto the shower curtain and gushed down the drain in what was once a pristine white bathtub. I had no idea what had happened or where I had cut myself, but had to make the bleeding stop; I immediately shut off the water and tried to clean up with the clean towel I had placed on the commode, but there was blood everywhere; by now, the towel was already drenched, and the bleeding continued. I yelled for Tommy in what must have been a shrieking tone since he suddenly appeared in the bathroom before I had finished calling his name; he was already awake, and in the kitchen. He opened the door and saw what he must have thought was a scene from the movie *Psycho*; looking at me startled, he said, "Ted, what did you do?" I replied, "I don't know!" He grabbed another towel from the linen rack to replace the one that I was still covering my face with. As I removed the blood-soaked towel, Tommy witnessed the damage, screaming, "Oh my God, Ted, you've shaved off half your face!"

Tommy worked diligently to stop the bleeding, then one of the homeowners stepped in to offer assistance and a first aid kit, which turned out to be not much help. At this point, my only consolation is that I had not kept my HIV diagnosis a secret from those attending the party, so at least that was one less thing for me to have to worry about. Luckily, once I was all cleaned up and the bleeding had stopped, it was just a small gash across the jawline on the left side of my face, but I had somehow shaved myself almost to the bone.

Unfortunately, the wound never truly healed properly and left a huge scar that I would have for life. I was often asked what happened, and always had a great story about the "peril" I was in when this accident occurred. My favorite anecdote was where I would tell people that I was working undercover with the DEA, and something really bad went down during a drug bust and a stray bullet grazed my cheek. Of course, that never really happened, but it saved me the embarrassment of having to admit I had simply cut myself shaving while hungover. On second thought, maybe what really happened is truly the better of the two. I'm just happy that Tommy was there to save me from my own idiocy.

Then one night in October that same year, my parents had decided that they were going out for the evening. I know that having me living in the house to which they had become accustomed to living in alone was beginning to frazzle them a bit; they deserved a night out. Because I was so frail, I asked Tommy to come and spend the evening with me. Without a moment of hesitation, he agreed; I was delighted.

That night just happened to be the airing of the Annual *Country Music Awards*, the one where Vince Gill and Dolly Parton performed "I Will Always Love You," a vocal performance that would win CMA Vocal Event of the Year in 1996. While Dolly and Vince sang, (*I just call them by their first names ... we good like that!*) Tommy and I reminisced about that time in 1989 that Dolly sang "He is Alive" with the full choir for a surprising and soul-searching ending; my skin tingled and my eyes teared up as the final refrain was sung, and the entire audience immediately rose to their feet for a well-deserved standing ovation. I jumped to my feet and yelled, "Oh my god, Tommy ... I have the video cassette," and ran over to retrieve the video from the storage cabinet and slapped it into the VCR (that's a Video Cassette Recorder, for you youngsters).

We sat next to each other on the single recliner in my parents' living room, and just enjoyed each other's company. We held hands and cried; not because we were sad, but because we were happy to be spending quality time together. I cherished moments like this the most; and am forever indebted to Tommy for the friendship and compassion that he so generously gave me even though we were no longer a couple. I am eternally grateful, mostly because even he didn't know that just his presence most certainly saved me from myself many times; it is a debt I can never repay.

That November, my family invited a few people over to the house to celebrate my birthday; of course, Tommy was there. It was a surprise party, and I was so happy to see so many friends, some of whom I had not seen in quite a few years. To see the joy on all of their faces really helped to lift my spirits, even if just for a little while. Sadly, I also recognized the fear and despair in their smiles as they hugged me (ever so gently, since my bones were brittle), and wished me a happy birthday. We were all certain that I would not see another one, but our veiled attempt to pretend that my health would improve and that I would soon be feeling much better failed miserably. There's no way to hide that amount of desperation.

In addition to the traditional fig cake my Mom always baked for my birthday, I received several wonderful gifts: a personalized blanket from my friends visiting from Houston, a "Man of the Month" calendar from my brother and his wife (wishfully thinking that I would somehow see all twelve months, but knowing that I wouldn't), a T-shirt with the word "WHATEVER" scrolled on the front from my four-month-old niece (she was quite the psychic at such a young age to know exactly how I was feeling), and a wonderfully comfortable and colorful recliner from my parents. Tommy's gifts were a knockout. They were both meaningful, and while one was meant to be a gag gift, he had no idea the inspiration I would get from a simple box of cereal. Tommy had bought me an autographed copy of bodybuilders Bob and Rod Jackson-Paris' autobiography, *Straight from the Heart*, and ... you guessed it ... a family-size box of Kellogg's Frosted Flakes! There's no way that Tommy could have known about my toxic relationship with Water Tiger, the owner of my power, my confidence, and my strength. Tommy had inadvertently given me a gift that suddenly forced me to see Water Tiger as a source of success rather than failure. He had no idea that the gift that was meant to be funny turned out to be the one gift that, through the laughter, helped me to see the person that I could become if I strived to never let those flakes get soggy. I was more than just okay, I was GR-R-R-R-R-EAT; I was also lying to myself, but many times that's what got me through the day.

And that got me to thinking, *If I was lying to myself about almost everything else, maybe I was also lying to myself about my own "fifteen seconds of fame?"* What if Andy Warhol's designation of fame was WRONG? What if I misunderstood the intent of his quote from the beginning? What if I was wrong about fame my entire life? What if fame was a feeling or an emotion rather than an achievement or an accomplishment? In the vein of his own verbiage, it would seem as though fame was whatever we decided it should be; being quoted and then misquoted sometimes had its advantages. So, what if the word *fame*, as defined by scholastic text, was no longer applicable when it was used to reflect upon defining moments in our own lives? Fame could mean many things: awakening, justice, honor, service, trust, redemption, pride, integrity, and of course, FABULOSITY!

What if I could just start over and try to re-experience all of those moments of fame that I had created and then missed? What if I could make my past life mean something different in my future life? What if I could create yet another "fifteen seconds of fame" over and over? Could we recreate our own fame in the image that we had envisioned our fame to be? Who was gonna tell us "no?"

I knew that I didn't have very long to live, but from that day forward, I was determined that the rest of my life—no matter how short or long—

would be FABULOUS! Fame no longer mattered, at least not by its old definition, but FABULOSITY did!

celebrating with Tommy Fontenot–1995

funeral crypt with inscription (just not the day I died)– 1995

CHAPTER 17

AWAKENING

(That Time I Was A Poster Boy)

I tested positive for HIV, the virus that causes AIDS, in Houston, Texas in July 1987 (patient number 026415). Meanwhile, in my hometown, a small group of gay men and straight allies volunteered their time and expertise helping those living with HIV/AIDS by providing food, clothing, toiletries, and other necessities, often from the trunks of their own vehicles. They named themselves "Lafayette Cares," but had no office space nor phone number; the volunteers kept in touch with each other, and "neighbors helping neighbors" is probably the best way to describe the services they provided. The Lafayette gay community was (and still is) very small, and the area in general was (and still is) VERY conservative; so, the HIV/AIDS community became its own nucleus and those offering to help were stretched to their limits very quickly. The generosity of both time and money dwindled even further when some of the volunteers soon became clients, and the caregivers became the patients needing care.

By the time I moved back to Lafayette in December 1994, this once tiny group of friends who just wanted to help the community to heal had grown into a non-profit organization called Acadiana CARES (Concern for AIDS Research, Education, and Support). I reached out for assistance, not knowing what kind of help I needed or wanted. I knew that I wanted to make a difference (at least that's what I needed to tell myself), but just didn't know how. I figured that if I would soon be dead anyway, then at least I could make the time that I had left actually worth something.

It was the staff and volunteers at Acadiana CARES that gave me the backbone I needed to continue believing in hope; it was the first time since my diagnosis that I believed that maybe there was a little more living to do before it was my time to leave this earth.

As part of my therapy, I told my story to anyone and everyone who would listen. I died just a little more every day, slowly becoming every other person with AIDS who would one day look in the mirror and not recognize himself; sooner rather than later this disease would ravage my body and my soul until I was dead; but until then, I was determined to somehow make a difference for those left behind. I knew what I looked like, and it was quite dreadful; I thought, *maybe if people SAW what AIDS looked like, then maybe more people would pay attention.* I was no longer afraid to be seen in public and getting out into the community and talking about things that I actually knew about was paramount to my survival. I wanted people to know what someone living with HIV looked like and what someone dying from HIV looked like: ME.

With the help of the case managers and volunteer coordinators at Acadiana CARES I crafted an informal "script" to help me to tell my story and to give a face to the horrid disease that was killing me. At the time, there were several speakers involved with the CARES mission who were doing their level best to educate the public and correct the misinformation and disinformation of the past; however, there was no one at the time (at least publicly) afflicted with AIDS to deliver the message that I so desperately wanted to share. Yes, I had AIDS, but was exhausted in allowing the virus to consume the definition of *who I was* rather than just a health condition with which I was living (dying). At the time, I didn't know the difference; living and dying, in my mind, had become warped synonyms of each other.

I kept that script. It began, "... Please be quiet and very attentive so that I don't have to speak so loudly," as my voice as well as my body had become frail and fragile. I continued, "I am what somebody with AIDS looks like. Here's my story." Immediately, I had peoples' attention, and for the next hour or so, in a concerted effort to stop the spread of the virus that was killing me, I intertwined my own life story along with facts about HIV/AIDS and focused on prevention. My first few talks were given to welcoming audiences in the gay community and in the medical profession. I made the disease more personable, more relatable. I wanted them to understand that, even though we knew that we were dying, we weren't dead yet, and our feelings were still very much alive. By the end of my talk, I was both physically and mentally drained, and the audience was mostly silent as they dried their tears. Evoking pain and raw emotion wasn't necessarily my intent, but their reactions to my talk proved that they were listening while simultaneously revealing their empathy. They flooded me with tears of love and caring.

As someone living with AIDS, and as I had seen others with AIDS die before me, one of the feelings that we missed so very much was the sense of touch. We still lived in a world (in South Louisiana) where people believed that AIDS was contagious, and that it could be spread by simply rubbing elbows or shaking hands. I was always comforted at the end of each speech by several of those in attendance wanting to give me a hug; I was happy to oblige. Feeling the caress of those soft, warm hugs more than compensated for my drained brain and weary body; sadly, they also reminded me of so many of my friends who had already died with no one to hold them.

Within a month or so of speaking, Acadiana CARES received repeated phone calls requesting my presence to teach a class. I was fortunate enough to give classes at elementary schools and high schools (though I was forbidden in Lafayette Parish Schools), the University of Southwest Louisiana (now University of Louisiana-Lafayette) psychology department and nursing department, and ... get ready for this one ... Catholic schools and Catholic churches. Scandalous!

I shared my own story, in my own way, in the way that it needed to be told; and always hoped to inspire at least one person to actually understand that I was giving them the benefit of having the life that I never had, and to live their lives to be better and to do better. Over the years, I received hundreds of letters from students; these cards and letters kept me going. These children inspired me to continue to do the right thing for the right reasons.

It was during this time that I made arrangements for final preparations for my death and burial. To everyone's surprise, I opted for what was left of my body (I'm an organ donor) to be placed in a plain pine box. I know you all thought that I would go with the Liberace collection, but not this time. What's the point of having glitz if nobody can see it? As for the glamour, I figure I brought just enough of that all on my own. You know, as they always say in Texas: "The higher the hair, the closer to God!" Well, as you may have noticed, I'm completely bald, so unless y'all put a damned wig on my head, I may need a little more help getting there. So, I bought this *"crypt"* (pronounced "crib") up on the penthouse level. (You would have expected nothing less from me.) I figured I might need a head start on to the rest of my life on the other side. But don't worry about me, I'm already singing and dancing with you! I'm already here, and I found **FABULOUSNESS** unlike anything I've ever seen before! And I love it!

[Sidebar: Knowing that I would never have children of my own, being called teacher, confidante, and uncle was always music to my ears, especially since I would not live long enough to be anything else. I treasured all of the time I spent with all of my students and other relatives, whether or not they considered themselves to be family.]

It was spring 1995 when Sharon Shupert Richard shared the exciting news that she was pregnant; this child would be my younger brother's first child, though he would later adopt Sharon's older daughter from a previous marriage. With love in their hearts, mixed with a bit of sorrow no doubt, I was asked to be the godfather for this new life about to be born; I would have yet another moniker associated with my name, *parrain*, which is French for "godfather." I was happy about being asked to be godfather, but lost as to why I was asked to serve a conservatorship-type role in this new child's life. The role of the godfather in the Catholic faith is to serve as a steward to ensure that, through baptism, this child will be raised to know ONLY the god of the Roman Catholic religion. I was honored that they thought of me and chose for me to play such a pivotal role in the spiritual development of their child, though ulterior motives abounded with questions. They knew that I was dying too, and perhaps this was their way of allowing me to feel special in my time of death, knowing that I would never really be able to fulfill the responsibilities of being godfather, especially since I don't believe in religion and am particularly abhorred by the Catholic church. Regardless, they asked, and I accepted ... for exactly the same reasons.

Ophelia Katherine was born in early fall 1995; since no one was ever gonna call me "daddy" (at least not on the familial level), I relished being Parrain Ted. I would never get to raise her, nor expose her to the Catholic religion, but made it my mission (whenever possible) to expose her to the spiritualities of the world, though her father made that purposefully difficult for me.

I recall that early on in the baby-naming process, the name Ophelia Jane had been considered for a while; I quickly stepped in to nullify that choice, "No, we ain't havin' no baby that you can nickname 'O.J.' Damn, just last year, that dude was chased down a California freeway in a white Ford Bronco claiming he didn't kill nobody … which we all know was *crap*. There ain't no way I'm gonna let y'all do that to that child." I loved the middle name of Katherine, since it was similar to her mom's middle name; as for Ophelia, I haven't a clue, but I thought it was pretty. Ophelia Katherine was the name under which she was baptized into the Catholic faith. Other than the stating of her actual name, I just mouthed the rest of the words in this sham of a baptism, pretending that they meant something to me. The "spirit of awakening" is what I planned to teach this child born into a family where dysfunction was the norm. I made it my ultimate goal that, as long as I was alive, my little Ophelia Katherine was always going to be "okay" (O.K.)

As a spokesperson for HIV/AIDS prevention, I was asked to do a story for Lafayette's local newspaper, *The Daily Advertiser*, in November 1995, but was emotionally torn about whether or not to allow my life story to become bigger than me. I was okay with sharing my story with students, nurses, faculty members, and others who had invited me to speak. But now, I was being asked to be a featured profile in my hometown's only newspaper. I wasn't ashamed anymore; I knew that I was dying anyway, and shame was one of those emotions I no longer needed. But it wasn't me that I was worried about, it was my parents.

Many years ago, my parents had bought a brand new dining room table (an upgrade from the Formica dinette from my childhood). Dad sat at the head of table, and Mom sat directly to his right; my assigned chair was to Dad's left. It was supper time, and my Mom had cooked cornbread. I love cornbread and milk coated with tons of sugar, my Dad often added figs, too (from that fig tree back on the farm). Once the clinking of silverware stopped and supper was over, my Mom would usually pick up the bowls and utensils to place them in the sink to be washed later. But on this night, no one stood up. My parents have always been very intuitive, and I think they knew that I had something to say. *Was it the tremble in my hands that they noticed, or my one eyebrow that always got a bit cock-eyed when I was nervous, or just the fact that I had not said a single word during supper, allowing the noise of the big spoon clinking against the cereal bowl to speak for me?* Mom asked what was wrong.

That night I had a very long talk with my parents about how excited I was to be featured in the newspaper, but I also needed to make them aware of the ramifications that the story might have on their own lives; both Mom and Dad encouraged me to do whatever I thought was best and they were unwavering in their support. (I know that they were hoping that by saving others, I was saving myself; they would soon learn that was not the case. I would learn that lesson much too late also.)

I remember telling them that: "Whenever this story hits the newsstands, you're gonna find out who your 'real' friends are." But it wasn't just that. I was worried that I would probably be dead soon, and that my parents would have to deal with not only my death, but the disengagement of and retribution from all of these people who they thought were friends, now willfully shunning them. Have you ever had a weird feeling (premonition) that something horrible was going to happen, and you knew it would happen, and there was nothing you could do to stop it, and you didn't want to be right, but you knew you were? If I agreed to do this feature story in the local newspaper, I knew that my parents would lose some of their best friends, and that there was nothing I could do to stop it. I didn't want to be right, but knew that I was!

Dad held Mom's hand and said, "Well, I guess it's best that we know now who our real friends are." That's what they needed to believe; I knew that they couldn't handle the truth. They were adamant that they wanted me to do whatever it was that I felt I needed to do, but even they could never have fathomed the amount of rejection they were about to endure. In this case, being wrong wasn't the problem. Being right was!

I met journalist Walter Pierce at a local restaurant in downtown Lafayette. I thought he was hot, then realized three things simultaneously: 1) he was probably straight, 2) I looked like death, and 3) I was only there for an interview. (*I wasn't wrong.*) I had conducted several radio and television interviews over the past two years (mostly about HIV education and not about my own diagnosis); but my meeting with Mr. Pierce was the first time that I felt as if someone actually listened to me as I spoke, and could actually feel some of the things I was feeling. I made it a point to let Mr. Pierce know about my concerns regarding the reactions and potentially negative responses from my parents' friends.

Mr. Pierce was a newspaper reporter, yes, but he was much more than that; he took the time to get to know ME ... all of ME, not just Colt Michael the stripper, not just Ted A Richard the retail executive, not just Colt Michael the drunken drug addict, and not just Ted A Richard, that guy with AIDS. Mr. Pierce and I chatted over lunch for several minutes before he even asked me a single question. Mr. Pierce was more than just a reporter chasing a story, he was real person who wanted to do his utmost best to tell the true story of another real person who just happened to be dying from this horrendous disease called AIDS.

Through his skillful wording and brilliant storytelling, Mr. Pierce made Ted A Richard a *real* person, and not just another gay dude with AIDS. He told my story with empathy and understanding instead of vilification and hatred (to which I had become somewhat immune). He shared my story in his words almost better than I could have told it myself. In the end, regardless of the words he used and my story that he told, it didn't even matter; my parents were still shunned by several people who they thought were good friends, though they had done nothing wrong. They just had the horrible misfortune of raising a once-successful son, who grew up to be an alcohol- and drug-addicted gay stripper who was dying of AIDS.

I was the featured profile on the front page of Lafayette's *Daily Advertiser* on Wednesday, November 15, 1995. I was happy to still be alive to tell my story, though I was now a mere skeleton of the man I once was. The story had an unintended consequence. I never meant for it to be misconstrued as being the *only* story of people living with HIV/AIDS; however, I was now the "poster boy" of HIV/AIDS in the Acadiana area. I didn't think that my willingness to open myself up to ridicule and ignorance was courageous; far from it. My main impetus for agreeing to do the article was somewhat selfish; I was tired of hearing the silent parts out loud. I heard many of the rumors around town; my parents even got a phone call from one of my "friends" because he had heard that I was dead (he only wished). I knew the gossip, and mostly chose to ignore it, but heard the whispers, where townsfolk babbled on about me as if I was invisible, saying things they hoped I wouldn't hear behind their cupped hands. *Did they know that cupping their hands magnified the sound? Were they merely pretending to whisper in hopes I'd actually hear them?* It's times like these that wished I could have shut off my hearing. Just like I never wanted to be the poster boy for Little League baseball, I never wanted to be the AIDS poster boy either, but that's what happened.

Fame, in this instance, I have defined as *awakening*. The story of my "unfortunate demise" was so sensationalized that the newspaper ran the article again the following Sunday, November 19, 1995. I spent the entire weekend mostly shuttered in, remembering Dennis Thetford's death just three years prior.

The awakening revealed itself that same weekend when my friends had planned a surprise birthday party for my thirty-third birthday. Yes, that's the same weekend that Tommy gifted me that box of Frosted Flakes. This birthday party was exactly what I needed to take my mind off of the stressors of the previous week. I had not planned on a simple newspaper article having such a huge impact on my life; it was not the attention I wanted either. Though I received many calls and well-wishes as a result of sharing my story publicly, unfortunately, the loudest voices were the ignoramuses.

But this awakening helped me to understand that my message had not fallen on deaf ears, and that my mission of HIV education was just beginning. This awakening also helped my parents to understand why I had, for so long, chosen to live the life I lived in secret. This awakening forced me to take a look in the mirror and see someone I had not seen in a very long time ... a strong, determined, and resilient young man who still had a lot to offer to this world. I still belonged here. Yes, I was dying, but the man I saw in the mirror decided that he was going to LIVE. I needed to continue spreading the message of HIV/AIDS prevention. I had to believe that in order to make the world make sense to me, because at the time, almost nothing else did.

As a kid, my own community laughed at me because I did a cartwheel onto first base. I no longer was afraid of ridicule, persecution, or any other emotion which, in the past, would have sent me into a downward spiral. Now I could hold my head up with pride, knowing that I was doing something good for myself and the community. And yes, I would do another frickin' cartwheel, but this time, at home plate!

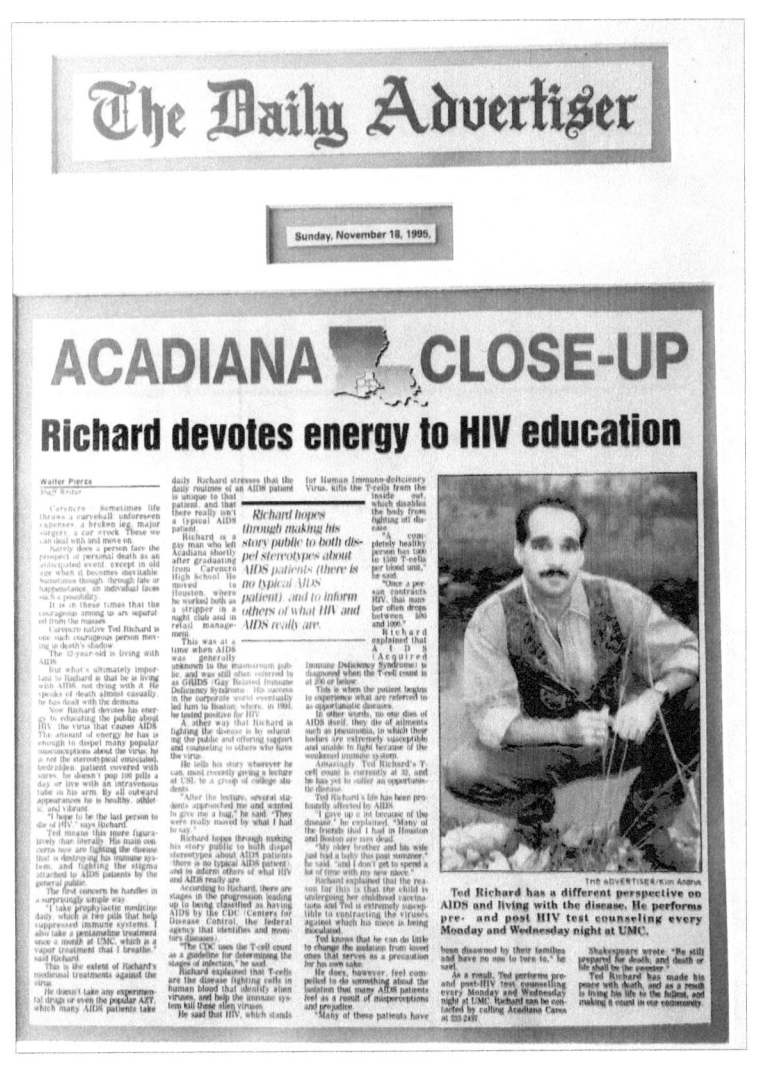

Daily Advertiser cover story – (courtesy The Daily Advertiser)

CHAPTER 18

JUSTICE

(That Time I Donated Blood)

During that same surprise birthday party, I received a surprise that no one, even my family, expected: a random phone call from my birthday twin, Kevin Nunez, who moved back to Louisiana to be with his family. We'd lost touch when I fled Houston, then failed in New Orleans, and moved to Boston. He read my feature in the newspaper and took a chance at calling me at my parents' house. As with many true friendships, we picked up right where we left off; the difference was that neither of us had told the other about our HIV diagnosis. I drove down to meet with him in his hometown the following week; we took one look at each other and both knew the decaying path we each were on.

I visited Kevin several times and even helped him to get set up at the local HIV clinic so that he could get the care and help that he needed; he was much worse off than I was, but neither of us knew that. We'd plan things to do together, like go to the zoo or maybe dinner and a movie, just to get us out of the house; but those plans almost never came to fruition because one or both of us would be just too fatigued. We'd usually end up spending the night together watching movies, eating popcorn, and sipping sodas before falling asleep.

It was during one of these visits that Kevin and I sat together on his couch watching the latest episode of *Dynasty* starring John Forsythe and Joan Collins. I was always so excited to tell the story of when I met Ms. Collins, and how she had her assistant take my picture and ask for an autograph; and I was certain to include the part where she railed on me for not properly greeting a lady. We laughed together as we scarfed down another bite of vanilla ice cream.

Due to our HIV medications, milk and other dairy products were usually off limits since they often created adverse reactions. But we didn't care; we were dying anyway. If we wanted to eat ice cream, we damned-well ate ice cream! We tried to pretend that we didn't know what was about to happen. We could only laugh at ourselves for the inevitable shit-show that occurred during each of the commercials; sometimes one of us wouldn't make it back to the couch in time, so we just decided to leave the volume up on the television. Heaven forbid we'd miss anything that Alexis Carrington said; Joan Collins would be mortified!

Kevin and I truly enjoyed spending time with each other, and the friendship we forged over the years never waned. But now, we needed each other more than ever, and we recognized that we needed to rely on each other, because no one else understood just exactly the emotional merry-go-round we were on. We were just happy when we awoke, and were aware that we could still *feel a brand new day*. [Did you really think I wouldn't have at least one "Dorothy" reference? This one is from *The Wiz*, a modern-day musical version of *The Wizard of Oz* starring Michael Jackson and Diana Ross.]

After one of those visits when I spent the night with Kevin, I needed to drive back to Lafayette the next morning for a doctor's appointment that afternoon; he knew that I was coming back on the following day. That was the last time that I got to hug him, and say, "Bye, see ya later." (I never told him the truth about my upcoming appointment.)

Having traveled the country, I was well aware of the jokes and false lore about the people of south Louisiana: no, we don't take boats to school; no, we don't (usually) chase our chickens for breakfast, and no, we definitely don't marry our first cousins (okay, there was this one time that I heard about, but nobody talks about it anymore). The tall tales of Cajun Country have been well-documented over hundreds of years; possibly the best known of these was Henry Wadsworth Longfellow's *Evangeline*. This epic poem recreated Evangeline's search for her long-lost lover, Gabriel, during *Le Grand D'errangement* (the expulsion of the Acadians from Nova Scotia). The setting for this beautiful love story was St. Martinville, Louisiana, where the "Evangeline Oak" still stands as an homage to celebrate the meeting place of the supposed real-life lovers Louis Arceneaux and Emmiline Labiche, of whom the poem was purportedly written about.

More than 240 years later, another pair of star-crossed lovers found each other in Lafayette, Louisiana. Only theirs was not the love of misguided travelers finding their way to each other; theirs was a story of forbidden love, mistrust, theft, and attempted murder.

In the early 1990s, there was a doctor at Lafayette General Medical Center (now Ocshner) who, on occasion, also treated HIV-positive patients. Dr. Richard Schmidt was married at the time, but had been secretly courting a mistress. The relationship was rocky at best, but they were in love, and nothing could keep them apart, at least at the beginning. But after about ten years of waiting for her Gabriel, his mistress, Janice Trahan, wanted to end the relationship. For nearly ten years, Dr. Schmidt had promised his Evangeline that he would divorce his wife so that they could be together forever. (*Oh, come on Janice, it's been ten fucking years! You're just now figuring out that he ain't leaving his wife?*) I guess ten years was her breaking point, and when it became clear that Dr. Schmidt would not leave his wife, Janice called it quits for good. Sadly, to deny proof of any extramarital dalliances, Miss Trahan was forced to have four abortions during the course of their romance, which later also produced one son.

Coincidentally, Dr. Schmidt also saw Miss Trahan as a patient, and administered B-12 shots to her on a regular basis; but once Janice ended the relationship, their doctor-patient "privileges" went away also. Until one random night (August 4, 1994), when Dr. Schmidt phoned Miss Trahan in a last-ditch attempt to salvage what was left of their tattered relationship; he was really going to leave his wife this time. (*Don't do it, Janice! Don't do it!*) Dr. Schmidt prepared a dose of B-12 to inject into Miss Trahan that night, in addition to their regular sessions, but things did not go quite as Janice had planned. (*I told you, Janice.*)

Within a couple of weeks, Janice became violently ill, developed chronic fatigue, and began losing weight for no apparent reason. It took only one blood test to reveal that Miss Trahan was now infected, not only with Hepatitis C, but also with the HIV virus. While it took her ten years and four abortions to realize that he was never leaving his wife, it took her only a split second to realize that she had been duped by her now ex-boyfriend's feeble attempt at reconciliation. Miss Trahan claimed that Dr. Schmidt purposefully injected her with Hepatitis C and

HIV-tainted blood while administering one of these "Vitamin B" shots; and that this was premeditated murder. (In Longfellow's *Evangeline*, Evangeline went mad when she discovered that Gabriel fell in love with another. Dr. Schmidt's anecdote for heartbreak was much more sinister; he would be certain that Miss Trahan would never fall in love again. She would be dead, at his hands.)

A look at Dr. Schmidt's medical files revealed that he had contact with only one of his HIV-infected patients on the date that Miss Trahan was fatally injected. That patient was a friend of mine named Donn McClelland, and Donn had given a blood sample during that day's office visit. It was alleged that Dr. Schmidt took that blood sample from Mr. McClelland, then mixed it into a B-12 shot, and later injected Miss Trahan with a lethal dose of Hepatitis C (from a different patient) and HIV. (*I'm worried about going to jail for not telling someone that I'm HIV-positive, and this dude is going around injecting his ex-girlfriend with it ... insane!*)

In preparation for Dr. Schmidt's arrest, all of Miss Trahan's former love interests were tested for the virus, and all were proven to be HIV-negative. This gave more credence to the fact that Miss Trahan was intentionally exposed to the HIV virus by Dr. Schmidt. (Being that Mr. McClelland was a gay man in a stable homosexual relationship, he was excluded as one of Miss Trahan's sexual partners immediately.) But how the prosecution was able to prove this theory is a true lesson in the advancement of forensic science. It was the first time in forensic history that viral DNA was used to prove a link (or exclude a link) between two persons with HIV in a criminal trial. Here's how it was done.

As I spoke about in my lectures on HIV/AIDS, I often explained the mutation of the HIV virus, and how it was constantly changing. But even with all of these continuous mutations, each strain of HIV has its own distinctive DNA marker. The prosecution had to prove "beyond a reasonable doubt" that the strain of the virus which infected Miss Trahan could ONLY have come from Mr. McClelland and COULD NOT have come from any other source.

To that end, a small group of thirty-two HIV-infected individuals were selected to have their HIV DNA markers distinguished from each other. All of those DNA markers were compared to those of Mr.

McClelland and Miss Trahan. There were no matches. It was then proven that the HIV DNA markers for Mr. McClelland and Miss Trahan matched almost exactly. Although much more evidence of this intentional infection of HIV was provided throughout the course of the trial, it was the DNA from those thirty-two donors which helped to build the foundation of the entire case against former Dr. Schmidt.

Schmidt was finally arrested on July 23, 1996, more than a year and a half after Miss Trahan had tested positive for the HIV virus.

Until today, no one knew the names of any of the anonymous HIV donors for this landmark case. Now you know that one of them was ME! Yes, that was the "mysterious" doctor's appointment that I could tell no one about, including Kevin. I am so very proud to have played a part in convicting someone of intentionally infecting an innocent person with HIV/AIDS.

Fame, in this instance, defined as *justice*, is one of the proudest moments of my life. I did my part in helping to convict a man who had committed a horrific crime and brought him to justice. And as for Miss Trahan, "Evangeline" has found the love of her "Gabriel," her real true love, and is still living the fairy tale of "happily ever after."

On October 23, 1998, Schmidt was sentenced to fifty years in jail for attempted second-degree murder. He is now serving out his sentence at the Hunt Correctional Center in St. Gabriel, LA (*ironic, huh?*).

[Update: In 2015, after seventeen years served, he was unanimously denied parole. He is eligible for early release in 2023. The Trahan family will most certainly contest.]

My sincerest hope is that Miss Trahan (purposefully not using her married name) will outlive the former Dr. Richard Schmidt and watch him rot in the jail cell he created for himself.

All these years later, I'm still wishing the exact same fate of justice for that former priest who took from me something that he knew I would never give willingly and lost my respect and trust in the process. Maybe they have green ropes in jail too!

disgraced former Dr. Richard Schmidt in handcuffs (courtesy The Acadiana Advocate)

CHAPTER 19

HONOR

(That Time I Saw a Rainbow)

I looked forward to seeing Kevin again following my "doctor's appointment for justice." But, on the very next morning of December 14, 1995, my parents received a phone call from his parents. Kevin had died during the night. I'd lost yet another friend to this horrible illness; I hoped (no, *begged*) that I would be next so that I didn't have to see anyone else die this way. We were only thirty-three years old.

When I arrived for his funeral, Kevin's parents pulled me aside; they had something that Kevin said he had wanted to give to me. They handed me a card that was ivory in color with fascinatingly detailed artwork of a rainbow of flowers including daffodils, gladioli, irises, and others that I didn't recognize. Inscribed on the card was the following message: "More and more, I realize that's just the way you are—sensitive, thoughtful, always willing to give of yourself with warmth and integrity. So, I hope you know that when I say, 'thanks for being you,' I sincerely mean it from the heart. Whenever I need your support, you're there to help out of genuine interest and concern." Then, I read Kevin's own words that he inscribed especially for me. He wrote: "This card says everything I can say except one thing, and don't forget it. 'I LOVE YOU'" Thanks for everything, KEVIN!

I was completely bereft by this point, but even Kevin's parents didn't know exactly why. In all of the years that Kevin and I knew each other, not once had either of us ever said those three little words to each other. I knew exactly what this "I love you" meant, which is something I would forever hold within my heart. It was impossible to put into mere words the impact these three simple syllables had on me, especially since we seemed to find it so difficult to say to each other when we were both alive. And I now realized he was never going to hear those same three words from me; at least not until the next life. How I wished my next life would begin sooner rather than later!

Kevin's parents informed me that one of his final wishes was that I would be a pallbearer for his funeral service. I nearly fell to my knees; to be honored in such a way as someone's final wish is yet another feeling I cannot find the words to express. At the end of the services, once all of the prayers had been said and well-wishers had given their final good-byes, I can distinctly recall pulling the blue rose boutonniere from the lapel of my suit jacket, and, placing it onto the casket where Kevin laid, I softly whispered, "I love you, too!" I know he heard me.

It drizzled earlier during the day of Kevin's funeral services, and I was invited to a family get-together at his parents' house afterwards. Sitting on the front porch steps, it wasn't long before we all noticed a full rainbow arching the clear blue skies. We were all certain that Kevin was sending us a message to let us know that he was okay. I concurred, but my brain-space was taking me somewhere else entirely. I wondered if a rainbow knew how beautiful it was. I wondered if a rainbow knew that it could only be created with just the right mixture of light and water. I wondered if a rainbow knew where it ended. And I wondered why I was wondering these things.

Vivid memories of the fun times that Kevin and I shared came flooding through my mind; yes, he wanted me to see that rainbow. *But why?* I thought to myself, *why don't rainbows have shadows?* That's such a silly question, but it's true ... they don't. Maybe it's because there was never meant to be any darkness in the brightness of a rainbow; maybe a rainbow is a reflection of itself; maybe I'm just making myself think these things so I wouldn't have to deal with the fact that my birthday twin was dead.

Kevin always told me that there was something that I needed to do; I never understood what he meant, until now. I wasn't so blind as to not realize that my time to wave good-bye to this earthly plane was nearing too. I spent the past year trying to make myself feel better by sharing my story; it was like a therapy session in real time. I relished those times that I got to share with strangers my experiences and how those milestones created the person that I became. But other than the educational component, I often felt as though the rest of my story was all lies. I ended each speech on a high note of hope and inspiration; I would say "living with AIDS isn't a death sentence," but I knew that it was. I just didn't want anyone to feel sorry for me anymore; I was tired of the endless barrage of fake sympathy and prayers. They all wanted me to die, and I still wanted to die too. *What the hell was taking so long?* Dennis was dead, Steven was dead, Patrick was dead, Naomi was dead, and now Kevin was dead too. *For fuck's sake, man; could it please be my turn next?* I couldn't do this by myself anymore.

However, in Kevin's death and rebirth, he somehow revealed to me (maybe rainbows can speak too) that I still had a lot of stuff left to do. Apparently, it seemed, Kevin knew that I'd be here for a while longer; I didn't know why, nor did he give me an explanation. I just knew that I needed to make some changes if it would be some time before I was pushing up daisies. Those words, "you still have stuff to do" reverberated in my dreams for several nights; Kevin wasn't going to let me sleep until I had figured it out.

The gift that Kevin bestowed upon me as his dying wish can never be repaid, and he planned it that way. He did what he could to ensure that I didn't spend the rest of my life believing that my *"fifteen seconds of fame"* had come and gone, and that I was living the rest of my life, without him, searching for something that never existed. He made certain that he honored me in his death the way that maybe he felt he couldn't while he was still alive. It was in seeing the rainbow and deciphering Kevin's message that I vowed to embrace the man I had become, understanding that *fame*, in this instance, defined as *honor*, was what was expected of me. By honoring my existence, I also honored his memory; maybe that's what his rainbow meant.

Kevin was right, and I knew he was right; I still had something left to offer to this world. My life wasn't over yet. For far too long, I searched for something, anything, to guide my journey of self-exploration to a place where I could be truly happy. I was determined, as I allowed the parts of my soul that I had never dared let see the light of day, to finally emerge from the shadows where I kept them hidden, recollections of a life I had once led began flooding my innermost memories. Yes, I lived through some extremely horrific times, but I had let all of that negativity overcome the joy that I had once felt when I was just being myself.

My incredible, FABULOUS self!

Voila, that was it, it was my FABULOUS; I lost it all somewhere along the way; I finally grasped only the first few sparkles of the fabulousness that was left in me, and I wasn't giving up. Thank you, Kevin, the *honor* was all mine!

I'd spent the past eight years or so hiding behind the virus that was certain to (pronounced "hoping would soon") kill me. I once thought that if I didn't say it out loud, then it couldn't be true. But I quickly learned that I HAD to say it out loud. When I contracted HIV, there was not much information available (if at all); the only known facts were that you got the virus and then you died. But I was now more than eight years into my diagnosis, and not telling my sexual partner was a crime (and still is).

As sickly as I was and as deathly as I looked, it would have been unthinkable that anyone couldn't just look at me and tell that "I had the bug." I missed the sensation of another man's touch on my skin, frail as it was. I needed to know that someone could still fall in love with me; I needed to believe that someone wanted more than just sex. I had felt the pain of rejection when I was in my early twenties and healthy; the fear of rejection hurt even more since I had begun to resemble the husked out pumpkin shell of this past Halloween. But as much as I didn't want to be turned away, yet again, I knew that I would much rather weed out anyone who was "scared" of me than have to deal with their ignorance later. Yes, it was hurtful every time someone who piqued my interest shunned me for someone else who wasn't quite as honest. I'd tell myself, "It's his loss," and "I can't blame him," but it wasn't, and I did.

Cleaning out my closet became more of a realization that the young man that I once was had no room in the body I now lived in. I had to declutter myself from myself. Then I remembered my coping mechanism from so many, many years ago … I began to write it all down. I was angry with myself for not remembering this sooner, but at least now I had another new starting point.

I would just lay back and think, I don't know if you would call regurgitating foul thoughts from your salacious past as *thinking,* but I couldn't remember anything positive to say about myself. So, that's what I started writing about … the things that I remembered. The final result was a poem called, *I Remember,* and it told the story of my life … at least the parts I chose to remember. Having encountered so much death for so many years, I needed answers, but was unaware of the questions. I remembered all of those times when I failed as a friend when I could have been stronger. I remembered all of those times when I wasn't there when someone who depended on me needed me. I remembered all of those times when I lacked the courage to stand up and fight when I saw someone being mistreated. I remembered those times because now, in my time of need, I was asking for the support of others, and many of the people whom I thought I could count on were conveniently unavailable. I forgave them because they didn't know any better (that's what I HAD to believe). I also recognized my own hypocrisy of putting unrealistic expectations on others, especially since I had been mysteriously absent when they had needed me.

Acadiana CARES sponsored the sophomore International AIDS Candlelight Memorial on May 19, 1996; yet another second of *fame*, again defined as *honor*, since I was asked to give the keynote address.

Sixteen years ago, on this same weekend, I was falling down drunk at my senior prom; now I was being given the opportunity to address an audience of people who looked up to me for inspiration ... that was quite a change. This would be the perfect venue for debuting my new poem; I hoped that through the negativity in my poem and my past that I could impart some positivity and sense of direction for their future. I wanted whatever little sliver of a person that was left of me to leave a lasting impression of inspiration for the future. It was my time to die; it was their time to live!

The work that I did on behalf of the HIV/AIDS community never really had anything to do with recognition nor celebrity. I lived the life I needed to live because I knew that I was dying; I didn't want this dreadful type of "circle of life" to continue. But because of my dedication to this cause and my strides for education, I received both the Acadiana CARES Volunteer of the Year Award and the Ramona Legé Humanitarianism Award in 1996. Though the recognition was much appreciated, I still had a lot more work to do.

I know that my birthday twin, Kevin, watched from the heavens; I was happy that he (and everyone else) got to see that I was actually doing something that could possibly help the rest of us living with HIV. I hoped that he was proud of me; I'm glad that I was allowed to show the world that I still had some fight left in me. (Kevin knew I was faking it.) Thank you, Kevin, for helping me through that night; I felt your hands on my shoulders and felt your kiss on the nape of my neck; "I love you, too."

But all of the volunteerism and all of the activism didn't erase the fact that I was still fighting the demons of alcoholism and drug addiction. As much as I tried to hide my shame behind my AIDS diagnosis, the only person I was fooling was myself. While I preached and taught health and education, I sabotaged my own well-being to finally be rid of myself once and for all. I regaled to everyone my stories of "living my own truth" and having "courage through consequences." Yes, it sounded like fabulous advice, if only I would have been living it while I spoke it. I owed an apology to everyone who knew me during that time when I was lost in my own misery and found a reason to blame everyone but myself. You all deserved better, and I couldn't find it within myself to give to you what I thought I didn't have to give. Of course, I wanted to fight, but I was exhausted, so I faked it. I faked it because faking it is all I was capable of. I wanted to die too, but I couldn't even get THAT right.

All of this harkened me back to my 1980 high school prom and the aftermath of my doomed dalliances with Mr. MacIntosh; especially when he and many of my other teachers warned me that my life would become an unmanageable mess if I didn't clean up my act. They told me that I deserved the honor, only after the accomplishment had been achieved. I always knew that they were right, but there was still nothing that I could find within myself to make the struggle worth the fight. All I ever wanted was for someone to be proud of me, to be honored and glorified, I never gave them a reason. I had to believe that too; it gave me yet another excuse for my alcoholism and drug addiction. Acadiana CARES had bestowed upon me the honor; only this time, I wasn't sure that I deserved it.

Kevin had been dead for exactly one year, and I decided to travel to his hometown of Delcambre, Louisiana to visit his gravesite and pray; I still didn't have a full grasp of prayer and why people did it. As someone who was more spiritual than religious, I never believed in the power of prayer, but I did believe that there existed a force stronger than ourselves permeating through our lives and creating outcomes based on the choices that we made. I parked my car and sat for a minute to finish listening to the rest of the Tony Braxton's "Unbreak my Heart" on the radio; that song always made me cry. I dried my eyes as I made my way to the cemetery and located his mausoleum plot; I just stood there for a moment in complete silence. I wanted to tell Kevin all of the positive work I had been doing on behalf of each of us and the rest of the HIV-positive community.

All of the things I wanted to say were swirling around in what was left of my slowly deteriorating brain, and I lacked the capacity to form a complete coherent sentence. It was the first time I visited him since he died. *Was he angry that I had taken so long? Was this his "b-ass-ackwards" way of messing with me just because he could?* I didn't have an answer; then suddenly, I felt a huge pressure pushing down into my shoulders, and tension like a rubber band tightening around my head. That sensation lasted less than a second, and all of the words that had been swirling around in my head miraculously began to form cohesive thoughts and allowed me to have the conversation with Kevin that I wanted to have with him while we were both still living.

I thought that I would be angry, which is probably why I waited so long to come and visit; I apologized to him for that. I told him that I had been very busy with all of the "stuff to do" that, through his death and rebirth, had been somehow assigned to me. I told him that I was happy to help others; I also told him that I was tired ... very tired. I asked him to help me to die; he seemed to not have heard me. I stood there waiting for some sort of response which I never received; I looked up to the heavens and realized that there were no clouds. It felt as though I was a part of the sky, and the sky was a part of me; I thought I felt Kevin's embrace in the arch of my back. I had to make myself believe that; it's the only way that I could make it make sense. I turned to walk away then quickly spun back around; I placed my hand where his name was engraved, and said, "Oh, I love you, too! Thanks for **everything**!"

I hopped back into my car, happier than I'd been in quite some time. I never thought that a visit to a gravesite could lift someone's spirits, but it did. I turned on the ignition, the radio blaring (I had forgotten to lower the volume); I heard the familiar rhythms of one of my favorite songs, "Macarena" by Los Lobos. (*Well played, Kevin. Well played.*) The smiles that I thought I had lost immediately reappeared, and I was back to being my own fabulous self, at least while that song was playing.

By this time, I was spending the majority of my disability monies on drugs and alcohol. I wasn't being charged for rent or food at my parents' house, and my only expenses were my car notes and the insurance, which left me extra funds to spend frivolously. I figured that I'd be dead soon anyway, so there was no need for me to save money for the future.

I went out to the clubs, still an alcoholic and drug addict, but if this was gonna help me die quicker, then I was all about it! I always wondered how I avoided the long arm of the law for so many years, I drove drunk and high consistently for the past decade and never got caught. Although I received my first and only DUI way back in 1982, and I hadn't even gotten so much as a speeding ticket in all of those years.

I left Kevin's gravesite, and "Macarena" was still blaring from the speakers as I drove out of the tiny town of Delcambre. Renewed with the spirit of Kevin's presence, I was invincibly fabulous. Until … I heard the sirens behind me. I pulled over onto the side of the road to allow the local police to pass, but he didn't. Instead, he pulled up directly behind me and instructed me to stay in the car. Same routine again: license, insurance, registration; I had them at the ready when he approached. He then asked, "Sir, do you know why I'm stopping you?" I said, "No, officer, I'm not from here, I was just visiting my friend at the cemetery." He replied, "Well, you just went straight through that red light back there." It is then that I remembered a joke that someone had told me a long time ago about how to get out of a red-light ticket.

The officer seemed to be a nice young man, and I was still full of "Macarena" spirit, so I gave it a whirl. I implored, "But officer, that light wasn't red when I went through it; it was pink, it was a pink light." Looking obviously puzzled, the officer queried, "A pink light, I've never heard of that!" I emphatically responded, "Yes officer, the light was pink. It was a-a-a-almost red, but not quite yet; so, it was a pink light." The officer, holding his sunglasses in his hands, now laughing, said, "You little shit, I wanted to give you a ticket so bad, but now

I can't. I have never in my life heard that story; now I can't write you a ticket. Damn, you're good." So, I told him about how a friend of mine had tried that joke once before, and it hadn't turned out quite so well for him. We laughed together, and he shook my hand, saying, "I can't wait until I tell this to the guys down at the station." I asked, "But please don't use my name, in case I need to use it again." We laughed some more; walking back toward his police cruiser, he turned around and pointed at me, "You be careful now, and no more pink lights." I gave him the "thumbs up" in agreement. *Well played again, Kevin! Well played!*

Kevin Anthony Nunez – November 20, 1962 – December 14, 1995

CHAPTER 20

SERVICE

(That Time I Watched a Cartoon)

So now it was more than ten years since my HIV diagnosis, and I still was not dead, but I did spend the past few years trying to drink myself to death. *Why the hell was I still here? I'm ready already, just let me die in peace!* I was trying to live a life that kept me busy with volunteering, giving speeches, and helping out at Acadiana CARES, but honestly, most days I felt like I was just here, but not *here*.

I thoroughly enjoyed my speaking engagements, but weakness forced me to schedule only one lecture per week because I needed time to recuperate. After each lecture, students wrote letters to tell me how my speeches touched them. I received letters from sixth-graders, high school juniors and seniors, and college freshmen and sophomores; I read each letter with the intent in which it was written. The love and support that flowed through the words in each of their letters encouraged me to continue teaching. It was important to me because it was important to them. Those letters kept me going.

I became extremely adept at faking my pain and hiding behind drugs and alcohol. I became so great at faking it that, in 1998, I was the very first HIV-positive person appointed by Louisiana Governor Mike Foster to serve on the state's Community Advisory Committee, and later became the first (openly) HIV-positive person to serve as Chairman of the Board of Acadiana CARES. For all of the accolades I received for my advocacy work for people living with HIV/AIDS and its prevention, there was no sense of joy or fulfillment; I just went through the motions because it made everybody else feel great about me, and that's exactly what I said I needed. But even that wasn't enough; there was still something missing. If I planned on sticking around any longer (which I didn't), it was imperative that I made some drastic lifestyle changes. Yippie! Y'all are thinking I finally quit drinking and drugging! Nope ...

far from it! And you all thought it couldn't get any worse ... just wait! Fabulousness, as it turns out, is sometimes not a good thing; it's all a matter of perception.

Finally, by mid-1998, my health improved, and I was ready to go back to work. My parents knew that something was up when they saw me leaving home in a suit and tie, but they didn't ask questions. There was an opening for an assistant manager's spot at a boutique retail store named Stein Mart; and although it was way below my previous pay grade, my five-year hiatus forced a step back on the corporate ladder. It was fine.

The question I always hated answering was, "Do you have any disabilities or limitations which would prevent you from adhering to the standards of the position you seek?" My answer was: "No," and in my head, I justified my answer. *Yes, I do have a disability, but no, it will not prevent me from adhering to the standards of this position.* I interviewed with the store manager, and when the question of my hiatus arose, my stock answer was, "I moved away in 1994 to take care of family matters, which are now taken care of, and I'm now excited to get back to my retail career."

Apparently, my successes in retail management preceded me, and by the time I got home Stein Mart management had called and offered me a wonderful career opportunity, though the salary was less than half what I made at Jordan Marsh. It wasn't important. What WAS important was that I would be finally free of the wrangling of the government peeking into my private life while I was on disability; I was now happy and healthy (at least that's the perception I gave), and looked forward to a new life and new adventures. I loved being back in the retail world and was so proud for putting myself out there again, even though the past five years or so had been incredibly challenging. I continued to break out of the struggle of the stigma of living with HIV; and I had to believe that I deserved better than the hand that HIV had dealt to me, but needed to prove it to myself too.

For me, with money always comes problems. Driving home from a bar one night after work, my blurry vision played tricks on me again; it can't have had anything to do with Jack Daniels and Goldschläger and a baggie of coke. I drove home on my usual route; the one with the least traffic. I saw one light turn green, but never noticed that the second light was still red (nowhere close to pink, either). I remember striking something really hard, then saw one of my tires rolling into the median of oncoming traffic before my car vaulted into a nearby parking lot. The next thing I remember is opening my car door and seeing four policemen with guns drawn and pointed directly at my head. I'd side-swiped another vehicle when I ran through the red-light going at least forty-five miles per hour. I was handcuffed and taken to jail. There was no need for a field sobriety test; and I told them I was drunk, in hopes they wouldn't search my car and find my cocaine stash. My parents bailed me out the next day, and I promised to quit drinking. I truly meant it when I said it, but my selfish mind had other plans.

In court, my DUI was reduced to a reckless driving charge (thankfully, my previous DUI from that obnoxious night at The Sting back in 1982 had fallen off my record) and I was sentenced to one-year probation, a mandatory Alcohol/Addiction Education Program, sixteen Alcoholics Anonymous meetings, and required to pay more than $3,000 in fines, penalties, and court costs. I was also advised that, should I get another DUI within the next ten years, that this reckless driving offense would be automatically upgraded to a first-offense DUI. I signed on the dotted line to agree to those terms of my release.

The news of my recent DUI made for quick gossip fodder at Stein Mart, and I was reprimanded by upper management, since my accident had been on the news and the negative impact could affect my performance as a manager and sully Stein Mart's good name. Honestly, that was just bullshit. I loved my job at Stein Mart, but I knew that my time there was limited; I had to get outta there, and fast.

Soon after this, in mid-2000, I received a great offer from VF Factory Outlet to move to San Marcos, Texas, and jumped at the chance to try something new with a change of scenery. It was still retail, but it was also something new and exciting, a different kind of retail. I started off as an assistant manager, but with my extensive background in retail management I was quickly recognized as an up-and-comer. As with many large, mostly male-driven corporations, many deals were made on the golf course. Problem was, I didn't play golf. One afternoon in the summer of 2001, the CEO of the company visited our store to meet with the regional manager and the store manager; then I was called into the meeting. I was nervous as hell. I had no idea why I would be a part of this meeting.

So, there we were just the four of us sitting in a very small office, and all three of them looking at me. The CEO looked at me and started asking me questions about how I liked the company, where I saw myself in five years, and what my aspirations were. And then the dreaded question came up. "So, Ted, we're going to play golf tomorrow afternoon, would you like to join us?" Without missing a beat I replied, "Look, I really don't play golf. I tried once but I hit my ankle with the club instead of the ball. I haven't played since. And I really don't understand how y'all can find that to be relaxing. Trying to hit a little bitty ball 200 or 300 yards into this little bitty hole. That's stressful as hell, I'd rather be at work." Then I continued, "Now I'd be happy to drive your little golf cart and be your caddy, but please don't ask me to put that little bitty ball into that little bitty hole." He said "Okay," and asked me to leave the room. There was an immediate a roar of laughter after I closed the door behind me.

The CEO called me two days later and offered me my first store managerial position. I was shocked, because no one ever received a call from the CEO unless it was bad news. He wanted to call me personally to tell me because; one, everyone at the store had spoken so highly about me; but two, because my story about putting "that little bitty ball in that little bitty hole" was so hysterical. He said he had almost never heard anyone be so brutally honest about not wanting to play a round of golf; and then he said, "You know, you're right, it is kinda stressful!" And no one ever asked me to play golf again.

A couple of years later, the late comedian Robin Williams summed up the game of golf even better than I could have; I wish I'd have thought of all this in that meeting with the CEO. You can check out his golf commentary from his 2002 show, *Robin Williams, Live on Broadway* on YouTube.

Regardless of my golf aversion, I moved up quickly in the company and soon became store manager of several of the largest outlet stores in the country. With the VF Corporation, which owned during my time with the company, Dickies, EastPack, Jansport, Jantzen, Lee, Nautica, The North Face, Reef, Vanity Fair, and Wrangler, I was able to live in the suburbs of Austin, San Francisco, Dallas, Fort Worth, and Baton Rouge, and manage some of the highest volume stores in the company. And even though I loved my new career path and enjoyed all of the new cities and experiences I was afforded by working with VF Outlet, my family still always came first.

Being the greatest uncle and godfather that I could be made me feel part of my family, and I had not been shunned by anyone in my family. All of them were educated on HIV/AIDS transmission, and they were not afraid of allowing their children to spend quality time with me. Over the years, I witnessed many victims of HIV excommunicated from their families, and witnessed the trauma they suffered as a result. Not only that, no one would even touch them (not even a hug or a handshake). Many of them ended up homeless and destitute.

My family made sure that fate never happened to me, and they took all the proactive measures they could to ensure that I was still loved and cared for. Never underestimate the power of a HUG! I got to spend so much time with my nieces and nephews; and I cherished each and every one of them. Because they were all still children, they never understood that I was dying, so they never realized what each moment I spent with them meant to me.

One day I was babysitting three of my four nieces; I absolutely LOVE them, but sometimes they could get to be a bit unruly. But one of the great things about being an uncle was that you could have all the fun with them, and very seldom need to be the disciplinarian. For some reason, the girls were feeling particularly rambunctious on this day, and I was tired, and needed to rest. I saw this weird cartoon come on the television, and I said, "Oh my gosh girls, it's *SpongeBob SquarePants*! ... this is Uncle Ted's favorite, favorite show! Let's watch it!" Within seconds, all of the girls were completely silent, and we watched a *SpongeBob SquarePants* marathon. I probably dozed off a couple of times without them noticing. From that moment on, I knew exactly how to keep the girls quiet.

And every year ... for my birthday, for Christmas, for Father's Day, Gay Uncle Day, or for any other special occasion, I would get *SpongeBob SquarePants* memorabilia. I had *SpongeBob SquarePants* pajamas, socks, ties, pins, shirts, towels, and almost any other thing that had a *SpongeBob SquarePants* reference. This tradition went on for years and years and years.

It was not until my nieces graduated from high school that I admitted I actually hated *SpongeBob SquarePants*, and that I had actually never even heard of the cartoon until that day it aired on the television. I finally told them the truth. "I just wanted you to be quiet, and that's what worked." We all had a great laugh about that, and we still do today. I call that "good uncle-ing!"

It wasn't until years later when I began watching *SpongeBob SquarePants* reruns that I realized how incredibly and fabulously gay it was. I mean, really? A frickin' sponge that lives in a pineapple on the bottom of the sea who's favorite pastime is blowing, er ... bubbles, a best friend named Patrick Star (that's a porn name if I've ever heard one), a boss named Mr. Krabs who has a daughter, Pearl, that's a sperm whale (you can't make this shit up ... pearl necklace, anyone?), and takes boating lessons from Mrs. Puff (translated to drag queen who loves "sea" weed). If I'd have realized the frivolity and campiness of the cartoon show, I'd have been a much more intent listener, knowing that my little nieces were much too young to understand all of the adult innuendo. Alas, now I get to enjoy *SpongeBob SquarePants* all over again.

Of all that I have accomplished in this life, being a fabulous uncle and a fantastical godfather are roles of which I am most proud. I am relieved to know that they were all too young to realize just exactly how sick *parrain* Ted was, and how he would probably be dead soon. They never knew that sometimes I wished that I was already dead, and that seeing their cute, little bubbly faces made me not think so much about death as an absolute, but as a destination. I am forever grateful for the borrowed time that I was able to spend with all six of my nieces and nephews; they will now know that they saved my life when it needed saving.

My first assignment was working at the VF Outlet in Gilroy, California (just south of San Francisco) where the manager was about to be fired, but she didn't know it yet (more on that later). I worked really hard to prove myself, but things just weren't going right. I was there for less than six months and struggled; Jack Daniels and cocaine helped to relieve the pressure of failure.

On September 10, 2001, I awoke with unbearable pain in my groin area; I looked down, and my balls were the size of grapefruits. I did a key of cocaine, then drove to work. After about ten minutes, I realized that there was no way I could make it through the day and drove myself to the emergency room. I was fast-tracked through triage as the nursing staff was frantic when my blood pressure seemed erratic. They hooked me up to a machine first, and the reading was 212/140 mmHg. The nurse said the machine must have been broken, so they hooked me up to another machine and the reading was almost the same. They sent in a different ER nurse who did my blood pressure manually, and the result was even worse ... something crazy like 310/201 mmHg. She quickly ran out of the room and told me to remain calm. (Really? I mean, I just broke the blood pressure machine, and you want me to remain calm?)

The ER assistant came into the room and turned off all of the lights; then he instructed me to just sit there as calmly as possible, but this became nearly impossible when I noticed all of the doctors and nurses running around collecting supplies. I asked what was up? One of the nurses said, "Mr. Ted, all of this is for you! Your blood pressure is incredibly high and you're about to have a heart attack and your T-cell count is two." He continued, "Oh, and you have epididymitis, which is why you're so swollen down there." Within minutes, I was hooked up to monitors and IV drips of saline and other medications, they also re-dimmed the lights in the room in an attempt to soothe my nerves. I was quite certain that the morning's key of cocaine had nothing to do with my ridiculously high blood pressure; and also quite certain that I couldn't hide my drug use from the blood tests, though no one ever questioned me. So yes, I was about to die and didn't even know it; I don't even remember if I cared. I was admitted into the hospital immediately.

[Sidebar: I also had a huge secret that I had told absolutely no one. I had not been taking any of my HIV medications, nor had I seen an HIV doctor for the past three years. The side effects of the drugs were taking a toll on my body, so I just decided to quit. I figured that if I was gonna die anyway, I wasn't gonna be miserable for the rest of my limited life. Instead, I actually started to feel better, and that's how I was able to regain the energy and stamina that I needed to go back to work and get off of disability. Little did I know that decision could come back to haunt me just a few years later.]

When I awoke the following morning, September 11, 2001 and the doctor walked into the room, she asked, "Have you heard the news?" I immediately got defensive; I knew that this was a Catholic hospital and would be damned if some doctor person would start my day by "spreading the good news" bullshit. I angrily said, "I don't need no news, I just wanna know what's up." Calmly, the doctor said, "No, Mr. Ted, they blew up New York City, it's all over the news." She turned on the TV, and for the next two weeks I was stuck in this hospital bed, and the only thing to watch was the tragic news every single day about the planes crashing into the World Trade Center in Manhattan, the attack at the Pentagon, and the United Airlines Flight 93 that went down in that field in Pennsylvania.

My parents were deathly afraid of flying, so they and Jocelyn Rae would instead call the hospital to check on me. Honestly, I was grateful for having absolutely no visitors for two weeks. Sure, people feel the need to visit their loved ones in the hospital, but I just needed extra rest to recover, and company would have severely hindered my beauty sleep. The doctors were also adamant that I needed to get back on HIV medication immediately. Thankfully, many strides had been made in HIV medicine in the late 1990s and early 2000s, and I tolerated this medication much better than in the past; even though it would take some time for my body to adjust to the new protocol.

At this time, knowing my dire health diagnosis, VF Factory Outlet also afforded me an opportunity that few people ever get.

My sister's husband, Christopher, served in the Air Force, and got called to duty on the day after 9/11. She (my sister, Cassie) had no idea where he was, nor for how long he would be gone. So, also needing a safe place to recover, I called her and asked if she needed help. She said "yes," and the following week I began my road trip up the Pacific Coast Highway to Spokane, Washington; this scenic route almost made me forget the dreadful situation that we were both in.

My company had offered me a paid leave of absence under the newly approved Family and Medical Leave Act, and I graciously accepted. I spent the next four months with Cassie and their two young boys, Dominic and Daric. We did so many fun things together; and each and every one of them was a special time for me. I thought death was imminent, and cherished every minute of the time I spent with them. But at the time, they truly did not have a grasp of the dire situation that our country was in, nor my downward-spiraling health. They just knew that they missed their dad. I knew that there was no way that I could ever replace Christopher, and Cassie did everything she could to make things seem as normal as possible, even though we both knew that none of this was anywhere close to normal. Still, we tried.

It was during this time that the school on the military base was having a father/son day in one of my nephew's English classes (he was in sixth grade). For the occasion, my younger nephew, Daric, wrote a special poem for his dad, but since his dad was away at some undisclosed location, "Uncle Ted" was both flattered and thrilled when he asked me to step into his dad's shoes for just a short time (and they were huge shoes to fill). Daric was so proud when he introduced his Uncle Ted to the class, though I was under no misconception that he would have much preferred his father being there; but today, Uncle Ted had to suffice.

I watched Daric shakily open up the paper he had stashed away in his folder. He began reading to me the most beautiful, poignant poem; one that he had probably spent hours, if not days, trying to put into words exactly what he wanted to say to his dad. I couldn't (no ... *wouldn't*) cry in front of him, instead hugging him tightly before leaving the classroom. I was so proud of Daric, and couldn't wait to get home to tell Cassie about our afternoon together, but I never did. The evening came and went, and we all went to bed happier than the night before; every night was happier than the night before because each day was one day closer until their dad (and her husband) came home.

I wanted to do something special for Daric since he allowed me to step in for his dad. He didn't have to ask me to be there for him, but he did, and that meant the world to me. I thought that the best thing I could do was to return the favor and write a poem just for him. I remembered an old story that my old boss at Foley's and Jordan Marsh, Mr. Billingsley once told me about being noticed. I reworded his anecdote especially for Daric; I called it *The Parade*. Until recently, Daric and I were the only two people who knew about this special poem shared between us; it is a memory that we still share to this day.

As my final gift to the boys before leaving Spokane, I surprised them with tickets to see Disney's *The Jungle Book on Ice*. That would have been enough for them, but I also invited all their friends from school. Coincidentally, Christopher returned from his tour of duty on the same weekend, so everything about this time was very special for everyone.

My leaving Spokane, Washington in January of 2002 was bittersweet, but now their real dad was home, and it was time for them to become a family again. Although the original reason I was there was very sad; it was actually one of the happiest times of my life. I got to help raise my only two nephews during a time when they needed someone. What they didn't know was that I needed someone too. It might have seemed as if I was helping them, but they actually helped to save my life that winter. And for that, I am forever thankful!

Fame, in this instance, defined as *service*, was being the Uncle Ted that everyone expected him to be, and to come out of the closet when real work needed to be done in the laundry room. (Dominic and Daric know exactly what I'm talking about.) And, while a horrible disservice had been forced upon my sister in high school at the behest of someone she called a friend, I hopefully rectified the pain and shame that she experienced at my expense. In high school, I couldn't be there to rescue her, but this was my chance at redemption. I owed this to her, but the obligation I felt was not to heal old wounds from the past (although I'd hoped that would happen); my responsibility was to rescue a family that needed my help during one of the worst times of their lives. Whatever health crisis I was going through was nowhere near the trauma that my sister's family felt when their dad was sent off to war. I'm just happy that I could be there to somewhat soften the blow.

As for Daric, he's doing great … he's married to an incredible woman, August, with two adorably smart kids (yes, I may be a bit biased);

he's also a high-ranking officer in the United States Air Force. I'd like to think that my little story, *The Parade*, played just a tiny part in encouraging him to strive for greatness, and not stopping until he's reached the summit and can see the horizon from the other side of his vast accomplishments. His *"fifteen seconds of fame"* are just beginning; I know for a fact that his *"sixteenth second"* will be spectacular! I'd like to take this time to thank his family and him for their *service* to our families, our communities, and our nation!

University Medical Center has new advisory committee

LAFAYETTE — Twelve area community leaders were appointed by the LSU Board of Supervisors recently to serve on the University Medical Center's new Community Advisory Committee.

The committee will hold its organizational meeting in Feburary, at which time an election of officers will occur. Members serve on a voluntary, non-salaried basis.

Act 3 of the 1997 Regular Session of the Louisiana Legislature — which transferred management of the public hospital system to LSU — also provided for the establishment of community advisory committees at each of the state's nine hospitals. The committees are to assess and make recommendations on community health needs, hospital performance in meeting patient goals and any hospital plans that would result in changes to services and patient accessibility to health care.

Those appointed to the committee are: Gerald Posner of the Opelousas/St. Landry Chamber of Commerce; Sandra Purgahn of Goodwill Industries in Lafayette Parish; Larry J. Richard of the Office of Public Health in St. Landry Parish; Ted Anthony Richard of the Lafayette Alcohol Management Program and Acadiana Area AIDS Legislative Outreach Network; Lise Anne Slatten of the Woman's Foundation in Lafayette Parish; Kent Andrews of Allen Correctional Center; Martin Ducote of Vildibill-Ducote Professional Medical Corp. in Lafayette Parish; Robert Louis Eastin Sr. of Eastin Pharmacy, Inc. and Tassin Clinic Pharmacy in Evangeline Parish; Ricky Hayes of Crowley Guest House; John Hughes of Employers Health Insurance in Lafayette Parish; Joella LeBlanc of Guidry's Quick Shop in St. Landry Parish; and Lydia Thibodeaux of the Council on Developmental Disabilities advisory board and member of Families Helping Families Network.

Hospital administrator Larry Dorsey and Medical Director James Falterman, Jr. also will serve on the committee.

Governor Mike Foster's Community Advisory Committee
(courtesy The Daily Advertiser) –1998

CHAPTER 21

LEGACY

(That Time I Was a Daddy)

While the reason I was in Spokane was quite tragic, the time that I spent with my sister and my two nephews was remarkably heartwarming, but now their dad was home and I quickly made my exit so as to not overstay my welcome. Driving away was one of the hardest things I ever did. *Don't cry, Uncle Ted,* I told myself, *You can't cry in front of the kids.*

The drive back to my parents' house was long, boring, and mostly uneventful (that's a big fat lie). My medication was messing with my stomach regularly (now, that's the truth), so I was forced to make several pitstops (shit stops).

Only six months after I was unexpectedly rushed into the hospital in California, I returned to work at VF Factory Outlet at my same salary, but in a new store; this time in Mineral Wells, Texas; a suburb of Dallas. While managing this store, I also became a member of the Board of Directors at the local Chamber of Commerce, and immediately put in charge of the Ambassador's Club, a sub-committee of the Chamber that welcomed new businesses to the city. My hard work and exhaustive efforts to help the city earned me the Ambassador of the Year Award and the Board of Directors' President's Award in 2003. This was the only time, to my knowledge, in the history of the Mineral Wells Chamber of Commerce that the same person won BOTH awards in the same year.

And while I was in Mineral Wells, Texas, I also learned that I had at least two children. SHOCKER! But it's not what you're thinking!

Every year in August, Texas held a tax-free weekend to offer a respite for parents' back-to-school shopping. This was a HUGE event for retailers, and VF Outlet stores always hired an additional fifty or so employees just to help us for the entire weekend. During this time, the store was open for twenty-four hours a day for three consecutive days.

Now usually, I did all of the hiring and firing for the store, but for this event, I let my two assistants take on the task of hiring all of the temporary staff. I usually never met any of the new staff until they showed up for training.

[Flashback: As Colt Michael, I had done many, many shows in the Dallas area while I was still working at Foley's in Houston. (Remember that promise to not dance in the Houston area after my promotion?)]

So, imagine my surprise when two of the new employees were named Colt Michael. As it happens, these two high school kids grew up together, and their moms were best friends, so of course, their last names were different; but I couldn't ignore that they were both named Colt Michael. Over the course of the weekend, I met their moms, which was pleasant at first, before becoming extremely awkward. I could see it in their eyes when they realized that I was the "Colt Michael" that both of their sons had been named after. We didn't ever talk about it, but their startled looks told me everything I needed to know; they knew exactly who I was. I am fairly certain that these women never told their husbands where the name "Colt Michael" came from. I'm sure they still don't know. So ... I have at least two "kids," which is a great honor. To their credit, both Colt Michael employees were incredible workers in addition to being HOT AS HELL! (Oops, I really wasn't supposed to say that about my "kids!")

More than twenty years ago, I, as Colt Michael, spent an afternoon all alone in a Houston condo sashaying, mostly naked, up and down a flight of stairs, high on cocaine, enjoying my body and the movements of the dance, and envisioning throngs of adoring men transfixed on me in amazement. More than twenty years later, I discovered that I had two namesakes, who would grow into incredible men to carry on the legacy of Colt Michael.

Fame, in this instance, defined as *legacy*, is the realization that I (Colt Michael) made such an impression on two complete strangers who decided that he (Colt Michael) deserved a legacy, a namesake, to carry on the fabulousness of the experiences they had at one of my performances. These young men would probably never know the fabulousness of the shoes they were destined to fill, nor the fame that would come with it. My sincerest hope was that they enjoyed their own *"fif-*

THE 16TH SECOND

teen seconds of fame" and lived up to the legacy in their own "*sixteenth second*" to which they were born.

My reputation and position with VF Factory Outlet was difficult to explain; over the course of my tenure, I was usually the traveling troubleshooter. When I arrived to work at whatever store was in need of help, the previous manager had been fired, usually the previous day. I was the fix-it guy. My first day at each store was always the worst because I was walking into a hornet's nest of hate. The employees didn't like me even before they met me, so I had to prove myself repeatedly. I was truly the "Real Slim Shady" of VF Outlet, just like Eminem, the guy that everybody hated for no reason, and it didn't matter why; but, in the end, I was proven to be right. While these constant promotions (only because I made more money) showed that the corporate executives appreciated all of my hard work and determination to get things right, it made me very disliked by the employees. But I am very proud to say, that by the time I left each store, the employees loved me; I actually made their jobs easier and gave them proper raises they deserved.

I think that what made me such a great manager, is that I showed the staffs that I believed in them. I got involved in their personal lives; I wanted to know what made them tick, why they worked here, what obstacles they had in their personal lives so I could accommodate their work lives. I helped one of my employees get out of an abusive relationship, helped another receive counseling for her son who was having depression issues, and even gave him a job, and changed schedules to work around their personal lives.

My biggest regret is that I never had the chance to give a proper good-bye to any of my previous staff. I always became so personally invested in each one of my employees that I felt as though they deserved a proper good-bye. In every store I was in, after I earned their trust and respect, these employees worked so very hard to be their very best every single day. It showed in their personalities and work ethics, and they were actually happy to come to work every day. My job was done. Now it was off to the next disastrous store for me to turn around and transform.

I worked in one store one night, hopped a plane the next day, and was in my next store on the following day. I could never tell my staff that I was leaving, or where I was headed next. Bad news travels fast; if I left any clue as to my schedule, my next store would have the "heads-up" that Mr. Ted was on his way, and that was something no one wanted to hear!

Living this way forced me to move a lot, and my personal life was lonely because I never invested very much of myself in myself. My time in each city was short-lived, usually a year or less, so I chose not to make time for a personal life. But I sure as hell drank a lot, and nobody knew (or so I thought). I totaled my truck twice when I was in Mineral Wells coming home drunk from the club. And one night, I was in a wreck that I don't even remember, instead awakening the next morning with the front part of my truck bashed in and a note on my front door from the police, demanding an immediate callback. Apparently, I was involved in a hit-and-run accident, but didn't even remember leaving my house. (Mixing drugs and alcohol can do that to you.) I made everything right with the victim, and paid a hefty fine, totaling more than $5,000 in damages. But that still didn't stop me from drinking.

Then, in 2004 I was offered a most fantastic opportunity. The store manager in Iowa, Louisiana, requested a transfer to Florida. My boss knew that Iowa was only forty-five minutes from my parents' house. It was perfect. I would finally manage a store with no problems and would be close to home. But that wasn't the case; my hard-assed reputation preceded me, and I had to work even harder to prove myself to the staff. After about six months or so, things calmed down, and the store ran like a well-oiled machine; so much so that I was able to leave my store once a month to help out at another store having troubles in Gonzales, LA, about 140 miles away.

I had a great staff and we had earned mutual respect for each other, but something happened in Iowa that never happened in any other store before. Roger, one of the assistant managers, was a strapping young man with jet black curly hair and ocean blue eyes. I definitely would have contemplated more than just a few trysts with him had I met him in a gay bar, but this was work, and work always came first. One day, seemingly from somewhere out of left field (but definitely not), Roger asked me: "So, Mr. Ted, are you gay?" To which I (quickly and emphatically) replied, "Roger, my sexuality becomes your business when I am sleeping with you, and since I'm not sleeping with you, I don't see that it's any of your business!" Then he retorted, "So you're gay!" And I said, "Of course, I'm gay ... and I'm fabulous ... and don't you ever forget it!" We laughed about that a lot during the course of my stay in Iowa, and I still believe that that conversation helped to facilitate the staff's perception of me; so, I guess I owe Roger a "thank you."

Anyone who has ever worked in retail can attest to the stresses of the annual or semi-annual corporate visits; you know the ones where you spend all night at your store trying to make everything perfect so that the big bosses can spend five minutes in your area, and tell you everything you're doing wrong? If you know, then you know! And, as store manager, I not only had to make sure that the store looked great, but I also had to provide spreadsheets showing my store's progress, identifying areas needing improvement, and plans to address those issues. I mean, really it was just an unnecessary exercise, since all of this had already been discussed in the monthly meetings with my boss. But they wanted a spreadsheet, so they got a frickin' spreadsheet.

It was during one of these corporate visits in Iowa that my store underwent extreme scrutiny. I didn't know why the CEO (the same one to whom I had told that golf story) was being so tough on me. He said, "Your store looks great! How late did you stay?" And I told him, "I left at 5:00 p.m. so that I could get my paperwork ready for today. My two assistants closed last night. I could check with them." And he said, "No, let's check their timecards." I obliged (why the hell didn't he believe me?). According to their timecards, both assistants had left around 7:30 p.m., only thirty minutes after the store closed, which meant that they didn't stay extra to get ready for the visit. When the CEO saw this, he was astonished. "Your store actually looks like this every day?" And I said, "Yes sir. I've worked in retail for a very long time, and I have always hated it when we had to stay until 3:00 a.m. to get ready for a corporate visit. I always told myself that when I got my own store, we would always be ready for a corporate visit." He then just shook my hand, and said, "Congratulations, this is the best store visit that this, or any other store, has ever had; and I'm even more impressed that your store looks like this every day. Ya done good!"

A few weeks later, I received yet another phone call from the CEO; he informed me that VF Factory Outlet would soon be opening a "new concept" store near Las Vegas, Nevada. He said, "We have selected only four store managers from across the country for this temporary position, and you are one of them. You have one of the only stores in the company that I feel could actually run well for one month without your being there. We will also compensate your staff accordingly." When I announced this to the staff, they were ecstatic. To this day, I still don't know if they were happy because they were all getting a bonus or if they were just glad to see me gone for a month. Anyway, I was happy for everyone—including myself—and proud that my legacy of outstanding retail management was recognized, and that many daily routines that I had created for my own stores would be introduced as company-wide policy.

Once I returned from Las Vegas, I decided to take a week's vacation before returning to work to visit with my family, some of whom I hadn't seen in quite some time.

The last time I had seen my nephews, Dominic and Daric, was in 2001. I was happy that Christopher had since retired from the Air Force and that he and Cassie and the kids were now living closer to my parents. While I was ecstatic to have my two nephews living so close to me, I was disappointed in myself that they had to witness the scourge of the embarrassing drunkard and druggie I had become. I hoped they didn't notice, or that they were shielded from my atrocious behavior, but when your name and mugshot are on the local news, it's kinda hard to ignore.

I know that the move from Spokane and the life of a military kid to Ossun, Louisiana and civilian life was torturous for both of my nephews and no amount of preparation could have made the move to Cajun Country any less of a culture shock. Dominic was in his junior year of high school in new surroundings without the comforts of the friends and relationships he had developed throughout his adolescence in the Pacific Northwest.

As Christopher, Cassie, and the kids moved into their new home, they knew that both Dominic and Daric, who was entering eighth grade, were going to require periods of adjustment. As any child in a military family can attest, moving around the country (and sometimes the world) is a fact of life, and changing schools was an adjustment that both Dominic and Daric had learned to accept as a part of their childhood development. They grew accustomed to new cities and new schools their entire lives, but this was the first time that the change was permanent. This time they recognized that none of their future relationships would be temporary (at least not due to military transfers).

Since Daric was younger and still in middle school, he would have a few more years to forge new friendships. Dominic's get-acquainted phase would prove to be a bit more challenging. I cannot begin to imagine entering my junior year of high school in a new city knowing absolutely no one, especially considering that almost all of the other classmates had known each other since elementary school.

And from chaos often comes great ideas. It was decided that, in an effort to help Dominic stay connected with his friends both near and far, he would have an entire wall of his bedroom dedicated as his personal wall of fame, where everyone could leave their signature. This way, every night he could go to sleep knowing that all of his friends were with him, and just seeing their handwriting on his bedroom wall would flood his dreams with the pleasant memories he'd shared with all of them.

I was extremely honored that Dominic asked me to sign his wall; I knew that I could never forget all of the precious moments spent with him and Daric. My heart melted that he would think of me as his friend. Over the years, I had autographed everything from magazines to napkins to a photo in Joan Collins' album, and maybe even an "eggplant" or two. There would, however, be no signature as important as this one was going to be. My inscription simply read, *Legacy of the Future, Ted A Richard.*

When Dominic saw what I wrote, he asked what it meant. I replied, not knowing myself exactly what I meant, "One day, you will know; and when you do, the rest of your life will suddenly make sense." He shrugged his shoulders, puzzled. He looked at the inscription again and then looked back at me. I winked.

Fame, in this instance, again defined as *legacy*, was the honor bestowed upon me (Ted A Richard) as an example of the definition of true excellence in retail management. I was finally lauded for my distinct attention to detail and for my human resources acumen in ensuring that my entire staff was included in all of the accolades that I received. I always included my staff in our victories; they deserved the rewards as much as I did. Their hard work was a direct reflection of me (Ted A Richard) and the concepts they had learned under my tutelage. I remain so very proud of them.

Twenty-three years ago, I was dancing nearly naked up and down a staircase, tweaked out on cocaine and whiskey, knowing that the person I was to become could never be anyone special. Twenty-three years later, I became a retail master and a daddy; my legacy of hard work, dedication, and perfection both preceded me and proceeded me; and I couldn't have planned it better myself.

Dominic would earn his *fame* as *legacy* later in life. Hopefully, I steered him toward a more direct path to finding his *"fifteen seconds of fame"* than the spirograph of a trail I took to find mine.

"Legacy of the Future" – Dominic's autographed wall–2001

CHAPTER 22

TRUST

(That Time I Almost Killed Her)

The best and worst days of my career with VF Outlet occurred at the same time. I was managing the VF Factory Outlet in Iowa, Louisiana when Hurricane Rita struck in September 2005. The south coast of Louisiana weathered Hurricane Katrina, but the Lake Charles area had been mostly spared. Hurricane Rita, however, was planning a direct hit to the southwest coast of Louisiana and threatened all of our livelihoods ... and our lives. The mall custodian was on duty when the emergency prompter activated and alarms began blaring. It was time to evacuate ... AND NOW! I was still in the store with the administrative director and an assistant. The custodian, a paunchy man in his late 70s, was a Vietnam war veteran; he ran to the front doors of my store, which we had already locked. He banged on them frantically, so I ran to meet him. He handed me the keys to the entire mall, and yelled, "My wife is home alone, and we gotta go! Please lock up everything for me ... don't worry about the keys, I'll know you got 'em!" Mall keys in hand, I urged him on to take care of himself and his wife. We could already hear the winds howling in the near distance. I thought to myself, *"Holy shit, this Vietnam vet knows that it's time to get the fuck out! We'd better hurry!"* but said nothing to the two women who were with me.

About thirty seconds later, we heard another emergency alert from the local radio station advising that: "Every person living or staying south of Interstate 10 must evacuate immediately." We rushed to secure everything in sight and locked all of the outer doors to the mall. I wondered, *Why the hell are we putting our lives at stake when the hurricane's gonna do what a hurricane's gonna do? There ain't nothing that we're doing that gonna stop that!*

Then, we heard breaking news from the same radio station; a listener had called in and asked, "I live just north of I-10, do I need to evacuate too?" And the meteorologist, without skipping a beat replied, "No sir, you're absolutely safe; the hurricane knows to stop at I-10." (I know that he wanted his next line to be "get the hell outta there, you fuckin' idiot;" I'll bet the censors would probably have let him.)

Within minutes, the three of us were out of the mall and on our way to safety wherever we could find it. I chose to go back to my parents' house near Lafayette. While the east side of a hurricane was usually the "dirty" side, I had no other options. Hurricane Rita was so huge that going north would have been a better choice, but I had not made prior arrangements, and I'd already spent my paycheck on Jack Daniels and cocaine.

It took more than two weeks before I got back to Iowa; a local Republican congressman, Dr. Charles Boustany, had erroneously claimed that the I-10 overpass in Iowa had been destroyed, but it was intact and undamaged when I arrived. As I approached Exit 43 in Louisiana, armed officers of the United States National Guard greeted me, and upon scrutinizing my driver's license, requested the nature of my visit. I explained that I was the manager of the VF Outlet, and was there to check on my store. Fortunately, I'd placed a phone call to the local Chief of Police (with whom I had had a few late night trysts), and he'd alerted the officers that I would be arriving soon, and gave them the "okay" for me to enter the premises. (It's nice to have friends in high places, too.)

The hurricane totally destroyed the entire mall, and, unbeknownst to me at the time, there was talk that the entire mall would be shuttered; VF Outlet was the anchor store for that mall, and if we didn't reopen, then the rest of the mall would be forced to close, and hundreds of people would lose their livelihoods. The state of affairs was grim, until my boss called me and asked if I thought I could get the store re-opened before Christmas. One of my assistants, who lived in Iowa, had been able to assess the damage with me that week prior after being escorted to the mall by the National Guard. The entire area resembled what I expected a war zone would look like; everything in sight was nearly flattened, and brown was the only color the eye could see, no matter which direction you looked. The air had a stench that reeked of rotting vegetables (if you've ever smelled the kitchen when your grandma was boiling cabbage, imagine that smell amplified by ten, or even a hundred); the smell knocked us off our feet, and we got the hell outta there. We returned, nearly one hour later, wearing N-95 masks (yes, the same ones we would use for the COVID-19 pandemic) and returned to the store. Unfortunately, the stink would get trapped in our masks, and twenty minutes later, we'd be running outta the store to throw up, switch out our masks, and get back to the task of surveying the damage, which was extensive, because most of the roof had collapsed.

I called my boss and described the damage and the awful stench (which was now embedded in my clothing), and requested help. "Ted, can YOU get the store reopened before Christmas?" I took this as a challenge, and said, "Definitely." I sounded confident, though, in my head and in my heart, knew it was a nearly impossible task.

Meanwhile, there was damage to my own apartment in Lake Charles. A huge pine tree fell and blocked the street to my apartment, and by the time I reached home—the city was still under National Guard control—the entire Lake Charles area had been without power for two weeks. As I walked into my apartment with my Dad, two brothers, and my nephews Dominic and Daric, who had come to help, I detected that same smell of rotten vegetables as I had smelled in the store. We all walked in slowly to try and assess the damage, which was minimal, except for the deep freezer full of rotting meat and seafood. Thankfully we were able to salvage most of my belongings.

Being the only restaurant open after a huge natural disaster has its advantages but can also create an environment of confusion and unsanitary habits in the rush to assist all of its incredibly hungry, needy customers. This day would be no different. McDonald's was jam-packed full of people, as the drive-thru was not open due to lack of staff. The rest of my helpers (family) ordered and I ordered last: a double cheeseburger, with mustard and ketchup only, no onions, large fries and a medium Dr. Pepper. As was my usual custom, I always watched as my burger was being made; again, today was no different. I saw their attempt at an assembly line wasn't very well-oiled ... bread, mustard, mayo (wait, didn't he say *no mayo*?) ... bread, mustard, ketchup, onions, (wait, didn't he say *no onion*s?) ... bread, mustard, ketchup, meat, cheese.

They finally got it right, but something else was wrong; I quickly asked for a manager. She asked, "What's the matter?" I informed the manager, (doing my best "Karen 2020" impersonation over fifteen years before its time) saying, "Well, Ma'am, other than the fact that absolutely none of the people making the food are wearing hair caps, I have another problem. That guy touched my meat!" She questioned, "What, what do you mean he touched your meat?" I retorted, "Look at him, just look at him. He's not wearing any gloves and he's touching my meat."

Suddenly I could hear hiccoughs and guffaws in the room behind me, but I couldn't figure out what the hell they saw that they thought was so funny. "That man touched my meat, he needs to make me another burger, and don't touch my meat this time." It is then that the laughter got ever rowdier, and I turned to discover that it was my two anti-laundry guys from Spokane, Dominic and Daric, leading the charge. (And after all I had done for them, they were gonna take this time to laugh at me?) I was crushed, until they repeated, verbatim, the words that "Karen 2005" had just said: "*Don't touch my meat.*" I fell over laughing with them when I realized how unintentionally hysterical I had been.

I was glad to have had those few moments of laughter, because the task at hand when we got back to my apartment would be anything but funny. We quickly finished loading the rest of my belongings into the back of my Dad's gooseneck trailer (ya' know, the one that all the redneck farmers have); we had cleaned up all the cow shit before leaving Ossun.

As soon as I got back into the store, the demolition began. My staff (only five of us at the time) worked tirelessly to meet our daily goals, which were extensive. By the beginning of November, the store was ready to be re-stocked with all new fixtures and merchandise. I called former store employees to ask for help; and was so overcome with emotion on that first day that I literally cried. My entire former staff showed up for work, and brought their children, relatives, and friends to help. Even retired employees, like Laura Goutreaux, then in her seventies, said that I was the only person for whom she would have come back to work. I was awed, and realized that my presence made an impact on these people to the extent they helped me when I was struggling. It was definitely one of the most humbling experiences of my life.

With their help, we got the store reopened nearly a month earlier than expected, and had our grand reopening on Black Friday (the day after Thanksgiving) 2005. We broke so many sales records that the CEO called to congratulate me. I put him on speakerphone over the store's intercom so that he could congratulate the entire staff; I had not done this alone.

Twenty-two years ago, I was specifically uninvited to a funeral because the family didn't trust the person I was in their son's life, but that's on them!

Fame, in this instance, defined as *trust*, was the fact that I was the single, solitary middleman that everyone depended on; and proved that I could be trusted as the person I became. Both corporate upper management and my own team and sales staff counted on me to perform a feat that apparently VF Outlet thought no one else could achieve; I had to reopen a store destroyed by a hurricane in fewer than six weeks; peoples' livelihoods depended on it, and my reputation depended on it. Trust is what I was given by every single one of my team members, along with corporate support, to allow me to make this miracle happen. Trust is what I earned by proving that absolutely nothing was impossible if Ted A Richard was at the helm.

Now that the store reopened, I could once again enjoy my pastime and renew my relationship with Jack Daniels and his friend, cocaine; how I had missed them so.

It was a given that every Thursday night, I could be found at Crystal's gay bar in downtown Lake Charles. I wasn't a very good billiards player, but there was a straight guy, Garrett, that I would meet up with each week. Garrett was a guy that we here in the south would call "oilfield trash." He stood about 6'2" with auburn-blond, curly, shoulder-length hair and dreamy greenish-aqua eyes. I'd swear that sneakily trying to catch a glimpse of those sexy eyes had made me miss at least more than one pool shot, but I don't think he ever noticed. We'd shoot a few rounds of pool, him drinking his Bud Light in a bottle, and me drinking my usual; I'd slip off to the bathroom for a key of coke trying to signal him to follow me, but he never did. I figured that if I wasn't gonna be having sex with him, then at least we could have a few good times together. But alas, a reverse to my unfortunate incident with Theresa DeLuca, this time I was "barking up a tree that had already been pissed on." And so, it went, week after week, month after month, Garrett and I could be found at Crystal's shooting pool every Thursday night.

On this particular night, the bar was very crowded for a Thursday, but for no apparent reason. Garrett seemed to be getting perturbed at having to wait so long at the bar for his Bud Light. He was about to take his turn on the eight-ball (billiards, of course) when he stopped mid-stroke and asked, "Do you live around here? Do you have beer at your house?" My response probably caught him off-guard when I said, "Yeah, I live just a few blocks from here, but I don't have any beer." He seemed shocked that I had no liquor at my house. He said, "Aw, that's all right." He sunk the eight-ball, then said, "Let's get outta here."

We'd just arrived at my apartment when Garrett excused himself to go to the bathroom. When he emerged, he had already ripped his shirt off, and I could see the strong arms and tight abs of an oilfield man who clearly worked very hard peering above his stealthily unzipped jeans.

An hour or so later, we returned to the bar; not noticing that we had exchanged shirts and he was now wearing the shirt that I'd worn earlier. Thank goodness no one noticed. Okay, that is such a lie ... *everybody* noticed, even the owner of the bar, who pulled me aside to gossip. I told him, in my charming, Southern enchantress voice, "A good girl never divulges her secrets." He laughed, "So you two hooked up?" With a slight nod of my head, my wink answered his question.

The bar owner informed me that several other patrons had tried to pick up Garrett over the past few weeks, and that he would always wait to shoot pool until I showed up; this is the first time I had been made aware of this. I guess both of us were missing the same thing on Thursday nights, and it wasn't an eight-ball (pun intended). We had many trysts over the next few weeks. I allowed him to believe that no one else in the bar knew that we would often times slip off to my apartment for a little "rodeo" action.

Then one Thursday, I showed up at Crystal's and he didn't; not the next week, and not the following week either. I was actually falling in love with a guy that I knew almost absolutely nothing about, and he knew even less about me (yes, he was aware that I was HIV-positive). We just knew that we were good in bed together. Our hookups had become so regular that we never even exchanged phone numbers; maybe he needed his privacy, and I never asked. In retrospect though, I don't think I would have ever called him. He wanted to be the one chasing me, and if I would have called him, even once, it would have totally screwed up the dynamic of whatever kind of relationship we were in.

I had no problem with that, but what happened when I really *did* want a relationship? Garrett walked away from me to what I hope was a better life for him, and him walking away gave me the opportunity to find true love elsewhere. Until then, there was always Jack Daniels and cocaine.

I continued my Thursday visits for months, until I realized that Garrett really wasn't coming back. My relationship with Jack Daniels got better, but I was still missing Garrett. I needed to find a new place to drown my sorrows. Crystal's, while it was the only gay bar in Lake Charles, constantly reminded me of the great times I'd had with him, but also depressed me a bit. I needed a new home.

I found that home at Rikenjak's, a straight bar featuring a logo of a pileated woodpecker. I had no idea how appropriate that was until I knew that these woodpeckers built their homes inside of dead trees; I certainly wasn't lost on the fact that I was also dead inside. My professional life was on a straight trajectory upwards, meanwhile, my personal life was in tatters.

It was a Thursday afternoon. I got off of work early and headed over to Rikenjak's to drink myself into near oblivion with Jack Daniels and shots of Goldschläger. Everyone there loved me. I was the token gay guy and always welcomed with open arms. I'm sure the fact that I often paid for rounds of drinks had nothing to do with the patrons' affection for me.

It was about 10:30 p.m., and I'd had my fill, so I figured I'd go home early and sleep it off. Tomorrow was another day, and I had the long weekend off. I hopped in my truck and headed home to my apartment about a mile away; it was basically a straight shot from the bar.

I was about halfway home when a sportscar ran a stop sign and I T-boned the driver's side. There was no way the driver could have survived the accident.

I quickly got my bearings, and slowly looked over at the totaled sports car, now perched on the curb on the opposite side of the road; all I saw was a lady's head hanging out of the driver's side window and blood dripping down the door panel. I screamed as the neighbors ran out into their yards to see what the commotion was all about. "Call 9-1-1, I killed her, I killed her, she's dead!" I cried. They all wanted to know what had happened. I told them that she ran the stop sign and although I slammed on the brakes, she was already in the middle of the road and there was nothing I could do. "I know I killed her! She's dead! She's dead!"

A neighbor rushed me into her house and gave me some water to try and calm my nerves, but even that didn't work. "I killed her! I killed her!" was all I could say.

The police and ambulance arrived in record time. I didn't need an ambulance, but the police were very interested in talking to me. I was immediately arrested, though I didn't really know for what. It was later determined that we were both legally drunk; her BAC (blood alcohol content) was 3.10%, and mine was 2.32%.

Even when I told the police that she was in the wrong, it didn't seem to matter to them; I was arrested for third offense DUI and informed that other charges were pending. It was my first felony arrest, certainly not my last. I again began scream-crying hysterically. I had killed her. I was going to jail for vehicular homicide. I was going to jail for life.

[Sidebar: My second-offense DUI had occurred when a local police officer found me asleep in my car in a gas station parking lot with the lights on and the car running (that seems to be a recurring theme) during one of my visits back to Lafayette while I was living in Austin (early-2001). I was arrested immediately. I knew that I'd be spending the night in jail, since that reckless driving charge from 1999 would now be assessed as a first-offense DUI. I don't remember much else about this unfortunate incarceration, but it sure as hell shows up on my Criminal History Report.]

Once booked into jail, I calmed down enough to call my parents. *How would I tell them I just killed someone?* When Dad answered the phone, I just began crying again and tried to explain what happened; I told him about the wreck, but left out the part about killing a young lady. My parents arrived the following morning to bail me out of jail; only then did the officers inform me that no one died. In fact, the woman *walked away* from the accident (and was also charged with third-offense DUI). I was pissed! How dare they let me spend all night in jail thinking that I killed someone? That was just fucking cruel! *Maybe they were trying to teach me a lesson about drinking and driving*? I once again promised my parents that I was going to quit drinking and (again) I really meant it this time!

When I arrived at work on the following Monday in a brand new (rented) truck, the news of my DUI had already made the rounds of the store. As it turned out, my drinking and drugging had been a concern of the staff for some time. There had been idle gossip since I arrived in Iowa that I had (at the very least) a drinking problem; but no one dared say a word. Drunkard or not, I had gained their trust because I enriched their lives by helping them to succeed in their retail careers. I asked my assistant Roger, regarding my drunkenness, "Why didn't y'all say anything?" He said, "Mister Ted, (I always liked when he called me that) we didn't know how." I lowered my head in embarrassment and walked away, promising myself to get better.

Twenty-six years ago, Kevin Nunez trusted me with a secret; a promise I kept until his dying day. In that brief five-minute exchange at Bennigan's on our twentieth birthdays, we knew that we had an everlasting connection. I learned the hard way that *trust* isn't easily earned and is rarely rewarded. I spent my life expecting the *trust* of others without the behavior to back it up. I still had a lot more work to do on myself. But Kevin also taught me that trust can sometimes be a wink of an eye and a secret to keep.

VF Factory Outlet, Iowa, Louisiana–2005

CHAPTER 23

REDEMPTION

(That Time She Died)

After the incredible successes of rebuilding an entire store that had been flattened by a hurricane, the "powers that be" decided that it was time for yet another challenge. For the past few months, I'd traveled back and forth to the VF Outlet location in Gonzales, Louisiana. The store manager had fallen off of a ladder, and the staff was struggling. My boss asked if I would be interested in becoming their new store manager, and I immediately declined because he'd promised that I could retire in Iowa without having to move again. He said that he understood, and the conversation was over.

The following week, he called again with the same question; and my answer remained the same. He called me an hour later, announcing that Brad, the CEO, would be calling me soon. Five minutes later, he was on the phone imploring, "Ted, we have an opportunity for you in Gonzales, I don't know why you keep saying NO."

One of the things I hate most about executive management is the constant barrage of corporate mumbo-jumbo, like "obstacles create opportunities," "when you see yourself winning, you're already a step ahead," "problems are possibilities," "see yourself as the person you want to become." I always hated that shit. Mostly because it's bullshit, and it's just a way for upper management to remind you that you could be doing a better job if you just applied yourself. In retrospect, my former boss' story about "the parade" was kind of a roundabout way of saying the same thing; the difference was that Mr. Billingsley recognized that none of the tried-and-true stuff ever worked on me. He never tried to prompt me by pointing out negatives that needed adjusting, rather he encouraged me by pointing out the positive; he knew what drove me and he pushed those buttons.

Brad knew that I hated that shit too, so he worded his next sentence very carefully, being certain to not use the words "opportunity" and "possibility;" he started by reminding me of the nearly impossible task that we had achieved by getting the Iowa store back up and running again (sure, go ahead and whisper sweet-nothings in my ear ... that never worked either ... he should have known that). Then he said, "Look Ted, I know you were told that you could retire in Iowa, but we really do have a situation in Gonzales; you've been there, you know it." I concurred. He continued, "Since you've already been to that store many times, the staff knows you and likes you; we thought you would be a perfect fit." My response was, "Of course they like me, they know that I'm leaving in a week; they definitely don't want me there full-time." He quickly retorted rather firmly, "Look Ted, it's not really about that, one of our most highly producing stores is beginning to fail with no constant manager. We don't know when, or if, the manager is coming back. I'm asking you to reconsider." I told him that I would think about it, but to give me a little time.

The following morning, corporate human resources called me: "Ted, Brad wanted me to call you to renegotiate your terms of employment." *Holy fuck!* I thought, *I'm about to get fucking fired!* But I was *so* wrong. The human resources manager continued, "We are aware that you were offered a lateral move to Gonzales, and that you refused." I quickly replied, "No, I didn't refuse, I just asked y'all to give me some time!" He responded, "Well, that's why I'm calling you. We'd like to create a benefits package that would enhance your move to Gonzales should you make that decision. Of course, we would pay all of your moving expenses, for temporary housing until you find a more permanent situation, and we will pay off the rest of your lease where you are currently staying." I inquired, "Don't y'all do that for everybody anyway?" He said, "Yes, but there's something else you need to know; you will also receive a substantial increase in pay." (Due to a non-disclosure agreement, I cannot divulge the amount; suffice it to say, it played a major role in my decision.) He continued, "Oh, and something else, if you agree to the new terms and conditions of your employment, Brad (the CEO) wants you in Gonzales next week. "WHAT?" I shouted into the phone, "It's Thanksgiving weekend and Black Friday, does Brad realize that?" The human resources director said, "Yes, he does, that's why he approved your salary increase, which, if he forgot to tell you, also includes a substantial bonus."

"BONUS? No, he never said anything about a bonus!" The human resources guy said, "Yes, you'll get an additional bonus for your sales increases in the Iowa store." *Holy shit,* I said under my breath, *This is insane*! realizing that the bonus was over $20,000. I hurriedly asked, "Can I please call you back in about five minutes?"

I really don't know why I asked for five more minutes; I already knew my answer, but I just needed a little time to gather myself. I wanted to call someone, but who? I picked up the phone so many times to make a phone call, but never did. The decision was mine alone to make ... right or wrong. Damn! I needed a drink and a shot; a little cocaine would have helped too, but I didn't keep any of that stuff at work. *Damn!*

I realize that money is not always the right reason for making a life-changing decision, but this salary increase was RIDICULOUSLY FABULOUS! There's no way I would turn down this opportunity. I made plans for a secret exit from the staff whom I loved so very much, who had helped me to achieve a miracle. The store would be in their very capable hands to continue the success that we together started, but my time there was over.

Thanksgiving 2006 was exciting and exhausting; I explained to my family what was about to happen. Two days after I last worked in the Iowa store, I showed up bright and early to my new store in Gonzales, Louisiana; the store manager had (conveniently) come back to work for one day and then quit, so I was thankful that I didn't have to fire anyone on the day after Thanksgiving. By 8:05 a.m., Roger, my assistant from the Iowa store called my cell phone; he asked, "Mister Ted, what happened? You weren't at the store, so I drove to your apartment and a moving van was there. Are you okay?" It was then that I informed him that I was now the new manager at the store in Gonzales. Without skipping a beat, he said, "I knew it! I knew it! I could tell you were acting kinda weird these past few days; I knew you were up to something." I apologized and asked him to give my love to the staff; they all understood the nature of my position and why I couldn't say that I was leaving; I only wish that the timing could have been different. I told Roger, "Please be sure to thank them; especially thank them for helping us to create the miracle we accomplished this time last year. Tell them that I'll be back to visit, and that I will miss them terribly. And then tell them 'thank you' again." Roger said, "Mister Ted, thank you too, and we love you too!" I heard the phone click as he put down the receiver; my new job in Gonzales had now officially begun.

My temporary home in Gonzales was luxury on top of luxury. I had no idea how much the company was paying for me to stay here. It was way out of my price range, but I relished in the fact VF Outlet had recognized that I "deserved" posh fabulousness. I stayed there for only a couple of weeks until it was time to move into my new apartment on December 10, 2006.

(And now you're wondering how the hell I remember the exact date that I moved into my new apartment so many years later. It's easy, my new store in Gonzales was (accidentally) set on fire on the very same day that I moved into my apartment. Yes, a damned FIRE!)

I had been at this new store barely three weeks, and my new store was now on fire. It was 10:15 a.m. and the moving van was loading things into my apartment when I got the call, and immediately jumped into my truck and raced to the store to find that firefighters already put out the fire. But there was extensive fire damage inside, not to mention the water and smoke damage. I checked on my new staff, and they were all okay. I was definitely having a "Bad Day." Even Daniel Powter woulda been proud of me. *Maybe.*

One half of the store was mostly destroyed; it was later determined that a child was playing with a lighter under one of the clothes racks in the children's department. *The children's department? Aren't all of those clothes supposed to be fireproof?* That was a lawsuit waiting to happen ... and that's the last I heard of it. I should have known better than to ask questions. [The culprit was never found, even after we aired the security footage on television.]

I called my sister-in-law, Sharon, and her husband to let them know what happened and that I needed help. Within two hours, they were at my new apartment unloading my furniture as I stayed at my store coordinating repairs and remediation. I stayed at the store until midnight, when my two assistants agreed to spend the night there with the remediation company so that I could get some sleep. By 5:00 a.m., I was back at the store and back to work.

With the restoration company still frantically working to remove all the burned clothing and clean the smoke smell out of the building, I was tasked with ensuring the safety of our staff, who all showed up that morning. Unfortunately, we were not able to open the store on time; however, only ONE HOUR late, at 10:00 a.m., we opened our store (with the exception of the children's department). My staff and I had, once again, achieved a miracle. And again, the CEO of the company called me; "Ya done good!" he said.

I said, "Look Brad, I went through 9/11 in Gilroy, an ice storm in Mineral Wells, a hurricane in Iowa, and now a fire in Gonzales. I think maybe there's something wrong with me." Laughingly, he replied, "I was kinda thinking the same thing, but I wasn't gonna say it." He asked if I was okay and how things were. I told him that it was quite a mess, but my staff and I would figure it out. He said, "Ted, if anybody can do this, I know it's you." I concurred, "Brad, I agree with you, but at this point, I'm kinda tired." We had a good chuckle, and you'd think that would be the end of it. But NO!

What I didn't anticipate is that we would have to do a physical inventory of the damaged goods—basically, the entire children's department—which brought back dreadful memories of the aftermath of Hurricane Rita that had destroyed my store in Iowa. I remembered the reek of wet, moldy clothing; but the vile stench of *burned*, wet, moldy clothing was even worse; and we had to touch each and every piece to account for them, *ewwww*! (And I was now sick with the flu! Thankfully, Sharon and her husband stayed to help with the inventory also; I was grateful.)

But what pissed me off even more than being forced to complete an inventory on burned, soiled, wet clothing, is that the company was well aware of my compromised immune system, yet never even considered the fact that this task could make me very ill. (Ted A Richard had a reputation for creating miracles and getting the job done ... that's all that mattered.) Still, I maintained my professionalism and completed the inventory for the insurance companies. I thought that a "thank you" would have been nice, considering all that we had done; but apparently that was just part of my job. I did, however, thank my staff.

Then on December 20, 2006 (only ten days later) I got a phone call from Sharon's husband, informing me that she had been missing since the previous night; I had not seen nor heard from her, and I hoped for her safe return. But that was not to be, it was determined that Sharon had died of an accidental overdose later that same night.

Sharon was a retired Air Force veteran who completed at least three tours of duty in Iraq during Operation Desert Storm. She and her husband built a home next to my parents after they had both retired from the Air Force. As a result of her service, Sharon suffered with chronic back pain in addition to major depressive disorder and post-traumatic stress disorder. She went to the Veterans Administration doctors in Alexandria, Louisiana (the closest one to Lafayette at the time) and was given several different medications for her illnesses; she kept returning to the VA to let them know the medications were not working. And their response was: "Just give it a couple more weeks."

Sharon did two things on her final day that were very poignant. First, she visited her daughter at school to say, "No matter what anyone says, I will always love you!" Second, Sharon went to the local Catholic church and prayed, where the priest simply waved at her, not knowing why she was parked in the front of his church. [Her final note should have clued him in.]

I thought long and hard before printing this letter, because it is extremely personal. I felt that the truth needed to be told; not to confirm the mental and physical abuse wrought by her husband, but because her daughters needed to know how much their mom really loved them. Sharon would want her story to be told. She was not allowed to voice her truth while she was alive due to the "alleged" physical and mental abuse of her husband, so I am giving her the voice now that she never had.

The note read:

Dear Father Harrington,   (dated: July 29, 2006)
I don't know what to do. I am in so much pain from my life and I can't bear anymore. I want to be with someone who loves me unconditionally. I want to be with God. This world is not working for

me anymore. I have had so many ups and mostly downs that I have reached my threshold.

I am on my third marriage. It's pretty much dead. I've struggled through my first two marriages financially and I can't put my youngest daughter (age ten) through that. My twenty-two year-old daughter paid the price for my first two marriages and now her life is one big struggle with two small kids of her own. In other words, I don't have the strength, will, or resources to start over again.

I have failed in every aspect of my life, except giving birth to two beautiful girls. I spent twenty-one years in the military all because I wanted to get away from my step-mom. After having kids, I couldn't get out because I needed to provide for them. My first marriage (lasted five years) happened on the spur of the moment in technical school in the Air Force. We didn't even date except a couple of times. When our friends announced they were getting married, my first husband suggested we do the same. I was afraid that would be my only chance at marriage, so I said yes.

My second marriage was to someone fifteen years older. I thought I finally had someone to take care of me. But, alcohol, many lies, and temperament ended that marriage. It also lasted five years. My third marriage has endured almost twelve years, the last nine going downhill. I had thought I finally met someone who loved me, loved my daughter, and loved God. I have suggested that we see a priest for counseling, and he said ok, BUT he doesn't know how a third party can help us communicate better, when the problem is between us. You see, once you find out who my husband is, you might be surprised. One of the many things I loved about him was his very strong Catholic beliefs and love of God and his past participation in the church. He is a wonderful man. However, at this time in our marriage, he is not so wonderful. Everyone thinks he's this loving, caring, and giving person who would do anything for anybody. That is true, but as a husband in this marriage, he is completely different. He told me that I am still here (at home) because I want to be here, not because he wants me here. I told him in the past I would not divorce him, so he thinks he is doomed to live a miserable life.

In the meantime, we put up a front to everyone in our day-to-day lives. If things are going all right, then the day is good. He stopped saying I love you several months ago after an event that I can't even remember.

Meanwhile, we have a ten-year-old daughter who loves me more than anything and has been the only reason I still exist. But it's not enough anymore.

What do I do? Counseling? Not if he thinks it's a waste of time. What good will it accomplish? Divorce? And lose the house we built on property his parents gave us? One person cannot afford that house. Go through a custody battle? I do not have the strength or the resources. My daughter deserves to live in that house, she does not deserve to live in substandard housing and struggle like my oldest one did with me. If it were just me, then I would cut my losses and start over, but it's not just me. I literally have ruined one child because of divorce and financial struggle; I will not do it again.

Suicide? Most preferred option for me. I won't have any more pain. I won't fail anymore. I truly doubt I would be missed except for my daughter. The only problem is, I don't want to go to hell, and suicide is a straight ticket to hell, or so I'm told. I want to be with God and Jesus NOW. I know they love me unconditionally, but I am human, and I need to feel loved and be told that I am loved. The only one who does is my daughter and now it's not enough. I don't feel I matter to anyone anymore except God. I know we are supposed to bear our crosses in this world, but mine is too heavy for me now. I am sorry I didn't call you or make an appointment.

By the way, my husband is Joey Richard and you came to our house for a meal and to bless it ... My name is Sharon Richard.

Please keep this letter to yourself and do not tell anyone about it. You are the only one I trust with this information. I haven't begun to cover every aspect of my pain and suffering. I've only touched highly on some situations. I am sorry to burden you with this. I am sorry to burden anyone, but I am literally at the end of my rope. If you want to speak to me, the best times would be Monday, Tuesday, or Wednesday mornings before 9:30 a.m. Joey comes home from work at 9:45 those days and is off on Thursday and Friday mornings.

I work Sundays and Saturday mornings I have my daughter with me. My cell is (xxx)xxx-xxxx. Thank you for your patience in reading this. I know you are an extremely busy man with more important things on your plate to take care of. I don't mean anything against you at all, but you are my last resort.

Father Harrington, the priest to whom Sharon reached out, never called her. Yet, he made sure to give the note to the police as they were investigating her death, where my brother was a prime suspect. And yes, Sharon's passing was a very, very sad time for all of us; yet, once again, a Catholic priest who was supposed to be there to serve his flock certainly let this stranded, battered lamb lose her way. *Did he not care, or was there just not enough time?* Either way, my hope is that there's a green rope somewhere out there for him too!

I felt cheated in Sharon's death in that, just as in Kevin's death, I didn't get to say good-bye. She knew that the last time she saw me would be the last time; I didn't and am constantly saddened that she felt she had no other choice.

Twenty-three years ago, I was specifically uninvited to the funeral of someone I truly loved. Twenty-three years later, my sister-in-law, Sharon was specifically uninvited to her own funeral. She lived a life in service to our country, and was rewarded with three broken marriages, the most recent of which was "allegedly" abusive. She wasn't even able to enjoy her final resting place, as my brother placed her in a mismarked grave.

[Update: Sharon Kathleen Shupert Richard was finally last to rest in her final burial plot on November 2, 2018, in a modified funeral service attended only by my brother and their daughter (my goddaughter). The tomb transfer was completed, in secrecy, without knowledge of the rest of the family.]

Fame, in the instance, defined as *redemption,* is my way of giving my sister-in-law, Sharon, the voice that she thought she never had while she was alive. She probably would never have had the nerve to speak the words of her letter out loud for fear of retaliation; but her death gave me the strength I needed to speak on her behalf. She deserved at least that! While this book was supposed to be about me and my life, one thing that I learned somewhere along the way, is that sometimes, it just isn't always about ME.

But there's something else about Sharon's death that makes my stomach churn every time I think of it. Every single person that serves in our country's military does so voluntarily; they work night and day to keep our country and our families safe. Yet so many of our veterans do not get the help they need once they retire. This is an outrage! I wish that Sharon, and so many other veterans, received the proper treatment that every human being deserves. Maybe we'd have fewer people being told to "give it a couple more weeks," and a lot fewer suicides of American veterans. *Maybe.*

Immediately after the Christmas holidays, I traveled back to Gonzales; my first order of business was to find a psychiatrist. Something was wrong, and I didn't believe it was just the alcohol and cocaine; it felt like random, sometimes vile, stuff spun around in my head. I found a local doctor in Baton Rouge, and we did a slew of preliminary tests. He didn't give me a diagnosis, but said, "We're gonna put you on the medication called Effexor XR. It should help to alleviate your mood swings." I told him, "But I don't have mood swings." Snarkily, he replied, "Well that's the medicine I'm putting you on. You can pick it up at the pharmacy and go back to work."

I felt defeated by this random psychiatrist who directly insinuated that I was faking mental illness so that I could get out of work. *Was he fucking kidding me?* I'd been down this road before and didn't want to have to leave my job again because of sickness! I picked up my medications from the pharmacy and went home.

Two weeks later, I told the doctor that I did not like the effects of Effexor XR at all because they turned me into zombie at work, and my staff assumed I was high on something. In the past, that might have been true; but this time, it wasn't! I had absolutely no emotion; I didn't feel happy or sad, excited or indifferent, delighted or angry, courageous or fearful ... my emotions had flatlined. I was just a body somehow standing up on its own without a thought or a conscience.

The psychiatrist suggested I give the meds a few more weeks to kick in. I'd heard that bullshit somewhere else. Yep, Sharon's VA doc told her the same thing! I refused to be yet another tragedy of horrible doctoring; I decided to stop the Effexor XR and get back to my old self. In hindsight, it was one of the worst decisions of my life; I had no idea that I was supposed to wean myself off of the medication but instead quit cold turkey. The withdrawals nearly killed me; but I survived and welcomed myself back ... albeit with those roller coaster episodes in my brain. I needed to find redemption *for* myself, and *from* myself.

Sharon Shupert Richard – November 17, 1962 – December 20, 2006

CHAPTER 24

FELON

(That Time I Was Santa ... Again)

Christmas 2006 was a difficult time in the Richard household, and I now had a godchild with no mother to comfort her; her father was useless, telling her only that "crying wouldn't make a difference." This made my job as godfather all the more difficult. The Christmas tree that Sharon decorated for the holiday season was never taken down; it was the only happy memory that Ophelia had of her Mom, and some morbidly warped reminder to my younger brother that, as stated in the note found in Sharon's dead hands, "You Win!" Indeed, he thought he won the battle, but this war was far from over. O.K.'s Mom was now dead; *Parrain* Ted needed to step in and salvage what was left of a shattered child and her memories. I had to fight for Ophelia. Sadly, her father's misguided parenting told her that no one else cared. But I *did* care; though his isolation of her never allowed me to show her the love and affection she needed. This wouldn't be the last battle I fought for her (many of which she never knew about), but I was determined to win the war for her future. I could use another drink and a key of cocaine, for sure.

I spent my entire life drinking and drugging because I was happy *and* because I was sad. It quickly escalated to where I was drinking and drugging "just because;" for no reason at all. I pretended to fight very hard to get sober and to get better (at least in my own mind, I knew I had a problem). But all of this fighting just led me right back to being drunk, high, and broke.

But now I had a devastated, ten-year-old godchild, and didn't know if anything that I did would make her feel any better or make a difference in her life. I drove back to Gonzales after those Christmas holidays and continued my mission of, once again, rescuing a store in distress ... this time after a failed manager and a fire.

It was during this time that I enjoyed an online fling with a young guy I met on Myspace. His name was John Trump (no relation to the idiot that was elected president; but, as it turned out, he had very similar characteristics of said idiot). On one weekend, I drove to his hometown of Opelousas, Louisiana. Oh, I forgot to mention that John was only nineteen years old (I was forty-four), had no job and no car, and no ambition. The red flags should have sent me running away immediately, but when I saw this Irish, strawberry-blond muscle god with arms the size of a small oak tree and thighs that could have cracked acorns, I was smitten. We spent that first night in a hotel in Lafayette then I took him to his first gay bar. To hell with all the red flags, I now had a trophy boyfriend.

Now you're wondering why I skipped over the part about all of the wild sex we had that night. Well, here's your answer. We didn't have sex that first night, not for his lack of trying. At some point in the past, I had been accused of not divulging my HIV-positive status to one of my sexual partners, which was bullshit. I was adamant to make sure that John was tested for HIV before we had sex. It was not my normal practice, but he was young, and I wanted him to know what to expect if we were ever going to have sex with each other, much less to be in a relationship. John told me that he had only been with one man in his life, but to make me happy, he'd get tested. I told him that it wasn't just about getting tested, it was about getting educated.

While in Lafayette, we drove to Acadiana CARES where they offered free anonymous testing (and still do). About fifteen minutes later, the counselor/case manager came into the foyer where I was waiting; she said, "John wants you to come in with him." I instinctively knew the results, but I just didn't understand; John had been with only one other guy (or so he claimed, and I chose to believe him). But when John told me the full story of this guy that he met in Alabama I was furious. This sick fuck infected John with HIV and never even told him that he was positive! This demented fucker needed to be tossed in jail for life. He destroyed the life of a nineteen-year-old; that is unforgivable! It was a rough few weeks for John in the beginning, but we got through it, and I made sure that he got the proper medical attention that he needed.

John moved in with me after that second weekend. (*What the fuck is wrong with me?*) I'd go to work during the day, and John would keep the house clean and do laundry (pronounced "play video games") until I got home. He was basically worthless as a companion, but the sex was great, so I continued to ignore the red flags.

I finally had enough of his "juvenile" delinquency and decided to start charging him rent only a few weeks into the relationship. I figured, *why was I letting this dude stay here for free if all he did was play video games all day and without even doing his part to keep the house clean?* John asked why I charged him rent, and I explained to him, "A long time ago, I learned to separate emotions from finances. I still love you, but we also have bills to pay." So, I gave him a job at my store to be sure that he could afford to pay the rent. Genius, right? (I had completely forgotten about my strict policy of not having sex with my staff.) I even taught him how to drive (*no, this kid didn't even know how to drive*) in my little red Ford Ranger.

Now that he had his own money, we'd go to gay bars together and I'd make him pay for his drinks. One of the perks of having stunningly great looks was that no one ever asked for his ID. I would learn, much too late, that he was making his own money on the side, too. (*I know, I shoulda seen that coming ... another red flag ignored.*)

It wasn't long before the stresses of a declining outlet mall, a store fire, and my continued alcohol and drug abuse began having a huge negative impact on my health again. I never really recovered from that case of the flu after the store fire, but even that couldn't stop me from hanging out with my friends, Jack and Goldschläger. The fact that I had willingly taken myself off of Effexor XR only served to make matters even worse, and I used cocaine to combat the withdrawal symptoms.

Even though I was taking my HIV medications as prescribed, my extra-curricular activities negated their effects. By March 2007, my T-cell count dropped to nine ... yes, *nine*.

I called my parents to see if, once again, the sunroom would be available, this time for me and John. They acquiesced, and we moved in by mid-March. My relationship with John lasted less than two years; the fact that it lasted that long still shocks me, but I always chose to see the better side of him (his body, not his mind), and avoided seeing the obvious flaws directly in front of me. The final straw came when I caught him in the act of side-hustling. We were at the local gay bar in downtown Lafayette. I was paying my tab, but John was nowhere to be found. With nearly everyone out of the bar, I realized that the only place he could be was in the bathroom. Sure enough, I was right; there he was, on his knees in the men's room, engaged with a complete stranger. I was furious!

We didn't utter a word on the drive home. When we arrived back home, John climbed onto the bed. I yelled, "What the fuck do you think you're doing? Get off the damned bed! Did you really think that you were sleeping with me tonight?" He stared at me, in shock, as if I was some sort of alien creature speaking to him. He seemed to not understand my anger, which I clarified next: "You need to be out of here by tomorrow. I don't give a fuck where you go or who you're with, but it ain't gonna be here!"

John grabbed a pillow and a blanket off the bed, and I made him sleep on the floor, but not before I yanked the pillow from under his head. I was not going to degrade myself by allowing a common whore to think that he could share a bed with me; it just wasn't gonna happen!

By noon the next day, John Trump was out of my life for good. I'd woefully allowed this arrangement to continue for far too long, later discovering that, for the past eighteen months, John had been telling everyone that we were in an open relationship, and that everyone in the bar knew exactly what he was doing but no one ever bothered to tell ME because everyone assumed I already knew. I was hurt and disgusted; they all knew me long enough and well enough to know that I would *never* be in an open relationship. My friends assumed that perhaps I changed my mind since John was so much younger than me. They thought it would be insulting if they told me what John was doing behind my back. So, I started hanging out with my other friends, Jack and Goldschläger, just a little bit (pronounced "a lot") more; at least they never lied to me.

[Update: In early 2020, John Trump was shot by his ex-boyfriend, for "allegedly" cheating on him in their shared bed while they were still a couple. John survived the shooting; his ex-boyfriend committed suicide while holed up in their former apartment following the incident.

Rumor has it that John is now in a committed relationship, though I must admit that I would have been committed (to an insane asylum) had I remained in a relationship with him. The worst I ever did to him was make him sleep on the floor and take away his pillow; I might have shot him too if I'd have caught him in my bed with a stranger. But, alas, a shot in the leg is better than a shot to the head; I'm glad I never had to make that decision.]

With that relationship over, it was time to re-evaluate my life and determine what was most important to me. My executive life was over, my personal life was in shambles, and I was still lost in my own misery; I needed something to get my mind off of myself.

By Christmas 2007, Sharon had been dead for a little over a year, and I found myself (or lost myself) single again. I was hurting, but I couldn't allow my sadness to overcome the responsibility I had to my goddaughter. This would be her second Christmas without her Mom, yet she had never been given the opportunity to properly grieve. *How does a ten-year-old deal with the death of a parent, especially when the surviving parent forbids you to cry for them?* I didn't know. *Could I fix this?* I didn't know that either. But I definitely had an idea! (I always "have an idea.")

[Flashback: Every year on the weekend before Christmas, my grandparents would have Santa Claus fly in on a helicopter and deliver candy and gifts to all the neighborhood children. At first, it was just a family event; I'm from a fairly large family, so there were usually 100 or more people there. Over the years, the celebration kept growing until the crowds reached around 500 people or so. That got to be very expensive to have candy and gifts for all of those kids; my grandparents paid for everything. As my grandparents got older, it became more stressful for them to organize such a huge event and it wasn't enjoyable for them anymore. They had heavy hearts when they had to discontinue the tradition. They were getting older and there was no one else who was willing (or could afford) to take on what had become such a huge yearly Christmastime event.]

I decided to start a new tradition. I knew that my Mom and Dad had purchased a new Santa suit to replace the old one from all those years ago. So, I decided that I would play Santa for the family every year at Christmas dinner (wherever it was being held).

[Sidebar: I had played the role of Santa once before; actually, Colt Michael had played the role of Santa once before. It was Christmas 1991, and our big, gay apartment complex hosted its annual Holiday Extravaganza which included a decorations contest. My neighbors David and Ray, always went above and beyond to make their holiday décor as festive as possible, and this year was no different. But Ray had a special surprise for this year's presentation ... Colt Michael.

David and Ray worked feverishly to outdo all of the other contestants and filled the street-facing apartment with merriment and joy, featuring a seven-foot undecorated Douglas fir (except for the tinsel) in the center of the massive picture window. A myriad of colorful and sparkly ornaments was strewn about the floor, ready to adorn the tree.

The judging took place on the Friday night before Christmas. The Westmoreland Square management selected its judges from local residents, ensuring that none of them would be biased since they knew no one who lived in the complex. Judging began at 9:00 p.m. so that everyone's lights would brighten the entire "gayborhood."

As the judges approached David's and Ray's huge picture window from the street, Colt Michael appeared from behind the shadows dressed as Santa, complete with hat and beard. He then removed Santa's red fur jacket and slung it over a nearby chair. Next, he removed his skirt, which was actually the tree skirt, and placed it around the trunk of the tree. Colt Michael revealed that he was wearing only a red and green-fringed G-string, then began dancing erotically as he picked up ornaments off the floor to decorate the tree. It was a rousing (pronounced "arousing") success.

The following day the winners were announced; as per my usual luck, the "Santa Decorates Tree" apartment won ... you guessed it, second place. But that's not the end of the story.

When I arrived at work, I was called into the store manager's office. Once the door closed behind me, I could tell that she could barely hide her laughter. I asked, "What's up, Mrs. Knott? What's so funny?" She could contain herself no longer, and said only four words, "How's Santa this morning?" My head spun in disbelief; my boss had been one of the judges at the previous night's contest. I could never have planned that. So, I asked her, "Well then why did we get second place?" She confided,

"Well, Ted, I had you in first place; I guess some of the others disagreed." I said, "Thank you very much Mrs. Knott. Whew, it's gonna be a busy day today and I've got tons of stuff to do. Ya know, Christmas and all! Have a great day, now." Grasping the awkwardness of the moment, she giggled to herself loudly enough so that I could hear her as I sheepishly walked out of her office.]

I remember that first year playing Santa for my family; I think I was even more excited than the kids. And even though they were all past the age of knowing that Santa Claus was a fictional person, it was always fun when "he" showed up to pass out the gifts and we took family pictures. When I walked back into the room after Santa left, everyone wondered where I had been. Santa had just left, and I had missed his appearance. Of course, it was all a ruse, but still it was lots of fun.

As the nieces and nephews got older, got married, and had children of their own, the role of Santa Claus became even more important. It was such a thrill to see the excitement on all of the kids' (and grandkids') faces when they heard Santa's sleigh bells ringing and heard the "reindeer hooves" on the roof. And every year I had the satisfaction of knowing that I did something for those kids that they would always remember. As those children grew old enough to know the shenanigans I pulled, we included them in on "the secret." I would let them help me get dressed, but only if they promised not to tell anyone; that trick always worked.

To this day, every year, after Christmas dinner, Santa Claus suddenly appears with candy and gifts for all the kids; I know that I get just as much enjoyment out of the event as they do. And I still do!

[Update: My time as Santa ended in 2019; I was so proud to pass along those duties to the eldest grandchild, Dominic (yep, my eldest nephew). I could tell that he was excited to continue the tradition which started with my grandparents when I was a child.]

Shortly after I was "officially" single, and after my award-caliber performance as Santa Claus, my parents gave me a parcel of land so I could build a house; but not just ANY piece of land. It was the land on which my grandparents' house had been many, many years before, so it had a very sentimental value to me since I had been extremely close with my grandma Yoila. Everyone knew that I was her favorite grandchild, and now I had the opportunity to create my own home on the place where she lived and turn it into something fabulous; I know she approved. That became my masterpiece of a home ... the home where I still live to this day.

I was so excited to finally have a house that I could call home. After living the life of a nomad for the past thirty-something years (moving from place to place for VF Outlet and other companies); I could finally settle down and begin the next phase of my life. I moved into my new home on my forty-sixth birthday, November 20, 2008.

My home was also chosen to be a featured in SLEMCO's (our local electric company) monthly magazine. I must say that it came as no surprise to me that my house was chosen; it was so different from anything anyone ever built in the area. I still remember random people just stopping by the house (even during the building process) just to see what my house looked like (and they still do).

I also remember the painters who painted the interior of my house. At the time, I had more than thirty-one different colors of paint in a 1,031 square foot house (kinda like Baskin-Robbins' thirty-one flavors of ice cream ... Go on, Millennials and Zoomers, "GTS!"). And they kept looking at me like, "Is this dude, crazy? I mean, we know he's gay, but is he for real?" By the time the painting supervisor came to do the final walk-through, I already had my furniture in place and all of my accessories installed. He told me, "Dude, I thought you were crazy as hell, with all those colors, but now that everything is in place, it really does look great!" All I could say was, "Thank you."

Because of all of the colors in my house, I decided that it needed to be called "Rainbow Ranch." All of my friends agreed; it was—and still is—definitely the gayest and most fabulous house in the neighborhood, so it certainly deserved an appropriate name.

Since March 2007, I had still been fighting with Social Security about the extent of my disabilities. Meanwhile the Social Security Administration was finding every way possible to establish that I was not, in fact, disabled. (It felt like a replay of the 1994 debacle all over again. As I've said before, I defined myself by the incredible work that I did; if there were any way possible, that's what I would have chosen, but I knew that continuing to work simply wasn't an option.) I was extremely thankful to have purchased both short- and long-term disability insurance with VF Outlet, which paid me eighty percent of my salary. My claim with their insurance company was approved immediately. (I suspect the company felt some sort of responsibility for forcing an HIV-infected patient with a compromised immune system to perform an inventory on wet, moldy, and stinky clothing, though I never questioned it at the time. I simply accepted the "generosity" of the long-term insurance for which I had already paid.)

The constant back-and-forth with Social Security, the stressors of building a new house, and the demise of a doomed relationship continued to take a toll on both my physical and mental well-being. Jack, Goldschläger, and cocaine were the friends I chose to rescue me from my emotional collapse.

[Sidebar: I owe you all some sort of explanation. You're probably asking, *"How are you so disabled that you can't work, yet you can go out to bars and get drunk?"* You would be absolutely correct for challenging me on that subject. Here's my explanation ... my disability stemmed not only from my HIV diagnosis, but on other factors, including chronic fatigue syndrome, anxiety, somewhat constant diarrhea, and the inability to function at a high mental capacity due to the side effects of the medication. I was wrong for using alcohol and drugs to mask the pain, but that was the only way I knew how. Once again, the medication for HIV was making me sicker than the virus itself. I needed relief, so I used the same tried-and-true method of the past. It worked then; I'd hoped it would work better this time. Maybe I would actually get to die this time! *Maybe.*]

I was driving home from the local downtown Lafayette gay bar in the late spring of 2009 when I reached a four-way stop near my house. Once at a complete stop, I noticed a car approaching quickly behind me, so I hurried through the intersection in case the vehicle didn't stop. As soon as I cleared the intersection, red and blue lights lit up behind me, forcing me to pull over. The policeman approached my truck and I was well-prepared; my license, insurance, and registration were already in my hand when he approached my window. He asked me to step out of the vehicle. When I asked why, he said that he smelled liquor on my breath. Knowing that I was not going to win this argument, I did as he requested. I also knew better than to tell him that the only reason I hurried through the four-way stop is because I had seen how quickly he was coming up behind me.

When the officer asked how many drinks I'd had that night, I was honest, and said, "One." He looked at me stunned, instinctively believing that I had lied. But it was true ... I'd had only one drink of Jack and Coke that night. I had conveniently left out that I had also done about eleven shots of Goldschläger. But the breathalyzer didn't lie at all; my BAC was nearly three times the legal limit.

I asked the officer if I could call my parents, who arrived about fifteen minutes later, and I attempted to walk away to get into the passenger's side of their vehicle. The officer grabbed me by the back of my elbow, "Hey boy, where do you think you're going?" I replied, "Well, my Dad's gonna drive my truck home, and I'm gonna ride back with my Mom." He laughed, and gave a wink to my parents, saying, "Well, boy, that's where you're wrong; you're coming downtown with me. They can come and get you in the morning." I was booked into the Lafayette Parish Correctional Facility for a second-offense DUI, which was later upgraded to fourth-offense DUI.

About a month or so later, I was out with friends at some straight bar behind the old racetrack in Carencro, Louisiana. How we ended up there, I have absolutely no idea; it really didn't matter, as long as Jack and Goldschläger were present. But after about two hours or so, even the liquor couldn't hide the fact that I really needed to be somewhere else. My truck easily found its way meandering down the backroads of rural Cajun Country until I made it to the frontage road of the interstate (some of y'all call them freeway access roads).

I immediately saw the police cruiser behind me; he'd waited in the parking lot by the side of the road as I drove up to the stop sign. Being it was so dark out, I opted to drive to a nearby well-lit parking lot. Of course, the officer was having none of it; he began revving his police cruiser behind me. Once again, I was ready ... driver's license, insurance, and registration. I handed them to the officer as I rolled down my driver's side window. He was already yelling, "Why'd you decide to run, boy?" I replied, "Run? Where'd you think I was going? I was driving twelve frickin' miles an hour!" (Probably not, but it sounded good at the time). As if he wasn't already sufficiently pissed off, I was about to make it worse. The officer informed me that I had not come to a complete stop at the intersection, and that I had cut in front of him on the service road. Being the smartass that "drunk me" could be, I had the perfect response, but not the perfect speech, "Well *occiffer*, if I cut you off, then how would you know that I didn't come to a complete stop; and if you were in the parking lot, like we both know you were, then there's no way I could have cut you off! You can't have it both ways!" He was extremely agitated—to say the very least—and asked me how many drinks I'd had that night. This time I was perfectly honest. I said, "Look, just put the cuffs on me, you know you want to; I know I'm drunk, you know I'm drunk; so, just take me to jail." After a few field-sobriety tests, which we both knew I would fail, he cuffed me. This time I was arrested for the latest in a handful of DUI arrests, and what made matters even worse is that I was now in jail for my fifth-offense DUI and I had still not been to court for my third-offense DUI that happened over three years before. My bail was set at $100,000. Cash only.

I called my sister, explaining, "Cassie, I'm in jail now, but don't do anything; just leave me here." With a knot in her throat, she asked if I was alright. I slurred, either from the booze, exhaustion, the fact that I knew I'd be there a while, or all three; "Yes, I have only one phone call, so I called you. I'll be fine. I just need to stay here and figure some stuff out." That was the only call to my family that I made during my first few days in jail. I called my parents the following week and told them I'd messed up again and wanted to make things right; and there was no way that I would ever ask them for that kind of money.

Twenty-five years ago, a young man named Ross found me and made me feel as though I was the only man in the world. Twenty-five years later, I was so lost and alone that I felt like the only man in the world living this dreadful existence. I was now a three-time felon, living my life in solidarity with the alcohol and drugs that now consumed me. This life of lonesomeness and abandonment I willingly brought upon myself. *Fame*, in this instance, defined as *felon*, is a moniker to which I had never wanted to become associated. How I wish that I could define this *"second of fame"* as anything else other than felon or convict, but I can't. This is my life story, and sometimes it's difficult to be honest with your harshest memories. I wanted this era of my life to be about encouragement, fulfillment, joy, and happiness (defined by the expressions on my nephews' and nieces' faces at Christmastime). Instead, I learned that honor is about honesty, that trust is about truth, and that legacy is about integrity, all of which I lacked. I mistakenly wielded the balance of justice upon others and failed to recognize that the judgement I needed to face stared back at me in the mirror this whole time. I had been both judge and jury in so many other people's lives that I was willfully oblivious to the failures in my own.

I was so very happy when Ross made me feel like I was the only man in the world; but now I was all alone in a world I had created just for myself; I made myself unbearable to me in spite of me. I was miserable, and had long ago forced myself to forget about much of my past, because there was no need for a future, even with the excitement of a brand new home. I was ready to die.

me sitting with myself dressed as Santa–2007

CHAPTER 25

RESPONSIBILITY

(That Time I Rescued Myself)

I spent that first night in jail in a holding cell with forty other inmates. I had been temporarily incarcerated at the Lafayette Parish Correctional Center on other occasions, but this time was different. In the past, I was held in a temporary cell, before being bailed out the following morning; this was definitely more of a permanent situation.

As I was escorted into the section in which I'd be spending most of the next few (pronounced "several") days, I was assigned a bunk (upper deck), surrendered my personal belongings, and now wore jailbird garb. I could tell that there had been an attempt to keep our pod clean, but the smell of old piss and sulfuric gasses still emanated from the shower area. To top it all off, one of the inmates was withdrawing from a suspected overdose of heroin and was convulsing and vomiting all over the floor.

I spent the next few days contacting those within the judicial system to determine if there was any way possible for me to get out of this jail cell. As difficult as it must have been for my family, I'm glad they didn't come to my rescue. My parents saved me on so many occasions, and each time, I promised—and truly meant—to stay clean, but never followed through.

Absolutely no one would save me this time. It was time for my life to change, and I was the only one who could change it. [*I'm three-fourths of the way through this book, and I still haven't figured out what the hell is wrong with me. It would take me a while to realize that I wasn't three-fourths done with my life, although many times I had wished it would have been.*]

There was a treatment program available for repeat offenders who wanted to get clean and sober. But there was a catch; there always was. I would be discharged from prison temporarily if, and only if, I wore an ankle bracelet (not an accessory I would have chosen on my own; I had no clothes with which to coordinate it) and submit to constant random monitoring. In addition, I was ordered to enter an addiction treatment program at the discretion of the court. Of course, I agreed to everything; I would have done almost anything to escape the vileness of my living situation for the past three weeks.

I submitted my request for treatment to Tyler Mental Health in Lafayette, Louisiana, and was immediately accepted. The intake procedure was fairly simple, but I'm sure the presence of my medical insurance most certainly played a role in my getting accepted so quickly.

[Sidebar: In the real-life-can-be-cruel department, the case manager who handled my DUI intake was my high school senior prom date. She was not surprised to see me there; the irony wasn't lost on her, either.]

My first appointment was scheduled for the following week; it was with a clinical psychiatrist. I was skeptical, especially since my last run-in with a psychiatrist landed me on medication that didn't work, and I never got a diagnosis of what my illness could be.

I sat in the doctor's office as he assessed my medical condition; he asked me questions and ended with asking if I'd ever considered suicide. I responded, "Yes, all the time; but I don't think that I could ever actually do it." Then I told him the story about my neighbor in Houston who shot himself and missed. I kinda laughed about it to make the story seem funny; his face fumed with anger. He sternly stated, "Ted, suicide is not something that we ever laugh about!" I told him that I only laughed because I was nervous talking about suicide; it made me uncomfortable. He calmed down and asked, "So, you said you think about suicide all the time?" I replied, "Yes, almost every day."

The room was deathly quiet, and he prepared to phrase his response with care and consideration, "Ted, I know that you've been through a lot in your lifetime. You're only forty-six years old, and you've been an alcoholic and an addict for more than half of your life. You're probably wondering, with your HIV and everything else that's happened why you're still here." I breathed a sigh of relief, saying, "FINALLY, finally somebody understands exactly how I feel!" He stopped me before I continued to speak, "Ted, yes, I do understand, and I certainly don't want to you to feel that I have no feelings for what you have been through and continue to go through. But I have seen thousands of patients during the course of my career in psychiatry, and I can honestly tell you that most of them do not ever think of committing suicide. You have come to me for help, and I am here to help, but we first need to determine the depths of your depression." I was shocked, "Depression? I'm mostly a very happy-go-lucky kinda guy. Of course, I get depressed sometimes, like most people, but I'm certainly NOT a depressive person. I don't understand." The doctor continued, "Ted, who you portray to be on the outside is not the person that I see on the inside. You claim that 'most people get depressed,' and that's not necessarily true. Of course, people mourn the loss of loved ones, or the loss of a job or income, or even experience the sadness of a friend or loved one moving away. But that is not depression, that is grief, and the two are not interchangeable." He continued, "You believe that depression is normal, because that's how you feel every day; you need to make yourself believe that. In reality, you've been using alcohol and drugs to manage your depression, but that's only making it worse. And even once you quit alcohol and drugs, your problems with depression will still exist. We need to get you sober and teach you how to cope with life on life's terms, and we will give you the tools that you need to learn how to make yourself happy without alcohol or drugs." (*"Life on life's terms"* was a phrase I'd heard at a few of the Alcoholics Anonymous meetings; my interpretation was that it was all bullshit!)

As I walked out of his office, he handed me a prescription, and a paper to bring to the front desk for my next appointment. I looked down at the green sheet of office paper; under the heading "diagnosis" it stated, "Major Depressive Disorder." I finally understood that the way I felt wasn't normal (*yes, I'm still gay, because that's VERY normal*), but had no idea that there was actually a name for it. I thought I was just a drunk and an addict, but there was much more to it than that; I just hated seeing those three words linked together ... Major Depressive Disorder ... basically, I was a fucked-up mess who needed lots of help to figure myself out.

The best way for me to describe my turmoil of emotions came from a conversation on the *The Golden Girls*. Rue McClanahan's character, Blanche Devereaux, was explaining her feelings to Bea Arthur's character, Dorothy. Blanche explained that the color "magenta" represented the way she felt when many feelings tumbled all around. She added that she wasn't quite sad or blue, and not quite green with envy or a yellow-bellied coward; however, she hated all those feelings and she hated the color magenta and just decided to call those feelings by that name.

Yep, that's kinda exactly what I felt. I was stranded in my own world of instant gratification and delusions of grandeur, and didn't know who I was anymore. Confusing fantasy with reality was my source of survival; obviously, that strategy wasn't working out very well for me. Magenta sucks!

July 11, 2009 was the night that I was arrested for my latest DUI and the last night that I had a drink or did any type of drugs. I was now in an intensive outpatient recovery program, and never thought I would make it past the first group meeting, but then something *happened*. It was before the start of that group meeting, and we introduced ourselves to each other along with stories of how we all ended up in a recovery program. I started, "You know, it's kinda like I'm on this roller coaster to nowhere. When I'm happy, I'm happy; but when I'm not, I'm anywhere from depressed to angry. And when I get angry, I just can't stop myself. It's like I know that what I'm doing, or about to do, is gonna be wrong, but I'm already on this ride and I ain't getting off until I'm finished." A few people nodded in agreement. "And I know that I'm probably gonna get in trouble, but at that point, it doesn't matter. Then, I finally calm down and I regret almost everything, especially because I can't take it back."

Nearly everyone in the room told a similar story; the counselor quietly walked into the room and allowed us all to continue without interruption. It was on that day, in that room, that I learned I wasn't the only one living this life (and lie) of reckless abandon without the common sense to simply get off the ride; I actually felt better. I'd lived most of my adult life thinking that I was the only one whose "emotional mind" was severed and separate from his "active mind."

I was so happy to have finally found a group of people with the same issues as me, and didn't feel so alone in my thoughts and actions anymore. There's a saying, "misery loves company;" this was the first time in my life that I truly believed that the rest of my life didn't have to be misery … that there were other options. Recovery wasn't gonna happen overnight, but at least I was now in a place where I had a starting point and could actually see a path forward.

[Sidebar: I knew the perils of alcoholism since I was very young, as I watched my excuse of an uncle become more and more abusive to his wife (wives) and children. I always swore to never be that type of uncle. I wanted to be the gay uncle that my nieces and nephews were proud of; not the uncle who was shunned at family functions and avoided at all costs by anyone who knew him well, especially me.

I distinctly remember on one hot summer afternoon when I was ten or eleven years old. My godfather's house recently had caught fire, and we gathered to repair the burned roof. As usual, all of his kids and nieces and nephews and neighbors showed up to help; that's how we do it here in Cajun Country.

As usual also, my drunk uncle was there. He was just drunk enough that he mistakenly thought that he could come at me. He blabbed some sort of indiscernible order at me and raised his hand as if to strike me if I didn't obey. I had been playing with the tools on the ground, and picked up the hammer and pointed the anvil part of the hammer directly at his face and screamed, "If you ever decide to touch me like you touch your kids, it'll be the last thing you ever do!" He walked away as if he'd "won;" he knew better. I don't know what gave me the audacity to retaliate in such a forceful way, but he knew that I absolutely meant every word. He NEVER approached me again, and I never spoke a word of the incident until now. (My parents always asked me if he "touched" me, since they were fully aware of my animosity toward him; I just said "No, he knows better," and left it at that.) It was a tough blow to my ego when I realized that I had actually become my uncle, minus the abusiveness; I was a HAPPY drunk (usually, or maybe just sometimes)!]

I thoroughly enjoyed our three-times-per-week inpatient meetings; there were some tough times, but the breakthroughs made it worth the pain. One of the most heart-crushing things that I learned was that "fame" or the lack of it, was a huge trigger point for me. I could handle the truth; I just couldn't seem to handle the fact that the fantasy of Colt Michael died a long time ago. It was true; as confusing a life as it may have been, I had to realize that Colt Michael no longer existed and could never be resurrected. I'd convinced myself that Colt Michael was everything that Ted A Richard could never have been. I lied to myself all of these years, believing that Colt Michael was somebody special. The truth was that Ted A Richard had already accomplished so much more than Colt Michael ever did; but I just couldn't let go of him.

Sadly, there was one huge obstacle to my sobriety that was nearly insurmountable; that obstacle was Alcoholics Anonymous. Please let me explain; I also want to be clear that these are my personal experiences at the time, and that perhaps things have changed in recent years. While I do realize that hundreds of thousands of alcoholics and addicts seek and find recovery through the AA program, it had the opposite effect for me. Once again, this is my personal story, and is certainly not meant to dismiss the achievements of those who have had success in the program, nor to disparage the program itself (if it worked for you); I just had a different experience; so did thousands of others just like me.

(*If you are a devout follower of Alcoholics Anonymous or any Twelve-Step program, you may want to skip to the next chapter; you're definitely not gonna like what comes next.*)

[Disclaimer: To my knowledge, SMART Recovery was not available in my area at the time of my sobriety. If it was, then it was not made available to me. At the time Alcoholics Anonymous and other Twelve Step programs were the only options offered.]

Okay, I'd like to have a serious conversation about my thoughts regarding my personal recovery, and why AA just didn't work for me. To say that I do not believe that AA is a great way to get sober would be an understatement. I believe that AA is one of the worst cults in American history except for, possibly, the Church of Scientology.

I am a spiritual person and definitely do not believe in God. Sure, I believe that there are unseen and unknown forces in the universe that create both opportunities and obstacles for all of us; however, the universe is not something or someone that I would ever pray to (the universe is not any form of god)—I just think that doesn't make sense.

It would help to remember, too, that I grew up in the very strict Roman Catholic church, and my parents believed the Catholic church was the ONLY church and that the pope received messages directly from God. (*There is so much that's so very wrong with that previous sentence.*) I also grew up learning the god we prayed to was a fearful god, and that we would be punished for any wrongdoing, yet I seldom heard or read about the good things that this god did. So, I ask, *"Why would I go to a church that preaches condemnation rather than forgiveness, and tells me that I'm going to hell every Sunday because I'm gay?"*—and don't even get me started on what's wrong with the Bible! Yet that's exactly what I was forced to do; unfortunately, my parents didn't know any better, and they still don't (though I don't love them any less).

To begin my thought process on why Alcoholics Anonymous didn't work for me, let's review using the Twelve Steps as a guide.

1) We admitted that we were powerless over alcohol, that our lives had become unmanageable.
2) Came to believe that a Power higher than ourselves could restore us to sanity.
3) Made a decision to turn our will and our lives over to the care of God as we understood Him.
4) Made a searching and fearless moral inventory of ourselves.
5) Admitted to God, to ourselves, and to another human being the exact nature of our wrongdoings.
6) Were entirely ready to have God remove all these defects of character.
7) Humbly asked Him to remove our shortcomings.
8) Made a list of persons we had harmed and became willing to make amends to them all.
9) Made direct amends to such people wherever possible, except when to do so would injure them or others.
10) Continued to take a personal inventory and when we were wrong promptly admitted it.
11) Sought through prayer and meditation to improve our conscious contact with God as we understood Him, praying only for knowledge of His will for us and the power to carry that out.
12) Having had a spiritual awakening as the result of these steps, we tried to carry this message to alcoholics and to practice these principals in our affairs.

This twelve-step mantra was recited at nearly every single AA meeting I ever attended. For an agnostic like myself to have to repeat the word "God" and "Him" as if it were something real was an absolute insult to my intelligence. I don't care if you add the words "as we understood Him;" the fact that you would capitalize "Him" dictates that you believe that this is an actual deity or god-like being. Of course, I don't believe in any of that, so I usually just kept quiet when the others were reading this garbage verbatim at each meeting; I disengaged from the pomp and circumstance. These meetings often made me feel as if I was stranded in a Catholic church with no escape. Sure, I could have walked out (and did sometimes), but I was ordered by the courts to attend these meetings, so I often had no choice.

The first thing that I took issue with was the distribution of "sobriety chips" at each meeting. I guess you could say that I'm not the type of person who bases his sobriety on a plastic trinket; it may be for you, but just not for me. But what really bothered me about the process was that it often turned into some sort of warped competition; nearly everyone bragged about their years of sobriety, and automatically created an atmosphere of hierarchy to any newcomer. (At one particular meeting, I sat next to a person who claimed to have twenty continuous years of sobriety, yet I could smell the liquor on his breath. No one questioned him since he was a long-timer. I found that to be degrading and disgusting to anyone else who actually DID have twenty years of sobriety, and it certainly did not help any newcomer who was there for their One Day sobriety chip.)

The audacity of reading the twelve steps before the meeting was supposed to remind members of exactly why they were there. Instead, once the meeting started (at least most of the hundreds that I attended), it became a cacophony of war stories; "I did this when I was drunk," "I did that when I was drunk." Yet, I heard very few people speak about their success stories of, and in, recovery. It all became a one-upmanship competition; who did the worst stuff when they were drunk or high. Damn, with all of those stories, I NEEDED a drink by the time I left the meeting, and immediately knew that AA would play absolutely no role in my recovery.

It concerned me when friends and acquaintances (people I'd known when I was drinking and drugging with them) would get involved in the program and immediately started living the "AA Lifestyle." Yes, I am an alcoholic and an addict, but I certainly don't need to be constantly reminded of the life I used to live; that's the life I threw away when I got sober, but I refused to let my addictions define who I was as a person. And the fact that we were to hold hands and say the Lord's Prayer at the end of each meeting made it even worse. I mean, if you supposedly tell your members to recognize "God as we understood Him," then why in the hell would you force its members to recite a prayer that is clearly based only in Christianity?

And finally, after the Lord's Prayer, while lifting each other's hands in unison, we'd say, "Keep coming back!" in emphatic excitement. *But WHY?* As I've previously stated, I've been to hundreds of AA meetings in my lifetime and have never felt more isolated than when I was within the four walls of those meetings. Sometimes I stayed for fellowship, but often found myself needing to get the hell outta there, for lack of actual fellowship. And while AA espouses itself to be open and welcoming, not one person ever reached out to me specifically to either help me or sponsor my progress. I thought to myself, *"Am I that unapproachable?"* (While it is not in the Twelve Steps, any AA member will tell you that you MUST have a sponsor in order to succeed in this program; so not only are you required to turn everything over to a Higher power, you must also be instructed by another alcoholic on how to do it. I'm really not that stupid; you may disagree, and that's okay, too.)

One of the mantras I often heard in those AA meetings was "don't be the victim." I found that to be rather hypocritical, since the very first step states that you must admit "that we were powerless over alcohol," confirming that we were victims such that "our lives had become unmanageable." Why aren't we teaching and showing alcoholics how to be stronger than the alcohol, thus making the alcoholic the victor?

Most of the people I met through the AA program, and now on social media, post graphics and memes of "inspiration" and "fortitude," sometimes speaking these mantras like a second language. To me, it's like the membership has been indoctrinated into the AA religion. It truly scared me!

In my opinion, AA only replaces your addiction to the alcohol and/or drugs with an addiction to its program; the entire concept of the program is structured to force you to depend upon someone else for your sobriety. While it may ultimately be a healthy addiction for the body, at least temporarily, I have to question its benefits to the mind, spirit, and soul ... where you need constant validation from others in the program to "approve" of your success. That's just not a system that works for me.

As a matter of principal, I felt that getting sober was much more about self-awareness and responsibility. We needed to learn why we fell into the throes of addiction, and what we needed to do to make ourselves a better person; it is a responsibility to ourselves and to others that we always present our best selves. That's not the vibe I got from Alcoholics Anonymous.

It seems as though every day was like a competition to be one more day clean and sober; if the competition was what kept you going, then the means to get there was worth the risk. For me, what worked was creating a competition between myself and tomorrow. I had to tell myself, "I need to be responsible today, because tomorrow, people are depending on me; I can't let them down and lose myself in the process."

I rode the "struggle bus" for far too long and allowed those struggles to consume me. And yes, although I was now in recovery, those struggles still existed; I was still an alcoholic and drug addict, and I still was HIV-positive. The former diagnoses I could change, the latter diagnosis I couldn't. So, I decided to no longer allow those struggles to occupy space in my quest for happiness ... and fabulousness!

Twenty-four years ago, I starred in a semi-pornographic video that I didn't even know existed. Twenty-four years later, I realized that I had been living a movie version of my own life without me in it; it was past time for me to take responsibility for my past, my current, and especially my future. I needed to show up and be present in my own life, which had been unraveling for years while I pretended not to notice. *Fame*, in this instance, defined as *responsibility*, is the journey that I had to take to be free of the addictions and worries of the past, and create opportunities for myself in a clean and sober environment.

I had to be responsible and accountable for myself at all times; admittedly, I failed a few times along the way and had to take the other fork in the road. That was okay, because I was still sober and clear-headed. Most importantly, I had to remind myself daily that being an alcoholic and an addict was somebody that I used to be, and I had the responsibility to leave that part of my life behind to find happiness and security for my future. To quote a meme I saw recently, *"If you're looking behind me, I'm not there anymore."* I agree!

It took only a few weeks in recovery to make the color magenta mean something else; I love the color magenta and always have, and I wasn't going to let Blanche's interpretation of that color make me dislike it. Magenta is the color of universal harmony and emotional balance, which I strive to maintain every day. And while magenta is actually equal parts of red and blue light, Blanche Devereaux saw it differently; now, I see it differently too.

When I see blue, I think of the vastness of the sky and constantly wonder about all of the things that I can't see behind the floating pillows of moisture. When I see green, I know that I am one with nature, and wonder about the expanse of life underneath the earth which we never see, recognizing that the survival of everything above depends on the health of everything below the surface. When I see yellow, it reminds me that even the brightest star in our universe can sometimes be dimmed for a moment when eclipsed by the rotation of the moon, but after those few minutes, the sun is shining again, even brighter than before. So, there, MAGENTA! I LOVE magenta!

Mardi Gras – drunk Ted with a rooster on my shoulder–2008

CHAPTER 26

MISSION

(That Time I Wore Orange)

In October 2009, I had to return to Lake Charles to face charges for my third DUI. I had an attorney, but nothing that he said could change the judge's decision; I was sentenced to five years in prison (and rightfully so). I immediately fell back into my seat and started crying, and dared not turn around to see the looks on my parents' faces. This was my fault alone and my journey alone; no longer could I depend on the kindness of strangers, though the character of Blanche DuBois from Tennessee Williams' play, *A Streetcar Named Desire* told me that I could. (*What was it with me and these "Blanche" women? "Blanche" is the French word for the color white, but these women were destined to be colorful; they were my rainbow spirit animals; their personalities and intuitiveness were far from being "blanched."*)

Then the judge said, "I see that you've been admitted into an intensive outpatient treatment facility and have been under house arrest; your records also indicate that you have excelled throughout the treatment process." (*Footnote: My therapist sent a special request to the judge to remove from my chart the requirement that I attend AA meetings.*)

Then the judge continued, "I will suspend all of the five-year sentence to thirty days in jail, which is mandated by the state of Louisiana. After that, you will be on mandatory parole for the remainder of those five years. You must also continue your treatment, and the facility will continue to send monthly reports to your parole officer."

At that point, my knees buckled in relief; I dried my eyes and thanked the judge for his consideration. The judge encouraged me just to keep up the good work and that he was glad that I was getting and accepting the help that I needed; he ended, "I don't wanna see you back here, okay?" I quickly responded, "I promise!" hoping that this time I could actually succeed. Thankfully, the judge also did not force me to go to jail immediately, and allowed me to complete my treatment program before serving my thirty days in jail.

Through Tyler Mental Health, I was admitted into Acadiana Recovery Center in November 2009. It was the first time in my life when I would spend both my birthday (my forty-seventh, for anyone who was keeping track) *and* Thanksgiving away from my family and without access to a phone. I didn't know if I'd be able to get through it; at least not without my friends, Jack and Goldschläger. Though I had already been in intensive recovery for several weeks before entering ARC, I always had a home to return to. I suddenly had the feeling of homelessness overwhelm me, but no valid explanation as to why.

On the first day in the recovery center I realized that the entire program was based on the principals of Alcoholics Anonymous. This really pissed me off, since the judge had specifically pardoned me from attending any AA meeting due to the fact that they normally triggered my addictions. Now, I was stuck here for twenty-eight days, being indoctrinated into the AA lifestyle and all of the "perks" that came with it, including the reciting of the lord's prayer (not capitalized purposefully) and the "keep coming back" bullshit. I mean, where the hell did they think I was going? We were locked up in a frickin' recovery center and being fed jail food. And yes, if given the chance, I might have run, even though I had no place to run to. I did, however, learn a lot about sober hierarchy in the recovery center, yet another problem that I have with this program. Exactly when did sobriety become a sport, where patients competed for "medals?" It was AA all over again.

Alas, I worked within the program as best I could, but always felt empty at night; I hated being forced to subscribe to a program I didn't believe in, at the risk of "failing" the course, and thus, violating the conditions of my parole. I worked closely with my assigned counselor, hoping that he'd never see my "Poker Face." (Lady Gaga always knows how to express exactly what I'm feeling.) Thankfully, he never did.

One of the benchmarks of recovery was in making reparations to people you have hurt in the past (Alcoholics Anonymous, Step 9). To that end, part of ARC's recovery program included a Family Day, which was touted as a reward for excelling in recovery; this was no treat at all. Unbeknownst to any of us in recovery, the program contacted everyone on our emergency contacts lists and invited them to attend; the visit would be more heart-wrenching than heartwarming.

Certainly, Family Day was not all it seemed. Chairs were set in a semi-circular pattern facing one way, with one chair facing the semi-circle. Those in the "hot seat" waited for their family and friends to tell them how badly they'd been hurt before affording the patient an opportunity to apologize for everything, and devise a plan for a sober future. This "intervention" bullshit never worked for me either; and badgering and belittling me in front of the rest of the recovery group caused me to become more angry than embarrassed and triggered my addictions. *I thought that recovery was about support and encouragement. When did recovery become about loathing and shame?*

I was surprised that most of my family members were not truly aware of how dependent I was to my addictions. Though they had been hurt by my constant arrests over the years, I never did anything to intentionally harm them personally (other than owing my parents money from all of the bailouts). While they hated seeing me suffer, it was time for me to share how I got so wrapped up in my addictions.

So my family started talking, but it was nothing like I expected. They did not fault me for any of my past indiscretions; they just asked me what they could do to help. I think that even the staff of the ARC facility were surprised about this new set of developments (probably because they were hoping for drama, which never happened).

Mom asked if I started drinking more after the HIV diagnosis. I explained that was a part of it, but also because I kept the diagnosis secret for five years. Further, for my entire childhood and young adulthood, my family forced me to go to Catholic church where it was drilled into me weekly that I was a horrible person because I was gay, and that I would rot in hell. The diagnosis just caused a faster downward, unstoppable spiral. It was also the first time that I told my family about the alleged sexual abuse by Fr Michael Guidry.

Then I continued, "I don't blame y'all for any of this, because I never had the guts to tell you what I felt inside; I just didn't want to hurt your feelings. I don't want you to apologize, because y'all didn't do anything wrong; I just never told you how going to church traumatized me."

Then my sister, Cassie, said, "Ted, you spent over four months with us in Spokane, and I never saw you have a single drink. I don't understand how you're an alcoholic." And I replied, "You're right, I didn't drink in Spokane because I was on a mission. You needed my help, and that was more important than alcohol at the time. I had a focus, and that was you and Dominic and Daric, so I really didn't have time to think about drinking." (As I said those words, even I didn't remember that I had not had a single drink for four months.)

"I guess you could call me an 'unintentional alcoholic;' my problem is that I would never go out with the expressed intention of getting drunk. It's just that once I have the first drink, I couldn't stop with only one, or two, or ten; it's best that I just don't even have the first one."

That was my *aha* moment; the epiphany that finally woke me up. It turned out that I needed a mission or a project to keep me focused on my sobriety, my health, and my well-being. Having a mission kept me sober and happy, and gave me focus and direction. Somehow, in the midst of all of the "Family Day" drama that the recovery center hoped for, it was actually my family who brought me down from the rafters; it was my family who chose support over condemnation.

I hardly slept at all that night, then I remembered that writing helped me sleep. This time I wrote about "Hiding Behind My Truth," even though I didn't know what my truth was anymore. For years, I kept forcing myself to believe things that weren't true for the sake of my own sanity. Yet it was these exact same "truths" that fueled my insanity.

When I told the counselor about my insomnia due to the "Family Day" massacre, I was told that my sponsor could help me deal with my trigger points once I get out. *REALLY, asshole? I am in fucking therapy in a recovery center to get help, and you're telling me to get help after I get out? What fresh pile of bullshit is this?* I kept my poker face since I needed to get the hell outta there, but not before I finished the program. I began counting the days; maybe I should have gotten a "chip" for that too—oh, and an Academy Award, too, for my acting skills.

I completed my twenty-eight-day treatment at ARC, then returned to Tyler Mental Health facility for continued follow-ups. Throughout the depths of my addictions, I'd allowed myself to become a spectator of my own life while I lived outside of myself. There was always a reason to drink and drug, and always someone or something else to blame. But I came to realize that, "Sometimes, it's just not about you; it really is about ME."

I was finally in a place (in my head) to focus on the positive and keep negative thoughts at bay. I also realized that I was responsible for my own sobriety, and that relying on someone else to keep me sober just wasn't going to work, although psychiatry and Xanax helped a lot. While in recovery, so many stories of other alcoholics and drug addicts being evicted, exiled by family and friends, and forced to live lives of destitution because of their addictions abounded. This was difficult to absorb, since my parents and family supported me throughout all my trials and struggles and never gave up on me. As much as I sometimes want to, there was no way to "blame" them for the monstrous failure of my life; rather, they saw me struggling and allowed me to "hit rock bottom" on my own, never knowing what my rock bottom was. I didn't realize that the struggle was not only mine, but theirs too. I hid my addictions from them for years, though, not very convincingly. My consistent lack of attempts to do anything to better myself took a toll on my family, more so than it ever did with me. I had to learn that my unwillingness to address my addictions caused nearly irreparable harm to my family and friends. Now that I was in (forced) recovery, my family recognized that, at least this time, I was trying everything in my power to become the person I should have always been. I now faced a new set of struggles unprepared: awakening the spirit still left inside to redefine the rest of my life, becoming a responsible brother, son, and uncle, regaining lost trust, and finally becoming clean and sober.

But stating that my mission in life was to stay clean and sober just wasn't enough; my mind needed stimulation and my thought processes needed rejuvenating. My mission had to be tangible with an achievable end goal. I decided to spend the rest of my life conquering obstacles that, in the past, had been unconquerable. That became my mission. Looking back on my life, all the failures became clear, and my mission was to rectify those failures and turn them into victories. But being sober and "not out" were not motivators for me either. I needed to remain clean and sober and know that I was completely "safe," and would spend the rest of my life working on that, too. Even with successes and failures, I never abandoned a mission, but always returned to try again. I began to understand that life was so much better on this side of addiction, and that I deserved to have the life I was creating in my own sobriety.

But first I had to do my mandatory thirty-day stint in jail. I showed up to the Calcasieu Parish (in Louisiana, we call them parishes, not counties) jail in early December, about a week after completing rehab. I still owe a debt of gratitude to the judge for allowing me to get help on my own terms, though the judge basically dictated what my "life's terms" would be for the next thirty days. He already saw all of the life changes I made before I appeared in court that prompted this latitude; and his speech to me at the trial proved to me that I was finally on the right track.

Since the drunkenness of what I used to call my life was now common knowledge all across south Louisiana, I knew better than to hide the fact that I was going to jail, instead finding the humor to let my family and friends know that I would be okay. I posted to Facebook a few days before I was scheduled to turn myself in; "So, it looks like I'll be taking a short mandatory vacation. I'm not very familiar with my new temporary housing arrangements (they all knew I was lying), but I have been informed that the only color we will be allowed to wear is orange. Here's the problem; I have absolutely NO accessories to match orange! It's just not a color I normally wear; though I have tons of accessories for black-and-white stripes. If any of you have any ideas for accessorizing orange, please send fashion advice, but please don't say 'black,' I don't wanna walk around looking like a Halloween advertisement."

Within minutes, one of my dear friends from high school responded, "I just love the fact that you're taking this going-to-jail thing in stride. I'm a straight dude (you know that), and I know nothing about fashion (my wife buys all my clothes); but Ted, I believe in you! I know that within the first week you'll have the place decorated and bedazzled to your liking!" I loved his post, especially because his response prompted hundreds of others to offer similar sentiments; they were all happy for me to get the help I'd refused for so long, and wished me luck on the other side of "my short mandatory vacation." I responded with, "Send ribbon and rhinestones, I got this."

While I spent my forty-seventh birthday and Thanksgiving in a recovery center that proved to be more harmful than helpful, I would spend Christmas in jail. I was counselled by former inmates (that I met in rehab and therapy) to get on a work detail. "That way you won't be stuck in your cell all day," they said. So, I of course, took their advice. WRONG CHOICE!

I thought that, for sure, with my management background and organizational skills, that I would be assigned an indoor job doing some filing or something like that. NO! I was sent out into "the field" to do weed-eating around the jail yards. *I don't even weed at my own damned house, and you think I'm gonna weed-eat here? Oh, hell no!*

So after about two hours I suddenly developed "heat stroke" (in December) and was immediately taken to the medical facility. When it was discovered that I was HIV-positive, I was immediately taken off of work detail and put into the "medically disabled" section of the jail. HEAVEN! It was the only time in my life that I used my HIV status for "preferential treatment;" but it worked, and I was grateful.

This sector of the facility where I was housed had about fifty inmates per pod, and I quickly learned to separate the good from the bad ... the wheat from the chaff. I got "acquainted" with just a few people that seemed trustworthy (as much as people can be trusted in jail).

Che' was the bad-boy type that would probably have been great for sex, but horrible for a relationship; something about him told me to stay away, though I hoped that I'd be in the bunk next to him. He was short, yet stocky, and had a body that was chiseled in exactly the places where he needed them to be (at least where I wanted them to be); sweatpants (even orange ones) don't lie. From the second I stepped into the medical pod, this Italian beefcake with the some of the richest black curly hair I'd ever seen already had my heart pumping (only because we can't talk about those other things in prison); I don't recall ever seeing someone stare back at me with ebony eyes so dark that I could almost see my reflection in them; though I didn't know if that glare was contempt, or if it was just an acknowledgement of my presence, or if it meant something totally different. I desperately wanted to find out, but there was no "gay section" in this jail. I would need to do my own detective work.

Che' reached out to me when he realized that I knew how to play Spades (thanks to those late night card games at Frank's); anytime the playing cards were being shuffled, Che' always made it a point to come grab me—to play cards, though I did allow him to "accidently" rub up against me a few times ... I think he enjoyed it too. That was perfectly fine with me. Che' shuffled the deck and dealt the cards. I got to stare into the ebony mirrored eyes until it was "lights out;" then his eyes melted into the background.

I quickly became trusted by the inmates in my pod, and got along with almost everyone. However, I was simply amazed by the easy access to drugs and contraband available within the confines of the jail, even while under constant watch in prison conditions. But I guess a true criminal will always find a way.

So, one day, while we were out on the basketball court during our random "outdoor hour" which occurred about once or twice a week, I whispered to a guard, "If you wanna know what's really going on, just let me know." That's all I said.

[Sidebar: Visitation day happened twice weekly, but I never had visitors. I specifically asked my family to not visit me in jail, explaining that it would only make me miss home even more. Besides, I put enough money into my commissary so that I could call them every day.]

The very next day, a guard came to our pod and called my name; I raised my hand and he said, "Come with me, your lawyer needs to see you." That made absolutely no sense to me, since all of my court dates were over (at least the ones in Lake Charles). *Could this be my attorney from Lafayette?* I followed the guard to the visitors' area, but we just kept walking; I knew better than to ask questions. We walked through another set of double doors and into an office too spacious for a prisoner to be in. Seated on the other side of the desk, though I didn't know it at the time, was the warden. He was a stocky, hirsute gentleman about my age who filled out his uniform extremely well; still seated behind his desk, he said, "So, one of my guards told me that I needed to be aware of what was really going on."

I was in shock; I couldn't believe that my message made it to the top so quickly. I asked, "Where do you want me to start?" He quickly responded, "From the beginning." So that's exactly what I did. I told him about cigarettes and marijuana being passed in between the pods using long pieces of string (though I didn't know where the string came from); how the inmates put aluminum foil in the microwave to spark a fire to light cigarettes; where all of the hiding places were in and around the pods (places they never looked during a shakedown), and how inmates would hide contraband in the waistbands of their orange elastic waist pants (and other places).

The warden was stunned at the sheer amount of information I provided. "Why did you decide to do this?" he asked. I let him know that one of the repeat offenders smoking them "fancy" cigarettes was sleeping in the bunk right next to me, and that I was afraid that the smell was getting on my clothing; I didn't wanna be blamed whenever some bad stuff went down.

Jail Warden McHottie stood up to shake my hand, and his 6'4" frame towered over me; his crotch was level with my eyes as I was seated, so I hurriedly stood up so that he wouldn't catch me staring. "Damn impressive," I said under my breath, hoping that he didn't hear that either. We shook hands, and I was escorted back to my pod.

The following morning, just after breakfast, "SHAKEDOWN!" The entire pod went collectively crazy as its residents tried to hide everything that didn't belong, and time was of the essence. We were removed from our pod to wait in the secure hallway, and once the strip search was over, re-entered single file back into our pod directly to our assigned bunks. An hour later, my next-door bunk mate was instructed to gather his belongings and moved elsewhere. No one knew why; but I did! Then, my Spades partner, Che', would shuffle the deck and deal the cards.

Surprisingly, twice each week, I had a "visitor," and almost twice each week there was another shakedown, and after each shakedown another inmate (or more) was removed from our pod. Still, no one knew why; but I did! Then again, my Spades partner, Che', would shuffle the deck and deal the cards.

The inmates were furious about the shakedowns and constantly tried to figure out who the "jail rat" was. Because of my congenial disposition and the fact that I'd always help out with my commissary, no one ever suspected that I could do something so devious. In addition, many of the inmates assumed that the jail rat must have been the person that was moved, for their own safety. No one ever realized that this "rat infestation" still had not been eradicated, and that I had outsmarted the rat trap once again.

While I understand that the moniker of "jail rat" is not a name to which most inmates aspire, I gained the trust and respect of all of the guards and I impressed Jail Warden McHottie; I could sleep well at night knowing that I did the right thing for the right reasons. My reward? An early release in time to spend Christmas with my family; Old St. Nick was surely coming to town to bring holiday cheer and presents (and my presence) to all of the good boys and girls.

Let's just be honest, I lived in the ludicrous irony that this former jailbird was now playing Santa, handing out gifts to everyone; I was not in a place to pass judgement over "good" and "bad" or "naughty" or "nice," while I had been the worst. I was much more at ease handing out the presents, especially since I felt I didn't deserve to receive any. No one questioned my wish to want to make all of the kiddos happy, and they all played along. The biggest gift I could ever give to them (and to myself) was something money could never buy: my sobriety. I hoped that this would be the first of many years to come that I was "sober Santa," not "drunk Santa."

In early 2010, the court dates came up for my fourth and fifth offense DUIs; thankfully they were combined into one case. The State of Louisiana charges DUI offenses in annual accruements; by the dates of my latest offenses, two of my previous offenses were not included in the new charges. So, my fifth offense DUI now became only a third offense DUI. Since I'd already been to treatment and remained clean and sober, my attorney got the charge reduced to a second offense DUI with the stipulation that any failure to maintain my sobriety would result in an immediate revocation of my probation, and I would spend the remainder of those five years in prison (pending other additional charges). The fines, however, were astronomical, since those fees were determined based on a fifth offense DUI ... I deserved it, and simply said, "Thank you, your honor;" the judge nodded in recognition of my accomplishments in sobriety and wished me luck.

[Sidebar: I am a firm believer in very strict DUI laws; I received so many DUIs (not even counting all those times I drove drunk without incident), yet never actually received the help I needed for many, many years. (I was lucky to never have killed anyone, but came close quite a few times.) We have a justice system that allows DUI defendants to "plead down" to a lesser charge. I think that this is completely unfair to the defendant and to the public at large. If EVERY DUI offender was sentenced to treatment on their FIRST offense, perhaps there would be many fewer second offenses. If I was forced to go to jail and attend treatment classes after my first offense DUI, perhaps I would have received the tools to make smarter choices regarding my drinking habits, and maybe I would have quit drinking at age twenty-six instead of age forty-six. *Maybe.*]

I needed to focus more on what people (not in AA) did to get better, to heal, and I surrounded myself with a small group of friends who understood what I experienced. They have continued to help me work through this process. (Thank you to Mike and Brian Galyean-Frederick.) With their help and my continuously long list of "unfinished projects" I have stayed sober until now. But something else was missing, so I kept looking for something else; I then realized that sometimes "looking for something else" was a mission of its own. My search for the next mission was what helped to keep me sober during what could have been very dark days.

Fame, in this instance, defined as *mission*, was the life path I chose (over thirty years too late), when I decided that it was finally time to grow the hell up, and be the man I was destined to be. Somewhere along the way, I lost that little boy with the smile on his heart that did cartwheels at that little league baseball game. I wanted to find him again; and yes, I can still do cartwheels (well, maybe just one at a time).

Twenty-three years ago, Theresa DeLuca was on a mission to conquer Colt Michael by forcing herself upon him and regrettably for me, succeeded. Twenty-three years later, my mission became conquering my addictions and forcing myself, through hard work and dedication, to my progress in sobriety, and to be a better man today than I was yesterday.

For the rest of my life, I would always be a convicted felon (and rightfully so), having allowed my addictions to consume me for far too long. Although I served my time and was now on the right path, even when I would finally be finished with my parole in five years, I would still be a convicted felon, and always would be. Now THAT'S a SOBERING thought!

Halloween–me dressed in orange preparing for jail–2009

CHAPTER 27

FAMILY

(That Time I Got a Tattoo ... or Two)

Now that the pressures of court dates and jail time and more court dates were behind me, I needed time to decompress from my past and figure out a path forward. I was forty-seven years old, and with all of the positive things I accomplished in this lifetime, I was still mired in the negativity of my past. I had become so complacent with blaming other people and circumstances for everything that I refused to see was wrong with me. I kept looking for my next mission but repeatedly drowned myself in self-hatred that I was too blind to see the path already laid out. *If finding a mission was truly the path forward, then why was I still circling the wagons around a life that no longer existed? Why did I continue to look for myself in the past?* I shouldn't be there anymore; but still was.

In the past, I searched to help others who I deemed to be worse off than me, figuring that if I spent time in an effort to improve their lives, then my life wouldn't seem so miserable. Recovery taught me that helping save someone else would never save me; it only shifted the focus outward rather than inward. I needed to see the broken parts of me and heal from the inside out. Though I had no specific plan of action, I decided to turn my attention to the one thing that mattered most to me ... family.

I was so very proud when, in 2010, both Dominic and Daric joined the United States Air Force. Each of them was starting new lives; Dominic became the father of his eldest daughter, Erica Renee, and Daric married his high school sweetheart, August Briella. Their lives were just beginning just as I thought mine was coming to an end. Yes, even though I was now clean and sober, the specter of AIDS still haunted me. If my time was short, I still wanted my best years to be remembered as great times spent with my family and not wallowing in the dregs of my past.

To that end, I decided to have a once-in-a-lifetime vacation to visit Daric and August at their new Air Force digs near Hurlburt Field in northwest Florida.

[Sidebar: During Daric and August's most recent visit to Louisiana, they each revealed their newest "addition;" they got tattoos to signify their love for each other. I thought the sentiment was so sweet, and I may have been just a little jealous; I had always wanted to get a tattoo, but I never could decide exactly what I wanted. I knew that this tattoo would be permanent body art, so it had to be something meaningful to me. I told them that the next time I visited them in Florida, I would get a tattoo. Of course, they laughed. I didn't.]

August picked me up at the airport, since Daric was on duty; as we were headed back to the Air Force base, I said, "Okay, where's the tattoo shop?" She thought I was kidding; I wasn't. So, as a joke, August pulled into the tattoo shop and said, "Alright, Uncle Ted, you ready?" She thought that she was calling my bluff, but it was no bluff at all.

I'd thought a lot about the exact tattoo I wanted. It had to have a *fleur-de-lis* to represent my Louisiana roots, the Scorpio scorpion and symbol to represent my birthday, and a rainbow ring in recognition of my gay pride. August also had no idea that I'd already drawn a rough draft of my tattoo.

We made an appointment for the next day, and August just watched in amazement as my creation came to life. To be honest, I was quite impressed myself! The tattoo artist was astonishing, and though the concept for the tattoo was entirely mine, I encouraged him to add his own artistic flair wherever he saw fit; after all, he was the artist, I was only a canvas. When he finished, I had a few tears in my eyes; not from the pain; but because it was so very beautiful. This tattoo was everything I wanted and even more than I could have imagined. I was so happy that I let the artist be the artist; and was proud to display his work on my body.

Those of you who have tattoos know that you need to take extreme caution with skin care for the next few days. Well, the problem was that the tattoo was in the middle of my shoulder blades; and I couldn't reach it. So, while Daric was at work, I would put on a swimsuit and August would put on her swimsuit so that she could properly clean my tattoo before I took a shower; it was all so innocent.

As fate would have it, one day Daric came home unexpectedly for lunch while August and I were in the shower. I didn't know why I felt so guilty, but I did. There we stood, his uncle and his wife with their swimsuits on, taunting him to join us in the shower. The look of sheer horror on Daric's faced immediately told us that he failed to find the humor in our tawdry escapade (as innocent as it may have been). Once August and I realized the seriousness in his demeanor, we quickly muffled our laughter and explained the situation to him. And even though he recognized that his uncle and his wife were simply engaging in basic tattoo skin care, we have never again spoken about "the incident."

But we did a whole lot more than just get a tattoo; this was MY vacation, but I wanted it to be a vacation that Daric and August would not soon forget. As with almost every vacation I took, I planned almost NOTHING. I waited until I arrived before making decisions about my schedule, and I needed to cross a few things off of my bucket list. As luck would have it, they were also on Daric's and August's bucket list. Many of these things were not cheap, and they were worried about our budget. I told them, "Look, I've been saving my money especially for this trip. (It's amazing how much more money you have when you stop drinking and drugging.) We can do whatever the heck we want to!" AND WE DID! It was definitely a vacation to remember ... the banana boat ride, parasailing, strolling the boardwalk and the beach; and to top it all off, we went to Pensacola where they saw their very first drag show!

While they were aware of my HIV diagnosis, I tried to never show them how horrible I truly felt and how my health was failing me worse and worse by the day. This vacation was about THEM, and not about ME. I never told them that this would probably be the last time they saw me alive.

Over the past several years I always tried to find different ways to let my family know how important they were to me; it was too late to make memories with my brother and sister, but it was never too late to make new memories with my six nieces and nephews. I was always the zany gay uncle who did crazy things like dressing up as an escaped convict for Halloween (though everyone knew I just got out of jail), pretending to be Santa at Christmastime, taking them somewhere unexpected on any random day, and even making bunny rabbit cakes for Easter. (It's a cake that's shaped like a bunny rabbit; NOT made from a bunny rabbit.) I knew that I would never have the opportunity to become a father, but being the fabulous uncle sufficed just enough for me.

I always relished the times I spent with the "kids" (even during those *SpongeBob SquarePants* days), and they never failed to let me know how much they truly loved me. My "Uncle Ted wisdom," often fell on deaf ears. I'd say things like: "You are destined for greatness, but that greatness comes in many shapes and forms," or tell them, "It is up to you to discover your own pathway to your own greatness!" At least it sounded good at the time, but they returned to watching their new favorite cartoon.

It was now July 4, 2012, and fireworks exploded like rockets all around my house to celebrate America's independence (though, honestly, I believe we have created one of the most co-dependent countries on Earth). Simultaneously, there was a huge thunder and lightning storm happening. Suddenly I saw a very large flash of light that looked as if it hit directly above my house. I was inside at the time, and my entire house shook. I immediately jumped from my couch and went to check things out; no damage inside, no damage outside, and I still had electricity. Close call.

About an hour or so later, I heard a crackling that sounded as if it came from the attic. *But wait, I don't have an attic. So, what was that noise?* Again, I went upstairs, looked all over downstairs, and I still had electricity. That light was so bright, and my house had shaken so violently, and I definitely heard crackling (like in a fireplace).

So, I ran outside, and that's when the horror struck me. Ophelia Katherine's house (next door to me) was on fire; things were definitely not OK! The garage door was open, so we knew that my brother wasn't home; but I didn't know where Ophelia (now sixteen years old) was. *Was she with her dad? Was she home alone? Did she know the house was on fire?*

I called 911 as quickly as I could. And you know those stories where people forget the number to 911? On that day, I completely understood how that could happen. Everything happening so fast. I just remember the operator saying, "911, what is your emergency?" Then I said, in a stuttering voice, "FFF-III-RRR-EEEE! TTTHe Hhhouse NNNNeeextt doooor!" I literally do not remember the rest of the conversation.

In the meantime, all the neighbors came out of their homes, and our neighbors from across the street came over to help; luckily, one of them worked for SLEMCO, the local electric company, and disconnected the electricity immediately. There was a sudden explosion from the side of the house, and both of our neighbors ran out of the way. The electricity was disconnected just in time; otherwise, the explosion would have been much worse!

I called O.K.'s father, but he was not answering his phone; we'd already determined that she was not home, and figured that she was with her dad. I phoned O.K., who answered immediately.

The conversation went something like this:

O.K.: "Hello."
Me: "This is *Parrain* Ted, are you with your Dad?"
O.K.: "Yes."
Me: "I need to talk to him right away."
O.K.: "He's on the phone."
Me: "O.K., this is very, very important, I need to speak to him right now!"

(Ophelia handed the phone to her dad)

Him: "Hello."
Me: "Your house is on fire."
Him: "I know, I'm on the phone with the insurance company right now. Lightning hit my flagpole and blew out my air conditioner. I'm making the claim right now."
Me: "No, you don't understand! Your house is ON FIRE!"

For their safety, he and Ophelia had gone to a friend's house, thinking that the extent of the damage was a lightning strike and that they would be out of electricity for a while; they had no idea that this lightning event was becoming a five-alarm fire. They got back home shortly after the fire trucks arrived (about five minutes), but by that time, the blaze was running the entire length of the roofline. The very, very thick, black smoke was seen from miles away. I received phone calls constantly, while my godchild's home and all of her Mom's memories went up in smoke.

My family and I clustered onto my front porch and just watched. There was nothing we could do. Ophelia just stood next to her dad; bewildered, shocked, sad and heartbroken; she was far from okay. And I don't even think that she was thinking about herself, nor the fact that her home was destroyed; I know that she was thinking about her Mom. Gone was the year-round Christmas tree, gone were her keepsakes from her childhood that were kept in the attic. She felt as though her mom had somehow just been erased; like she never even existed.

It was now Thanksgiving 2012, and we were having dinner at Christopher and Cassie's house. At one point, it was just Ophelia and me sitting and talking. I could tell that she had a heavy heart. She said, "*Parrain* Ted, I don't understand why people spend all this money on all of these Christmas decorations, and spend all these hours putting them up ... and then they have to take them all down a month or so later. Why can't it just be Christmas all year long?" I knew that she was missing her Mom; that permanent Christmas tree had been the only constant reminder of her Mom that always made her happy, and now that was gone too. I *needed to do something. But what?*

I immediately had an idea; *Parrain* Ted always had ideas! The Dollar General store was open and only about a quarter mile from the house. There was virtually no traffic, so we walked to the store, and I bought more than $300 worth of Christmas ornaments and decorations. (That's hard to do at the dollar store!) I even brought the shopping cart home. My house was too small for a large Christmas tree, so we decorated all of the trees on the outside of my house; we took out ladders and stepstools and everybody helped; especially O.K., and I told her, "Now it can be Christmas at *Parrain* Ted's house all year long, and you can have good memories of your Mom every time you walk outside and see my house next door!" Those same ornaments stayed up for about three years or so, and lots of people always asked why I never took down my Christmas decorations. When I told this story, they would always respond that I'd done something special. To me, it was no big deal. I loved Sharon and I love Ophelia ... it was a no-brainer. Over the years, many of the ornaments since fell off or blew away after a few Louisiana hurricanes. I guess it was time for me to redecorate my trees. I promise to get around to that very soon. And if I don't, y'all can do it for me!

[Update: For Christmas 2021, I purchased another $300 worth of ornaments and we—meaning me, O.K., and her new husband, Axel—decorated all of the trees (now fully-grown) around my house.]

In addition, something no one in the family knew, was that I had kept photo albums for all my nieces and nephews since they were children. (Many of these photos were taken before cell phones were invented, so I had kept old photos of them in an album.) Also, in this album, I kept mementos from over the years, especially the ones that had a special remembrance for me, and planned to give each child their photo albums when they were older. For some reason, this particular Christmas season seemed special. So I gave each of the nephews and nieces their photo albums. I met with each of the kids separately. I wanted this to be special for them too.

Of course, Ophelia was the first, and when she saw the album, was speechless with astonishment. There were photos and mementos in her albums that she didn't even know existed; there were photos of her with her Mom that she had never seen. Now I know that there was nothing that I could ever have given her to bring back lost memories of her Mom, nor to restore anything that was lost in the fire, but hopefully I was able to put that sparkle back into her eyes, even if just for a little while! Maybe it's that sparkle that I missed too.

Then, in January 2013, I attended a birthday party for a friend. I'm usually not a big fan of birthday parties, but this one was special. This friend having recently survived a suicide attempt, was depressed about his own sexuality, being shunned by his family, and his recent HIV-positive diagnosis. It was difficult to be at a party with his family whom I knew hated me just because of who I was (an out and proud gay man living with HIV). I felt the tension in the air as I walked in, especially because the family had not invited me; rather, my friend had. In retrospect, his invitation was probably two-fold; he wanted his family to know he was no longer ashamed, and that if they truly accepted him, then they would also accept having me as his friend. (NOTE: To assure his privacy,

I have not named him or his family. My friend endured a lifetime of shame at the hands of the people he still calls family. Unfortunately, I had to minimize my contact with him, since he could not let go of the family purse-strings, and still fosters their belief that "gays don't go to heaven.")

We sang "Happy Birthday," which I always found to be such a dreadful song. *Why was it that when we're singing what is supposed to be a joyous, celebratory song, it always sounds like the droning hymns at a funeral home?* I've always hated that song; maybe that's why I hate birthday parties too.

But in the middle of the drawn-out "happy birthday to you," I saw what I thought was an apparition through the windows of the restaurant. *No, it couldn't be! Was that Dominic? No way! He was supposed to be in Afghanistan or Iraq or Syria or some other far away place. Wait! It WAS Dominic! Nope, it's my eyes playing tricks on me again.* I swear I'm not even drinking; only pineapple juice for me these days.

Then the apparition walked in through the front doors of the restaurant and headed straight toward me. Indeed, it was Dominic, who was as surprised to see me as I was to see him. We both had that deer-in-the-headlights stare; neither of us believing this twist of fate that had us finding each other in a random place on a random night in January.

Dominic gave me a warm embrace; there were no words that needed to be said. Slowly releasing each other from the hug, Dominic declared, "Uncle Ted, I know what it means, I know what it means!" I could hear the excitement in his voice; and as quickly as he appeared, he was gone. He was meeting other folks for dinner later. He waved good-bye again as he saluted his way out the front door. Proudly, I saluted him back and winked. Now we both knew.

The following day, I received a phone call from Dominic. He said, "Uncle Ted, I'm going get a tattoo tomorrow, you coming?" "Absolutely, buddy; see ya there." Now, both Dominic and I have tattoos that say *Legacy of the Future*. Of course, mine has a rainbow owl too, but you would have expected nothing less. And out of love for my nephew, I wrote him a poem about the origins of the saying, appropriately titled, *Legacy of the Future*. The poem tells the story of a dream where a rainbow owl appeared to me to guide me toward finding a path that kept me wandering through life with purpose and kept me wondering if what I left behind was the legacy that others would cherish.

It was the last day of school for Ophelia and her first cousin, Katrina Todd; I decided to surprise them and picked them up from school. My other in-town niece, Etta Mae, had to work, so she missed out. But I took O.K. and K.T. out to eat at one of my favorite Mexican restaurants in downtown Lafayette. All of a sudden, we all jerked our heads back like a synchronized dance move. It was as if we planned it, but we didn't; we were all staring at the same thing. There was this really, really hot guy riding his bicycle without a shirt and only a guitar strapped to his back, catching all of us by surprise that somebody this gorgeous would just be randomly riding a bicycle downtown. Of course, I paid a little more attention than they did; maybe not.

I noticed that he snuck into the business next door; I'd eaten at this place many, many times, and had never noticed that there was a bicycle shop right next door. While they weren't looking, I rushed over to the bike shop and spotted him; he was very easy to find. (I was disappointed to find that he had put his shirt on.) In my gay nervousness, I said, "Look, I know you don't know me, but my nieces and I saw you on your bike earlier with a guitar." He nodded his head inquisitively. So, I asked what, in retrospect, was a stupid question, "Do you happen to play the guitar, or sing, or anything?" Quick to catch my faux pas, but clever enough to not call me on it, he said, "Of course I sing!"

I didn't realize that he worked at the bike shop, and that the young lady standing behind him with a Cheshire cat-like grin on her face was his boss. I apologized to her for interrupting his work, and then made this request, "It's my nieces' last day of school, and I was wondering if you could come and sing them a song or two, kinda serenade them or something." With his boss' encouragement, he instantly agreed. I sneaked back into the restaurant, telling the girls that I had been in the restroom.

They were shocked when they saw that same bronzed, muscled guitar guy walk directly up to our table and introduce himself, "Dustin Gaspard," he said, "your uncle asked me to sing for you." O.K and K.T. looked at me with equal amounts of excitement and embarrassment.

Though I don't know why they were so shocked; Uncle Ted always did crazy stuff like this.

Dustin began by strumming his guitar and humming a few bars to a song we had never heard. What none of us expected, was the voice that sprung forth once this soulful and bluesy crooner, with a range wider than the Mississippi delta, began singing. We all just sat there in amazement; I didn't understand how this incredible talent was being kept hidden somewhere in the back of a bicycle shop.

I gave him $20 for his efforts, though that was not nearly enough. I promised him that if I ever had the opportunity, I would put him on the stage where he belonged. Dustin stayed and chatted with us for a while as we exchanged contact information; I knew it was just business, but I intended to keep the promise I made. (Damn, what is it with me and these straight guys?)

Fame, in this instance, defined as *family*, is the culmination of a lifetime of memories, both good and bad, that continued to shape the manner in which I chose to live the rest of my life. I learned that my family means more to me than the wicked blood that runs through my own veins. I lived the first part of my life wanting my family to love me in spite of my faults, and because I just assumed that I deserved it. I wanted to live the rest of my life wanting my family to love me, not because I felt it was owed, but rather, because I earned it. I wanted the prophecy of the rainbow owl to lend credence to the rhythm of what would become the rest of my life. I owed that much to myself.

But I also learned a sad truth; the recognition that sometimes life is about the company you keep. It had been stated many times that just because you are related by blood doesn't mean that they deserve to be included with the people you call your family.

One of the things I learned in recovery was the need to change the people, places and things from my past that contributed to the delinquency of my lifestyle. Unfortunately, one of the people who needed replacing was my younger brother. For most of my life, I tried to have a cordial relationship with him, ignoring the countless lies and acts of aggression, only to realize that I was upholding *both* sides of the relationship. I tried to sever ties with him on several occasions, but once Ophelia was born, I knew that if I exiled him from my life, then it would be easier for him to tell her that I just didn't care for her anymore, and I refused to allow his demented narrative to be the definition of the relationship between me and my beloved godchild.

Twenty-eight years ago, I was so completely lost in the oblivion of my HIV diagnosis that I couldn't understand my purpose anymore, nor even know if it really mattered. I always swore that I would never take one pill to offset the side effects of another pill, but that's exactly where I found myself. I took between twenty to forty pills a day to subdue the virus, manage my side effects, and save my kidneys from being ravaged by the toxic HIV virus. I was gonna die soon anyway; this would be my legacy.

Twenty-eight years later, my eldest nephew, Dominic, found me in the most unexpected place, and in his excitement for the family he was creating, discovered the beginning of his own legacy. The rainbow owl was right!

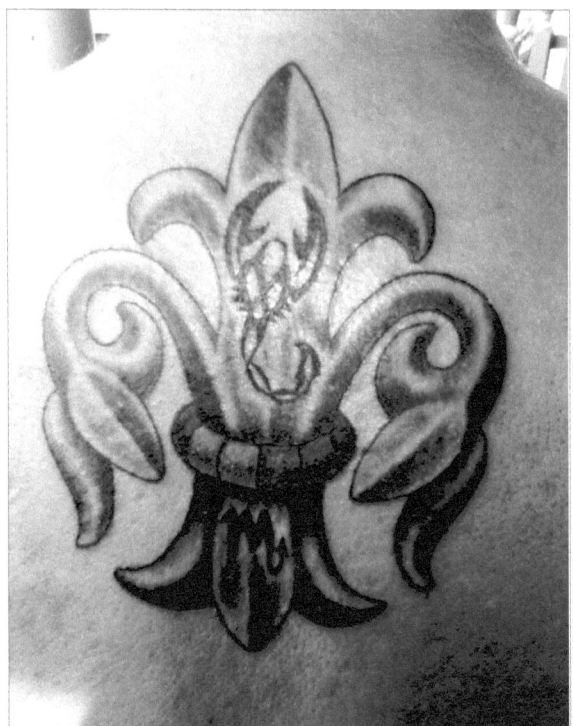

Fleur de Lis tattoo–2010

Rainbow Owl tattoo–2013

CHAPTER 28

PRIDE

(That Time I Loved a Biscuit)

In March 2013, I was approached by my dear friend, Louis Toliver, Jr. to help with the Inaugural Acadiana PRIDE (People Representing Individual Differences and Experiences) Festival. It would be the Acadiana area's very first gay pride celebration; I jumped on board immediately and was elected vice-president at the next meeting. While Louis focused his efforts on marketing and promotions, I took on the task of actually building the entire festival from the ground up.

It was exhilarating to have a brand new project to work on; I was handed a real mission with an end goal, which is exactly what I'd been searching for. Together with the board, we wrote a set of by-laws and set up a non-profit organization, which was a huge task. We spent an entire meeting discussing whether or not to include the letter "Q" in LGBTQ. Yes, it was *that* serious! (It is important to remember that I grew up in a generation where the word "queer" was recognized as a gay slur. I had been labeled "queer" before, in addition to "fag," "faggot," and a few other colorful names. While it took me some time to understand that many of this younger generation identified as "queer," rather than "gay" or "lesbian," I was proud to see that they had taken back the word "queer" from the vocabulary of hate and changed its meaning to love. Within one month, we completed the by-laws, and six weeks later, our non-profit status was approved. (This became truly helpful when trying to obtain sponsorships.) Getting all these details completed in under a year was simply unheard of. But we were doing something important, and the personnel at the Louisiana State offices were extremely helpful, as they recognized the speed at which we needed to make things happen. [A very big THANK YOU to my "special friend" at the IRS for fast-tracking the 501(c)(3) status for us!]

We decided on producing a four-day festival event with music and activities for everyone, and that the entire event would be family friendly. We chose our theme, "Celebrating Family," that focused our events on the diversity of the definition of family. I decided to build the entire festival around music and its diversity to encourage folks from all walks of life to attend, and hoped that music would transcend hate, and that, regardless that it was considered a "gay" festival, people would come to hear the music; I hoped I'd be right.

We knew that such an ambitious festival would need a substantial budget; I decided that $100,000 was appropriate; the entire board was flabbergasted at the amount, but I remained unphazed. We set the dates for the last weekend of March 2014. ("But wait," you're saying, "Gay Pride is in June." And you would be correct. But if you've ever visited south Louisiana in the middle of June, you'd know that sweat drains under your man-titties faster than water from a fire hydrant. So *no*, we would not be having the festival in June.)

Many people, especially other board members, thought I was absolutely insane, and that my budget proposal was soundly unattainable, thus leaving most of the fundraising efforts in the hands of just Louis and me. I went to different businesses and organizations requesting sponsorships and donations. After reviewing my projected budget to our state tourism commission, the proposed sponsor asked, "What is your Plan B?" To which I quickly replied, "There is no Plan B!" We received a substantial check from them the following week, and with Louisiana's Office of Tourism now an official sponsor of our festival, Acadiana PRIDE now had clout as we presented our proposal to other would-be sponsors. Apparently, word got around fairly quickly that we were serious about putting on a one-of-a-kind festival, and we quickly received more sponsorships and more donations. The local news media also got involved and covered almost all of our events throughout the year.

As soon as the bones of the festival took shape, one very important phone call remained. The person who answered sounded surprised when he heard my voice; I asked, "Dustin?" He said, "Mr. Ted, I can't believe you're calling me? What's up?" I told him all about the inaugural Acadiana PRIDE Festival and my role on its board of directors.

I immediately offered him the guest spot on the *Festival International* stage on the opening night of the festival.

[Sidebar: For those of you not familiar with Lafayette, Louisiana, it is the home of the world-famous *Festival International de Louisiane* held every year at the end of April. Musical acts from across the globe perform on several stages set up throughout the downtown area. The largest venue is the *Festival International* stage; many local artists spend their entire lives entertaining crowds, and never get the honor of showcasing their talents on this main stage.]

I was giving Dustin the gig of a lifetime, and we both knew it; I let him know that it was his talent that got him the gig, and not necessarily how he looked without a shirt.

Dustin thanked me profusely, saying, "You know, Mr. Ted, so many people say they're gonna call, but they never do!" I was very happy to keep my promise! Dustin was pleasantly surprised to learn that his boss, Hub City Cycles, the place where we first met, sponsored his performance that night; we kept that secret from him for some time.

One of Louis' brilliant ideas was to make sure that the festival remained at the forefront of everyone's minds throughout the year; Acadiana PRIDE Festival held at least one fundraising event every week leading up to the weekend of the festival, and it created buzz and excitement throughout the community.

Prior to the Acadiana PRIDE Festival, Louis Toliver, Jr. had already created a writer's workshop called "Louisiana Words" that helped many in the LGBTQ community express themselves in forums that were open to the public. It was a very healing and cathartic workshop. In 2013, Louisiana Words became the launching pad for the 2014 inaugural Acadiana PRIDE Festival. Both Louis Toliver and I agreed that the community, whether gay or straight, could be unified through self-expression. With Louis as the creator and me as the producer, Louisiana Words: The Reading Series was created. In addition to the writing series of Louisiana Words, Louis also developed venues for other forms of visual expression such as "Feet" for dancers, and "Rhythms and Visions" for musicians and artists.

During that first year of Acadiana PRIDE, I hosted a weekly singing competition called "Acadiana PRIDE Idol," a twelve-week preliminary elimination process followed by another twelve weeks of semi-finals and finals. The contest culminated with the winner receiving $1,000 and a spotlight showcase at the Acadiana PRIDE Festival. This event also kept the LGBTQ community engaged in the festival for more than six months prior to the actual festival. The finals were held the week before the festival, and the entire community was kept in suspense. We witnessed the huge amount of talent from Acadiana; every Wednesday night at FAME Nightclub we saw unbelievable performances from people that we knew, but didn't know that they could actually sing. (And most of the time, even they didn't realize how good they were.) It was a rousing success, and it helped to reinforce the fact that music could unite a community. We had contestants who were straight, gay, bisexual, and transgender challenging each other in the same competition. Music transcends sexual identity and sexual orientation; and that is the message I tried to send. I guess it worked.

[Sidebar: I had plenty of reservations hosting the Acadiana PRIDE Idol competition because it was held in the local gay bar. Throughout my sobriety, I avoided bars, thus alleviating the trigger that a club atmosphere could induce. I found my solace in the bar owners and bartenders; it was no secret that I recently got out of jail and that I was "on the wagon." (I had no clue where the wagon was going, but I was definitely on it.) I alerted each of the bartenders that my drink of choice was pineapple juice, and all of the bartenders were ecstatic about my sobriety, although they also took great joy in reminding me of my outlandish antics during my drunken blackouts of years gone by. They were more than eager to serve me pineapple juice, and often didn't even charge, just so that they could play their part in keeping me sober. Turns out the bartenders hated the drunk me too; they were happy to encourage sober Ted.]

That year, a young lady named Hannah Johnson won the competition. She was an amazing woman in her own right, with a voice unlike any other. So soft and beautiful sometimes, and loud and powerful at others, but even she was shocked when she won. The competition was so fierce, but she faced her fears and challenged herself each week. What she didn't know was that, on the night of the finale, her father sneaked in to watch her perform. He heard that she was in a little singing competition at a gay bar, and that she was doing fairly well; he didn't want her to be nervous to see him there, so he hung out all alone in the back of the bar. (Obviously, he had never been to a gay bar either.)

Up until this point, he'd only heard Hannah sing from behind the closed door of her bedroom. And when his daughter got up to sing and he actually "heard" her, I saw tears welling up in his eyes. He was such a proud father. And when she was announced as the winner, he was right there in the front row to congratulate her. It was definitely an unforgettable experience.

I also timed the Acadiana PRIDE Idol competition to have a break in between the preliminaries and the finals; this afforded me the opportunity to help another non-profit agency that had been extremely helpful to me in the past. Acadiana CARES, the local HIV/AIDS support agency, was there for me when I needed it the most, and this was my opportunity to say "thank you."

For years, Acadiana CARES hosted an annual fundraiser for HIV/AIDS prevention and education; I'd volunteered for a few of those fundraisers in the past. At one of our weekly PRIDE board meetings, I was informed that Acadiana CARES would not be hosting the "Red Ribbon Ball" this year due to staffing shortages. (Clyde Jones, one of the original members of the Acadiana PRIDE Festival board of directors was also, at the time, employed by Acadiana CARES.) I knew that we had to step in, and after relating my personal story to the PRIDE board, it was resolved by unanimous vote that Acadiana PRIDE would organize and host that year's Red Ribbon Ball event. We worked diligently to put together a drag show and gather items for silent and live auctions.

[Sidebar: I want to sincerely thank all of the drag queens (female impersonators), who, over the years, donated countless hours helping to raise funds for HIV/AIDS causes and Gay Pride causes. Female impersonating is a JOB, and I believe that, for far too long, we in the gay community have taken advantage of drag queens by continuously asking them to "donate" their time and talent for one cause or another. I intended to right that wrong. I was proud to announce that for EVERY fundraiser that Acadiana PRIDE held, including the Red Ribbon Ball, we paid every single entertainer that performed. It might not have been their full fee, for which I was grateful, but I insisted that these entertainers needed to be paid. I just needed it to be known that I find it incredibly hypocritical when people in the gay community make fun of drag queens simply because of what they do for a living. Yet, when the gay community needs a fundraiser, they are the first people expected to donate their time; that's what I would think about every time I did a fundraiser of any kind. At one point, one of the drag queens told me that they were doing it for free because "I" had asked. And I told her that I appreciated the sentiment, but that I knew that doing drag cost a lot of money; so, I at least want to "pay you enough to cover your costs" for the evening. And she agreed. But what bothered me in particular was that, in some cases, those drag queens who would not donate their time and talents (usually because they couldn't afford it), were sometimes shamed by some in the gay community for not doing so. Think about this ... what if you were asked do your job for free, for some random fundraiser for one cause or another, almost every other weekend? Would you do it? Probably not! So, think about that the next time you ask a drag queen to do their job for free!]

I am very proud to say that on that first year that Acadiana PRIDE organized and hosted the Red Ribbon Ball, we were able to donate $2,100 for Acadiana CARES! That night made me proud of my community!

Louisiana Words soon became one of the most anticipated PRIDE events each week; allowing many who felt that they would otherwise not have a voice to share a piece of themselves helped the LGBTQ community get together and celebrate life in all of its forms. It also kept everyone looking forward to the upcoming festival.

It was the weekend after the Acadiana CARES Red Ribbon Ball that I received a phone call from one of our volunteers. His name was Kristopher Hebert, but he went under the pseudonyms of "Biscuit" and "Bisquita Stevens." Biscuit—as he preferred to be called in male form, was an outcast. He was shunned by the community, and most people barely talked to him, or talked at him or about him, or just ignored him, and even worse, just pretended like he wasn't there.

It was a horrible scene to witness, though I think that even he would have agreed that he brought some of this upon himself; but it wasn't his fault at all. Biscuit had both a physical and a mental disability that prevented him from behaving in a manner most would call "normal." He sometimes lacked "filters" and spoke without tact. But he was extremely talented and always strived to achieve his dreams. He knew his time on this Earth was not long, so he made the most of every day.

DAMN, he was on *American Idol*! Were you? Probably not. (Of course, he was singled out as "what NOT to do on *American Idol*," but he was on frickin' national television in a singing competition. And I ask again, "Were you?") I always admired him for that.

Biscuit told me that he wrote a poem for Louisiana Words, but that he was scared to present it. I assured him that there was nothing to be scared of, that I would emcee the show that night, and that I'd stand right next to him for moral support.

On this particular night of Louisiana Words, Biscuit showed up in drag as Bisquita Stevens, and she had something to say. Biscuit had remained in constant contact with Louis and me over the previous week, but neither of us had any idea what he was writing. He just told us that it was important and that he was scared. It became apparent once Bisquita began speaking that she no longer needed me standing beside her to give her the permission she previously felt she needed. No, tonight was her night, and on this night, Bisquita Stevens brought the house down.

Her poem was titled *The Colors of the Rainbow*. She spoke so eloquently about love, nature, and life; she spoke of colors and how each of them shimmered like prisms when the day would go from morning to dusk to night.

She spoke about how each of the colors made her feel.

And then she got to the color red, and she said,

"When I see the color RED I see HATE.

You all look at me as if I am some kind of a monster,
and you all make fun of me behind my back.
I am a human being just like the rest of you.
And you purposefully hurt me.
Why? I don't understand.
I just want to be loved like the rest of you.
RED should be for LOVE
And I don't feel that from my own community.

What I am I supposed to do when my own
community doesn't even want me?
I don't like feeling HATE but I do, and it's your fault.
Please show me some LOVE.
I think I have earned it!"

(I am crying now!)

And that night, the entire room went completely silent for about five seconds. And then, the thunderous roar of applause from the audience came, one clap at a time. I, then Louis, then the rest of the audience gave Bisquita Stevens exactly what she needed ... **LOVE** ... and a standing ovation. Bisquita Stevens was absolutely right, and she had just called everybody out in public about the way she was treated by her own community. You see, Bisquita was one of those drag queens that many people made fun of; and though they thought it was behind her back, she heard everything. She told me later, "I hear all the horrible things they say about me; they think I can't hear them, but I do, only I hear it twice as loud as they think they said it. It hurts!"

And it shook me to my core to realize that, at some point, I had been one of those people who hurt her; and I apologized to Bisquita Stevens. It made me feel better, because I did the right thing, but I don't think she felt any different at all; she already understood that tomorrow, nothing would have changed, and that hurt me even more, because I knew she was right. I think that Bisquita Stevens felt the **LOVE** of her community for that one night, but she also recognized that one night couldn't change the world.

Well, Bisquita Stevens, that night certainly changed MY world. And I will always love her for that. Kristopher "Biscuit" Hebert died on February 12, 2019; may you, Biscuit, rest in peace knowing that, in ONE NIGHT, you may not have changed the world, but you certainly changed more than just a few hearts.

[Sidebar: So, let me vent! Every community has a "Biscuit," someone who is constantly ostracized for being "not like the others." We are taught to live our lives as individuals and to freely express ourselves, yet, when someone expresses themselves differently than what is the accepted "norm," they are shunned for being the exact person we encouraged them to be: themselves. On that night, I was taught to love a biscuit, whether it was plain, or nutty, or bedazzled, or anything else. Not all biscuits are the same, but they all deserve to be loved.

And for those of you who still make fun of our beloved "Biscuit;" you need to know this. Kristopher Hebert did more advocating for persons with disabilities than many of you will probably ever advocate for anything in your lifetime. He spoke to Congress in Washington, D.C. on more than one occasion, and he actively worked with the Louisiana legislature advocating for equal rights for people with disabilities. As a matter of fact, Louisiana's then-Governor John Bel Edwards attended his funeral and handed a proclamation to his family in honor of his service to our community and our state.

I wanted to be certain to include this in "my story" because nobody ever got to tell "his story." So, the next time you think of making fun of someone because of their disabilities, think about what YOU have done to make the world a better place for EVERYONE! Hopefully it will change your mind (and your heart), before you say something negative about something or someone whom you know nothing about! I say all of this knowing that, in the past, I was one of those shameful people. Rant over! *Mic drop!*]

I also wanted to focus a portion of the festival to feature local gay culture; to that end, I produced a play written by Dennis Ward named *Chez Gisele* which was about the first gay cabaret in downtown Lafayette. It celebrated the life of Gisele Carriton who opened this club, and chronicled the amazing life of a vivacious young French woman who brought "Gay Paris" to Lafayette, Louisiana. She was a straight woman but understood that gay men and women needed a safe place to visit, so she created "membership" cards to enter the building. She was a generation ahead of her time, and an incredible woman.

Chez Gisele also tells the story of Clarence Aucoin, one of the club's bartenders, and his 1971 murder, which remains unsolved to this day. It seems that the death of a gay man whose body was discarded in a local ditch was not that important to the Lafayette Parish police department in the early 1970s. (Seems as though times haven't changed much here in south Louisiana.)

Sometimes it takes a generation to change a generation, and I wanted those young men and women who were coming out to understand the struggles that previous generations went through to get to where we are today. I wanted them to know that everyone's coming out was not the same, and that there was no handbook to this life, but I also wanted them to know that everything would be okay. Generations previous to mine made it easier for our generation to face our fears head-on. They taught me that I was okay, and that, if I needed, they were there to help; they welcomed me with open arms and challenged me to be a better person as a gay man than I ever was as a confused and questioning boy in high school. They guided me to a path of understanding and empathy.

No, coming out will never be easy, and often, everyone else knows before you do; I just needed to be honest with myself. I thank them for teaching me that it was part of my responsibility as a gay man to try and make it easier for the next generation, and hopefully, I have done that. Damn! I actually BUILT an entire four-day festival from the ground up; that was just the beginning.

Without the paths scored on the backs of those who came before us, I would not have had the abilities afforded to me to even dream of something as monumental as a gay pride festival in the middle of downtown Lafayette, much less have a community who felt as though it was safe to attend. Without these history-making men and women, PRIDE would have never come to Lafayette, Louisiana. And that brings us to the Inaugural Acadiana PRIDE Festival.

By the time the festival happened, taking into account all cash, sponsorships and other in-kind donations, we had raised over $110,000 through our fundraising efforts. (I guess we didn't need a "Plan B" after all.) The next task was to actually create the festival; the entire structure of the four-day festival included gathering vendors for shopping and food, and contacting local and national talent to fill two entire days of music at Parc International in downtown Lafayette. That was the hardest part; getting contracts signed with major talent is a huge deal. It was a very tedious process and required tons of time; oh, and they all needed to be paid in full, up front. Somehow, I was able to get at least ten performances together for both the Friday and Saturday of the festival, flanked by performances of the play *Chez Gisele* on Thursday and Sunday with music and *hors d'oeuvres*.

I did everything I could think of to ensure the success of this festival; Louis and the rest of the board did their part too. I made some mistakes, and there were definitely things that I would have done differently. But it was too late now; the show had to go on.

With nerves of steel, a heart of gold, and the voice of rhythmic mastery, Dustin opened the festival on Friday night. His performance was so incredible that the other upcoming performers just stood and watched in silent amazement from backstage, videotaping his entire performance. I am happy to say that Dustin and I remained friends over the years, and I have been fortunate to see many more of his performances. I only wish that one day he could be in the right place at the right time. His voice deserves to be heard!

Friday night's headliner was Nakia, who became famous as a recent finalist on *The Voice*. He was open about his homosexuality on the show and was an easy choice. Nakia was actually the second act confirmed and booked thanks to a friend of mine who went to college with him in Alabama.

The headlining act for Saturday night was Steve Grand, a famous gay pop artist whose first major song, "All American Boy," got the attention of television host Larry King. I worked for almost the entire year to ensure that I booked him early and paid early, so that he wouldn't get booked by someone else. We were the first show of his nationwide tour that year, and Steve Grand's first performance at a major gay pride event (I think). In retrospect, the fact that I was able to get Steve Grand turned out to be quite an accomplishment. I had PRIDE festivals from across the country calling me to find out how I did it. In the next three years, Steve Grand performed at each and every one of those PRIDE festivals (thanks to me ... and Steve Grand, of course!) But we were the first!

Steve and I ended up talking almost all evening, both before and after his performance. I found him to be quite interesting, but he was actually more interested in learning about me! That shocked me. He actually took the time to get to know me and learn about the festival and asked how he could do more to help. He was a huge hit that night, and I explained that just showing up was plenty; he stayed for the entire festival. By the end of the night (nearly midnight) we were both exhausted, and it was time for him to get back to his hotel. On the way there he asked, "Well, where is everybody else going?" I said, "They're probably going to FAME (Nightlife) for the after-party. Raven from *RuPaul's Drag Race* is performing." He then asked if it was on the way. It wasn't, but of course I said that it was. We stayed, along with Nakia and Jason Dottley and a few of the other festival entertainers until the club closed at 2:00 a.m.; I was truly exhausted.

I drove Steve back to his hotel, but he still wanted to talk. I don't even know how long we stayed in the parking lot in front of my truck once I brought him back to his hotel; what stayed on my mind was the manner in which he chose to end the night.

We'd attempted to end our conversation several times, but it seemed as though neither one of us wanted it to end. Suddenly, Steve reached out to caress each side of my face; in the same sweet motion, he surprised me with a kiss so passionate that I was nearly brought to my knees. I don't even think that he actually planned it; it was really quite spontaneous. The openness of it all sent shivers up my spine; we were in the middle of a hotel parking lot, savoring a kiss that neither one of us had expected. I don't know if it was the shock of it all or the fact that this kiss spoke volumes to me; his embrace told me a story of true compassion and gratitude. It wasn't meant to be sexual. It came from such a natural and organic place that it just felt appropriate. And that's how we left it. Just the way it should have been; a sincere kiss from a grateful artist to one of his biggest fans. My night was now complete; I was wide awake. The stars were trying to say "good night," but I could already see the crescent sun on the horizon.

And just like that, the festival was over. It seemed like I had worked so hard for so long and the entire weekend went by in a flash. I didn't even have time to enjoy the entire festival that I helped put together. I am eternally grateful to everyone who helped, volunteered, donated a dollar or two, attended even one fundraiser, and donated their time, money, experience, and equipment. Thanks to their efforts, our Inaugural Acadiana PRIDE Festival was a success; and I made a promise to myself to re-create another fabulous festival the following year.

I knew that I would be President for the Second Annual Acadiana PRIDE Festival; Louis was moving to Austin, and I already created the platform, scheduling, and fundraising criteria from the previous year, so it just made sense.

Fame, in this instance, defined as *pride*, was the wealth of knowledge I attained in my short one year as vice-president of Acadiana PRIDE Festival. The education of a younger queer generation helped to influence my progress as I continued to make the word "community" actually mean something.

Twenty-five years ago, I spent the new year in a drunken stupor, embarrassed to be seen by my long-time boyfriend, and simultaneously shattering his dreams of the relationship he thought he had. Steven had become my family, and I committed the mortal sin of not being with him to ring in the new year. The legacy Steven created for us became twigged, because my addictions became more important than the root foundation of our relationship.

Twenty-five years later, I learned the hard way that I wrongly judged others all of my life without knowing the facts, the same way that Steven had wrongly judged me (though rightfully so). I also learned the difference between love and acceptance. Simply stated, they are not the same. (*Thank you, Bisquita Stevens!*)

Ribbon cutting at the inaugural Acadiana PRIDE Festival–2014

Inaugural Acadiana PRIDE Festival Poster—2014

Acadiana PRIDE Festival Poster—2015

CHAPTER 29

INSPIRATION

(That Time I Met the GOAT)

Now that the inaugural Acadiana PRIDE Festival was over, I decided to take a little time for myself to recuperate and relax. I was beyond ecstatic to receive word that our festival had been voted one of the Top Five festivals of the year. (For those of you not from south Louisiana, this area hosts well over 100 festivals each year, so to be voted as one of the Top Five was a major accomplishment, especially for a first-time festival.)

After emceeing the entire festival on both days, I realized how much I missed singing. Sure, I sang during all of the weeks of Acadiana PRIDE Idol, but always wondered if I could be something more than just a host and emcee. Luckily for me, *The Voice*, a popular nationally televised singing program, was holding auditions in Houston during the summer; if Biscuit could be on *American Idol*, why couldn't I be on *The Voice*? I submitted my video, and by the end of the following week, received an e-mail confirming my live audition (along with 1,000 or so others).

As a kid, I always loved taking train rides, so I definitely used this excuse to hop on a train to Houston. And ... another big plus ... I met some incredible people with fantastic stories of their own journeys, and had the honor of sharing my story with them. This included one very special young man named J.D. Baker, though not on the train; and that brings me to my next story.

I met J.D. Baker at a gay bar in Houston on the night before the auditions; he was straight, but his gay friend drove, so he was stuck. He was hot as hell, and you know I am immediately attracted to young muscle men with tattoos. But there was something else. When we met, we had no idea that the other was there to audition for *The Voice*. However, we found other things to talk about for almost two hours, and during karaoke night at EJ's Bar, the subject never even came up. I thoroughly enjoyed my evening at the bar drinking pineapple juice, and enjoying a great conversation with a hot guy. (*Ted, get your mind outta the gutter, he's straight!*) My night couldn't get any better, right?

We were deep in conversation when the karaoke emcee called his name. Then I heard him sing! *Holy bat crap ... incredible!* That coarse nasal, raspy voice with a hint of a country twang got me every time, so that gave us something else to talk about for the next hour or so.

Our audition times on the following day were different, so we didn't see each other on the day of the tryouts, and *The Voice* rules prohibited us from using our phones during the audition process, but we did text each other "good luck" on that morning. We were each about to have an experience of a lifetime, but for different reasons.

My scheduled audition time for the second round was in the early afternoon; after waiting for what seemed like forever, a producer informed us that the preliminary judges' lunches ran late, so there would be a short delay. And then she said, "Oh, y'all sing something! What's a song that you all know?" Then someone else suggested "Amazing Grace."

And there we were; nearly 500 people in a completely empty Reliant (now NRG) Stadium, standing up to sing "Amazing Grace," and just so very naturally, everyone matched their voices to each other; it was a synchronization of sound that I had never heard before or since. The echoes of our own voices were awesome on their own, but when you heard the inspirational lyrics as they reverberated through an entirely empty stadium, it was both a chilling *and* humbling experience. That one performance on that one day in Houston made the entire trip worth it. Even those waiting outside applauded for us when we finished. It was truly amazing!

From there, the contestants were whittled down, first into a room of about 200, then into groups of ten to audition for one of the producers. We were each given wrist bands to signify that we were prospective contestants, and as long as we wore wristbands, we were able to move forward in the competition. One by one, we sang our songs. As each person sang, I could see the producer moving contestants' info sheets to either a stack on her left or a stack on her right; we had no idea which stack was the "good" one.

I opted to sing Kid Rock's "Blue Jeans and a Rosary," which was quite a stretch from my normal karaoke repertoire, but it gave me a better opportunity to showcase my range. I not only knew what the lyrics meant, but I knew how they felt; it was the life that I had been living since the unfortunate night that my pajamas were soiled. I thought of Steven Meert the entire time; he was my savior when I didn't even know that I needed one.

The talent in that room was so great that any one of us could have been selected to go on to the next round, but only one of us did, and it wasn't me. The nine remaining, unselected contestants made our ways to the exit; the assistant waiting at the door cut off our wristbands, and our journeys on *The Voice* were over.

J.D. Baker made it further in the competition than I did, but he didn't make the televised program. We connected through country music, and stayed in touch throughout the years. I promised to book him for next year's Acadiana PRIDE Festival, and definitely kept that promise.

I do also need to thank Biscuit for giving me the courage to take that leap and opening myself up to judgement and criticism. I learned more about myself during those few hours in auditions than endless days in rehab. We were thousands of wanna-be entertainers all encouraging each other, regardless of gender, race, sexuality, background, or anything else; we all just wanted to be heard, and my ears were opened.

Although I didn't get very far during my auditions on *The Voice*, I considered my appearance there to be a success. I returned to Lafayette with a renewed spirit and vigor to make next year's Acadiana PRIDE Festival even better than its first.

I continued to build on the accolades of the previous year; Louis had moved to Austin, Texas, and I had a new vice-president in Kay Jeansonne, along with an almost entirely new board of directors. We chose the motto "Unity Through Diversity" for the current year's theme.

In the event's second year, we worked more like a slow-moving engine that gained momentum at just the right time. Almost everything worked in the prior year, so we just stuck to the original plan and tried to work smarter. We had that "if it ain't broke, don't fix it" attitude, and it worked, as we garnered even more sponsors and raised nearly $125,000 for our sophomore festival.

I produced another play to further educate the gay community about gay south Louisiana and our generation's storied and questionable history. This year I chose a play entitled, *UpStairs: The Musical*, the story of a famous New Orleans bar that burned down on June 24, 1973. The mystery of the fire was never fully investigated, and no arsonist was ever charged. But thirty-two people lost their lives that day (three of which were never identified because the families would not claim the bodies of their family member(s) found burned to death in a gay bar). The play (including original songs) was written and co-produced by Wayne Self, a Louisiana native, who flew in from his home in California for opening night.

We also brought back the fan favorite Acadiana PRIDE Idol, except I didn't want to host the competition anymore; it was just too difficult sending someone home every week, especially as the competition dwindled down to the final ten or twelve contestants. There was so much heart and passion put into each and every performance, and on any given night, everyone had their moment to shine. I just couldn't bear to see those sad faces; knowing that I was the one to tell them that their "moment" had passed. So instead, I became a judge.

In retrospect, that was a really stupid decision. I didn't want to host because I didn't want to have to send anyone home, but now I was part of the reason they were going home. Doesn't make sense, really. However, sitting at the judge's table taught me a lot about viewing things from "the other side." I got to see the courage it takes to get up and sing for an audience. I'd done it many times before; as the host of last year's competition, I sang every week at Acadiana PRIDE Idol, both solo and with the judge's panel; but many of the contestants had never really performed in front of a large crowd. Yes, they had done karaoke before, but they had never been put in the spotlight. As a judge, I got to help them along on their journeys; I helped them with song choices, and worked with them to select songs that not only showcased their voices but challenged them vocally. Many of them were surprised at what they accomplished, and it was truly a pleasure to see each of them grow and learn more about themselves through the Acadiana PRIDE Idol experience.

I invited last year's winner, Hannah Johnson, to judge. It was after one of those nights that she pulled me aside, saying that she had something really important to discuss with me. I was rather taken aback; her expressions told me that whatever it was, it was very serious.

We found a quiet place to sit outside of the club; she seemed as if she wanted to cry, but I couldn't figure out why. As she began to speak, I could hear the tears in her voice. She told me about a spiritual retreat that she recently attended. At this retreat, they were all asked to create an "inspiration list" of the ten people who had most impacted their lives. I felt honored that she would have thought to include me on this list, especially since I'd known her for less than a year.

But I was jolted by what she said next; with that same lump in her throat, she sheepishly said, "But Ted, I really wanted to include you on my list, but I just couldn't. You've done so much for me and my confidence and self-esteem that I couldn't think of a single reason for you to not be on that list. I still don't know why I didn't include you, and now I kinda feel bad. I'm sorry."

Seeing the defeat in her eyes, I immediately consoled her. "Hannah," I said, "I am so very proud of you and all that you have accomplished. Don't feel badly just because I didn't make the cut on your list; that's your list, and many people are inspirational to you for many different reasons. To be honest, yes, I would have been honored, but just you telling me about your experiences and how far you've come in the past year is thanks enough for me. I'm just happy to play just a teeny, tiny part in that."

We held each other for a long embrace, one of those embraces that neither one wants to release first, but it would have been weird if we hugged for too long. In those moments, we basked in the knowledge that we inspired each other, and that's all I ever wanted.

Our very special guest for the 2015 Acadiana PRIDE Festival was Greg Louganis; for those of who do not recognize that name, please allow me to enlighten you. Greg Louganis is, undisputedly, the "Greatest of All Time" in the sport of Olympic diving, and all of his records still stand today. He is the most decorated diver in Olympic history; and only the second person to win gold medals at two consecutive Olympics in both the three-meter springboard and ten-meter platform events, setting a scoring record for men's platform diving in 1984.

The incident that garnered international attention came when Greg hit his head on the springboard during the preliminary round of diving at the 1988 Olympics in Seoul, South Korea. At the time, only Greg and his coach were aware of his HIV status. Greg bled into the water, and there was fear that other divers could be infected by diving into the same pool. But those fears were laid to rest, as doctors assured them, "the small amount of blood had already been diluted by the thousands of gallons in the pool and chlorine kills the HIV virus, and the human skin is a very large barrier to the contraction of HIV."

Greg proceeded to compete and made the final cut through the preliminaries even with the missed dive, which was testament to just how great a diver he was. This accomplishment, among many others, earned him the *ABC Wide World of Sports* Athlete of the Year honor in 1988.

Greg's autobiography, *Breaking the Surface*, originally published in 1995, spent five weeks at No. 1 on the *New York Times* bestseller list; the book was later produced as a made-for-television movie starring Mario Lopez.

This was aside from the fact that Greg had always been a role model for me; I always lived my life struggles in private and with my family and friends. I never could have imagined what it must have been like to have to live in the public eye, but figured, if Greg could handle all of this in an internationally public forum, then I certainly could handle it on a personal level.

And with that, I decided to have Greg Louganis at our 2015 Acadiana PRIDE Festival. Greg's then-husband, Johnny Chaillot, was originally from Crowley, Louisiana, so I started doing some research. Within a couple of weeks, Greg signed on as our Grand Marshal for the festival. (That sounded like it was too easy but booking celebrities was always a task unto itself. I accomplished it, and remain very proud of myself.)

[Sidebar: Many years later, my mom was looking at different posters and pictures on my living room walls, and commented, "Never in my life did I ever think that I would meet somebody famous like Greg Louganis." My heart continually smiles because I made her dream come true. I had no idea she was such a fan! Mom admitted she saw a lot of "me" in Greg Louganis; I'll take that compliment any day!]

At the time, Greg was promoting his new biopic *Back on Board*. The national première of the movie was held in New Orleans only a few weeks before the Second Annual Acadiana PRIDE Festival, and Greg and Johnny invited me. There was a pre-party for the première, and they invited me to that too; I was extremely nervous. But Johnny was right there to welcome me to the event. I was introduced to the small gathering of their family and friends, who cheered for me and made *me* feel like a celebrity. It was so surreal; there were no words to explain that feeling. When I met Greg for the first time, he was so inviting and welcoming; and he was so excited to meet me and thanked me for taking the time out of my busy schedule to attend this event. Greg and Johnny made feel as though I was the one being honored and not them.

We chatted for a while and found that we had lots of things in common; not only our HIV status and alcoholism, but the fact that Greg was also quite shy. He was sincerely curious and wanted to know more about ME. I was just not used to celebrities being interested in me, but Greg and Johnny made me feel like family. It was just what I needed to calm my nerves.

There were already hundreds of people waiting in line to attend the movie, and I stood in line behind everyone else. Greg and Johnny found me and graciously pulled me into their party so I wouldn't have to stand in line. I walked the red carpet, took photos for the event, and was interviewed by one of the local papers, as well as promote both Greg and the Acadiana PRIDE Festival.

The following week, it was time to once again focus on the festival; but we all know that nothing ever goes according to plan, at least not in Ted's world. It was the semi-finals night of Acadiana PRIDE Idol, and I was hungry. On the way to the venue, I stopped at one of my favorite college joints, Judice Inn, to have a cheeseburger. I ran into one of my neighbors, who asked, "Hey Ted, did you notice that someone hit the building on the corner by the roundabout by our house? It must have happened last night." I told him, "I just drove by there on my way here, and I didn't notice anything." I finished my meal and drove to the venue, judged the semi-finals of Acadiana PRIDE Idol, and headed home; I needed some rest.

But on my way home, my curiosity got the best of me. When I arrived at the roundabout near my house at about 2:30 a.m., I wanted to see what my neighbor was talking about. I pulled over into the abandoned parking lot and got down out of my truck. Sure enough, someone had run into the building with their vehicle and caused extensive damage. I did a little more snooping around just because I was curious, then got back in my truck and headed straight home, one quarter of a mile away.

As I pulled into my driveway, I noticed red and blue flashing lights directly behind me, and hurriedly parked my truck so the police could bypass me. Well, as it turns out, the destination was my house; I became totally startled and began shaking tremendously.

Why did he follow me? Did I do something wrong? I hadn't been drinking, so it couldn't be that. Why were the police at my house?

The lights now blinded me, and I heard the words I'd heard many times before, "Please remain in your vehicle, and put your hands out the window where I can see them!" I followed his direction verbatim. The police officer pulled up to my truck and asked why I was snooping around the roundabout.

Now, when I get really nervous, I start talking really fast, and that's exactly what happened. I regaled to him the story about running into my neighbor at the restaurant and found out about the car hitting the building, and that I was just a curious neighbor ... and I began slurring my words.

Then a second question I'd heard many times before followed; "Sir, how much have you had to drink?" And I replied, "I had several drinks, all pineapple juice. I haven't had alcohol in over five years." That smart-assed remark could have gone either way. Then I could see that he really wanted to start laughing (reminiscent of the "pink light" policeman), but he maintained his composure. We chatted for a little bit longer and then he left.

On the following weekend, I returned from a Saturday night Acadiana PRIDE Festival fundraising event around 2:15 a.m., and saw a car in a ditch just a few miles from my house. No one was there to help, so I called 911 before offering to help the victim. The drunk lady driver said, "No, I'm walking home!" So, there I was, all alone, waiting for the police to arrive so that I could give a report. When the police arrived, he said, "You must be one of the only sober people on the road at this time of morning!" I agreed and set off for home. It had been a long night and I nearly fell asleep putting my pajamas (boxer shorts) on.

Suddenly, I heard a very loud bang, a honking horn, and some other kind of unknown raucousness outside my bedroom window. I jammed my left hip on the bedpost as I ran outside only to see a car that had run through the fence between my house and my goddaughter's house and was stalled ten feet from my bedroom with the engine running and all the lights on. A man, maybe the driver, ran across my yard to get away from the accident, but my hip was hurting so badly that I couldn't chase him.

So, again, I called 911 to report the accident. And the 911 operator said, "Wait, didn't you JUST call me about another accident?" And I laughingly replied, "Yes ma'am, it's been that kind of night!" Then she promised to say a prayer for me before dispatching the police to my house.

The police arrived to find me, dazed and dressed only in my boxer shorts. (It had happened many times before, but I was drunk ... however, this time I was completely sober.)

As the police began poring over the accident situation, they started asking me questions.

Police: "Did you see what happened?
Me: "No!"
Police: "Did you see the driver?"
Me: "Yes!"
Police: "Can you describe the person?"
Me: "Yes, he was a dark-skinned man; but not black and not Hispanic, about six feet tall, maybe 185 pounds. He wore heavy work boots, a dark denim jacket, and blue jeans with holes in them."
Police: "You saw all of that?
Me: "Yes, I tried to chase him, but my leg was hurting!"

As the police continued the investigation, they discovered that the driver had not only left the engine running; the police found his telephone, his wallet with his driver's license, and $51 hidden in the dashboard of his vehicle. They conducted a manhunt to find the driver, but came back empty.

And even with all of this chaos going on, I found something funny to laugh at.

Of course, the police blocked off the street in both directions for safety purposes. But apparently, many of the drivers on the road thought that this was a DUI checkpoint. It was so funny watching cars reroute toward the "backroads;" it's exactly what I probably did hundreds of times before. (By this time, it was about 4:15 a.m.) When I pointed out the vehicles turning around to avoid the DUI checkpoint, even the police chuckled a bit; still the driver was nowhere to be found.

We had no idea where the driver was, but when the police pulled his license, they found something startling. When I reappeared from my house after putting on some shorts, the officer immediately called me over to the police cruiser and showed me his photo. He said, "Mr. Ted, is this the man that you saw?" And instantly, I said, "Yes." The startling part is that I had described the gentleman PERFECTLY! The police officer told me that he had never heard a witness give such a perfect description of a defendant.

The driver of the vehicle (according to his driver's license) was 6'1" tall, weighed 185 pounds, and was of Egyptian decent. All of the officers were in complete amazement that I was so "spot-on" with my description. (I guess my point in telling this story is that, had I not been completely sober, I could never have identified the driver of the vehicle.)

As we waited for the policemen to complete their investigation, one of the officers pulled me aside and asked, "Mr. Ted, do you recognize me at all?" I said, "Look, it's almost 5:00 a.m., and I still haven't had any sleep, and I've had to report TWO separate accidents tonight; neither of which I was directly involved in, and when you got here I was still in my underwear. I'm having a hard time remembering my own name at this point. So, no, I do not recognize you!"

The officer immediately started laughing, and then said, "Do you remember last week when you got pulled over for stopping at the corner by the roundabout, and the police followed you home? Well, that was ME!" And then I started laughing too. It was such a small world, and it was nice to laugh for while even though my leg hurt more and more. But the story got even better.

The next day, the driver arrived at the repo lot at the Lafayette Parish Police Department to retrieve his car. He gave a statement explaining that his vehicle had been stolen, thanked the police for finding it and requested assistance in trying to find the person who stole his car. As it happened, that same police officer who stopped me on the corner by the roundabout and worked the scene on the previous night (with me in my underwear), was at the station when the suspect attempted to claim his vehicle.

The officer read his statement, and then told the guy, "Sir, do you remember that you almost hit a house last night?" And he replied, "No, somebody stole my car!" The officer then informed him that I saw him fleeing the scene of the accident and that I identified him perfectly. "Would you like to change your statement?" And the defendant said, "Okay, give me another piece of paper."

If you've ever heard the *cliché*, "If it weren't for bad luck, I'd have no luck at all," that was kind of the story of my life. Weird (and true) things like this have happened to me throughout my lifetime. Somehow, I always found humor in whatever happened, but this time I actually got hurt. That's why attendees of the second annual Acadiana PRIDE Festival noticed my limp. I never told anyone what had happened, the festival was more important. Yes, I was hurting, but the show must go on!

As with the previous year, we had two full days of music to entertain the crowds, and our event was a huge success. Jocelyn Rae even flew in from Washington, D.C. to help me, for which "forever grateful" doesn't even begin to suffice.

One of the most memorable moments of the festival was watching the crowd react as J.D. Baker and his band performed. (Remember my friend from *The Voice* auditions?) He'd worked so hard for this, and I felt badly that we didn't have a chance to visit before he and his band took to the stage. Their performance was astonishing, and I think that even J.D. was surprised by the audience's overwhelming reception.

Once his performance was over, I walked up to the stage, reintroduced everyone to the crowd and presented him with one of our programs. I opened it to the page featuring his picture and asked for his autograph. Taking a cue from my backstage encounter with Joan Collins, I said, "J.D. Baker, you're going to be a big star one day, and I want your first autograph." He immediately started crying while signing my brochure, and the hug we shared seemed longer than normal, but it just showed me his appreciation for "giving him a shot." I was happy to oblige.

And that's one thing that I have always tried to do with the Acadiana PRIDE Festival. Acadiana has so many talented people that never got a chance to be heard. I always included local and up-and-coming artists in our festival, in addition to national recording artists, to give them that chance.

Music, laughter, love, and joy surrounded the events of the weekend, and again, more than 10,000 people attended our "little" festival. Christopher and Cassie came to listen to the final band of the day and stayed to help me clean up and close the park. I then headed to Fame Nightlife for the after-party, where Jujubee and Raven from *RuPaul's Drag Race* were scheduled to perform. I was exhausted, but, as president of the festival, attended every single event. Tomorrow would be the final day of the festival; a salute to Greg Louganis.

Fame, in this instance defined as *inspiration*, was my continued striving to showcase the talents of many people who I felt were not being given the exposure they deserved. Dustin Gaspard, Hannah Johnson, J.D. Baker, and many others have always moved people with their music; I was just happy to give them a stage so they could share their gifts with the world.

Twenty-six years ago, I attended the memorial service of my boyfriend, Steven Meert; although I'd dated periodically since his death, no one could ever replace him. Steven always inspired me to be someone better than the person I thought I was, but he died before I ever figured out what that meant. Perhaps the fact that I compared all my relationships to the one that I had with Steven was the reason they all failed. The alcoholism and addictions, I'm sure played no role in their demise.

Twenty-six years later, I had been clean and sober for nearly six years and was finding *inspiration* in the voice I gave to others. For so many years I assumed that my voice lent credence to my convictions, and that if I spoke loudly enough, people would believe me and reward me with the compassion I thought I deserved. It wasn't until I learned to be silent and listen—truly listen—that I understood that sometimes the quietest people have the most to say; they just needed a platform. I'm honored that I was able to inspire them to speak their truth. I wished I'd learned that lesson in listening a long time ago.

I once read that "if art is how we decorate space, then music is how we decorate time." I finally understood that it was the music of the soul, the rhythm of the rivers, and the voices of the unheard that spoke to me the loudest.

me with Johnny Chaillot and Olympic Diving Champion Greg Louganis–2015

CHAPTER 30

ADVOCACY

(That Time I Was an Idol)

In addition to Greg Louganis' appearance at the festival, we held a luncheon on that Sunday to view the Acadiana première of *Back on Board*; the venue was completely packed. The luncheon was buffet style, and the menu was exquisite and very upscale (you know us gays can be bougie sometimes). After the luncheon, it was time for the movie.

Before we started the movie, I made all the necessary introductions, and wanted to recognize a very special person, whom I had made great strides to ensure would be at this event. Throughout my own struggles with HIV and addiction, there was one person who was a true inspiration to me; that person was Claude Martin, the executive director of Acadiana CARES. I presented him with the very first Acadiana PRIDE Legend award, and wanted him to know the impact that both he and Acadiana CARES had on my life and the lives of many others struggling with HIV, alcoholism, and drug addiction. It truly was a "full circle" moment for me in giving back to the person who had helped me so very much, and it felt incredible. Many times, we never get to recognize those who had a tremendous influence on our lives, and many times, even they don't realize the impact that they had on our lives. I got that chance. Under the leadership of Claude Martin, Acadiana CARES and its staff saved my life on many occasions; he will forever be a legend to me and to the Acadiana PRIDE family.

As I introduced Greg, I also let him know how he and his struggles helped me with my life and what a powerfully positive impact he made on my life before awarding him with the first ever Acadiana PRIDE Icon Award. He thanked me and Acadiana PRIDE, then spoke about his journey and how special he felt to be in Lafayette. To many, that might sound like a canned response, but when I saw the look in his eyes, I saw a tear through the smiles, which only confirmed his sincerity. I will never forget when our eyes locked on stage; it's was as if we saw each other's souls. We had both been through so much in our lives, and there was a true common bond. *Sympatico!*

The viewing and the entire event were another huge success. Greg and Johnny invited me to stay with them anytime I visited Los Angeles, and while I knew that was "Hollywood speak" for "We'll probably never see each other again," this time was different. Both Greg and Johnny were absolutely sincere, and I sometimes regret never taking them up on their offer. The weekend was one of the highlights of my life.

During his visit, I heard about a petition to get Greg Louganis on a box of Wheaties Cereal; we even circulated a small petition during the festival to encourage those efforts. Greg was finally featured on a Wheaties cereal box in 2016 (over twenty-eight years since those gold medal diving performances). I was so excited when I saw his cereal boxes in one of our Lafayette grocery stores, and proudly sent him a photograph!

Once the festival was over, I could finally address my hip pain. My orthopedic surgeon discovered that I had a condition called avascular necrosis (AVN). I told the doctor, "Look, I have no clue what that means, but I know that 'necro' means 'dead,' so what the hell is DEAD in my body?" He explained that AVN happened as a result of bone deterioration. Apparently, I had this condition for some time (possibly the result of a cartwheel in little league baseball), but when I hit my hip against the bedpost, it fractured that part of my hip since the bone was already weak. (I really wanted to insert some kind of demented bedpost joke here, but I could never think of anything that was as funny as what I know you're thinking about right now.)

It was time to have my entire hip replaced, and the operation was completed successfully within the month. As I told my parents when the surgery was over, "Look, now my leg goes all the way behind my head." They both rolled over with laughter. I pressed the button on the morphine drip; it was that funny.

Over the course of my two years with Acadiana PRIDE Festival, I met some very incredible people, including the members of a group called Equality Louisiana. It was EQLA's mission to work with local and national political leaders to advance equality for the LGBTQ community. I had the pleasure of working with gay and trans influencers such as Bruce Parker, Tucker Barry, Dylan Waguespak, and a host of very savvy young people; even though I was the one of the oldest members of the group, these very young, very intelligent individuals taught me a lot. Times had indeed changed since I came out. With so much left for me to learn, this younger generation proved to be my best teacher.

It was during an EQLA retreat that several LGBTQ advocates from across the state united to discuss the upcoming legislative session, and were ecstatic that one of the guest speakers was a local out-spoken lesbian who worked on behalf of EQLA in the past, Annaise Jameison. However, my joy turned to disgust when she informed us that the ONLY way to get positive LGBT-inclusive legislation in the current Louisiana congressional culture was to avoid using the terms "gay" and "lesbian." I was completely taken aback by this plan of attack; to state that it was possible to advocate for our community without actually stating the communities we represented was absolute idiotic fuckery to me. I refused to see that as a plausible way forward, but she was the guest speaker, so I said nothing.

As the Acadiana area advocate for EQLA, I spoke with our local political leaders to further educate them about the plight of the LGBTQ community for equality in all forms, and was invited to speak before a committee of the Louisiana state congress when a legislator tried to pass legislation that would have moved Louisiana backwards in regards to the issues facing the LGBTQ community. As a part of this "re-education" process, we began a campaign called *"Not My Louisiana."*

The legislation at hand was Louisiana House Bill #707 that would have allowed discrimination based strictly on anyone's "perceived" homosexuality. This was my speech before the committee; notice that I never shied away from the words "gay" and "HIV."

To the honorable members of this committee:

I love my Louisiana, but HB 707 is not the Louisiana that I know and love.

I grew up in south Louisiana, raised by a loving family and a supportive neighborhood as a Roman Catholic who was taught to live by the Ten Commandments, and that we must always love our neighbors as we love ourselves. I was raised to treat everyone equally.

I grew up knowing that I was Acadian, and I was always proud of my heritage. But I also learned that the fact that why we were here in Louisiana was not part of the original plan of our ancestors. Cajuns grew up in a culture where we knew what it was like to be discriminated against. That was how we ended up in Louisiana.

My family told me stories of how difficult it was for our forefathers to bear the brunt of being exiled from the country they loved, simply because of who they were and the way they were born.

I was also a part of the onset of integration of schools in the early 1970s. Of course, I did not know what that meant at the time, since I never saw anything wrong with going to school with or being friends with someone of a different race. They were all my neighbors.

To be honest, I never really knew what discrimination felt like until my senior year in high school, when I realized that I was born gay, and later came out to my family and friends only to be shown lots of love and support. No, I did not feel discriminated against by my family and friends. They were my neighbors. The discrimination came in the form of governmental laws.

As the grandson of an army medic who was killed in World War II, I always wanted to serve my country. And this is where I learned exactly what discrimination felt like after being told that I was not eligible to serve my country, simply because of the way I was born, and the people I loved. The recruiting officer informed me that my homosexuality was incompatible with military service. I did not understand how a country that I wanted to serve could deny me that right. And having been denied the dream I always longed for, I was left wanting more, but couldn't find the answers I looked for here in Louisiana.

So, I did what many young men and women did in the early 1980s and moved to another state, where I learned that things are different everywhere. I hid behind what I thought others thought I should be, or what I thought they perceived me to be, instead of just being myself. I reinvented myself to become someone that others could "accept," rather than being "accepting" of who I truly was.

I lived a mostly transient life working for a company that allowed me to travel this great country and live in some of our most wonderful cities. But when I retired in 2007, I always knew that Louisiana was my home. And that this is where I wanted to be. And when your parents give you an acre of land, you build a house on it.

And something great had happened during my thirty years away from my Louisiana. I watched my Acadiana home grow into a place that I truly loved to be in and a place that I truly belonged in. It is a place of acceptance of our past and recognition that we must do our best to make our futures better. It is a place where the neighbors from my youth are still the same neighbors in my adulthood. It is a place steeped in culture and rich in its diversity. I no longer have to hide behind a façade of whom others perceive me to be. I am my own man, and can stand proudly as a gay man who also happens to be living with HIV. Louisiana is now a place that I truly do love again, and we are all neighbors.

But now HB 707 stands before us and infringes on the very rights that I have come to love about my Louisiana. HB 707 is not my Louisiana. This bill, even with all of the amendments, restricts my rights as a human being to live my life fully. This bill allows discrimination purposefully directed toward others' perception of my homosexuality and my ability to make adult decisions regarding my own finances, living situation, schooling, marriage, and children. And that is one of the reasons that I left Louisiana in the first place. When I moved back to Louisiana, I knew that I was home. But the passage of HB 707 would make me have to rethink my reasons for staying. Because this is definitely not my Louisiana.

I used to run away when I did not understand the discrimination in front of me and wanted to get away from social and legislative injustice. But not anymore. I want to stay in Louisiana and make it better! I want my Louisiana back. It is my duty as a gay man and my responsibility to my community to strive for equality for all, regardless of gender identity and sexuality. The passage of this bill would be a hinderance to us all and create a Louisiana where people like me would continue to feel unsafe.

And now I can stand before you as a Cajun, an Acadian, and as a proud gay man living with HIV.

I am your neighbor, and I AM Louisiana!

I love my Louisiana,

Please vote against HB 707, and tell the rest of the country that this bill is NOT MY LOUISIANA!

Ted A Richard, Acadiana PRIDE President

Due to all of our tireless work, this legislation failed to pass the committee and never saw the light of day again.

[Update: The legislator who proposed this bill, the "dishonorable" Mike Johnson, was later elected to become a Louisiana State representative in Washington, D.C. It is abhorrent to me how many of us in the deep south continue to vote against our own best interests simply because "What would Jesus do?" The Jesus that I used to pray to fed the sick, helped the poor, supported those in need, and loved his neighbor. Apparently, Mr. Jesus had changed since I left the shackles of the Catholic church.]

From 2013-2015, I worked continuously with these incredible young people, and we made inroads into Louisiana politics to further ensure that the LGBTQ community continued down the path to true and honest EQUALITY for ALL people, regardless of sex, race, sexual orientation, gender identity, and gender expression. Yes, Louisiana still has a long way to go to ensure equality for us all, and I have continued my advocacy work to improve the lives of my LGBTQ brothers and sisters; hopefully their lives can be lived fully without fear of repercussion for simply being the people they were born to be. As a group, we accomplished a lot but recognize that there is still plenty more to be done. And I continue to do my part.

In addition to representing our communities at the Acadiana PRIDE Festival, EQLA always had a very large presence at the Baton Rouge Pride festival. As in previous years, EQLA sponsored the annual Equality march—a one mile walk from the venue of Baton Rouge Pride to the Louisiana State Capital Building. It was an event meant to unite our community in solidarity, share recent victories from the previous year, and rally the troops on upcoming legislation that could negatively impact the

LGBTQ community. I'd attended the Equality March in the past, but with my hip in "recovery" mode, I had to miss the event as well as an opportunity to speak there, until Tucker Barry reached out: "You just HAVE to be here! But we'll understand if you absolutely can't make it."

That invitation made a difference. I was still on crutches, so my parents drove me to the capitol steps. Tears welled up in my eyes as hundreds of people merged from the side streets and walked up the promenade to the event. Rainbows appeared from nearly half a mile away, and as the crowd got closer and larger, it was certainly an unimaginable spectacle. If my prose *The Parade* could have been something from my imagination that came to life, this display would have been it. And for the first time in my life (I think) I found myself speechless! I was completely overwhelmed with emotion; and a renewed sense of PRIDE in myself and my community!

In short order, I realized the real reason that "I just HAD to be there." To my surprise, I was honored with the 2015 EQLA Outstanding Community Advocate Award for the state of Louisiana. And, with tears in my eyes again, I rose to my feet (on crutches, of course) and stepped up to the podium to receive my award. Receiving the award and speaking on the steps of the Louisiana State Capitol was incredible in itself, but having my parents there to witness the event was mind-blowing. They were always unconditionally supportive of my efforts to extend equality to everyone; but I know that they always wondered just exactly what I did. Finally, they understood that my labors of love created change in the community that could erase the wave of homophobia that would certainly have happened had we not won over the Louisiana congressional committee with our "*Not My Louisiana*" campaign.

By the fall of that year, I was forced to have yet another hip replacement; so I turned the event over to two other individuals on the board of directors, Matthew Credeur and Coye Kidd, in hopes they would continue to build on the successes of the past two festivals. I gave them ALL the information they needed to make planning easier for them. About one month later, Matthew and Coye showed up at my house, unannounced, and returned almost ALL of the merchandise, the secretary's minutes, and treasurer's reports I had given them. But there was a HUGE problem.

Much of the merchandise was missing, there were no updates on the treasurer's report, none of the bills were paid, and the checking account was empty with no receipts to show where the money went. And Matthew and Coye had no explanation as to how it all happened.

I immediately shifted in to damage control mode, and phoned the few businesses to which Acadiana PRIDE Festival still owed monies to and explained what happened. Of course, an explanation always sounds like an excuse, and because of this, the relationships that I built with these businesses on behalf of Acadiana PRIDE Festival were now ruined irreparably.

I have always been an effective communicator, and worked very diligently to forge relationships with these companies to benefit their business and the Acadiana PRIDE organization. Matthew Credeur's and Coye Kidd's actions were not only detrimental to the future of Acadiana PRIDE but served as an attack on my reputation as an honest businessperson.

However, I settled everything with these businesses, and because I had personal relationships with their owners, they agreed to not press charges against me, nor against Acadiana PRIDE Festival with the caveat that they would no longer support Acadiana PRIDE, and that, in the future, our bills would need to be paid in full and up front. How could anyone blame them?

All the business relationships that I worked so hard to foster and nurture were ruined forever. It was unconceivable that people I trusted could do this, and to make matters worse, Matthew and Coye blamed ME for the situation, and took NO responsibility at all.

Once again, the future of Acadiana PRIDE Festival rested in my hands, and I wasn't even on the board of directors anymore. I needed answers and I needed them fast.

No one I reached out to was interested in taking on this monumental responsibility. I found it to be very disconcerting that all of these people who had initially wanted to be on the board of directors (because it looked good on a resumé), were suddenly unavailable when they realized that it actually took real work to get it done. Such a shame.

But then, a group of young people including Tara Guy and Beyoncea Black came to my rescue. I gave them a crash course in running the festival and handed over all of the remaining merchandise with a promise to help as much as possible given my limitations during recovery. They did an amazing job.

I was excited that the new board of directors decided to continue the tradition of Acadiana PRIDE Idol, even though it was a scaled down version of what was originally created and held for one night only. On that one night, ALL the contestants would sing two songs, and the six contestants with the highest scores would move on to the finals. From that point on, it would be a voting-driven contest. Each contestant had two weeks to garner as many votes as possible from the general public, and the winner would be the contestant with the most votes.

Although I was still on crutches, I attended the competition to support the contestants, many of whom I had judged and mentored at the two previous Acadiana PRIDE Idol competitions. It gave me such a sense of pride knowing that these kids were still chasing their dreams, and I was certainly happy to see all of them.

I had no intention of entering the competition, and was only there to cheer on everyone else; though the emcee implored me to enter. I finally relented and sang my signature song, "Never Been to Spain" by Three Dog Night in the first round. I was amazed at how much better all of the Acadiana PRIDE Idol alumni had become. They sounded like professional performers. I was so proud of them, and it was an honor to see that they had grown and prospered to further their singing careers.

For the second round, I sang "Like A Cowboy" by Randy Houser. It conveyed the story of a rough-and-tumble guy who hitched his horse from bedpost-to-bedpost; it was the life I once lived when my journey spun out of control like the tornado I was living in. The song was about cherishing loved ones but realizing that relationships could never be permanent. It mirrored my life when I destroyed my relationship with Steven Meert. Since he died, I'd lost my soul in the rodeo of what was left of me; this became my love song to Steven, hoping that we could ride together again on the other side of the rainbow.

After a brief intermission, the six finalists were named; four were Acadiana PRIDE Idol alumni. And then the final two contestants moving on were announced; the first name called was a newcomer to the

Acadiana music scene, and the second name ... you guessed it ... Ted A Richard.

Of course, I was happy that I made the finals, but was sad that there were two of the Acadiana PRIDE alumni who did not make the cut. In addition, it just struck me that I would be competing against the same people whom I had previously judged and mentored; it certainly was an awkward position to be in. But, now that the cards had been dealt, I really did want to want to win.

I kept a daily voting tally and suddenly felt as though I was back in elementary school. Once again, I came in second place; something I had become used to. Then, on the final night of voting, my friends Mike and Brian Galyean-Frederick hosted a voting party to support me; they knew how badly I wanted to win. Over the course of the next few hours, we added an additional 500 votes to my total, though I wasn't sure if that would be enough.

The voting ended at midnight, and on the following morning I received a phone call from Tara Guy informing me that I had won the 2016 Acadiana PRIDE Idol competition. I was beyond excited, especially knowing that all of the former Idol contestants voted for me. Just as I thanked Greg Louganis and Claude Martin for the inspiration they gave me, these mentees took it upon themselves to figure that the best way for them to thank me was by supporting me in my quest to be the next Idol.

The 2016 Acadiana PRIDE Festival was a scaled-down version of the four-day festival I initially created; it was a smart decision. This single-day event was filled with entertainment, vendors, and sponsors, featuring those from across the Acadiana area while welcoming talent from across the country. The set-up was very intimate, and because the venue was much smaller, the optics made it seem like there were lots of people in attendance. While the two previous Acadiana PRIDE Festivals logged more than 10,000 visitors, it always seemed as if the venue was empty because the (*Parc International de Lafayette*) was so massive.

It was such a humbling experience to win the 2016 Acadiana PRIDE Idol competition. In just three short years I graduated from being the host, to being a judge and mentor, to being the winner. Once again, my parents, forever two of my biggest supporters, were there to cheer me on as I sang; they even danced together, celebrating fifty-eight years of marriage. The day could not have been more perfect.

Once the elation of being the Acadiana PRIDE Idol fizzled, it became evident that I was no longer needed or wanted, by the Acadiana PRIDE organization, and the reason why came more quickly than I expected. One of my concerns was that there were absolutely no records kept on merchandise sales, monies collected from the sale of rental booths, or documentation that vendors had the correct credentials to conduct business within the state.

The main reason for my concern was that I specifically impressed upon Tara Guy and the organization the crucial importance of compliance with the IRS and local tax enforcement agencies. I continued to offer my assistance but was reminded repeatedly that I was no longer the president and that my help was no longer needed. That was my first clue, among many, that Acadiana PRIDE Festival was not being run like the true 501(c)(3) non-profit organization it was intended to be.

Regardless of the circumstances that led to the Acadiana PRIDE Festival becoming synonymous with bad bookkeeping, stolen monies, and back-handed business transactions, I was blamed for its demise. Though I had tried to remain an outside advisor, it became very evident very quickly that Tara Guy and the new board of directors had ideas of their own (but no plans in place to accomplish them). They also made it clear that my ideas and suggestions were neither wanted nor needed at any further meetings. Oh, and the new president of Acadiana PRIDE was Annaise Jameison, the anti-LGBT vocabulary proponent. Regardless of my thoughts on the future of the festival, I still wanted to see it be successful, but unfortunately, that was not to be.

Fame, in this instance, defined as *advocacy*, was the exceptional pride that I had in speaking on behalf of the LGBTQ community in our fight for true equality. The advocacy that pumps my blood is also what encouraged me to fight tirelessly for the success of Acadiana PRIDE Festival even when I knew they were headed in the wrong direction; I had to learn that sometimes advocacy, especially when it was unwanted, fell on deaf ears.

Twenty-six years ago, I was lying naked and tethered to a leather sling begging for someone to rescue me. My advocate angel, Wayne, showed up just in time to save me from the hellish scenario where others took advantage of me to spite my own lack of self-respect.

Twenty-six years later, I found the dignity and self-respect I had been searching for, and had a backbone and the strength of the LGBTQ community pushing me to make this generation, and even the next, proud of who they were. My mission was to make my hometown in south Louisiana better than the racist and homophobic area where I grew up, as we deserved to be seen and heard. Maybe this time someone would listen. *Maybe.*

me (Acadiana PRIDE Idol) with Mom and Dad– 2016

CHAPTER 31

INTEGRITY

(That Time I Attended a Funeral)

With all of the chaos surrounding the ultimate demise of Acadiana PRIDE, I needed another mission to focus my energies, and *voila!* The opportunity of a lifetime fell into my lap.

Back during the time of the inaugural Acadiana PRIDE Festival in 2013, I produced a play called *Chez Gisele*, written by my dear friend, Dennis Ward, who was also writing a new play called *Big Daddy's Last Dance*. It was about a funeral home director, named Mr. Pinkmink, whose job was to determine "who had the money" when Big Daddy suddenly died in a very compromising position. I was invited to do a cold reading of the play; this was just a read-through, not actual acting, just so that the playwright could get a sense of how the play flowed and make any adjustments. It was so much fun and very cool so see a playwright at work. I read the part of Mr. Pinkmink by complete accident. One of the lines read something like, "We put the 'fun' back in 'funeral'." But I misread the line and said, "We put the 'fyun' back in 'fyuneral." And the whole room just went into hysterics.

After the cold reading, Dennis asked me if I ever thought of acting. I told him, "I've never acted before, I don't know that I could do that." And Dennis, without missing a beat said, "Ted, you act every single day. You are your own character. I want you to play Mr. Pinkmink." And I said, "Sure Dennis, I'm a character, but that's not acting! Nobody writes that stuff down for me. I just make it up as I go!" We laughed, and Dennis asked me to at least consider auditioning; I agreed.

A few years passed, and I'd forgotten about Dennis' play. I had been so busy with Acadiana PRIDE and Acadiana PRIDE Idol that it was not a priority for me. Then one day, Dennis called to inform me that auditions for *Big Daddy's Last Dance* would be on the following weekend; he encouraged me to audition. I said, "Of course, but I'm not promising anything." He sent me a copy of the script, and to my surprise, Dennis had rewritten parts of the play to fit my personal character almost perfectly! I was ecstatic. I showed up at the audition, and was the only person who auditioned for the part of Mr. Pinkmink. The part was, it seemed, written just for me!

Then the rehearsals started, and the play took on a life of its own. As we rehearsed, we changed some things and reworded some lines which further enhanced the hilarity of the play. Many times, we were barely able to make it through an entire rehearsal without breaking into thunderous laughter. Sometimes we'd even ad lib, as long as it made sense in the play. The fact that one of the antagonists in the play was portrayed by Tara Guy only added to the animosity she had for me; I used her hatred for me to fuel my performance and never let on to her that I knew about the false gossip she'd been spreading about me.

My character, Mr. Pinkmink, was the executive director at Stiff and Moody's Funeral Parlor. He was an outlandish character and had a wardrobe to match his personality. Mr. Pinkmink wore a pink tuxedo bedazzled from head to toe with rhinestones and fringe; and his accoutrements included a pink glittered broom with matching dustpan, pink rhinestone feather dusters, and a coordinating ruffled apron. We played to sold-out performances nearly every night.

My favorite part about playing Mr. Pinkmink was that I was the only character in the play allowed to interact with the audience; in acting, that's called "breaking the fourth wall." Each night of the play was entirely different for me since every audience was different. The energy of the audiences only enhanced my performances by allowing them to "guest star" in the play for that evening.

The show closed as the "mourners" did a "second line" dance at Big Daddy's funeral; of course, Mr. Pinkmink made a final appearance anchoring the family, complete with his pink-and-white lace parasol with matching bedazzled lace handkerchief.

That year I was nominated for a "Rosie" award for Best Actor in a Comedy Play; it's the Acadiana Community Theater's version of the Academy Awards. When you hear people say, "It's just nice to be nominated!" it's really true! I was humbled just to be nominated for my very first play; to be included amongst veteran actors of the community was indeed an honor. I didn't win, and didn't expect to win, but did frame the postcard announcing my nomination. It is a reminder of one of the most fulfilling experiences of my life, during a time when I needed my mind to be rerouted from the world around me for a while. I do look forward to acting again in the future. Maybe even a musical version of *Big Daddy's Last Dance*? Stay tuned!

June 12, 2016 might have seemed like just any other day to most of you, but to me it was significant. On that day, forty-five people senselessly lost their lives due to a vile act of cowardice, gunned down at a gay bar named PULSE Nightclub in Orlando, Florida. I am tired of and disgusted by people saying, "That's so sad," and "We're sending you our prayers," and "Our hearts are with you." But sometimes all you can do is give your sympathies to those who are hurting so very much; and prayers and even millions of words of sympathy can never make that pain go away. I do have hope for the future, but those whose lives were destroyed by one night of targeted hate and violence can find a little solace knowing that the world is watching, and that the world will stand behind them through this struggle. That became my next mission.

Within twenty-four hours, I and a large group of volunteers put together an impromptu memorial for the victims of this hate crime; I found it strangely ironic that Tara Guy and Annaise Jameison contacted me to help spearhead the event, especially since I was *persona non grata* at Acadiana PRIDE. But my integrity allowed me to dismiss their animus toward me, since my mission had nothing to do with personal triumph, but rather, with organizing an event to help a community that needed to heal and move forward.

In late 2014, a new art installation was created for downtown Lafayette, where the word LAFAYETTE is spelled out in seven-foot letters minus the "Y;" tourists were encouraged to take photographs with their hands outstretched to the sky in the center of the artwork to create the letter "Y." As a part of our "Remember Pulse" memorial, we knew we would hold the event in downtown Lafayette. Using my former credentials as the president of Acadiana PRIDE Festival, I obtained permission from the Downtown Development Authority to paint the "Y-LAFA_ETTE sign. It was during this meeting with administrator of the DDA that I said, "Now, you know we're painting it in rainbow colors, right?" She quickly replied, "Ted, I'd expect nothing less from you!" I winked at her with a sly laugh; we knew there was drama to follow, and we'd be ready for it.

The paint and supplies were donated by a local Lowe's center; now all we needed were people. I got started that same afternoon by priming the sign white and measuring and scoring where the different colors of paint would go, so that we had a starting point for the next day. I slept restlessly for most of the night.

By 7:00 a.m., I was back at the park to finish prepping the sign for painting, but I was the only person there and began to worry. By 8:00 a.m., two or three more people showed up. By 9:00 a.m., another five showed up. By noon, thanks to social media and the community's outpouring of support, there were at least fifty volunteers helping to paint the Y-LAFA_ETTE in rainbow colors. Some people had made plans to be there, but the majority of the volunteers were just passers-by who saw the event on social media and were eager to help when they realized that there would finally be a rainbow sign in downtown Lafayette, even if just for a while.

Once the sign was completed, I wept from exhaustion and elation, and was in awe of what our community had accomplished. This was a true testament to the passion of the LGBTQ community of Acadiana and our commitment to always strive to do the right thing, even when it went against grain of those in government who opposed it.

The event was to begin at 7:00 p.m., and everyone was encouraged to wear yellow to the event. Yellow was our message to Orlando that, even through the darkness, there was light.

[Sidebar: National recording artist, Jason Mraz, was performing that night at Acadiana Center for the Arts. When he arrived into town, he recognized that we were planning a memorial that night for the victims and survivors of the Orlando Pulse Nightclub shooting; when he saw the Y-LAFA_ETTE sign painted in rainbow colors, he immediately made himself the "Y," took a picture, and posted it to his thousands of Twitter, Instagram, and Facebook followers. Within minutes, the world knew where Lafayette, Louisiana was; more importantly, Orlando knew that it was not alone.

Jason Mraz did something even better; he delayed his concert so that anyone who wanted to attend the concert could do so after the memorial was over. And that, Mr. Mraz, was the definition of class! I thank you, Acadiana thanks you, and we know that the great people of Orlando thank you and love you for showing your support from a thousand miles away!]

As I arrived at the venue later that night, my face flushed in sheer joy at the sea of yellow before me; standing right there, in the middle of the Y-LAFA_ETTE sign, my parents were "the Y." I don't know why I was surprised to see them there, because they have always supported anything I have ever done, and with all of the anger in my heart over that nightclub massacre, seeing them there brought me a sense of peace.

The memorial began with a moment of silence; then, as I stood before the microphone for Lafayette and Orlando and the world to hear, these were my words. And you may ask why I am including their names in my book. The answer is simple ... they are a part of me, and I am a part of them forever. It's easy for me to say that now, but it was not so easy to say it then.

My welcome speech began, "One of the strangest feelings in the world is having NOTHING to say and having EVERYTHING to say all at the same time. Nothing that we say can change the past and everything that we say will certainly change the future; and while the victims of this viscous terrorist attack in Orlando can no longer speak to us, I know that the power of their silence speaks volumes and that they are with us here in spirit."

I continued, "As I read the names of each of the deceased individuals who fell victim to this senseless act of terror, please listen carefully; as their voices will speak to us through their silence. They will give us the words to everything that needs to be said to make their unfortunate deaths a milestone to something much greater for all of us! Because they know that even through the darkness, they and we can always be the light. So, LISTEN to them ... because tonight MY voice and MY name is not important ... THEIRS ARE!"

Stanley Almodovar III, 23
Amanda Alvear, 25
Oscar A Aracena-Montero, 26
Rodolfo Ayala-Ayala, 33
Darryl Roman Burt II, 29
Angel L. Candelario-Padro, 28
Juan Chevez-Martinez, 25
Luis Daniel Conde, 39
Cory James Connell, 21
Tevin Eugene Crosby, 25
Deonka Deidra Drayton, 32
Frank Hernandez Escalante, 27
Leroy Valentin Fernandez, 25
Simon Adrian Carrillo Fernandez, 31
Mercedez Marisol Flores, 26
Peter O. Gonzalez-Cruz, 22
Juan Ramon Guerrero, 22
Paul Terrell Henry, 41
Miguel Angel Honorato, 30
Javier Jorge-Reyes, 40
Jason Benjamin Josaphat, 19
Eddie Jamoldroy Justice, 30
Anthony Luis Laureanodisla, 25
Christopher Andrew Leinonen, 32
Alejandro Barrios Martinez, 21
Brenda Lee Marquez McCool, 49
Gilberto Ramon Silva Menendez, 25
Kimberly Morris, 37
Luis Omar Ocasio-Capo, 20
Eric Ivan Ortiz-Rivera, 36
Joel Rayon Paniagua, 32
Jean Carlos Mendez Perez, 35
Enrique L. Rios, Jr., 25
Jean C. Nives Rodriguez, 27
Xavier Emmanuel Serrano Rosado, 35
Edward Sotomayor Jr., 34

Yilmary Rodriguez Sulivan, 24
Shane Evan Tomlinson, 33
Martin Benitez Torres, 33
Jonathan Antonio Camuy Vega, 24
Franky Jimmy Dejesus Velazquez, 50
Juan P. Rivera Velazquez, 37
Luis S. Vielma, 22
Luis Daniel Wilson-Leon, 37
Jerald Arthur Wright, 31

Once the shock of the shootings in Orlando subsided a bit, it was time to move on to something more positive. I contacted DDA to offer my services to repaint the Y-LAFA_ETTE art installation to prepare for the annual July 4th Uncle Sam's Jam.

As I primed the sign white, a passerby walked past and I heard him say underneath his breath, but *loud enough* to make sure that I heard him, "Thank God they're covering up that fag shit!" I kept my head down and started crying; this was a very bittersweet moment for me, since I had designed the sign that I was now covering up. We received so much support from the Acadiana area in the aftermath of the Orlando shootings that I was shocked that there were still people who would be so vocal about having a rainbow painted on the Y-LAFA_ETTE sign; I thought we'd moved past the vitriol and hatred, but I was wrong. And regardless of your thoughts on Gay Pride, the LGBTQ community in general, or the Orlando shootings, anytime I see a rainbow, it makes me happy. *How could something that makes most people so happy cause such hatred?* It just didn't make sense.

About twenty minutes after this incident, another person stopped to ask why I was covering up the sign. I explained that I was repainting the sign for the upcoming July 4th festivities. The gentleman insisted that I didn't have the right to do that and called the police. (I must admit that I was not very pleasant to this gentleman.) When they arrived, I explained that I had the approval to repaint the sign, but that gentleman still insisted that I was "vandalizing" the Y-LAFA_ETTE sign. He was so upset that he posted his disgust on social media, and the story went viral from there; this guy thought that I was vandalizing the sign, and there were even stories on local radio and television stations.

I reached out to that gentleman, because I wanted to thank him for what he did. I wanted him to know how much I appreciated his concern about the purported vandalism, *and it worked*. Within an hour or so, we contacted each other and had a long conversation about the series of events that caused this chaos. I apologized for being so rude to him, but then explained the event that occurred just moments before his arrival on the scene. He said, "I noticed that you kept your head down, but I thought you were just trying to avoid me." And I replied, "No, I was still crying from what had happened earlier, and frankly, I was still very angry."

In light of what happened, this gentleman posted on social media for people to please supply me with water and food so that I would remain hydrated and well fed during the extreme summer heat; I even got some extra help in painting the sign from one of my former *Big Daddy's Last Dance* castmates (not Tara Guy ... *though I know that you were sinisterly hoping for drama*). The outpouring of support from the community was overwhelming; strangers stopped by all day long for the next two days to make sure that I had cold water and hot food. It was an amazing show of love from a community that I didn't even know, nor did they know me. It just goes to show how easy it is to take something negative and turn it into a positive. It's all about communication, response and integrity. And it's like I've always said, "In the end, *LOVE WINS!*"

I'd spent a few days designing the new sign, and had this great idea to use *fleur-de-lis* instead of stars on the blue field to represent the states. So, as I prepared to put the *fleur-de-lis* stars on the sign, I contacted the DDA administrator, to tell her about this idea. She immediately shut it down, saying, "Look Ted, we took so much flak for painting the sign rainbow colors; I don't want Lafayette Parish Government getting any more phone calls complaining about it. Just use regular stars, and don't create more chaos over the sign." I was so mad that I said, "Okay, why don't you make me a template of the exact star that you would like for me to use, and I'll be sure not to ruffle any feathers." She knew I was angry, and she knew that I had the right to be, but in her defense, she was just trying to keep the peace. Censorship of art, in any form, is a sort of discrimination that I couldn't swallow. The Y-LAFA_ETTE sign was designed to be the centerpiece of artistic expression, yet the local government had not put its "rubber stamp" on the rainbow colors, so any deviation from "the norm" would have been considered blasphemous. *What an outrage.*

I was discouraged that I couldn't use my original design because of a few "haters" who were too closed-minded to accept the present as-is and unwilling to listen to the opinions of others. It's always easy to express your hate anonymously in a phone call; maybe if more people took the time to understand the purpose and the meanings behind why people support the causes that they support, they might learn something.

For all of the confusion and chaos surrounding the rainbow sign/stars and stripes sign, I was still very proud of the work I did to help beautify Downtown Lafayette. I learned that even though some people will never change, there are still those who show empathy and compassion in the Acadiana area, especially for people trying to affect positive change. I will always be proud of my hometown, many times in spite of the governance we elect. We still have a long way to go, but this one incident proved to me that we were moving in the right direction. And for that, I am grateful. *LOVE WINS AGAIN!*

For the next few years, I continued to work closely with Equality Louisiana to strive for justice for all people in all forms; it was in working with some of these young individuals that I got much more accomplished through education rather than through ridicule. I learned that many legislators voted a certain way simply because they were not fully aware of how their votes would impact the LGBTQ community. I became adept at using my status as a gay man living with HIV to my advantage, and to give a face to whichever bill they were voting on. I made it difficult for them to vote against me while they looked directly at me. I was just as proud of the work I did behind the scenes as I was of the issues that were publicly televised, maybe even more so.

Fame, in this instance, defined as *integrity*, was realizing that I could be a spokesperson for the local gay community when no one else was doing so. I became aware that I no longer needed the moniker of "president of Acadiana PRIDE," nor any other title, to encourage the community to come together behind a specific cause and challenge them to seek equality for themselves. I was shown that, though I had been ostracized by the current Acadiana PRIDE board, my integrity spoke volumes to the community; I rose above the scandal and the drama to, once again, become the person they trusted to speak on their behalf.

Twenty-two years ago, I lay sprawled half-naked across a bed in Provincetown, Massachusetts, though I could have been anywhere. My drunkenness once again consumed the person I became. Though I knew that I was loved by both Jocelyn Rae and her husband, Baxter, I was untrusted, disliked, and most certainly unwelcomed.

Twenty-two years later, I became the media darling of the gay community; a voice that was not only welcomed, but liked and trusted. The gay community turned to me for comfort, guidance, and stability. I learned that integrity had power, and I used that power to educate, not humiliate. I lived through a scandal not of my own making, and my integrity proved that I was exactly the man I claimed to be ... honest, sincere, and compassionate, and that I was finally growing into the man I always knew I could be.

performing as Mr. Pinkmink in "Big Daddy's Last Dance"–2016

CHAPTER 32

BE YOU-BE FABULOUS
(That Time I Ran for Office)

Dustin Gaspard's song, "Just a Little," asks, "Am I living longer or just dying slower?" There have been many times that I've pondered the same thing. I spent twenty-seven years trying to recreate my first *fifteen seconds of fame* by devoting my second attempt at success in life to making my next *fifteen seconds of fame* mean something different; I succeeded each time, but different didn't necessarily mean *good*.

Beginning the journey of my second life was also the beginning of my downfall into the abyss of alcoholism and substance abuse. My life spiraled out of control and I refused to do anything to make the rest of it any better; I was dying anyway, so it really didn't matter.

A movie called The Help changed the trajectory of my life in only my second year of sobriety. There was a line where Allison Janney's character, Charlotte, told her daughter, Skeeter (played by Emma Stone), that, she "decided not to die." Those four little words helped shape what would become the rest of my life. Once I decided I was no longer dying, I actually began living. Once I became sober, I more clearly saw the path that was laid out before me, and decided to not let the mistakes of my past determine my future. Sure, I took many forks and detours that prolonged my trail, but the destination remained the same; I was now living in my own fabulousness.

I refused to let the rest of my life become a punchline to a homophobic or racist joke. By actually owning up to all the things I did in hurting myself and others, I learned that my life and my story of recovery and survival could help others see that there was a better life on the other side of addiction, and that the reward was well worth the fight.

Even after all these years of sobriety, I still get triggered every time someone in recovery states that they have "overcome addiction." Alcoholism and addiction are triggers that I deal with daily, sometimes hourly—it is not a condition that I will ever feel comfortable saying I have overcome—rather, I see it as a condition from which I am constantly healing.

If I allow myself to believe that I have overcome my addictions, I know myself well enough to realize that I could easily fall into a false sense of achievement that has not yet been fully accomplished. Yes, recovery is an achievement, but to me, it is not something that is in the past that I've already overcome. Each day when I look into the mirror, I am reminded of the man that I used to be; the man that I never wanted to be; and the man who looks back at me is only one drink away from destruction. That is what keeps me clean and sober.

I had lived through two incredible lifetimes, and it was time for my third act. I still had more fight left, and was determined that my story was going to continue; I decided not to die.

The next event that changed the course of my life happened on June 18, 2019. On that day, there was a resolution coming up for a vote and approval to recognize June as Gay Pride Month in Lafayette, Louisiana. As usual, the news outlets called me for my thoughts on the issue. Although I had been out of the "gay spotlight" for a few years, the local media still considered me their go-to guy when it came to LGBTQ issues. I relished the honor.

I called my local council representative, Kevin Naquin, and explained that it was important for him to show his support for this resolution by voting "YES" on it. He then explained to me that he represented a very conservative district (the same homophobic and racist district where I was born), and that he would need to vote to represent his constituency. Although I disagreed with him, I understood, but still wanted to voice my support for this resolution at that night's council meeting. I delivered a speech that night in an attempt to tug at the heartstrings of those council members who were still undecided, but to no avail. Here is that speech:

Good evening, my name is Ted A Richard and I am a very proud gay man living in Lafayette Parish. I graduated from Carencro High

School in 1980 but moved away after high school because I did not feel safe as a young gay man living in this area.

I moved back to the Lafayette area after I retired in 2007 and felt that the city changed a lot in those twenty-seven years. It became more urban and more accepting of the LGBTQ community. I finally felt safe in the space where I grew up, and was glad to be "home." However, I quickly learned that there were still more hurdles to overcome regarding my own equality amongst others.

Fifty years ago this month, riots erupted at the Stonewall Inn in Manhattan. The Stonewall Inn was a bar known to be frequented by members of the LGBTQ community, and police raids became more and more routine. Finally, on June 29, 1969, enough was enough, and the patrons and supporters of the bar and its clientele rebelled against the anti-gay police establishment. The Stonewall Riots sparked outrage across the country, and by 1972, many of the largest cities in America, including Atlanta, Buffalo, Detroit, Washington D.C., Miami, Minneapolis, Philadelphia, and San Francisco held celebrations commemorating the Stonewall Riots and urged for continued progress for LGBTQ equal rights. Over the years, these celebrations have come to be known as Pride Festivals and June has come to be known as PRIDE Month.

In 1999 and 2000, President Bill Clinton declared June as "Gay and Lesbian Pride Month." Then in 2009, recognizing the 40th anniversary of the Stonewall Riots, President Barack Obama declared June as "LGBT Pride Month," and did so every year through 2016.

In 2014 and again in 2015 I was charged with helping to produce and coordinate the first two Acadiana PRIDE Festivals. As vice-president in 2014 and president in 2015, we brought a four-day festival to Lafayette for the first time in history. The festival included music, of course, but it also included educational and interactive components ... and it was family friendly. The festival was assisted and partially sponsored by both the city-parish government and by the Louisiana Bureau of Tourism. The festival was attended by both the LGBTQ community and by the straight community as well as LGBTQ allies.

On May 31, 2019, in recognition of the 50th anniversary of the Stonewall Riots, President Donald J. Trump became the first Republican president in history to acknowledge LGBTQ Pride Month through a series of Tweets.

And that brings us to where we are today ... before you is a resolution that recognizes the triumphs and achievements in attaining LGBTQ equal rights over the past fifty years. It acknowledges, just as President Trump did, that June is PRIDE Month.

The passage of this resolution would show that the Acadiana area is in lock-step with what is being acknowledged on a national stage. Recognizing June as LGBTQ Pride Month is not something new and it is not something other cities and regions across the country haven't done before. Passing this resolution simply states that the Lafayette City-Parish government recognizes June as LGBTQ Pride Month just like the rest of the country does.

So, you may be asking, if it is already acknowledged federally, why do we need to duplicate it at the local level? And my answer is simple; this could be a very valuable teaching moment for our community.

Many people talk about ignorance with a negative connotation. But I do not. Ignorance to me is simply a lack of knowledge. Let us take this opportunity to educate others about the history of LGBTQ rights. Perhaps if you knew a little bit of the history of our discrimination, then you would understand why Pride Month is so important to us. Many of you do not understand the need for equal rights, because you have never had to fight for them.

As a gay man, I still do not have the same rights as many of you. That is why it is important to share our history with others, so that they can understand where we have come from, where we have been, what it took for us to get here, and how to become truly equal in the future. We, as the LGBTQ community will never be "a part of" as long as we continue to be viewed as people who are "apart from."

Now I turn to you, the members of the city-parish council. I completely understand that for some of you this is an extremely difficult vote, and that you were voted into your position on this board to represent your constituency, but there is another reason that you were elected to your position: LEADERSHIP!

There will come many times as you serve your constituency that you will need to make difficult votes, such as this one maybe. And sometimes the correct vote is not the popular vote. At those times, it is up to you to stand up and be a leader for those of us who are often not heard.

The LGBTQ community will ALWAYS be in the minority, and those in the anti-LGBTQ community are always the MOST vocal, but those in favor of LGBTQ equality are currently at a historic high of nearly seventy percent.

We are only asking to be recognized on a local level for our past achievements and triumphs; and we look forward to working with you in the future as we continually strive for equal rights for ALL.

In conclusion, all I can ask of you is that you take these matters into consideration as you cast your votes tonight. I can most certainly assure you that your vote FOR this resolution will further garner you the leadership responsibilities into which you were elected. I can also assure you that you have unmeasured support from the LGBTQ community and its allies (even those who remain silent).

Thank you all so very much for allowing me to speak this evening.

            Ted A Richard— June 19, 2019

But something else happened that night when it was Kevin Naquin's (City-Parish Council representative from District 1) turn to vote; he decided that he needed to explain his vote. BIG MISTAKE! Kevin proceeded to give one of the most homophobic speeches I have ever heard in my life. He spoke about having gay family and that I was one of his friends (yes, he called me out by name) in an effort to prove that he was not homophobic. He even mentioned the fact that he performed at the Acadiana PRIDE Festival the year that I was president (which is true).

But then he started talking about his religious background, and how his father raised him to have strong morals and high values, and the that the strength of his moral compass would not allow him to vote for this resolution. At that point, I was livid. *How dare he*! Here was a person who divorced his first wife while she was fighting a battle with cancer, then "allegedly" cheated on his second wife to be with his third wife. Yes, he definitely got his morals from his father! Kevin Naquin voted "No" on the resolution.

I wondered, *how can anyone be so disingenuous and speak of values and a moral compass (especially with his own past), and still have the nerve to call me a friend?*

Apparently, he was not thinking about his moral compass when he played at the 2015 Acadiana PRIDE Festival and was paid $2,000. (I must include here that HE contacted ME and requested to play at this festival. Almost no one showed up for his performance, and he was the headlining act! So, Acadiana PRIDE Festival actually lost money during his performance. But I digress!)

Ever since that night, I was blasted and bashed by many in the LGBTQ community who questioned my "friendship" with Kevin Naquin. Many questioned my sincerity to the LGBTQ community, especially when, by all appearances, I was still supporting Kevin. I felt that I had let down the same community which, for many years, I tried to raise up. And they were right! (Sometimes even those of us with the best of intentions can be blindsided by the obvious; that was definitely me in this situation.) Once I realized that Kevin Naquin's moral compass was apparently only as short as his own stubby penis (so I've heard), it was time that I sprang into action, AND I DID!

My morals always dictated that I not associate with anyone who didn't have my best interests at heart. So, in an effort to uphold my own morals and defeat the hypocrisy of someone I once thought of as a "friend of Dorothy," I decided to run against Kevin Naquin in the upcoming election to fill the newly created seat of the Lafayette Parish Council (District 2). I didn't really have a great chance of winning, but if I could get my ideas into the mainframe of conversation, then, even if I lost the election and my ideas were acted upon, I still won!

And yes, I did lose the election. But I fared much better than I thought. By all local polling data, it was expected that I would receive maybe 500 votes. However, on election night, I received 2,239 votes (nearly twenty-five percent of the vote). While that might have seemed like a "landslide" victory for my opponent, I looked at it a bit differently. I received more than four times the votes expected, which meant that my message resonated with at least 2,239 local constituents. My job was not over; there was still more to do. My loss, though, was probably the best thing that could have happened because I later realized that I could accomplish a lot more in the community from "this side" of politics.

[Side note: It was so exciting to see my family posting pictures of themselves as they voted for me. It made me smile just a little more that day, even though I lost the election.]

For many years, I was affiliated with Acadiana Open Channel (AOC), a local non-profit television station, and became a contributing member. After losing the election, I understood that I still had a voice, and that people were actually listening to what I had to say. I decided to host my own television show, called *JUST THE FACTS with Ted A Richard*, which aired as a live, call-in program every Wednesday at noon.

I decided to call this show *JUST THE FACTS* because I was so exhausted from the media always putting a spin on the news of the day. I just wanted to hear the news, and didn't need anyone to tell me what to THINK about the news. It frustrated me that on many news programs, there was always some type of "spin" or commentary that was woven through the news stories, sometimes it was subliminal, other times it was downright blatant. Either way, it was WRONG!

It is partially the media's fault for the political and cultural divisions that abound in this country. Anyone can watch the "news" based on their own beliefs. If you lean more to the liberal side, then watch MSNBC. If you lean more to the conservative side, then watch FOX. The CNN network often fell somewhere between the two. I have always prided myself on watching ALL of the news, because I knew that the truth was actually somewhere in between. And that led to my decision to focus on *JUST THE FACTS*.

I tackled subjects such as racism, homophobia, and xenophobia, and discussed the effects that national issues had on our local area. I also addressed local issues, worked from behind-the-scenes to ensure equality for ALL, and fought diligently for pay raises for our first responders, Lafayette Consolidated Government employees, and Lafayette Utilities System employees (all of which passed). I continue to fight for our Sheriff's Department to get their employees an equitable pay schedule, and was also instrumental in the fight to raise the minimum wage in Louisiana to $15 per hour. It continues to be an uphill battle. But I continue to fight for EVERYONE to have a decent living wage.

My shows varied, depending on the issues most concerning our constituents, and I used my voice to send a message to the community that someone was in their corner. And I did exactly that by simply stating *JUST THE FACTS*!

Unfortunately, I was injured in a vehicle accident on December 7, 2019, and had to indefinitely postpone further shows due to my injuries. It was just my luck that I was on my way to see Dustin Gaspard in concert when a large truck reversed into the road directly in front of me. Only eight episodes into its run, *JUST THE FACTS* went on hiatus. I had every intention of reviving the show once I recovered, but other community issues arose and it became clear that I could accomplish a lot more by being a part of the solution instead of just talking about the issues on a television show.

My time at Acadiana Open Channel was a joy, and I'll always cherish the friendships I made through its mentorship and community programs. I learned a lot at AOC, and those lessons proved valuable as I continued on to my next journey. Because of all of my exposure in the community, through the Acadiana PRIDE Festival, running for public office, and my own television program, I met some incredible people.

One of those people was Aileen Bennet, who initiated a program to recognize community members who inspired others by just being themselves, being proud of who they were, and what they had accomplished. This is how Aileen Bennet describes her "BE YOU" attitude.

> "BE YOU started as a small project with some friends ... and grew (as things do in LFT). One day my (not so) evil plan is that Lafayette officially becomes the BE YOU city in the BAYOU State (how perfect is that?). It's the story of many people who live here, including the Cajuns – people just looking for a place where they can be themselves, where they can share values, good times, music and of course, food."

I was honored to be chosen as a "BE YOU" person of the week in December 2019. An introduction from Aileen Bennett read:

"Ted Richard is the busiest, brightest retiree you may ever see! Ted A Richard tells me he is retired, but he's a busy man. He has a weekly live call-in television show called JUST THE FACTS every Wednesday at midday. In a typical Ted way, he wanted to do it because it needs to be done. He wants it to be a place where people can find the truth. Ted has lived an interesting life, to put it mildly.

He was diagnosed as HIV-positive in 1987 ... yes, he's still here, and classed as healthy and undetectable. Ted has spent his life standing up for others, he believes simply that "right is right" and that we should all take care of each other.

He was one of the driving forces behind the PRIDE Festival in Acadiana and has helped many people gain the confidence to be themselves, mostly by leading the way.

Ted is wearing rhinestones as usual; they match the sparkle in his eyes and give you a glimpse into the joy he finds in his life and community. He is always ready for an interesting conversation and to do his part to make the world a better place."

Here are my responses to just a few of the interview questions. No doubt, many caused controversy, but I wanted to prompt a dialogue with others who were unaware of some of these issues.

What advice would you give the younger you?

Never be afraid to tell your own story! Often times we can't be honest with ourselves, and tend to be selectively oblivious to wrongdoings being done to others for fear of the risk of incriminating ourselves. If you are honest with yourself and own your own truth, then you can more freely talk openly with others without feeling the need to hide anything. When others see you living in your own truth, it hopefully encourages them to do the same.

We live in a society where anyone can sit behind a computer screen and spread untruths about anyone. I look at it this way: It is inevitable that people like to gossip. And gossip, by definition, has a negative connotation. People use gossip as a bullying tool to "hold something over you" which, in their eyes, empowers them. I say, "Take their power away." When you tell your own story, then it is no longer "gossip." It is just another story in the chronicles of your life. And life just gets a little bit easier.

What event in your life most shaped who you are now?
July 1987 changed my life forever. That was the month/year that I found out that I was HIV-positive. Weird thing is, that I actually wasn't shocked by the results.

It was "the gay disease" of the 1980s, and I already had friends dying from this disease. But to hear the actual words, "You tested positive" is a feeling that I would wish on NO ONE!

This revelation led me down a path of self-destruction for many years, since I figured I was going to die soon anyway. But twenty years later, I was still alive, and I was like, "Holy crap, I need to refocus ... and fast!" So, I re-purposed my life, got clean and sober, and my life has been a constant whirlwind of conquering challenges ever since then. And encouragingly, I have been healthy and undetectable (non-transmittable) for the past ten-plus years.

What values do you live by?
Loyalty and consistency are values I treasure. No one ever has to guess where I stand on any particular issue or in any particular situation. No matter whether you agree with me or not, at least I am consistent. I live by and stand by my core beliefs and strive to be a better person every day.

"Values" are not the same as religion, although many times, people conflate the two. I am constantly affronted by those persons who claim to have "Christian values" who are not very "Christian-like" at all. It makes me wonder what "values" they are really learning in their church.

What do you most appreciate?
Life-long friendships. I have had the same best friend since high school. I have had many great friends over the years, and thousands of acquaintances, but only one truly best friend. Those are hard to find!

What is your favorite journey?
I have had an amazing life! And every day that I wake up to another glorious morning, I am reminded of how fortunate I am to be able to have had so many wonderful experiences in this short lifetime.

And I challenge myself everyday to take the time to smell the roses. I have lots more life in me, so I am still learning more about myself and becoming a better person.

My entire life has taken on a journey of its own: some of it due to sheer circumstance and some of it due to careless mistakes and my sometimes feeble attempts to overcome them.

I have learned through this journey that I cannot survive without having a mission or a purpose to keep my mind occupied. I have reinvented myself many times in this lifetime, which has allowed to me to explore facets of myself that I didn't know existed. The term "shine bright like a diamond" has a somewhat different connotation than its intended meaning. It's not always about "the sparkle," even though I love the bling. To me, it is more about discovering the brilliance emitting from each of its facets. You must explore the facets to discover what's beneath and release the brightness from within.

Where is your favorite place to be alone?
On my front porch swing

How do you "let the good times roll?"
Since I don't drink, I don't find the bar scene to be very fun, although I am comfortable being a non-drinker in a bar atmosphere. (I love pineapple juice, so my friends always say, "Drink your juice, Shelby!")

When I always have the most fun is on vacation. I love going on vacation alone. I enjoy meeting the locals at wherever my destination is, and I can create my own schedule as I feel like. I relish the spontaneity of living life "on the fly."

How would you like to be remembered?
How you remember me will be based on our shared memories. I want to be remembered for taking the time to help others.

In the words of the incomparable Naomi Sims (Miss Gay US of A 1978, Miss Universe 1980, Miss Gay Universe, National Female Impersonator of the Year 1983 and Miss Gay America 1985), "If only one person remembers my name and remembers me with love and kindness, then I will truly live forever!" I would never place myself on the same pedestal with my idol, Naomi Sims; I just hope that she can still see me doing some good in the world. We can chase rainbows together when I get there, but I'm not in a hurry.

The year 2019 was a banner year for me (among others). In that one year, I got involved—again—in local government, continued the fight for equal rights for all and equal pay for all, ran for public office for the first time, and started my own television show. *Whew! That was a lot!*

And even though 2019 ended on a sour note, with me totaling my favorite little red Ford Ranger, I had a phenomenal year of successes! Who'd have thought that, at the age of fifty-seven, I could re-invent myself all over again? BUT I DID! And it was an exciting time.

And you never know who's paying attention to all of the work that you are doing for your community. In recognition of all that I recently accomplished for our community, I was one of only 10,000 people invited to the Inauguration of Louisiana Governor John Bel Edwards. [Consider this: Louisiana has nearly 2.3 million registered voters, and John Bel Edwards received almost 475,000 votes. That means that I was selected as one of the top two percent of John Bel Edwards supporters who was invited to attend the Inauguration. THAT'S QUITE AN HONOR!]

While this may seem a bit conceited, I remember some great advice by Mike Billingsley. Mr. Billingsley always noticed that I accomplished a lot in a very short time, which showed in my management style. But he also noticed that I never really took the credit for those accomplishments. I always credited my staff for their incredible job performance.

Mr. Billingsley's advice was this, "Ted, you are an incredible manager and a wonderful person, but in this life, you need to start owning the things that you have accomplished in your lifetime. If you don't take the credit for the part that you played in 'making things happen,' then someone else will certainly be next in line to take that credit away from you." I remember telling him that I was uncomfortable with that, and that as long as people noticed that I was doing a great job, then good things would continue to happen to me in my career. He replied, "What top executives notice is that great things are getting done, but they need to know that YOU are the person responsible for making them happen."

From then on, I took pride in accepting responsibility for my accomplishments, but strived to never forget to thank all the other people who helped me along the way.

There is a line from one of Dustin Gaspard's songs that states, "I can't see the side of me that everyone holds a candle to." I never realized that people looked to me as a role model of some sort, and never saw myself fitting in to that category, especially during my active alcoholism and addictions. It would take me a very long time to understand that the person I became after I got clean and sober was one that people could look up to; I was only doing what I thought needed to be done, both for my community and for my continued sobriety.

I soon became more accustomed to being called a trailblazer, though I would never be so presumptuous as to call myself one. If others saw me as a one, then I was certainly very proud to OWN it. Though I held that honor in an embrace of esteem, there were many others who were also deserving of this title who preceded me and allowed me to be the trailblazer I ultimately became. Upon further reflection, I realized that I have accomplished lots of "firsts" in my lifetime. I was the very first Mr. Royal Order of Unicorn. I was the first openly gay and openly HIV-positive person to teach HIV education in Lafayette Parish public schools and in the Roman Catholic Diocese of Lafayette. (Yes, I taught HIV education in the same halls where I attended catechism as a youngster.) I led the effort (with Louis Toliver, Jr.) to bring the first (and second) Acadiana PRIDE Festival to our extremely conservative community, an effort that succeeded beyond our wildest dreams. I was also the first (and only) openly gay and openly HIV-positive person to run for public office in the state of Louisiana (of which I am aware) and garnering twenty-five percent of the vote was truly a phenomenal feat. In addition, many of my platform ideas raised during that campaign are now being addressed by the current parish council, though I received, nor asked for, any of the credit. A heartfelt thanks goes out to everyone who believed in me and my abilities as a true leader, even though I often questioned myself. I achieved great things because of all of you.

Who I became in life was not a result of all of the good and bad experiences that happened in my life; how I responded and reacted to those experiences is what made me who I am. And, yes, I made some bad decisions (lots of them), but haven't we all? I spent most of my life mistakenly running toward the sadness that I told myself I was running away from. I learned, much too late, that when you're looking for sadness, you will always find it. I never looked for sadness, sadness just always seemed to find me.

People tend to hide all the bad stuff, yet that's what others talk about behind your back. I have always believed that telling my story was the best way to get the story right. This way, it's not gossip, and regardless, no one ever has the right to gossip about anyone else. Gossip is a tactic that bullies use to wield power over you. If I tell my story FIRST and you decide to repeat that story, it's just a story ... it's not gossip. Furthermore, your gossiping about me only reinforces your own insecurities. It didn't—and doesn't—hurt me.

And that's the message in this story of my life. I have told you almost everything about me. Hopefully, I have answered many of your questions, but what you think about what I have written really doesn't matter to me.

I lived this life, and I own the life I led. If it happened, then it happened. There's no reason to ever hide behind the truth. OWN IT! You will find that it makes you a much stronger person as you continue on your journey in this place called Earth. It certainly led me to the path I am now on. Now to begin my next act!

For the record, I DO believe in a life in the hereafter, and also in reincarnation. It may sound like a contradiction of thought, but I don't think so. Why can't there be both? I firmly believe that we are given the opportunities for several lifetimes, both here on this planet and in the heavens of the universe. And I believe that we are allowed to have multiple lifetimes on both planes.

I believe that the way we handle our lives during one existence has a direct bearing on the type of life we will live in the next. But I see things a bit more clearly than that. I believe that we are born into each lifetime as a clean slate. While we may not always be given the same tools and opportunities, it's what we DO with those tools and opportunities that can change anyone's course; even across lifetimes.

So, for those of you who are still here in this lifetime, please know this: No one will EVER be perfect. We can only be perfectly imperfect.

It took me a very long time to figure this out, but I finally discovered that seeing other people happy is exactly what makes me happy. I spent so much time focusing on myself that I never noticed the world around me and the impact it was having on my life. That is, until I hit rock bottom and had to learn it all over again.

If you are reading this now, then YOU are one of the people who have always made me HAPPY. And I want you to know that your life has always had a place in mine and always will. Please join me for my next *"fifteen seconds of fame,"* and let's create our next *"16th Second"* together!

Be You – (courtesy The Daily Advertiser)–2019

AFTERWORD

Thank you for reading about, what some would say, an extraordinary life. Regardless of what you think of me or the choices and often bad decisions I have made, I hope that you can learn from my mistakes and seek your own personal growth through my successes. We all have different life paths, and because our goals are constantly changing, we must learn to adapt to our new lives with new visions for our future.

I originally planned for this book to be released after my death. But as my death, happily, grew further and further away due to new advancements in medication and treatments for HIV/AIDS, addiction, and depression, my family pursued me to write and publish this book so they could read it before I die. I warned them that there were several stories in this autobiography that I had kept hidden from the family my entire life, and thus decided to make a "kid-friendly" version of the book called *Out Loud*, which will be printed upon my death to distribute at my funeral. But until then, I wanted to share my life with the rest of the world. And I am bringing my FABULOUS book to a store near you!

Happily, I was never able to completely dismiss Colt Michael from the rest of my life; Colt Michael does now, and always did, have a very special place in my heart. He had adventures and experiences that, at the time, Ted A Richard would probably never have had the courage to do. And my years as Colt Michael were some of the happiest days of my life. Yes, sometimes I DO miss Colt Michael! He was my savior, but sometimes also my downfall. I learned so much (both good and bad) through being Colt Michael that were it not for "him," the Ted A Richard you know today would be someone totally different. And for that, I am eternally thankful.

As I promoted my autobiography, *The 16th Second*, an acquaintance, Mike Skywark, whom I'd been chatting with on social media posted, "You're writing a book? But why? You're not even famous!" Immediately going into defense mode, I replied, "That's the exact premise of the book! I am not famous, but I have lived an extraordinary life." And when I regaled to him the story of the unintentional prostitution that became rape, he inquired, "So is that what turned you gay?" Those words coming from someone who claimed to be gay was asking a question that I thought had been answered ages ago. Having someone ask me about "being turned gay," prompted me to weigh my response somewhat delicately and with sympathy as well as just a hint of skepticism. *Why would a gay man ask that sort of question?* Perhaps he was still in the closet. Perhaps his religion taught him differently. I didn't know the reason, so I hesitated for a moment before responding. Then came the words I wanted to say.

In direct response to his previous query, I firmly stated, "Hell NO, I was having sex with my teacher in high school. Oh, and by the way, no one and nothing *turns you gay*. You're either born FABULOUS or you're not!"

Immediately the pace and tone of the conversation shifted as if a monstrous weight was lifted from his weakened shoulders and troubled mind. He told me about his horrible kinder years as an adopted child in a biracial family. He was of Mexican heritage; his white stepmom thought he "wasn't white enough," and his Black stepdad thought he "wasn't Black enough." After he'd heard enough of their bickering, he retorted, "I'm fucking Mexican, can't we just split the difference?" It astounded me that biracial parents would be racist against their own adopted child. And I thought we were going to have a conversation about his homosexuality or non-homosexuality, or whatever sexuality he felt comfortable with. But no, he needed to address his racist parents first.

That was important to him as a baseline, because as we continued the conversation and broached the subject of sex and sexuality, he continually mentioned how he felt discriminated against in the gay community. He felt as if he wasn't white enough to fit in with the white crowd (stepmom was right), and he wasn't Black enough to fit in with the Black crowd (stepdad was right). Furthermore, he was ostracized by the local Hispanic community for not being Mexican enough because he was raised by biracial parents who weren't Mexican enough (whatever the hell that meant).

Now I completely understood why such a seemingly well-educated man who once worked for a major law firm would ask such simplistic questions regarding "being gay" and what it meant. By being made to feel that he didn't belong anywhere, he began to think that perhaps he belonged nowhere. I was happy that he was comfortable enough to have a conversation with me that, to him, might have been life-changing.

He told me that he journaled for most of his life, just as I had. "Why don't you compose your journals into book form?" I asked. And his retort was, well, rhetorical, "But I'm not famous!" And I said, "Exactly my point, no one will ever know about your fabulous life unless you tell them. You are a very interesting and accomplished young man; perhaps others could learn from your hardships and your struggle to triumph. Find your FABULOUS and write about it! Even if it never gets published, someday, someone will read it, and know that you lived a life that was, indeed, FABULOUS, too!

We talked about the media phenomena of Instagram and TikTok and people who were considered "famous" based on their number of followers and how today's definition of fame diminished the dedication and sacrifices that previous artists worked so hard to achieve while still earning little notoriety in their fields of interest. Sadly, many of the younger generation are attempting to mold themselves into someone with no discernible life skills other than the ability to take a "selfie" or create a short video where they're the "star." Social media is whatever we, the public, make it out to be. "Reality" television has never been real. The sooner we discover ourselves without the world of fantasy-driven "fame" and social media "stardom," the sooner we will begin to see our own fifteen seconds of fame and see the importance that our own existence provides to the success of others. And THAT, my friend, is FAME!

There is a scene from the 2013 movie *Getting Go–The Go Doc Project*, where the two main characters have a conversation about their definition of fame. Sam Camp's character, Go, tells Tanner Cohen's character, Doc, that Doc doesn't want to be normal, he wants to be an artist. Doc responds that being an artist is overrated, that everyone's an artist, or at least they think they are. He continues, saying that most people believe that the only thing separating them from fame and fortune is a reality show and notes that he doesn't know that his voice is more unique than these other peoples'; he conjectures that fame is the new American "birthright," that people would do anything to achieve it and would feel cheated if they didn't obtain it.

Doc then references Andy Warhol and the "Campbell's Soup Can" exhibit. Go commented that those soup can paintings were *"about the mundane life of the (19)50s."*

Doc replied that Warhol not only wanted to be famous, but that he wanted to lead by example, adding that Warhol wanted people to lose the parts of themselves that made them less than ideal.

This discourse of the "art of being famous" is the exact premise of this book. Andy Warhol wanted to be famous, and he decided exactly what fame meant in the context of his own life. He taught us that we all had the opportunity to be famous, if only we followed his example. *If everyone was normal, then would normal still mean the same thing? If everyone was famous, then would fame mean the same thing?* As for myself, I enjoyed being somewhere in the middle of the two, not so normal that I didn't stand out in a crowd, but not so famous as to be above the crowd. I wanted to be famous for the multitude of my accomplishments, but never forgot that I would probably always end up in second place. I'm fine with that.

It was this social media conversation alone that taught me yet another valuable lesson. Sometimes it is the responsibility of those living in the realms of their own *"16th Second"* to help others find their first! And maybe, just maybe, I helped someone else FIND THEIR FABULOUS in the meantime so they could relish in their newly-found *"first second of fame!"*

During our last conversation, he finally told me his real name ... Colt Michael. Now it all made sense. He tried to experience life vicariously through the fictitious Colt Michael that I created. Now the "new and improved" and REAL Colt Michael could begin his journey to experience life and not just live it. He could create his own successful version of the Colt Michael that he aspired to become.

Over the past few years, I lost touch with this person who had reminded me that I wasn't famous, so I don't know if he ever wrote the book that we talked about. I would read it if he did.

Since publishing this book, the question I'm most often asked is, "Why are you still single?" My response is always the same. "I am selectively single. I choose to be single because I enjoy being single. I've lived life long enough to know what I expect from others and what I can and cannot accept from others. I inform interested "applicants" that "my inclusion in their lives must benefit each of us, and is a necessity for neither of us!" I firmly believe that if every relationship followed this guideline as a testament to the strength of their loves' bonds, there would many more happy and gay marriages!

Life is always worth living. Don't just be a spectator in this parade we call life. BE THE PARADE! And, yes, there is definitely room in my life for a future partner, a man who understands that I enjoy having him in my life because I see the rainbow in him, and he sees the sparkle in me.

I encourage each of you to re-evaluate the life you are living and acknowledge your own fifteen seconds of fame. My sincerest hope is that after reading this book, you learn to embrace the thrill of living life to the fullest in the *16th Second*.

Ted A Richard / Colt Michael

POETRY

A HAIKU COLLECTIVE

The rapture of life
Begins, breathe in and breathe out
Searching, exploring

A life borne with an
Infant's imagination
Breaking obstacles

Fragmented standards
Dreams and determination
To become famous

Searching for fame that
Didn't exist until we
Discovered ourselves

Learning that our lives
Are intertwined with threads of
Faith, and hope, and love

Inspired by the truth
Yearning for inspiration
Reaching for the stars

Believing that I
Deserve the accolades of
The Sixteenth Second

Ted A Richard – January 2021

ABOUT THE AUTHOR

Ted A Richard was born and raised in Ossun, Louisiana and graduated from Carencro High School in 1980. Shortly after graduation, he traveled all over the country working in retail management, later creating an alter-ego dance phenom named Colt Michael. He has lived in Austin, Boston, Dallas, Houston, New Orleans, Spokane, and San Francisco. He retired in 2007 after working more than thirty years in retail business management, and currently resides near Carencro, Louisiana.

He has been HIV + since 1987 and formerly served as president of Acadiana CARES, the Lafayette area HIV/AIDS service organization, as a consumer advocate, and he has spoken on hundreds of occasions to schools and community organizations to raise HIV/AIDS awareness in the Acadiana area, and advocates for HIV prevention.

He has also been a rarely outspoken advocate on behalf of the LGBTQIA+ and HIV+ communities for several years, having given speeches in the Louisiana Congress on pertinent issues regarding our rights as equal citizens.

He was instrumental in organizing Lafayette's first-ever Acadiana PRIDE Festival as its vice-president in 2014 and president in 2015. "We want to be the beacon to the rest of the state and our country, to shine the light on what true family, togetherness, and diversity means in Cajun Country!" Ted is also an avid singer and was voted the 2016 Acadiana PRIDE Idol.

Ted continuously strives to bring LGBT-relevant theatre to the Acadiana area. He has produced two plays for Acadiana PRIDE; *Chez Gisele* written by Dennis Ward, and *UpStairs: The Musical* written by Wayne Self. Both plays were performed at *Cite des Arts* (in 2014 and 2015, respectively), and both received high accolades from the theater and performing arts community. In 2016, Ted made his acting debut as the star of Dennis Ward's original comedy, *Big Daddy's Last Dance (at the Stiff and Moody Funeral Home)*. He was nominated for a Rosie Award for his performance.

REFERENCES

Page 44

His real name was Joseph David, or J.D., but Texas knew him as David Prejean, the reigning Mr. Gay Texas 1982. I preferred to call him Shirtless Joe. (*This Week In Texas*–Volume 7, Number 38, December 11-17, 1981)

Page 49

And then the drum roll, and the emcee announced that the first runner-up was Colt Michael, and the Winner of the Male Stripper of the Year for 1982 was Peter Casares. (*This Week In Texas–Texas' Leading Gay Publication*, Volume 8, Number 23, August 27-September 1, 1982)

Page 75

The following week, the bar used my picture for its weekly advertisement. (*This Week In Texas–Texas' Leading Gay Publication*, Volume 10, Number 12, June 8-14, 1984)

Page 82

Joe and I lost touch for a while when I was dating Dennis, but we reconnected on the night of JR's male stripper finals in 1983; he won, and I was first-runner up (second-place loser again). (*This Week In Texas–Texas' Leading Gay Publication*, Volume 9, Number 34, November 11-17, 1983)

He would go on to become the current third runner-up to Mr. Gay Texas, and, coincidentally, had been sponsored by JR's. (*This Week In Texas–Texas' Leading Gay Publication*, Volume 9, Number 39, December 16-22, 1983)

Joe and I continued to see each other on each of my subsequent visits to Houston; though we never officially dated, he held a very special place in my heart and I was excited when he was chosen as the next TWT cover model. (*This Week In Texas–Texas' Leading Gay Publication*, Volume 9, Number 45, January 27 – February 2, 1984)

Page 89
I was waiting at the bar for my good friend, Chuck Roberson, yet another *TWT* cover boy, (*This Week In Texas–Texas' Leading Gay Publication*, Volume 10, Number 7, May 4-10, 1984)

Page 91
In mid-December, I finally got a call from one of the managers at Heaven; Chuck Roberson, fresh off his much-deserved win as Mr. Gay USA 1986 (*This Week In Texas–Texas' Leading Gay Publication*, Volume 12, Number 25, September 5-11, 1986)

Page 100
(HIS name would have been Coulter Anthony-Thomas in honor of my friend Colt Thomas, 1983 Mr. Gay Texas (*This Week In Texas–Texas' Leading Gay Publication*, Volume 8, Number 38, December 10-16, 1982) and 1983 International Mr. Leather, who would become the very first model for the cover of *Advocate MEN* (Premier Issue – 1984). I first met Colt shortly after his *TWT* cover story (*This Week In Texas–Texas' Leading Gay Publication*, Volume 8, Number 9, May 21-27, 1982)

Page 105
It's not until The Lazy J bar manager pointed it out, that I noticed how big and beautiful my dark brown eyes were. (*This Week In Texas–Texas' Leading Gay Publication*, Volume 12, Number 45, January 23-29, 1987)

Page 106
There were three other entertainers that night, all drag queens (using the term loosely), and I was the featured performer and

only stripper. (*This Week In Texas–Texas' Leading Gay Publication*, Volume 12, Number 45, March 13-19, 1987)

Page 109
On Friday, April 3, 1987, the worlds of Ted A Richard and Colt Michael would soon collide; and my "double-life" escapade would be blown when the *TWT* magazines with me on the cover were circulated across the state of Texas. (*This Week In Texas–Texas' Leading Gay Publication*, Volume 13, Number 3, April 3-9, 1987)

Page 118
In 1976, Mr. Tag Kowis (aka "Flash Storm") and a few of his friends began hosting "The Garden Party" in his back yard, an event principled on the reasoning that it would be a day when it didn't matter what your outfit consisted of, whether you were "real" or just "convinced," as long as it pertained to DRAG, and you had a great time in doing so. (*This Week In Texas–Texas' Leading Gay Publication*, Volume 11, Number 18, July 19-25, 1985)

Being on the cover of *TWT* magazine did, however, come with its own perks; by the following week, I was suddenly welcomed with open arms at all of those Pacific Street clubs who shunned me after my recent New Year's Eve debacle. (*This Week In Texas–Texas' Leading Gay Publication*, Volume 13, Number 8, April 10-16, 1987, page 65)

Page 132
The photographer, Rob Weatherly, called me during the first week of February 1989 to say he spoke with the owner of the soon-to-be-open gay bar, Kaleidoscope/S.R.O., in Odessa, Texas. (*This Week In Texas–Texas' Leading Gay Publication*, Volume 14, Number 48, February 10-16, 1989)

Page 141

I only wish that I could have been the rose that he wanted with fewer thorns. (*This Week In Texas–Texas' Leading Gay Publication*, Volume 15, Number 31, October 13-19, 1989)

Page 149

What a surprise when, in March 1990, my former *TWT* cover photo was featured in the Classic *TWT* section of its magazine, stating, "If you could get past this gorgeous man on the cover, Houston's Ted A Richard, you were sure to find something to satiate your appetite for entertainment and news shaping the gay community within the pages of Texas' gay gazette." (*This Week In Texas–Texas' Leading Gay Publication*, Volume 16, Number 2, March 23-29, 1990)

Page 156

And then, Texas' newly elected governor, Ann Richards, appeared from behind the "rain." (*This Week In Texas–Texas' Leading Gay Publication*, Volume 17, Number 9, May 10-16, 1991)

RESOURCES

National Suicide Prevention
1-800-273-8255 (1-800-273-TALK)

RAINN (Rape, Abuse, and Incest National Network)
1-800-656-4673 (1-800-656-HOPE)

SNAP (Survivors' Network of those Abused by Priests)
1-877-762-7432 (1-877-SNAP-HEALS)

www.ingramcontent.com/pod-product-compliance
Lightning Source LLC
Chambersburg PA
CBHW020346170426
43200CB00005B/71